PLATO'S ANIMALS

STUDIES IN CONTINENTAL THOUGHT

John Sallis, editor

Consulting Editors

Robert Bernasconi William L. McBride
Rudolph Bernet J. N. Mohanty
John D. Caputo Mary Rawlinson
David Carr Tom Rockmore
Edward S. Casey Calvin O. Schrag
Hubert Dreyfus †Reiner Schürmann
Don Ihde Charles E. Scott
David Farrell Krell Thomas Sheehan
Lenore Langsdorf Robert Sokolowski
Alphonso Lingis Bruce W. Wilshire
David Wood

PLATO'S ANIMALS

Gadflies, Horses, Swans, and Other Philosophical Beasts

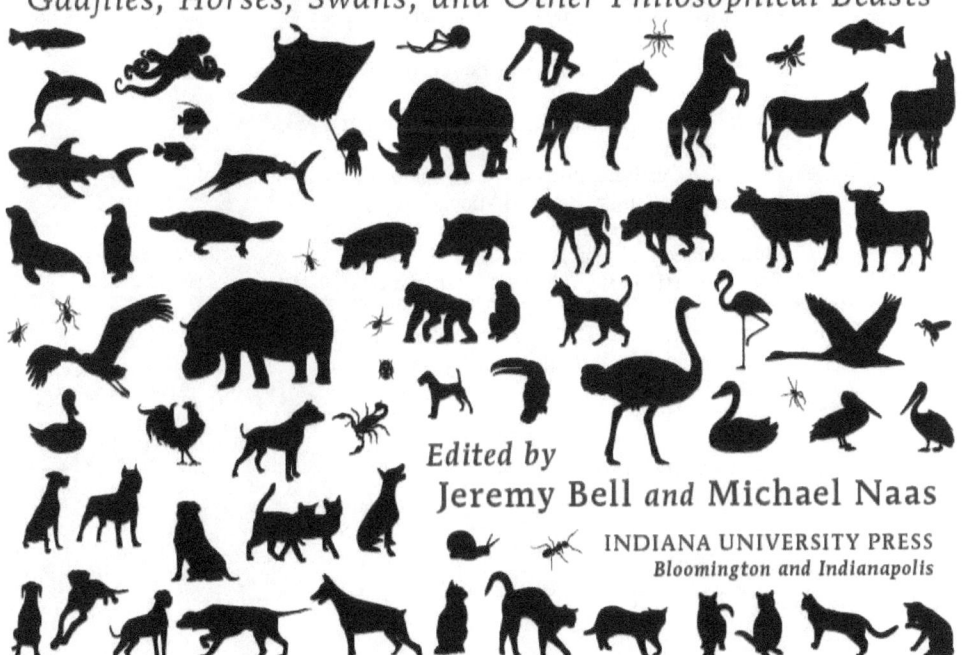

Edited by
Jeremy Bell and Michael Naas

INDIANA UNIVERSITY PRESS
Bloomington and Indianapolis

This book is a publication of

Indiana University Press
Office of Scholarly Publishing
Herman B Wells Library 350
1320 East 10th Street
Bloomington, Indiana 47405 USA

iupress.indiana.edu

© 2015 by Indiana University Press

All rights reserved

No part of this book may be reproduced or utilized in any form or by any means, electronic or mechanical, including photocopying and recording, or by any information storage and retrieval system, without permission in writing from the publisher. The Association of American University Presses' Resolution on Permissions constitutes the only exception to this prohibition.

⊖ The paper used in this publication meets the minimum requirements of the American National Standard for Information Sciences—Permanence of Paper for Printed Library Materials, ANSI Z39.48-1992.

Manufactured in the United States of America

Library of Congress Cataloging-in-Publication Data

Library of Congress Cataloging-in-Publication Data

Plato's animals : gadflies, horses, swans, and other philosophical beasts / Edited by Jeremy Bell and Michael Naas.
    pages cm. — (Studies in continental thought)
    Includes bibliographical references and index.
    ISBN 978-0-253-01613-3 (hardback : alk. paper) —
ISBN 978-0-253-01617-1 (pbk. : alk. paper) — ISBN 978-0-253-01620-1 (ebook) 1. Plato. Dialogues. 2. Animals (Philosophy) I. Bell, Jeremy, [date] editor. II. Naas, Michael, editor.
    B398.A64P53 2015
    184—dc23

2014039533

1 2 3 4 5   20 19 18 17 16 15

Contents

Editors' Introduction: Plato's Menagerie   *1*

Part I. The Animal of Fable and Myth

1. Making Music with Aesop's Fables in the *Phaedo* / Heidi Northwood   *13*

2. "Talk to the Animals": On the Myth of Cronos in the *Statesman* / David Farrell Krell   *27*

Part II. Socrates as *muōps* and *narkē*

3. American Gadfly: Plato and the Problem of Metaphor / Michael Naas   *43*

4. Till Human Voices Wake Us and We Drown: The Aporia-fish in the *Meno* / Thomas Thorp   *60*

Part III. The Socratic Animal as Truth-Teller and Provocateur

5. We the Bird-Catchers: Receiving the Truth in the *Phaedo* and the *Apology* / S. Montgomery Ewegen   *79*

6. The Dog on the Fly / H. Peter Steeves   *96*

Part IV. The Political Animal

7. Taming Horses and Desires: Plato's Politics of Care / Jeremy Bell   *115*

8. Who Let the Dogs Out? Tracking the Philosophical Life among the Wolves and Dogs of the *Republic* / Christopher P. Long   *131*

Part V. The (En)gendered Animal

9. The City of Sows and Sexual Differentiation in the *Republic* / Marina McCoy   *149*

10 Animality and Sexual Difference in the *Timaeus* / Sara Brill   161

Part VI. The Philosophical Animal

11 Animal Sacrifice in Plato's Later Methodology / Holly Moore   179

12 The Animals That Therefore We Were?
    Aristophanes's Double-Creatures and the Question of Origins /
    Drew A. Hyland   193

Part VII. Animals and the Afterlife

13 Animals and Angels:
    The Myth of Life as a Whole in *Republic* 10 / Claudia Baracchi   209

14 Of Beasts and Heroes: The Promiscuity of Humans
    and Animals in the Myth of Er / Francisco J. Gonzalez   225

    List of Contributors   247
    Plato's Animals Index   249
    Name and Subject Index   257

PLATO'S ANIMALS

Editors' Introduction
Plato's Menagerie

As every student of philosophy well knows, Socrates was truly a beast, a philosophical animal par excellence. In the *Apology*, he compares himself to a gadfly who has spent his entire life stinging the lethargic horse that is the city of Athens in order to keep it from falling into slumbering ignorance. In the *Meno*, Socrates is portrayed as a stingray or, more accurately, a torpedo ray who shocks or benumbs his interlocutors and causes them to question all their previously held beliefs, while in the *Symposium* he is compared to a venomous snake whose philosophical discourses strike at the heart or soul of those who hear them. In other dialogues, Socrates compares himself not to some stinging or biting beast, some predatory animal, but precisely the opposite, to a fawn at the mercy of a lion in the *Charmides* or, in *Alcibiades I*, to an old stork who hopes to be cared for by his young, that is, by his students. And then there is the *Phaedo*, the dialogue that takes place on the day of his execution, where Socrates compares himself to a prophetic swan singing his most beautiful song—arguments about the immortality of the soul—in anticipation of his imminent death.

Gadfly and horse, swan, snake, stork, fawn, and torpedo ray: this is already a pretty impressive and diverse assembly of animals. But it is really just the beginning of the enormous bestiary contained in Plato's dialogues. Indeed, animal images, examples, analogies, myths, or fables are used in almost every one of Plato's dialogues to help characterize, delimit, and define many of the dialogues' most important figures and themes. They are used to portray not just Socrates but many other characters in the dialogues, from the wolfish Thrasymachus of the *Republic* to the venerable racehorse Parmenides of the *Parmenides*. Even more, animals are used throughout the dialogues to develop some of Plato's most important political or philosophical ideas. In the *Republic*, for example, the guardians of the ideal *polis* are compared to trained guard dogs who must protect the state from marauding wolves, that is, from tyrants and sophists of various kinds. In the same dialogue, the human soul is itself compared to a composite animal with a human head, a lion's torso, and nether parts like a multiheaded beast, while in the *Phaedrus* it is likened to a charioteer and two horses, with the former ruling over and guiding the latter.

It is thus often through images or examples of animals, along with the analogical relationships that come along with these, that Plato is able to develop a hierarchy not just between humans and animals but between rulers and the ruled, men and women, adults and children, free men and slaves, and so on. It is not too much to say that animal references are employed to help characterize, explain, or value almost every aspect of human life. In the *Republic* and the *Phaedo*, we even hear Socrates argue that the character and destiny of animals pursue humans beyond life right into the afterlife, since it is suggested there that a human soul that does not devote itself to a life of philosophy is likely upon its death to pass into the body of a donkey, hawk, kite, or wolf, or, if it is lucky, a bee, wasp, or ant.

Plato's dialogues are thus teeming with animals of every kind, not only gadflies, horses, swans, snakes, and torpedo rays, but wolves, dogs, pigs, donkeys, hawks, bees, roosters, bulls, foxes, monkeys, locusts, oysters—and the list goes on. By our reckoning, there is but a single dialogue (the *Crito*) that does not contain any obvious reference to animals, while most dialogues have many. What is more, throughout Plato's dialogues the activity or enterprise of philosophy itself is often compared to a hunt, where the interlocutors are the hunters and the object of the dialogue's search—ideas of justice, beauty, courage, piety, or friendship—their elusive animal prey. Hence animal images, examples, metaphors, and tropes are used throughout the dialogues to develop not just Plato's dialogical characters, and not just the differences between the human and the animal, but many of the most important aspects of his ontology, epistemology, ethics, aesthetics, and political theory. To understand Plato's dialogues, then, it seems necessary to explain the presence of all these animals in the dialogues, their strategic or rhetorical necessity as well as their philosophical significance.

Plato's Animals is an attempt to give an account of the scope and importance of this remarkable bestiary in Plato's philosophy. It is a first attempt not just to gather or collect the many animal references into a single volume but to explain their function or purpose in the dialogues. While there have been numerous books in recent years that have treated the question of the animal in contemporary thought, or else the presence and significance of animals in a particular thinker, for example in Nietzsche, there has been nothing of the sort on Plato—whose bestiary is, we believe, just as rich and important for understanding his work as Nietzsche's bestiary is for his.[1]

This collection demonstrates that Plato's many appeals to animal images, analogies, and examples are not, as most commentators have treated them, mere rhetorical embellishments of otherwise independent philosophical ideas and arguments but essential elements of Plato's philosophy. The essays gathered here demonstrate that without such animal references Plato would have been unable to develop a full and coherent account of human society, human sexuality, human virtue, or the human soul. Even Plato's account of the nature of the cosmos itself would have been incomplete without such references to animal life. In other words, without this appeal to an animal world that is, for Plato, essentially without philosophy, Plato would have never been able to delineate a sphere for philosophy itself. *Plato's Animals* thus demonstrates that, without his animals, Plato would have never been able to develop a philosophy as coherent, comprehensive, and authoritative as the one he has.

Plato's Animals brings together contributions from scholars in the field of ancient philosophy on the theme of animals in Plato with a view to illuminating these larger aspects of Plato's philosophy. The volume is thus much more than a sophisticated lexicon for Plato's many animal references. Each essay in the volume looks at Plato's use of animals in the dialogues to help explain Plato's conception of philosophy and philosophical method; his understanding of politics and sexuality; the hierarchy he establishes between beasts, humans, and gods; his depiction of the afterlife, and so on. Some of the essays here concentrate on a single animal (e.g., the gadfly, horse, swan, or torpedo ray) in a particular dialogue or series of dialogues in order to show how Plato's use or characterization of this animal informs or is informed by his epistemology or his ontology, his ethics or his politics, his aesthetics or his general approach to philosophy. Other essays look at the various animal images used by Plato to characterize Socrates, at the way the soul is portrayed through animal images, at the way animals are used in Plato's reincarnation myths, at the manner in which political organizations are understood through animal analogies, at the way Plato distinguishes humans from (other) animals, at the question of animal sacrifice, or at the general question of just what an animal—a *zōion*—is in Plato.[2]

The fourteen essays gathered here are organized under seven headings, each illuminating a different aspect of the animal in Plato's dialogues. The first looks at the role animals play in myth and fable in the dialogues. The next two parts consider the various animal images, from the gadfly to the swan and the torpedo ray, used in the dialogues to characterize Socrates. The next three parts are devoted to particular aspects of Plato's depiction of animals: the political, the gendered or the sexual, and the philosophical. The volume concludes with two essays that consider the question of the continuity between human and animal life, specifically the question of whether, for Plato, human souls can be reincarnated as animals or animal souls as humans and, if so, what implications this has for Plato's philosophy as a whole.

The volume begins by recalling that, in the *Phaedo*, the dialogue in which Socrates tries to prove the immortality of the soul, Plato puts an implicit reference to animals right on the threshold of that work. As Heidi Northwood recalls in her essay "Making Music with Aesop's Fables in the *Phaedo*," Plato has Socrates say at the very outset of the dialogue that as he was awaiting his execution in prison he began for the first time in his life to compose poetry and to set Aesop's fables to music. But why Aesop? To answer this question, Northwood examines the many parallels between the lives of Socrates and Aesop, parallels of which Plato himself would have surely been aware. She then considers several points of intersection between Aesop's fables and Plato's thought, particularly with regard to the frequency of animal references in both. This leads Northwood to consider similarities between the various techniques Plato uses in his dialogues—myth, elenchus, and, especially, analogy—and the kind of critical self-examination that results from readings Aesop's animal fables.

In "'Talk to the Animals': On the Myth of Cronos in the *Statesman*," David Farrell Krell looks at animals not in fable but in myth. He considers especially the enigmatic myth recounted in the *Statesman* where it is suggested that in a mythological golden age humans not only got along peacefully with animals, neither killing nor being killed by them, but perhaps even conversed with them. This reference to "talking animals" allows Krell to reconsider many of the things said about the close relationship between humans and animals in other dialogues (such as the *Menexenus* and the *Timaeus*). Finally, the fact that the universe or cosmos is itself called a *zōion* in the *Statesman* allows Krell to ask about the nature of the body itself—the body of the cosmos, of humans, and of other animals—and the possibility of a "primordial disharmony" of the body, an originary chaos that precedes and conditions all living beings.

The next four essays all consider the animal analogies used to characterize Socrates throughout the dialogues. In "American Gadfly: Plato and the Problem of Metaphor," Michael Naas looks at perhaps the most memorable animal in all of Plato's dialogues—the image of Socrates as *gadfly*. Naas considers the various associations of the Greek word *muōps*, commonly translated into English as *gadfly*, in order to argue that this translation is at once uniquely appropriate and potentially misleading. Insofar as the term *gadfly* has come to have a metaphorical as well as a literal meaning in English, naming not just an irritating fly but an individual who acts as a productive, critical stimulus within society or the state, it seems to translate very well the metaphorical transformation that Plato would have wished to bring about in his depiction of Socrates. But since the metaphorical meaning of *gadfly* has an almost exclusively *political* meaning in English, and especially in the United States, Naas argues that this translation tends to conceal other potential meanings, including a uniquely philosophical one.

In "Till Human Voices Wake Us and We Drown: The Aporia-fish in the *Meno*," Thomas Thorp looks at perhaps the best known image of Socrates after that of the *muōps*, namely, the image of Socrates as a *narkē* in the *Meno*, that is, Socrates not as stingray, as this term has often been translated, but as *torpedo* ray. As Thorp demonstrates using both contemporary and ancient sources, the torpedo ray, as opposed to the stingray, does not actually sting its prey but "electrifies" its surroundings or its milieu, benumbing all the living beings in close proximity to it. This torpedo ray, rather than the stingray, is thus, Thorp shows, a more appropriate image for Socrates, who narcotizes his interlocutors and brings them to the point of torpor or perplexity, that is, to the place of *aporia* where all genuine learning begins. Thorp demonstrates that Plato's depiction of Socrates as a torpedo ray helps us understand both the psychological and philosophical effects of dialectic and, especially, of the Socratic elenchus.

In "We the Bird-Catchers: Receiving the Truth in the *Phaedo* and the *Apology*," S. Montgomery Ewegen appeals to the comparison that Socrates in the *Phaedo* draws between himself and the prophetic swan in order to reveal the complex relationship between *logos*, interpretation, and truth. By means of this comparison, Ewegen argues, Plato develops a conception of philosophical *logos* that does not simply express truth claims or propositions but prophetically signifies a truth that precedes and exceeds all reason, a truth that is not simply given but instead requires interpretation for its disclosure. Reading the *Apology* and Socrates's many claims in that dialogue to speak the truth in light of the image of the swan as a prophetic animal in the *Phaedo*, Ewegen argues that Socrates was, in effect, always singing his swan song, a song that ultimately aims to reveal and underscore the nature of truth and human finitude.

In "The Dog on the Fly," the final essay devoted to Socrates, H. Peter Steeves returns to the same image of Socrates as gadfly from the *Apology* in order to contrast it with the description of another philosophical provocateur from the same period, Diogenes the Cynic. Steeves reads Plato's depiction of Socrates as a gadfly in relation to the popular portrayal of Diogenes of Sinope as a dog in order to examine how and why, despite the remarkable similarity between these two thinkers, Plato valorized the former and vilified the latter. Through this examination, Steeves argues that Plato's attempt to cast Socrates as the paradigm of not just philosophy but humanity has the paradoxical effect of turning Socrates into a nonhuman animal who both fails to teach others to care for their souls and deprives his interlocutors of their humanity. Hence Steeves exposes a schism running through the Platonic corpus, where Socrates comes to embody values and goals that explicitly conflict with those that Plato intended to express.

The next two essays, gathered under the title "The Political Animal," look at the way in which animal images and analogies are crucial to the development of Plato's political philosophy. In "Taming Horses and Desires: Plato's Politics of Care," Jeremy Bell demonstrates the centrality of the example of horse training for Plato's political philosophy and, as a result, for Plato's philosophy more generally. Beginning with Socrates's comparison in the *Apology* of Athens to a large, lethargic horse, Bell demonstrates that Plato consistently deploys the image of the horse as an analog for the duality of human nature, which is characterized by the potential for both wildness and tameness, and which therefore requires practices of care in order to attain the good unique to its nature. Having determined that, for Plato, the highest form of such care is found in the practice of philosophy, Bell shows that philosophy, as the only true form of statesmanship for Plato, is best understood as a politics of care. To underscore this, Bell points to the depiction of the soul in the *Phaedrus* as a chariot and charioteer drawn by two horses in order to argue that, for Plato, it is philosophical education that tames the unruly desires of the human soul and makes that soul as divine as it can be, while the absence of such education renders human beings, as the *Laws* puts it, "the wildest of earth's creatures."

In the following essay, "Who Let the Dogs Out? Tracking the Philosophical Life among the Wolves and Dogs of the *Republic*," Christopher P. Long offers an account of Plato's political theory in such dialogues as *Republic* and *Statesman* by examining the opposition between well trained dogs, an image of the guardians of the state, and wild wolves, a figure for the tyrant and all those who threaten the state. Long begins by appealing to the dual nature of wolves—at once cooperative pack animals and savage beasts—in order to examine both the foundation and dissolution of the city and so reveal the proper path to the philosophic life. Long tracks the wolf from its earliest appearances in Book 1 of the *Republic*, where its savagery is set in opposition to the tameness of the just person, to the contrast in Book 2 between the wildness or savagery of the wolf and the tameness and gentleness of the young dog. Only this latter, Long shows, can be a model for the guardian/philosopher who must learn to be gentle toward his own and harsh toward his enemies. Long argues that this movement from savagery to tameness represents throughout the *Republic* the development of the possibility of true friendship and the progression toward a genuinely philosophic life.

After "The Political Animal" come two essays devoted to "The (En)gendered Animal." In the first, "The City of Sows and Sexual Differentiation in the *Republic*," Marina McCoy provides a feminist interpretation of the *Republic* by explaining precisely why Glaucon not only rejects Socrates's nonluxurious city or city of necessity in Book 2 but characterizes it as "a city of sows." Because, as McCoy argues, the Greek term for "sows" was commonly used as slang for female genitalia, Glaucon's rejection must be understood as a rejection of feminine *eros* more generally in the name of more masculine forms of desire. After demonstrating that much of the imagery used to characterize the city of sows is explicitly borrowed from the Thesmophoria, a gynocentric festival associated with the goddess Demeter, McCoy argues that Glaucon's emphatic dismissal of this first city amounts to a rejection of any city that would be built around feminine practices rather than founded on masculine principles. Setting these two cities in a dialectical relation with each other, McCoy argues that the philosophical task of the

Republic is to negotiate the extremes of each in order to demonstrate that Platonic philosophy resides in the tension between feminine and masculine forms of desire.

Sara Brill continues this inquiry into the sexual implications of Plato's thinking of the animal in her essay "Animality and Sexual Difference in the *Timaeus*." Brill begins by offering an at once expansive and detailed reading of the cosmogony presented in the *Timaeus*. Because mind and mindlessness can be presented to thought only through animality, Timaeus must, Brill contends, construct his cosmogony as a zoogony. But this attempt to articulate the origin of humanity in cosmological rather than political terms ultimately fails to account for the flourishing of the quintessential animal, that is, the human animal. Thus, Brill concludes, the *Timaeus* works to expose the shortcomings of a philosophical cosmogony that aims to provide a nonpolitical anthropogony. By reminding us that, in the *Timaeus*, the term *zōion* is used to name not only the many animals within the universe or cosmos but the cosmos itself, Brill's essay also raises the question of sexual difference at the level not just of different animal species, including the human, but at the level of the cosmos that contains or embraces all these different species.

The next two essays look specifically at Plato's philosophical methodology in relationship to his thinking of the animal. Holly Moore in "Animal Sacrifice in Plato's Later Methodology" argues that Plato's *diairesis*, that is, the method of division and definition that is developed in the *Phaedrus*, *Sophist*, and *Statesman*, is modeled on the Greek religious practice of animal sacrifice and dismemberment. Close examination of this practice is thus necessary for a richer and fuller understanding of Plato's philosophical methodology. Moore thus demonstrates that when Socrates in the *Phaedrus* argues that ideas or categories must be divided along their "natural joints," he implicitly compares not just the dialectician to a butcher but the conceptual world or landscape to a living animal. This insight has many implications, Moore argues, for the relationship between organic life and being itself, since classes or ideas must now be not simply identified and analyzed but domesticated, sacrificed, and expertly carved up. Hence Moore argues that there are, in effect, no natural kinds but only classes or ideas that have already been domesticated and marked as sacrificeable wholes to be divided along their natural joints. There is thus, Moore concludes, an inherent anthropocentrism in the very processes of collection and division and, therefore, in Plato's ontology at its most general level.

In "The Animals That Therefore We Were? Aristophanes's Double-Creatures and the Question of Origins," Drew A. Hyland reads Plato's *Symposium* and *Phaedrus* in order to determine exactly where Plato draws the line between the human animal and other beasts. Hyland argues that Plato locates this line not, as is commonly thought, between pure reason, which would be the privilege of humans, and *eros* or desire, which would essentially be the province of animals. The line is to be drawn, rather, between a uniquely human form of *eros*, on the one hand, and animal or animal-like desires, on the other. Hence Hyland demonstrates that while Aristophanes in his encomium of *eros* in the *Symposium* presents humans as little more than desiring animals, Socrates will argue that what sets humans apart from animals is their participation in a uniquely *rational* form of *eros* that goes beyond desire and makes philosophy possible.

The final part of the volume, "Animals and the Afterlife," brings together two essays on the role animals play in Plato's conception of death and the afterlife. Both begin by focusing on Plato's account of humans being reincarnated as animals in the concluding myth of the *Republic,* the Myth of Er. In the first of these two essays, "Animals and Angels: The Myth of Life as a Whole in *Republic* 10," Claudia Baracchi explores Plato's conception of justice through an examination of the circular and regenerative nature of the life of the soul. Baracchi argues that insofar as the soul retains traces of its previous lives, traces that span both human and nonhuman forms, Plato's myth of death and regeneration suggests that nonhuman animality always underlies and marks human life. This account of the way in which nonhuman animality is retained within the human soul is perfectly consistent, Baracchi shows, with Timaeus's account of the lively, organic, and regenerative nature of the cosmos itself. Baracchi concludes that Plato's understanding of the circularity and regeneration of all life opens up new possibilities of empathy for and community with both human and nonhuman animals.

In "Of Beasts and Heroes: The Promiscuity of Humans and Animals in the Myth of Er," Francisco J. Gonzalez contrasts the account of reincarnation given in the Myth of Er with that offered in the *Phaedo,* where it is said that humans may indeed be reincarnated as animals but not animals as humans. In light of the difference between these two accounts, Gonzalez examines the Neoplatonist concern that the account of reincarnation in the *Republic* undermines any fundamental distinction between human and animal souls and, thus, any fundamental distinction between humans and animals. Gonzalez demonstrates through a close reading of Plotinus, Proclus, and Ficino's commentaries on Plato that the question of the animal in Plato has a long history in Western thought and has profound implications for both philosophy and theology.

From Plato's conception of the philosophical life to his depiction of the afterlife, from his politics to his ontology, from his psychology to his understanding of sexual difference, these fourteen essays demonstrate that almost nothing in Plato's dialogues goes untouched by the animal. If the human is, for Plato, a philosophical animal, the philosophical animal par excellence, it could not have been defined as such without a distinction between what is proper to the human and what belongs to other animals or to the animal within the human. *Plato's Animals* demonstrates that if Plato places animals rather far down on his hierarchy of being, intelligence, beauty, and truth, far below gods and humans and just above plants, animals nonetheless occupy a central place in the drama, architecture, rhetoric, and argumentative structure of the dialogues.

Because the theme is so vast and has so many implications, this volume makes no pretentions to having exhausted the theme of "Plato's Animals." On the contrary, it is meant to be just a beginning and, hopefully, a provocation to scholars and students of Plato. It is for this reason that we have included at the end of the volume an index of all the animals or explicit animal references in the dialogues, not just those treated by the essays in this volume. The reader will find there hundreds of references to more than three dozen different animals, an indication of just how ubiquitous this theme is in Plato's dialogues and how crucial it is to his thought.

Given the recent proliferation of works in philosophy on the relationship between humans and animals, on vegetarianism, animal ethics, animal rights, and so on, we hope that this volume will serve as further impetus to ask such questions in the context of Plato's dialogues. What is one to make, for example, of the comparison referred to at the beginning of this introduction between Socrates and a stork, that is, not some biting, stinging, or goading animal but one that hopes to be cared for by its offspring? Or else—to stay just with Plato's birds—what is to be made of the fact that a plover is the privileged example in the *Gorgias* of a life of pleasure, or the fact that in Plato's myths of the afterlife birds such as the nightingale and the eagle appear to be favored choices for Greek heroes, or the fact that, in the *Laws*, the Athenian argues that insofar as birds, unlike human beings, cannot "perceive order," insofar as they have no number and thus no rhythm, they are incapable, despite every appearance, of having song? What does it mean, in short, for Plato's philosophy that no other animal beside the human can sing or dance? While the question may initially appear tangential to Plato's overall philosophical project, our hope is that the reader of *Plato's Animals* will understand it as a potentially crucial question for asking, for example, about the importance of number and mathematics in Plato's philosophy, about the relationship between order and disorder in his cosmology and ontology, about the opposition between reason and unreason, and about the line that is drawn—the line that Plato seems to have thought had to be drawn—between the human and the animal on the basis of these categories or these attributes.

Notes

1. See, for example, Cary's Wolf's edited collection *Zoontologies: The Question of the Animal* (Minneapolis: Minnesota University Press, 1998) and Matthew Calarco's *Zoographies: The Question of the Animal from Heidegger to Derrida* (Columbia University Press, 2008), as well as *A Nietzschean Bestiary: Becoming Animal beyond Docile and Brutal*, ed. Christa Davis Acampora and Ralph Acampora (Lanham, Md.:Rowman and Littlefield, 2004). The closest work to

any of these is Jean Frère's *Le bestiaire de Platon,* a single-authored (French-language) work that looks at the theme of animals in Plato from a quite different perspective.

2. The noun *zōion* has in Plato, as in many other Greek authors, both a general and a more restricted meaning. In a first moment, it designates anything that "partakes of life [*zēn*]" (*Timaeus* 77b), an animal or living creature in the most general or generic sense. Such a *zōion* is alive to the extent that it is "ensouled," its body held or possessed by a soul, a *psychē* (*Timaeus* 87e), and it is "mortal" insofar as this union of body and soul is of finite duration (*Phaedrus* 246c, *Sophist* 246e, *Timaeus* 77b). But in addition to this more general sense of *zōion* as any living, ensouled, mortal creature, whether plant, animal, or human being, *zōion* (or *ta zōia* in the plural) can suggest animals (including humans) as opposed to plants (*Protagoras* 334b; *Statesman* 261b–c, *Gorgias* 516b), but then also, in an even more restricted sense, animals as opposed both to plants, on the one hand, and humans (or *anthrōpoi*), on the other (*Phaedo* 111a–b, *Republic* 466d, *Protagoras* 321c). Finally, the word *zōion* is used in a couple of dialogues to characterize the cosmos as a whole, the universe itself as a "living creature" (*Timaeus* 30b, *Statesman* 269d), and in the *Laws* there is speculation about whether the stars, as apparently self-moving and therefore "ensouled" bodies, can also be considered *zōia* or living beings (*Laws* 899b).

PART I

The Animal of Fable and Myth

1 Making Music with Aesop's Fables in the *Phaedo*

Heidi Northwood

AT THE BEGINNING of the *Phaedo*, Socrates contemplates the relationship between pain and pleasure after having been released from the shackles that had bound his legs: "'What a strange thing, my friends, that seems to be which men call pleasure! How wonderfully it is related to that which seems to be its opposite, pain, in that they will not both come to a man at the same time, and yet if he pursues the one and captures it he is generally obliged to take the other also, as if the two were joined together in one head'" (*Phaedo* 60b).[1] This makes him think of Aesop: "'And I think,' he said, 'if Aesop had thought of them, he would have made a fable telling how they were at war and god wished to reconcile them, and when he could not do that, he fastened their heads together, and for that reason, when one of them comes to anyone, the other follows after. Just so it seems that in my case, after pain was in my leg on account of the fetter, pleasure appears to have come following after'" (60c). Here Cebes interrupts Socrates, having remembered that Evenus had asked him to find out why Socrates had been composing poems—"metrical versions of Aesop's fables [λόγους] and the hymn to Apollo"—while awaiting his execution in jail (60d). Socrates answers that it was to test the meaning of certain recurring dreams that said, "Socrates, make music and work at it [μουσικὴν ποίει καὶ ἐργάζου]" (60e). To this point, Socrates had thought these dreams were encouraging him to do what he was already doing, since "philosophy was the greatest kind of music and I was working at that" (61a). But just in case the dreams really meant that he should make music in the ordinary sense, he thought he should compose some verses (61a). So first he composed a hymn to Apollo whose festival was causing the delay in his execution, and after that, "considering that a poet, if he is really to be a poet, must compose myths [μύθους] and not speeches [λόγους], since I was not a maker of myths [μυθολογικός], I took the myths [μύθους] of Aesop, which I had at hand and

13

knew [προχείρους εἶχον καὶ ἠπιστάμην], and turned into verse [τούτους ἐποίησα] the first I came upon [ἐνέτυχον]" (61b).

Socrates downplays his choice of Aesop. He is quite serious about following the message of his dreams "to make music," but the choice to "make music" out of Aesop seems to be one of convenience: a poet must compose myths; Socrates doesn't do this; Aesop's myths were "at hand"; off he went. But there is good reason not to take Socrates too seriously here. In addition to Plato's artistry, which makes any seemingly offhand remark in his dialogues suspect, there is Socrates's claim that he does not compose myths when he had himself just created one about the nature of pain and pleasure. This alone should make us pause and wonder why, really, Socrates chose Aesop's fables to make into music. And it's not at all obvious; on the surface Aesop was no particular favorite of Socrates or Plato; he is mentioned in only one other dialogue in the Platonic corpus, in *Alcibiades I*, where the fable "The Lion and the Fox" is used to point to the Spartan's hidden love of wealth.[2]

Others have considered this question. Compton, for example, has argued that Socrates chose Aesop because Plato wanted to remind his readers of their parallel lives and deaths, that Plato was "assimilating Socrates to Aesop."[3] The similarities between them as they are portrayed in the works of Plato and the *Life of Aesop* are indeed striking. While the version of the *Life of Aesop* that survives was likely not written until the first century CE, there is evidence that it was based on a number of stories about Aesop's life and death that were widely known in the time of Socrates.[4] The portrayal of Aesop in Aristophanes and Herodotus is consistent with the later story, as is a representation of Aesop on a fifth-century BCE Attic cup.[5] The parallels are these: both are extremely ugly (indeed both are compared to satyrs); both are righteous critics of an unjust city; both are found to be intolerable by members of this unjust city and are consequently brought to trial on trumped-up charges; both, in their defenses, use animal parables to criticize their accusers; both prophesy doom for the city after they receive their death penalties; both comply with their death penalties; and both have a relationship with Apollo. Compton concludes:

> That these parallels are not accidental is shown by Plato's having Socrates versify Aesop in the last days of life. Versifying beast fables would seem almost a trivial thing to do, taken at face value, but our respect for Plato's conscious and subtle artistry will not allow us to leave it at that. Immediately before we learn that he is versifying Aesop and the hymn to Apollo, he tells a fable that he describes as Aesopic.... Socrates makes up Aesopic fables and (re-)writes Aesop's fables.... [Socrates] is being assimilated to Aesop by Plato, and surely Aesop's death is being adumbrated here, in the dialogue of Socrates' death, the *Phaedo*.[6]

Edward Clayton takes this line of thought a step further.[7] He agrees with Compton that Plato means for us to see the similarities between the lives of Aesop and

Socrates, but he invites us to notice the differences as well. For example, while both are righteous critics of a city, Socrates criticizes the Athenians for thinking they know when they don't and being too fond of money, reputation, and physical pleasures. Aesop, on the other hand, criticizes the people of Delphi because they don't honor and pay him after his performance. Socrates can compel others to goodness because of the beauty of his own soul; Aesop's intelligence and good advice can help people to get on in the world and solve some of their practical problems. Socrates's motives in talking to others are pure; he is attempting "to turn people from injustice to justice and vice to virtue."[8] Aesop, however, always seems to be motived by self-interest, whether by his desire for freedom when he was a slave, or for money and fame at other times.[9] Socrates is nearly always immune from pains and pleasures of the body, whereas Aesop has sex with his master's wife nine times.[10] In prison, awaiting his execution, Socrates is remarkably calm, even happy; Aesop is far from tranquil and, on the way to the cliff from which he is to be thrown, tries to escape his death by seeking sanctuary in a shrine to the Muses. Finally, Socrates never wavers in his service to Apollo. Aesop, however, neglects to properly honor Apollo when building a shrine to the Muses.[11] Plato's purpose, then, in having Socrates versify Aesop at the beginning of the *Phaedo* is to remind readers of their parallel lives, and through the comparison, notice the differences. Clayton's conclusion: Plato wants us to see that it is Socrates whom we should emulate, not Aesop. Socrates is wise and good; "Aesop is a good man, but he is no philosopher."[12]

I do not disagree with Compton or Clayton as far as they go (although the characterization of Aesop that Clayton points to makes it difficult to see Aesop as a "good man"). It is clear both that there are surprising parallels between their lives as found in these texts and that there are differences that Plato may have wanted us to think about at the beginning of the *Phaedo*. But there is an omission in both. The arguments of both Compton and Clayton rest almost entirely on a comparison of Socrates's life as found in certain Platonic dialogues with Aesop's as found in the *Life of Aesop*. There is very little mention, and no detailed study, of the fables themselves. Granted, it is difficult to know the "message" of Aesop since the history of each fable involves a complicated story of transmission and rewriting by various compilers at different times. And for the most part one cannot know whether a particular fable is "genuine" or invented later and merely ascribed to Aesop. But if one wants to understand why Socrates chose Aesop to versify, the fables do need to be explored, if only with the modest goal of seeing whether there are general themes repeated in many myths, themes that could give us a hint about why Socrates chose Aesop. Indeed, Clayton himself (without much if any evidence) writes that there is one such general message, and it is at odds with the message of Platonic philosophy.

Clayton mentions the fables in the context of his enumeration of the various ways that Socrates and Aesop are different. He seems to be in the same camp as

Blackham and Rothwell, who believe that overall the fables have a political message.[13] As Clayton argues: "Their basic message is that the strong survive and the weak suffer, and the highest goal one can pursue is the preservation of one's life in the face of a world that is hostile or at best indifferent."[14] Consequently, for the powerful, these "Might makes right" fables would "reinforce the rightness and naturalness of their power and actions and would allow them proudly to compare themselves to lions and other powerful predators able to impose their will on others with impunity."[15] The weak could identify with the weaker animals in the myths and find helpful advice about how to stay out of trouble.[16] Thus, Clayton writes, "fables can reveal important truths and provide useful, practical advice for conducting one's affairs, but they are not useful for bringing people to an understanding of virtue or vice, nor is that their purpose." And so the message of the fables "is not the message found in the Socratic teachings."[17]

If this is the message of the fables, it is indeed very different from Plato's. But we need to be cautious about accepting this too quickly. First, it would be very strange for Socrates to put a fable with this message to music, even if all he was concerned to do was "make music in the common sense" by putting some fable "at hand" into verse. That general message—that "the politically strong survive and the weak suffer"—is antithetical to what Socrates had argued for in the *Apology* and *Crito*, and it is opposed to "the message" in the *Republic* and *Gorgias* where Socrates takes on Thrasymachus, Polus, and Callicles for holding that "Might makes right." Imagine, for example, Socrates putting something like Hesiod's "The Hawk and the Nightingale" into verse and dedicating it to the author of his dream; it seems more than a bit of a stretch. It seems like blasphemy.[18] Having Aesop's fables "at hand" or "in memory" would hardly be enough reason to choose them if that's what they were about.

But there is an additional reason to be cautious: this view of the fables can be defended only by ignoring a large number of them. While there are a number of fables that, arguably, support the "Might is right" thesis,[19] there are also many ethically themed fables that have a different moral. For example, in "The Hare and the Lion's Justice" a good-tempered lion king creates peace between the powerful and weak by bringing all the wild animals to justice, making each pay penalty for what it had done to its prey.[20] Admittedly, such images of justice are rare in the fables. More common (and more famous) are those fables that show the value of friendship and fellow-feeling between the powerful and the weak. In "The Shepherd and the Lion," for example, a shepherd helps a lion who had a thorn stuck in his paw.[21] Later, the lion returns the favor when he saves the shepherd, who has been convicted of a crime that he didn't commit. Similarly, in another, a mouse accidentally runs over a sleeping lion and wakes him.[22] The lion grabs him but decides to let him go, since "to kill such a tiny creature would be cause for reproach rather than glory." A few days later the mouse repays the kindness by freeing the lion when trapped by a hunter. And there are others that tell a similar tale: good deeds and fellow-feeling will be rewarded.[23] While one could argue that the message of such fables is not the enlightened morality of Plato, since they highlight the practical rewards of friendship and gratitude, they nonetheless give a different message than "the strong survive and the weak suffer." (One might wonder if Aesop's "might makes right" fables are not in fact a criticism of such a view.) But even with a more complicated version of what Aesop was about, we still don't have much to go on. We still have no answer to the question: "Why Aesop?"

There are, in fact, quite a number of animal fables in the Aesop collection that contain stronger echoes of Platonic thought. Some of them are quite interesting even if not profound. For example, a wolf, a cat, and a lion are cast as doctors whose patients (a donkey, a hen, a pregnant sow, and a horse) are really their prey.[24] These fables echo some of Plato's own comments about doctors as unnecessary if one leads a moderate life,[25] and, stretched just a little, perhaps Plato's criticisms of the Sophists.[26] Aesop, in a number of charming fables with disputing foxes, monkeys, crocodiles, and fishes shows how ridiculous it is to boast about one's ancestors, which sounds quite a bit like Socrates's own criticisms of this in the *Theaetetus* digression.[27] Yet another group of fables points out the distinction between appearances and reality: camels are in fact gentle despite their size;[28] frogs and crickets are in fact quite small, despite the noise they make;[29] the sea can be quite dangerous even though it can also be tranquil,[30] and so on. Other fables (and these are, by far, the most numerous) have rather "obvious" "Greek" ethical messages that are also found in Plato: don't be boastful, vain, self-deluded, or hubristic.[31] But these connections, while making it less shocking that Socrates would versify Aesop as he awaits execution, don't get us very far. They don't suggest a clear answer as to what Plato is trying to tell us with Socrates's choice of Aesop.

We need to look at the *Phaedo* more closely with a view to exploring the similarities and differences between "the messages" in the *Phaedo* and the messages in the fables. That Plato wanted us to do this is, I think, indicated by references to animals in a variety of contexts throughout the *Phaedo*, all of which are likely to have called Aesop to mind for a contemporary reader/listener of the dialogue. The first, found in Socrates's explanation of why philosophy is the practice of death, describes the different afterlives likely available to humans, depending on the kind of lives they have led. The pure soul will dwell with the gods (80d–81a), but the soul that has mingled with the body and has come to love its pleasures will be held fast to this world and be reincarnated into another body (81b–e): the followers of gluttony, wantonness, and drunkenness into asses; followers of injustice, tyranny, and violence into wolves, hawks, and kites; and the happier followers of the civil and social virtues into bees, wasps, ants, or even men (81e–82b). While the details are different, a similar idea is found in Aesop in "Zeus and the Ant": "Long ago, the creature who is today an ant used to be a man who was always busy farming. Still, he was not satisfied with the results of his own labor, so he would steal from his neighbor's crops. Zeus became angry at his greedy behavior and turned him into the animal that now has the name of 'ant.' Yet although the man changed his shape, he did not change his habits, and even now he goes around the fields gathering the fruits of other people's labor, storing them up for himself."[32] This is not a reincarnation story; the punishment of being turned into an ant for being greedy happens to the farmer in this life, not the next. Nonetheless, the general structure of being turned into the animal that one resemble as an appropriate punishment for one's vice is the same, as is the underlying belief/assumption that animal species have souls and characters that are typical, that these animal souls can resemble human souls,[33] and that the character of a creature's soul will not be altered even after "transmigrating" into another species.[34]

In Socrates's second and third references to animals—swans and bees respectively—it is a particular trait of these animals that are common to both. Intending to reassure Simmias and the others that his situation is not a misfortune, Socrates compares himself to swans, which, when seeing that they are about to die, sing even more passionately than before. Socrates argues that they are not lamenting (as was commonly believed) but instead "sing most and best in their joy that they are to go to the god whose servants they are [Apollo]" (84e). The swan and its song are mentioned in two of Aesop's fables. In one, a man tries to slaughter a goose, but in the dark, grabs his swan instead. Its song saves it.[35] In another, a man buys a swan to sing for guests at a dinner party. But the swan doesn't perform, the man not realizing that the swan sings only at death. It is only later, when the swan is singing its "funeral dirge," that the man realizes his error.[36]

Bees and their stingers come up in the misology passage (89c–91c). Fearing that he might be deceiving his friends in his enthusiasm for the argument—persuading them to believe something that is not true—Socrates hopes that he is not like a bee that leaves its sting in them before he dies (91c). Aesop gives an etiology of the bee and its stinger in "Zeus and the Bee."[37] Zeus, delighted with the bee's gift of honey, grants her anything she wishes. She asks for a stinger so she can protect her honey and herself. Zeus grants her wish, but out of his love for humans arranges it so that she will die as soon as she uses it.

Finally, at the very end of the *Phaedo*, in his description of his conception of the earth and the heavens, Socrates compares the region around the Mediterranean and its inhabitants to "ants or frogs about a marsh" (109a–b). He goes on, in an extended allegory, to suggest that there are many other "marshes" or "hollows" about which humans live—spoiled and corroded, full of mud where nothing can grow nobly—and all those who live this way are deceived, thinking that they live on the surface with true light (109b–110a). Part of the original image, frogs about a marsh, is very common in the Aesop fables. Of the thirteen fables with frogs, nine make explicit reference to the swamp or pond, and in most of them the swamp is significant.[38] For example, in one, frogs scoff at a donkey for complaining when it falls into their swamp;[39] traitorous frogs drown unsuspecting mice in their ponds;[40] Zeus gives a floating log to frogs as their king;[41] and there are more.[42]

So why would Plato want us to think of Aesop throughout the dialogue? We need to return to where Aesop is first mentioned in the *Phaedo* to be reminded of Socrates's purported purpose in versifying Aesop's fables: it was to "make this which is ordinarily called music" (61a). Recall: Socrates thought he had been "making music" his whole life in his pursuit of philosophy since "philosophy was the greatest kind of music" (61a). But what does this mean? What else is said about the connection between music and philosophy in Plato?

Music and philosophy are put together in many places in the dialogues.[43] But perhaps the most straightforward is in the *Sophist* (253a–254b) where the methods and goals of the arts of music and dialectic are compared. The Stranger and Theaetetus are discussing three possibilities: "either all things will mingle with one another, or none will do so, or some will and others will not" (252e). The first two are impossible: if all things can mingle, then "motion is at rest" would make sense (252d); if no things mingle, then one could not attribute being to anything (251e). Thus, the third possibility, that some things will mingle and some not, must be true. It is much the same, the Stranger says, as "the letters of the alphabet: for some of these do not fit each other, and others do," and the vowels "run through them all as a bond, so that without one of the vowels the other letters cannot be joined one to another"; and one needs a specialized kind of knowledge, one needs the art of grammar, to know how to join the letters properly (253a). The same is true with music and in fact all the arts (253b). Knowledge of each art is just knowing what things go with what, and which ones do not, and why. The same is true for philosophy:

> Now since we have agreed that the classes or genera also commingle with one another, or do not commingle, in the same way, must not he possess some science and proceed by the processes of reason who is to show correctly which of the classes harmonize with which, and which reject one another, and also if he is to show whether there are some elements extending though all and holding them together so that they can mingle, and again, when they separate, whether there are other universal causes of separation?—Certainly he needs science [ἐπιστήμης], and perhaps even the greatest of sciences [τῆς μεγίστης]. (253b–c)

Philosophy is like music (and grammar) because both arts are concerned with the fitting together of things (their "harmony") and the reasons why things fit together in the way they do. Philosophy is concerned with which ideas go together, which ones do not, and why, just as music is concerned with which notes go together, which not, and why. Perhaps philosophy is the "greatest" music because of the importance of what is put together, and what "fitting together" means here: namely, that something is true. But, in any case, to say that philosophy is the greatest music is to say something about the fundamental nature of philosophy.

Is there, then, something special about Aesop that would make him a good choice to be put to music "in the common sense" when music here is understood to be about investigating what goes together and what does not? That Socrates found it natural to refer to animals as both positive and negative exempla in the *Phaedo* is helpful. First, it suggests that we should look to Aesop's fables to see what he thought made particular animals worthy of emulation (like the swan who is not afraid of death) and other animals eschewed (like a bee who leaves its stinger in another when it dies, etc.). Secondly, it should make us wonder about the vehicle of the animal fable itself.

First, the animals that are held up positively are those that know what's true, know themselves, and what's what. The tortoise in "The Tortoise and the Hare" is a good example of this; here is an animal that knows its own limitations but uses this knowledge to beat the hare in the famous race.[44] In another fable a wasp tells a butterfly that the most important thing is what one is, not what one has been.[45] When shown the splendor of the city mouse's plate, a country mouse is still satisfied to eat only acorns if it means he has his freedom and can live without fear.[46]

There are many more fables that ridicule animals for not knowing what's right, true, or appropriate. Various animals are punished for attempting to perform tasks for which they are not suited or for trying to be something they are not. An earthworm splits into pieces for trying to be as long as a snake.[47] Tortoises and beetles die as a result of their desire to fly like eagles.[48] A crab tries to be a land animal and is eaten by a fox.[49] A raven wants to be like a swan and starves to death.[50] A monkey drowns trying to catch fish with a net.[51] A donkey is beaten to near death, having acted like his master's favorite puppy,[52] or, in another fable, having danced on a roof like a monkey.[53] A hare is captured and killed when given stag's horns by Zeus.[54] A frog tries to be as big as an ox by puffing itself up and explodes.[55] And there are more.

If these are taken in isolation from other fables, they might seem to support the view that Aesop's message is, for the weak, "keep your head down; don't get any ideas about becoming more than you are." But not all of the creatures in these sorts of fables are weak. The strong, like the weak, are capable of doing things out of ignorance of what is fitting and how things work. A fisherman, for example, unsuccessfully tries to woo fish onto land by playing a flute.[56] A fox is ridiculed by a bramble for thinking that the bramble was a good thing to grab to prevent a fall.[57] A greedy woman, thinking that if she gives her hen more food it will lay more eggs, ends up with none.[58] A wolf loses his dinner for acting like a musician instead of a "butcher."[59] A middle-aged man with two age-inappropriate mistresses becomes bald.⁶⁰ The problem in these fables is not that the creatures are trying to overstep their bounds in a political sense, but that they do not understand the natural order of things: things have natures that make them what they are but also limit what they can do. Acting as one should—within one's own nature, performing one's own work—is appropriate and right. This is a metaphysical point about what fits together and what does not; it is not a political one.⁶¹

Aesop's fables, however, do not merely assert a natural order of things; a large group of them also explain this order, or *why* things go together in the way they do, just as in the art of dialectic. And given that the Aesopic fable that Socrates "composes" at the beginning of the *Phaedo* is of this sort—not an animal story, but an allegorical explanation of the nature of pain and pleasure—this would appear to be particularly significant. Some of these fables explain the characters or characteristics of certain animals and plants: why they eat what they do, why some plants have thorns,⁶² why they live where they do,⁶³ why some birds don't sing or sing well,⁶⁴ why tortoises have shells,⁶⁵ why camels have short ears,⁶⁶ and why she-goats have beards.⁶⁷ The fable about why bees die when they sting is also of this sort.⁶⁸ Often the explanation involves some sort of punishment: the creature is the way it is because of some transgression, greed, or vanity. Kites, for example, can't sing because they lost their voices trying to neigh like horses.⁶⁹ As we have already seen, ants gather and store the "fruits of other people's labor," having once been greedy farmers who were changed into ants as punishment.⁷⁰ Others explain certain characteristics of human beings (e.g., the different periods of human life),⁷¹ why humans cry,⁷² why some humans prefer the same sex,⁷³ why short people are smarter than tall ones,⁷⁴ and why some humans act like animals.⁷⁵ One even explains humans' ability to speak and reason.⁷⁶

But it is not just a similarity in message—a shared conception of wisdom and recognition of a cosmos—that is found in these animal fables and etiologies; the vehicles used to express this wisdom and teach others—the fables, allegories, and analogies themselves—are also similar to what is used by Socrates and Plato. Leslie Kurke has argued that this similarity actually points to the fact (sometimes even acknowledged by Plato) that Socrates's use of *epagoge*—induction by analogy—has its roots in Aesop.⁷⁷ In many dialogues—not only in the *Phaedo*—Socrates uses animals to point out the motives and manners of humans in order to praise them or else ridicule them as not worthy of a human being. Ants, bees, cattle, cows, cranes, dogs, fish, frogs, foxes, gadflies, horses, sheep, lions, nightingales, oxen, oysters, swine, plovers, roosters, snakes, and, more generally, beasts are all used in this way.⁷⁸ But according to Kurke, it is Socrates's use of analogy per se that has its roots in Aesop's animal fables. And, of course, Plato's use of allegories and myths is also widespread.⁷⁹ Indeed, Kurke sees the other part of what Charles Kahn has called "the old Socratic tool-box" foreshadowed in Aesop as well: the elenchus. And while she, like Compton and Clayton, focuses exclusively on the *Life of Aesop* and the fables that are included there as part of the narrative, her point is only strengthened by an exploration of the fables themselves.

It is significant, I think, that these two forms of Socratic discourse require a kind of engagement that other forms of early philosophical writing do not. An analogy requires the reader to make the connections, to see what is the same and what is different in the terms. Likewise, showing someone that their beliefs involve self-contradiction—the hallmark of the elenchus—goes beyond this to active, sometimes very disturbing, self-examination. Kurke makes the connection between the elenchus and Aesop on the basis of stories in the *Life of Aesop* where opponents are reduced to self-contradiction in public demonstrations. I would like to push this a little further and suggest that ridicule itself—the most common method used by Aesop in his "negative exempla" animal myths—can work in a very similar way to the elenchus.

The elenchus works, when it does work, by making manifest to the interlocutor that her beliefs do not add up; she thought she knew something (what goes with what), but in fact she does not. The most common reason for the failure of the elenchus is that the interlocutor is not open to examining her own beliefs or entertaining the possibility that she does not know what she thought she did; she becomes defensive, angry. While ridicule is nastier, it too can teach if you are open to the possibility that the person laughing at you really does know what you do not. Likewise, it can fail to teach for the same reasons as the elenchus.

Now, one cannot teach an animal by ridiculing it. But of course that is not the point of the fables. The fables are meant to be didactic for humans. And if they are to teach us, and not merely reinforce what we already know, they must teach us something new. But we are already removed from the ridicule. It is not we who are ridiculed, but the animals. So we have to identify with the animal that is being ridiculed. We must go from "What a stupid animal" to "Oh! I see myself in that stupid animal" to "I guess I didn't know what I thought I did." The process is vital. We need to take the steps for ourselves; we need to identify with the animals and then engage in self-examination. Otherwise, what we take away from the myths is likely to be nothing more than an opinion (not knowledge) about what is right. Interestingly, a promythium or epimythium was later added to most of Aesop's fables to spell out what the compiler thought was its "lesson." The compilers did not want to leave it up to their readers to figure it out. But this is to take away a very important step for the reader or audience, and it makes the fables more like a set of moral rules than the engaging fables that can help one examine one's own life. This kind of engagement is, of course, also the goal of Platonic dialogue itself. Instead of merely telling a person what to believe, the dialogue form hides its author's message, and so the reader must engage. She must figure out which character or what idea makes the most sense; she must think for herself. Likewise, a fable that ridicules an animal for doing something stupid does not include along with it an explanation of the "joke" (at least if it has no promythium or epimythium). The reader has to figure it out on her own: for example, what did the fox do wrong? Why didn't the fox see it beforehand? Will the fox learn his lesson? Am I ever like that stupid fox?

Why then did Plato have Socrates choose Aesop? The mention of Aesop at the beginning of the *Phaedo* might very well point to a connection between the lives of Aesop and Socrates, and by comparing them—and seeing the superiority of Socrates's—we might learn something about how to live rightly. But it seems that by digging more deeply into the fables themselves, we might also learn something if we examine the similarities and differences between Aesop and Plato. Perhaps Aesop was not as virtuous as Socrates in "real life," but he did seem to share a conception of philosophy and teaching with Plato. To love wisdom is to make music. It is to strive to see what goes with what—to catch a glimpse of the natural order of things—and to show this to others indirectly: showing what happens to a fox who ignores this order, illustrating how a person can be confused in their beliefs. While fables, dialogues, analogies, ridicule, and the elenchus, all of which require engagement, might not be successful in teaching something to someone, they still have a better chance than direct admonition. And what better way to have others think about this than to have Socrates put Aesop to music?

Notes

1. All translations are from the Loeb Classical Library unless otherwise indicated.
2. *Alcibiades I* 122e. "The Lion and the Fox" is Fable 18 in Gibbs (Perry 142). In what follows, I will use Gibbs's numbering to refer to the fables and Perry's number in parentheses following. Because there is no one standard way to refer to the fables, I have chosen to use Gibbs's translations and numbering since her translations are excellent, she has grouped the fables in a very accessible way, and she includes all the known fables: Laura Gibbs, *Aesop's Fables* (New York: Oxford University Press, 2002). I also include Perry's numbers since they are both traditional and complete.
3. Todd Compton, "The Trial of the Satirist: Poetic Vitae (Aesop, Archilochus, Homer) as Background for Plato's *Apology*," *American Journal of Philology* 111, no. 3 (1990): 330–347, especially 341. Leslie Kurke has also considered this question in her article "Plato, Aesop and the Beginnings of Mimetic Prose," *Representations* 94, no. 1 (2006): 6–52. I shall consider her arguments later in the paper.
4. See Compton, "The Trial of the Satirist," 331–332, for a detailed discussion of this.
5. See ibid. 331.
6. Ibid. 341.
7. Edward W. Clayton, "The Death of Socrates and the Life of Aesop," *Ancient Philosophy* 28, no. 2 (2008): 311–328.
8. Ibid., 319.
9. Ibid.
10. Ibid., 320.

11. Ibid., 324.
12. Ibid., 314.
13. H. J. Blackham, *The Fable as Literature* (London; Athlone Press, 1985), and Kenneth S. Rothwell Jr., "Aristophanes' *Wasps* and the Sociopolitics of Aesop's Fables," *Classical Journal* 93, no. 4 (1995): 233-254. I say "seems" because this is not the view that Clayton takes in his article "Aesop, Aristotle, and Animals: The Role of Fables in Human Life," *Humanitas* 21, nos. 1 and 2 (2008): 179-200. While agreeing that the message is predominantly that "Might makes right," he argues that "the fables can point towards a means for escaping that world. They can actually point towards democracy, equality, and justice rather than hierarchy, power, and exploitation" (183).
14. Clayton, "The Death of Socrates and the Life of Aesop," 314.
15. Clayton, "Aesop, Aristotle, and Animals," 183.
16. Ibid.
17. Clayton, "The Death of Socrates and the Life of Aesop," 314.
18. This is silly, but I think it makes the point: "There once was a Hawk who was mighty/ Had caught him a nightingale who was whiney/She lamented her fate/Hawk said 'Shut up and wait./If it strikes me you might get off lightly.'" Talk about needing to recant!
19. See, for example, Gibbs 15 (149) and 16 (514).
20. Gibbs 20 (334). At the end, a timid hare proclaims: "Now has come the day for which I have always prayed, when even the weak creatures are feared by the strong!"
21. Gibbs 69 (563).
22. Gibbs 70 (150).
23. See, for example, Gibbs 71 (235), 72 (395), and 73 (296).
24. Gibbs 309 (392), 310 (7), 311 (547), and 313 (187).
25. See *Republic* 405a-408e.
26. See, for example, *Protagoras* 311b-314b.
27. Gibbs 188 (14), 189 (20), 190 (584), and Plato's *Theaetetus* 174e.
28. Gibbs 268 (195).
29. Gibbs 270 (141), 271 (397).
30. Gibbs 275 (207).
31. For fables about boasting, see Gibbs 206 (315), 207, and 208 (different versions of 368), 209 (33), 210 (541), 211 (349), 212 (332), 213 (377), 214 (244), 215 (300). Fables about the dangers of vanity and self-delusion include 216 (484), 217 (151), 218 (292), 219 (531), 220 (62), 228 (132), 229 (49), 232 (407).
32. Gibbs 513 (166).
33. Aesop's "Zeus and Prometheus" explains that some humans act like animals because Prometheus made too many animals at first and was ordered to turn some of them into humans (Gibbs 515 [240]).
34. See Gibbs 350 (50), 351 (107), 352 (463) for fables that tell of animals being changed into other species but being "found out" because their characters gave them away.
35. Gibbs 303 (399).
36. Gibbs 284 (233).
37. Gibbs 509 (163).
38. Frogs are characterized as so cowardly that they give comfort to a band of hares ready to drown themselves in the frogs' pond (238 [138]); a frog comes out of its swamp and surprises a lion because it is so small when its sound is so loud (270 [141]); one frog's pond is too close to the road and he gets crushed by a wagon wheel (490 [69]); frogs are afraid of the sun since it can dry up their swamp (436 [314]); when the frogs' swamp dried up, they had to find a well (445 [43]); frogs are fearful when bulls battle near their pond since it will affect them (12 [485]).

39. Gibbs 377 (189).
40. Gibbs 139 and 140; these are two versions of Perry's 384.
41. Gibbs 27 (44).
42. There is at least one other moment in the *Phaedo* that would likely have called Aesop to mind for contemporary readers/hearers: when Socrates argues that, although philosophy is practicing dying, the philosopher should not commit suicide since that would be like leaving a good master. Aesop too has a number of fables in which the clear message is that while one gives up a lot when one has a master, good masters also offer protection (5 [411]) and rejoice when one is prospering (9 [465]). And in a long fable entitled "Aesop and the Runaway Slave," Aesop himself convinces a slave that it is wrong to escape even a cruel master (7 [548]).
43. Examples are *Sophist* 234b–236e and *Philebus* 16c–26c. These are the most famous extended treatments of the similarities between the art of dialectic and the art of music. Usually grammar is mentioned as well, as we shall see in our examination of the *Sophist* passage. *Phaedrus* 248d is also very striking. Socrates says to Phaedrus that the soul that has seen the most of the eternal realities shall enter the body of a philosopher, musician, or lover.
44. Gibbs 237 (226).
45. Gibbs 199 (556).
46. Gibbs 408 (352).
47. Gibbs 348 (268).
48. Gibbs 331 (230) and 332 (650).
49. Gibbs 333 (116).
50. Gibbs 335 (398).
51. Gibbs 337 (203).
52. Gibbs 338 (91).
53. Gibbs 339 (359).
54. Gibbs 511 (658).
55. Gibbs 349 (376).
56. Gibbs 290 (11).
57. Gibbs 306 (19).
58. Gibbs 433 (58).
59. Gibbs 356 (97).
60. Gibbs 584 (31).
61. Perhaps it is this preoccupation with the natural order of things that explains an interesting group of fables that tell of the wiliness and untrustworthiness of "ambiguous creatures," as Gibbs calls them. Ostriches (having the head of a bird but the feet of a beast), bats (being both birds and mice), hyenas (which were thought to change their sex every year) can trick others because of their dual natures; they are not to be trusted (Gibbs 362 [418], 363 [566], 364 [172], 365 [242], 366 [243]). There is one fable, "The Satyr and His Guest," that has a satyr, himself ambiguous, shaking with terror at his guest's ability to warm his hand and cool his mulled wine by blowing breath from the same mouth (368 [35]).
62. Gibbs 500 (171).
63. Gibbs 505 (277).
64. Gibbs 506 (396) and 507 (509).
65. Gibbs 508 (106).
66. Gibbs 510 (117).
67. Gibbs 512 (516).
68. Gibbs 509 (163).
69. Gibbs 506 (396).
70. Gibbs 513 (166).

71. Gibbs 502 (105).
72. Gibbs 516 (430).
73. Gibbs 517 (515).
74. Gibbs 520 (108).
75. Gibbs 515 (240).
76. "Zeus and the Ant," Gibbs 514 (311). It is worth including it here in its entirety given the resemblances it bears to the versions of this myth found in Plato's *Protagoras* (320c–322d) and alluded to in the *Philebus* (16c–e): "They say that in the beginning, when the animals were being formed, they received their endowments from Zeus. To some he gave strength, and to some speed, and to others wings. Man, however, was still naked so he said to Zeus, 'I am the only one that you have left without a gift.' Zeus replied, 'You are unaware of the gift you have obtained, but it is the greatest gift of all: you have received the gift of speech and the ability to reason, which has power both among the gods and among mortals; it is stronger than the strong and swifter than the swift.' Man then recognized the gift he had been given and bowed down before Zeus, offering his thanks."
77. See Kurke, "Plato, Aesop and the Beginnings of Mimetic Prose," 23–35.
78. See this volume's animal index.
79. Wonderful examples that have a very Aesopic flavor are to be found in the *Symposium*.

2 "Talk to the Animals"
On the Myth of Cronos in the Statesman

David Farrell Krell

PLATO'S DIALOGUES ARE filled with references to animals—cicadas, crickets, bees and birds, stingrays and oysters—and, by the dog! many of these references are humorous. Quite a few are also intended as insults. Recall Plato's *Timaeus*. At the very end of that dialogue, the Pythagorean astronomer, Timaeus of Locri, says this about animals, *all* the animals, including, for example, women. He says:

> On the subject of animals, then, the following remarks may be offered. Of the men [i.e., males] who came into the world, those who were cowards or led unrighteous lives may with reason be supposed to have changed into the nature of women in the second generation. And this was the reason why at that time the gods created in us the desire of sexual intercourse, contriving in man one living creature [ζῷον], and in woman another.... Wherefore also in men the organ of generation, becoming rebellious and masterful like something alive [οἷον ζῷον], yet not heeding speech, and maddened with the sting of lust, seeks to gain absolute sway, and the same is the case with the so-called womb or matrix of women. The living creature [ζῷον] in them passionately desires to make children, but when it remains barren long past the proper time it often suffers fretful irritation; and wandering everywhere throughout the body, obstructing the respiratory passages, it prevents them from taking in breath, drives the body to the worst extremes, and produces all sorts of illnesses, until passionate desire and love from each side gather together, plucking fruit from the trees, as it were, sowing in the fields of the matrix living creatures [ζῷα] that are invisible because they are so small and have no shape, letting them develop there and come to maturity within, and after all this bringing them to light, thus fulfilling the generation of living creatures [ζῴων ... γένεσιν].
>
> In this way, women and all that is female were made. Now, as for the race of birds, they were created out of innocent light-headed men who, although their minds were directed toward heaven, imagined in their simplicity that the

clearest demonstration of the things above was to be obtained by sight; these were remodeled and transformed into birds, and they grew feathers instead of hair. The race of land-animals and wild beasts [πεζὸν καὶ θηριῶδες], in turn, came from those who had no philosophy in any of their thoughts. . . . And the most foolish of them he made without feet to crawl upon the earth. The fourth class were the inhabitants of the water . . . , the race of fishes and oysters and other aquatic animals, which have received the most abyssal habitation as a punishment for their outlandish ignorance. (*Timaeus* 90e–92c)[1]

The combination of misogyny and, if we may coin a term, "misozoony," is dismaying. It is difficult to imagine Plato taking his astronomer as anything other than a birdbrain—especially when we examine other dialogues. In particular the one called "The Politician," or, if things go very well, "The Statesman," Πολιτικός.[2]

A foreigner or stranger from Elea, a city famous for its philosophical tradition deriving from Parmenides, is talking about politics with a young man named Socrates. The older Socrates, the famous one, is also present but is mostly silent. Another young man named Theaetetus, who looks a bit like the famous Socrates, is also present, but he too is largely silent. The stranger, who guides the entire conversation, interrupts it at a certain point. They have been talking about the possibility of finding a good politician, indeed, a statesman, but they have arrived at an impasse. They must seek another path, set out on a new beginning, and they will do so by hearing an old story, a myth. The myth, like all the old stories, will involve "child's play," which in Greek is a peculiar pleonasm, one we might translate back into a bastard Greek as παιδεπαιδιά. There will no doubt be some silliness to it, but also something serious: the Stranger tells the Younger Socrates to pay close attention, the sort of attention children pay when you tell them a story. This should not be all that difficult for the Younger Socrates, who has only recently left his childhood behind. Herewith a brief recounting of the myth.

We tend to think nowadays that the evolution of the universe moves in one direction, but this is not so, says the Stranger. Rather, there are serious reversals in that evolution. The universe is like a yo-yo, or like you and me when we reach the end of our tether. When the cosmic yo-yo comes to the end of its string, it reverses direction and spins backward toward the hand that originally guided it. At the apocalyptic turn, all of life dies and, buried in the shattered earth, must wait upon a new eon for rebirth. We today live in an anthropological age. That is, we have left the guiding hand of all gods and goddesses behind; no tutelary spirit or daimon nurtures and shepherds us. That explains why in our own time so much fecal material strikes the ventilation system. But there was an earlier and a better eon. The Stranger calls it the Age of Cronos.

During the Age of Cronos, an age more remote than that of the Egyptian kingdoms, things went very well for humankind. Human beings emerged from the crust of the earth, not from the bodies of their own kind. Born of the earth, the human beings of that eon grew younger each day instead of older. During the Age of Κρόνος, Χρόνος, or time, was on our side. Time was not "stupid," as Aristotle reports Paron the Pythagorean as complaining, but smart. And we too were smarter then than we are now in our anthropological age, cut off as we are now from all gods. Why, smarter? How, smarter? For one thing, and a very important thing it is, *we could talk to the animals,* even the wildest of them, for they were not so wild back then, *and they could talk to us.* Animals did not merely *react* to the needs of their sovereign masters; they *responded* to the queries that we fellow mortals put to them. Human beings and other animals shared their leisure: the σχολή of animals was ours too. We went to school together, as it were, and all our possibilities were held in common, which befits a community of friends. Human beings were able to "mix with" and even "grow and develop with" the animals, συγγίγνεσθαι. Moreover, our conversations all went in the direction of philosophy, ἐπὶ φιλοσοφίαν, and especially of practical wisdom, "life" wisdom, φρόνησις (272c). Humans and other animals told one another their stories, their μῦθοι, and all were alike in their enthusiasm for insight and for the riches of language, ἐπιθυμίας ... περί τε ἐπιστημῶν καὶ τῆς τῶν λόγων χρείας (272d). No wonder we were all a thousand times happier back then! and a thousand times smarter! Our cats and dogs told us what they saw in us, and, while we had to blush a bit, at least we learned who we were.

That at least is what the Eleatic Stranger tells us. Is Plato's Stranger playing Dr. Doolittle? Is Plato here disguised as Rex Harrison? Let us confess it at the outset: there is not a shred of evidence in the other dialogues that would lead us to take seriously the talking animals of the *Statesman* myth. And yet the story is so elaborate—humans and other animals conversing with one another at their leisure, their possibilities of growth and development being shared, their conversations eminently philosophical, focusing on how life should be lived, one and all displaying their enthusiasm for knowledge and language—that one has to wonder whether the tale can be mere whimsy. (Of course, there is whimsy throughout the dialogues, and, as you know, the history of philosophy consists of a series of footnotes to the earnest matter of Platonic whimsy.) Plato's *Timaeus*, which was taken for a millennium or two to be Plato's scientific treatise on cosmology, is whimsical to the point of hilarity or even hysteria. Plato's whimsy, the Pythagorean caprice of *Timaeus*, is all about life—universal life, the life of gods and men, plant life, and, at the very end, even female life and animal life, with women, birds, terrestrial animals, and oysters marching onto the scene more or less in descending order. What complicates the Timaean story is that, at least to our way of thinking, mortals of many different kinds appear to be borne by and born of women. Immortals too, for that matter, and right from the start. Would it simplify matters if we were all born of the earth? The dialogue called *Menexenus* suggests that woman and earth are not opposed to one another—but let us call a halt to these rambles and return to the *Statesman* fable.

Cronos the Titan rules over an earlier age of humankind, the age of the earthborn humans. During this age, recounted only in dispersed bits of stories that the Stranger must now weave together, human beings did not procreate with other humans through love but arose from the soil. They emerged fully grown, indeed as elderly folk, soon after the universe reversed the direction of its development. As we have heard, the cosmos repeatedly spins out first in one direction, then, having arrived at the end of its tether, spins back in the other direction. It does this as something "living," a ζῷον, guided by a kind of life-wisdom, φρόνησις (269d). What sort of wisdom is that? Because the cosmos consists of body as well as mind, it cannot be perfectly divine; the closest thing to unending autokinetic circular motion is this metabolic, periodic, forward and backward spinning motion. No matter how proximate to wisdom and blessedness the cosmos may appear to be, however, the momentum that presses ahead when the forward spin runs out wreaks havoc on all that lives, both other living creatures and humankind (270c: τῶν τε ἄλλων ζῴων, καὶ δὴ καὶ τὸ τῶν ἀνθρώπων γένος). The positive aspect of such mayhem, for older folks at least, is that every dead creature from the earlier age, now reborn, grows younger instead of older, younger and "more tender." Gray hair finds its youthful color restored and stubbly cheeks grow smooth and rosy. Young men go back to being little boys, boys presumably capable of listening raptly to the tales they are being told. Yet all is not as rosy as it appears: the children grow ever younger, until they dwindle, diminish, wilt, evanesce, and—it seems—disappear altogether.

"But how did living things first come to be, back in those days, and how did they reproduce themselves?" asks the Younger Socrates.

There was no reproduction as such, answers the Stranger. Rather, those that succumbed in the prior anthropological age emerged now from the earth. Moreover, the ruling god saw to it that daimons protected each species of life, so that none served as prey for the others. Neither war nor conflict nor predation raged among them. As for human beings, a god protected them, "just as now human beings, as the more divine among living beings, protect other lesser species of life" (271e). For all living beings, whether human or otherwise, there was no memory of ancestry and no family, hence no sense of clannish pride or loyalty, no rivalry or feud. The earth yielded everything they needed for their sustenance, and they lived outdoors, roofless, with grass for their bedding, naked to the moon and sun. Such was life under the protectorship of Cronos. Life under Zeus, says the Stranger to the Younger Socrates, "you yourself know," as though the reign of Zeus were nothing other than the anthropological age in which human beings have severed their relations with all gods. The Stranger here seems in accord with pseudo-Aeschylus's *Prometheus Bound*, in which Zeus is named the upstart god whose new laws do nothing to protect the welfare of humankind. In fact, Zeus plots the destruction of our species, which has only Titans and heroes as its friends. The Younger Socrates, asked whether he would prefer the Age of Cronos to that of Zeus, delivers a resounding affirmative, and the Stranger then regales him with further particulars about that now vanished Golden Age.

It is at this point that the Stranger refers to the talking animals by name: καὶ θηρίοις διὰ λόγων δύνασθαι συγγίγνεσθαι (272b). And it is here that the details mentioned earlier about our intercourse with the other animals appear. The talking animals, with whom human beings share virtually everything, enter on the scene immediately after the account of the rejuvenation of the earthborn. Is there something about this growing ever younger of mortals that implies communication with other animals? Is there some sense in which, at least in this anthropological eon of ours, which is the Age of an angry Zeus, the animals are seen to have arrived before us, are "earlier" than we are, and, therefore, in the perspective of the Earthmother, are immeasurably "older" than we are? Would our ability to talk with them and listen to them be a bit like catching up with our older siblings, on whom we have always counted for guidance and protection? The fact that in our own time we still tell one another animal stories, fables of talking animals, animals who often outsmart one another and us—stories of coyote, wolf, dog, and dragon, of snake and eagle, of flying elephants and Miss Piggy—indicates that, as the Stranger says (272d), we surely were happier and smarter back then when these fables were all true histories. Precisely because the animals were enthusiastic for knowledge and language, the Stranger adds, he and the other interlocutors will have to reflect on why this detail concerning the Golden Age—that during it we conversed philosophically with the other animals—has been brought into the discussion.

In the fulfillment of time, all living things in the Golden Age passed into whatever forms were appropriate to them, and, as though having exhausted all those possibilities, they left behind seeds of themselves to be planted once again in the earth. The cosmic μεταβολή was about to take place, with all its accompanying devastation, so that only those tiny seeds or σπέρματα, protected by the earth, would survive to inhabit our more forsaken age.

Perhaps one detail of the Age of Rejuvenation needs to be noted: it is impossible for us viviparous beings to imagine any destination for the earthborn, as they grow tinier, more fragile, more latent, almost dormant, than the womb of our mothers. Yet this flight of imagination forgets that we are speaking here precisely of the earthborn, not of mothers' sons and daughters. Aspasia would insist that "the woman in her conception and generation is but the imitation of the earth, and not the earth of the woman" (*Menexenus* 238a), and a formidable woman like that is to be believed. Even so, however, we will want to know when mothers were made, or first arose, and how the transition from earthborn to womanborn occurred. For if the earthborn rise from the earth only to return to it, whence in all the world the birth of the first woman, the woman who, as Aspasia says, models her life on the life of the earth by becoming a mother? Timaeus, as we heard, tells us that the first woman springs from a cowardly male, and that is very funny, except to women like Aspasia and to anyone else born of woman, so that we will surely clamor for a more serious answer. For neither *Timaeus* nor *Statesman* tells us where it all began, back in an eon that is earlier even than the Age of Cronos, the eon we may have to call the Age of Chaos, when the human body—the very form of the body—first took shape, perhaps in the womb of the sea. If the cosmos only spins about and reverses direction, if the hourglass of existence is merely inverted over and over again, as Nietzsche's demon tells us it is, when does the human fetus exchange dry land for amniotic seas? Whence that narrow yet astonishingly supple and expandable birth canal? Whence that glorious gateway? What memorious animal will tell us this?

All we know is that once the cosmic crises occurred seeds were planted in the earth, age after discontinuous age. Our own viviparous age began when the gods and subsidiary daimons stopped caring for their portions of the cosmos. True, we of the new age, after the seismic cataclysm, learned to get on, but only by means of the process of fickle memory, recalling at first how things in the prior age transpired, imitating the care and concern of our now vanished daimon, but eventually growing lazy and forgetful. The painful fickleness of the memory process, says the Stranger, is caused by the presence in humans of the "form of the body [τὸ σωματοειδές]," which humankind "has brought along from its older nature [τὸ τῆς πάλαι ποτὲ φύσεως σύντροφον]" (273b).

Now, this is very strange. Whence the idea of the body? Is not "the form" of "the body" the ultimate oxymoron, at least for all metaphysics from Plato onward? Is the very word σωματοειδές a *possible* word? And is that older, disordered bodily form to be found first of all in the Age of Cronos? Clearly not. It belongs to an earlier eon, an older nature, some primeval upsurge. Inasmuch as the cosmos is itself embodied and alive, we have to wonder when and how the human body first found its form in this time prior to the rule of Cronos the Titan. All we know, or all we are told, is that, from the very first, even before both our own disordered age and the age of the Titans, the body was afflicted with disorder, ἀταξία. Yet if things went so well for embodied humankind during the reign of Cronos, the disorder, stemming from a still earlier time, seems to have been somehow held in check during the Golden Age. That earlier time would be, to repeat, a time prior to the earthborn, a time when human beings were once again or perhaps for the very first time viviparous. As the viviparous humans of our own age grow more and more forgetful of the Golden Age, they regress two stages back, as it were, degenerating to creatures of that earlier age of chaos and confusion. In our own time we see shades of it, and we know the signs: human beings suffer the disorder that Hölderlin at the end of the *Rheinhymne* calls *uralte Verwirrung*:

> . . . oder auch
> Bei Nacht, wenn alles gemischt
> Ist ordnungslos und wiederkehrt
> Uralte Verwirrung.

... or also
In the night, when all's a jumble
Devoid of order, and what recurs is
Primeval confusion.

These are lines that Hölderlin seems to have drawn precisely from *Statesman* (273d): τὸ τῆς παλαιᾶς ἀναρμοστίας πάθος. Ancient disharmonies, which have as their ostensible cause the shapes and vicissitudes of the human body, threaten once again to wreak havoc on the anthropological age, until a friendly god or hero (Prometheus? Heracles? Christ? Dionysus? Osiris? Demeter?) takes the yo-yo in hand. Yet if the spinnings of the cosmos forever reflect the primeval disharmony marked in and by the human body, as also of the bodies of other animals, it will be important for us to ask about the primordial age of the viviparous body. Or, more correctly, *bodies*. For are there not, for our species and for many others, at least two, rather different, bodies? Is that the disorder? Is that the source of cacophony? What memorious animal will tell us this?

As the Stranger now (273e) tries to draw out the points of the fable that are especially relevant to matters of kingship and statesmanship, as though the beast and the sovereign could have anything in common, he mentions that in our current age human beings are born no longer from the earth "but from and by means of their own parts [τοῖς μέρεσιν αὐτοῖς δι'αὑτῶν]" (274a). It would take too long to report on the animals, he says, on how each one developed in complex ways, but it would be shorter and more to the point to talk about human beings. The only thing one can say is that when the good daimon let things drift animals became wilder and human beings weaker and more defenseless. Prometheus and Hephaestus came to the rescue—precisely in this ostensibly anthropological age, which is cut off from all divine assistance, at least from any that might have come from Zeus. The Stranger seems to have forgotten that these two, the Titan Prometheus and the Olympian Hephaestus, are themselves gods.

Yet we may have stumbled upon the reason that the *Statesman* myth appears at the precise moment in the dialogue when it does. For the earlier discussion of kingship, prior to the recounting of the myth, has made the mistake of thinking that the search was proceeding during the earlier age, the Age of Cronos; in their search for a king or statesman the interlocutors have been looking for a divine sovereign, an avatar of Cronos, "a god rather than a mortal [θεὸν ἀντὶ θνητοῦ]" (275a). They must reset their sights considerably lower. Let us see now, with apposite brevity, whether the participants succeed in this readjustment of their common purpose.

The stated aim of the dialogue, declared at the outset, is to divide insightful knowledge—which one presumes the statesman must have—into its various types, in accord with its sundry objects, until one arrives at a very specific definition of the wise πολιτικός. This is the same method employed during the previous discussion, the one that attempted to snare the *sophist,* with what success one may hotly debate. Statesmanship should be some sort of commanding and even self-commanding gnosis that guides action, and so the divisions proceed—perhaps too confidently. As in the dialogue called *Sophist,* what remains forever obscure is the initial gathering that precedes all the divisions. For example, early on in the discussion in *Statesman* "everything that has come to be" is divided into the living and unliving, the ensouled and not-ensouled, τὰ ἔμψυχα and τὰ ἄψυχα (261b). But what initial gathering lets *all* becoming lie before us? The Stranger looks for an analogy. Perhaps the insightful action of a statesman is that of a herdsman who must see to the welfare of his flock? If the Younger Socrates says "yes" to this too quickly, the Stranger warns him (and himself?) not to be too quick, not to be fooled by names. For this is the very mistake they have already made, imagining that they were living in the Age of Cronos, in which a shepherd god guards his flock. Clearly, all such analogies and divisions must occur along the lines of natural joints, with each joined member having its own form or εἶδος. The painstaking carving of dialectic is not a hacking away. Schleiermacher translates the Stranger's warning quite beautifully: *Aber Lieber, schnitzeln ist hier nicht sicher* (262b), which we might translate into American as the gentle admonition, "We're not doing fricassee today, darling." The Stranger therefore admonishes that it will not do to divide ensouled humankind into Greeks and barbarians, as though the latter were all alike. It would be more seemly, he suggests, to carve humankind into male and female, since that division would presumably apply in foreign lands as well as in Greece.

The search for the primeval men and women, the originals of the species, continues upon the model of weaving. Once again the Stranger invites the Younger Socrates to cut and divide all the technical arts in order to separate out the particular strand that would go into the art of weaving. The problem, the very same problem that arose at the heart of the search for the sophist, is that weaving is all about συμπλοκή, that is, the art of uniting sundry strands into a richly patterned textile. Diacritical dialectic is insufficiently dialectical, even when it takes its time and concentrates, and even if it cuts in accord with the natural joints and separates everything in accord with its proper idea. The synthetic art requires some other sort of metrics, some finer sense of the great and small, a sense honed on the necessity that rules in the things that become, κατὰ τὴν τῆς γενέσεως ἀναγκαίαν οὐσίαν (283d). We ought to pause to reflect on how un-Platonic this phrase seems. If the Demiurge of Plato's *Timaeus* looks to the ideas or forms themselves in order to shape becoming—and this is Timaeus's initial supposition—then why should mortals choose any other way? Should we not model statesmanship on the perfect idea of the same? In one sense, yes, in another, no. When we are dealing with actions or deeds, any sort of praxis, we must gauge it on its own terms, "as it actually comes to be [ὡς ὄντως γιγνόμενον]" (283e). We expect to read the phrase as ὡς ὄντως ὄν, "as it actually *is,*" but in this we are frustrated. Here it is a matter of *becoming* rather than *being*. As with the infamous σωματοειδές, the ὄντως γιγνόμενον leaves us in perplexity. That perplexity will require us once again to commit patricide, to insist against Father Parmenides that nonbeing in some way *is*, at least in all that *comes* to be. The proper measure for weaving will be found somewhere in the middle of being and nonbeing, which is where everything "having to do with action [περὶ τὰς πράξεις]" (284c), prevails. For its part, statesmanship, which has to do with deeds and practices, cannot be measured in terms of absolute opposites—big and small, good and evil, and so on. Everything we expect of a statesman lies in between these extremes, somewhere in the middle, εἰς τὸ μέσον. And what do we expect of a statesman? Precisely the measuredness that characterizes the proper philosophical method, πρὸς τὸ μέτριον καὶ τὸ πρέπον καὶ τὸν καιρὸν καὶ τὸ δέον (284e), that is, appropriate behavior, conduct befitting a statesman, performing the right action at the right time, and doing whatever needs to be done—all those traits that Zeus has so much trouble with.

Yet weaving cannot proceed without a prior combing and separating out of the strands, so that it is difficult—if not impossible—to say whether gathering or distinguishing comes first. A search for all those traits in the middle cannot do without paying attention to differences, "all the differences [τὰς διαφορὰς πάσας]" (285b), even if this seems to take an inordinate amount of time. How much time? That is a matter for a deferred decision, a decision that haunts every discussion, and the answer is always the same: the method demands the proper amount of time, the time called for, the time that skill alone can promise—though never guarantee. Again Plato writes that the proper road to be taken, the method, must be πρὸς τὸ πρέπον (286d), which Schleiermacher translates as *nach dem schicklichen,* "in accord with a fateful skill." Skill of the kind the Stranger is trying to impart to the Younger Socrates is something that is more destined than earned or learned after even the most diligent practice. This we will have to remember when the interlocutors later discuss education. For the moment, what the Stranger insists on is that method must be respected above all things; only through speeches of the kind he is making will the Younger Socrates grow more skilled in dialectic and more "inventive" or more "capable of discovery" when he turns to beings themselves (287a).

Much later on in the dialogue it becomes clear to the Young Socrates that in our anthropological age many traits of the statesman will have to be inherited—and from both the maternal and paternal lines. The wellborn statesman's task in turn will be to weave together the contrasting yet equally positive natures of the best human beings—especially by means of training and by arranged marriages, uniting those who tend to be courageous (but who border on the bold) with the cautious (but who border on the overcautious). How is that to be done, asks the Younger Socrates, and the Stranger replies, not altogether clearly, "First of all, he [the statesman] unites with a godly bond those who are likeborn with respect to the everborn being of their souls, and then, after the godly bond, he unites the creaturely born by means of a human bond" (309c). "Likeborn" hopes to translate συγγενές, those who are related or are of the same family—as human beings once were with the other animals. Schleiermacher translates, *wie es der Verwandtschaft gemäß ist*, "in accord with their [natural or familial] affinity." Meant here are the two types of virtuous persons in the city, the first type courageous and brave-hearted, those whose yarn has been warped and twined to a tougher tensile strength and who will therefore serve as the yarns that are set up lengthwise on the loom; these persons constitute the warp of the woven cloth of the city, and J. B. Skemp is able to make the wonderful pun that these stouthearted persons are "warplike." By contrast, the woof of the tapestry consists of yarn not so tightly twined, yarns richer in natural emollients, more pliable and flexible, guided as they are by "temperance" or "moderation" (σοφρωσύνη) rather than "courage" or "manliness" (ἀνδρεία). (If we insist on keeping up with Skemp, we may say of the "wooflike" that their bark is worse than their bite.) "Everborn," no doubt an oxymoron as well as a neologism, tries to translate τὸ ἀειγενὲς ὂν τῆς ψυχῆς, "the everborn being of the soul." Worse than any oxymoron or neologism, here a genuine anachronism, "creaturely born," tries to translate what Schleiermacher calls *den tierischen [Teil ihrer Seele]*, "the animal part of their soul," τὸ ζῳογενές αὐτῶν.

All three genuses will give us trouble—the genus of those who belong together by virtue of their allegiance to the good, the everlasting portion of the souls in them, and the living or animal portion of those same souls. A Christianizing translation can of course obfuscate all the problems: "He first unites that element in their souls which is supernatural by a divine bond, since this element in them is akin to the divine. After this supernatural link will come the natural bond, human ties to supplement the divine ones" (J. B. Skemp). Is it not strange that Skemp can translate the third genus, ζῳογενές, as "natural," Schleiermacher as *tierisch*, "animal," if not "bestial," whereas one would most accurately translate it simply as "living"? True, τὰ ζῷα are often animals (as opposed to plants), but the word also refers to living beings in general, including humans. Timaeus uses this word to designate the impulses planted within male and female human beings to mate, as though tiny living creatures with a mind of their own were embedded within human beings, who are themselves embedded in the "living" universe. Animals within animals!

The trouble becomes more apparent when the Younger Socrates asks the Eleatic Stranger what in the world he means by the "everborn." The Stranger replies, "The truly true opinion one has of the just, the beautiful, and the good, as well as of their opposites, when it dwells securely in the soul, is what I call the divine that has come to be in a daimonic race" (309c). The daimonic genus, the genus "in-between" immortal and mortal, is—especially when we think of the daimonic

Eros of Plato's *Symposium*—nonetheless superior to the human; appropriate to all inquiries concerning the daimonic and divine is an appeal to the Muse for assistance, an appeal that the Stranger now makes (309d). One has to wonder whether the principal lesson of the myth here has been forgotten: the Eleatic Stranger, even after having left his Parmenidean patrimony behind, invokes being rather than becoming and does not shy from defining the divinity that should inhabit the soul of the statesman. Nor does he shy from specifying how the perhaps daimonic marriages of the elect should go: the "warplike" must mate with the milder natures, lest the progeny become all-too-savage, all-too-bestial, πρὸς θηριώδη τινὰ φύσιν (309e). One is reminded of the Older Socrates's modest proposal in *Republic* concerning marriage in the ideal polity, which requires what one might call the ignoble lie in contrast to the noble lie, the latter concerning the postulation of an afterlife for the meting out of rewards and punishments. The ignoble lie is the rulers' deceiving the entire citizenry by fixing the lots of those who apply for marriage, so that only the select few can actually mate and bear children, the losers of the lottery blaming chance instead of the rulers for their bad luck. Socrates admits that this is "strong medicine," but he insists that the good of the city requires it (*Republic* 459a–460b). Here too, in the Stranger's polity, mild must mate with wild—this alone would secure the "more divine bond [θειότερον σύνδεσμον]" (310a), an odd comparative form. And here too the Stranger admits that this is "strong medicine" for the state, a φάρμακον so strong, to be sure, that it may prove to be a poison. It will not be difficult to fool the men, even the most warplike of them, with these rigged hymeneals. But the women? Will they be fooled?

The problematic nature of the elect, of those whose souls seem by birth and by education to partake richly of the divine transcendentals, comes to light when the Stranger reflects on what would happen if, instead of weaving mild with wild, one let the wild choose for themselves. After several generations one would have not bravery but insanity, παντάπασι μανίαις (310d). If weaving serves to rescue diacritical dialectic from an all-too-arbitrary cleaving in twain of sundry groups and genuses, that same art would also serve to rescue the state from the deterioration of those who are courageous and those who are moderate. These divine qualities *of themselves* degenerate unless a fragile metrics is applied to them, in human terms, perhaps even in animal terms, here on Earth. Yet how are we mere humans to estimate, or guesstimate, the instant when courage is about to become foolhardy or when moderation verges on sheer vacillation? If our statesman himself derives from one or other of these genuses, or even from a happy mix of the two, can we be certain that he will apply the proper measure, always choosing the right mix at the right time? The truth is that people are hard to judge.

Which is where the story of my Crazy Uncle Bill comes in. Now, Plato's stories and myths are almost always made up out of whole cloth, and it is often difficult to see exactly what point he is trying to make with them. By contrast, my own stories are always to the point and are altogether true and certain, ἀληθῆ μετὰ βεβαιώσεως (309c). My mother had three sisters, and all four Farrell girls had something of the divine about them—so said my father and virtually everyone else who knew them. They were the perfect mix of feminine fortitude—not timid wallflowers these girls!—and remarkable moderation, even wisdom. Accordingly, their judgments were virtually impeccable. At least until Crazy Uncle Bill came a-courting the oldest girl, Catherine, who had helped to raise the other three, who were therefore especially devoted to her. Crazy Bill was of course not yet Uncle Bill, but was at that point merely applying for the post. All three of Catherine's sisters, however, demurred. No, the man was by birth and training simply too low for Catherine; to describe him they used a word that was not far removed from the Greek κακός. Yet Bill persisted and Catherine consented and so, against the will of the three sisters, the two were wed. Whereupon, lo and behold, Crazy Uncle Bill turned out to be *kalokagathia* in person, a courageous, gentle, and faithful partner during his and Catherine's entire life together. He continued to be Crazy Uncle Bill, of course, a safety engineer who stuck his fingers in the fan and who drove like a lunatic, but a princely husband and father. Years down the road the divine sisters had to admit it: divinity notwithstanding, they had made a mistake.

Can we hope for better judgments from the Stranger's statesman when it comes to the good, beautiful, and true—or, by contrast, the bad, the ugly, and the false? Are the transcendentals any less liable to a misreading than courage or moderation? Or has not the Stranger forgotten what he wanted the Younger Socrates most to remember, namely, that they must search for a statesman who is suited to our anthropological age, and not go beating the bushes for some god?

The Stranger must leave Cronos and even Zeus to their own devices. Where can he turn for counsel? If only he could talk to the animals, his search for an excellent class of future statesmen and stateswomen would surely bear fruit! A second story, once again an eminently true one. A friend of mine, at that time the assistant dean of faculty at one of the great German universities, was to hold the annual Christmas party at his home. Many faculty members were present that evening, and all were waiting for the newly elected dean of the faculty to arrive. He was as yet untested, so that a sort of "honeymoon" mood prevailed among the faculty. Several semesters later would they discover that they had elected a scoundrel.

Now, my friend had a dog, a cheerful, amiable mutt, whose only pedigree came from the streets, his only papers from the university of life. Lowborn, he was also not the best educated. His name, if I heard my friend aright, was Phaido. On that night Phaido was lolling on the rug, reveling in the fondlings and ear-scratchings of the assembled faculty, when the doorbell rang. The new dean. The dean entered and greeted the crowd heartily as he doffed his fedora and overcoat.

Phaido came to greet him as well, and, perhaps acting on a canine hunch, sensing that an investigation was called for, he placed his snout precisely in that place on the dean's person that you are no doubt thinking he must have placed it. Phaido inhaled noisily, pulled back, and reflected. He then snorted and sneezed, shook his shaggy dog's head, and, if ever a dog was able to grimace, Phaido grimaced. Months later the faculty agreed: they would insist that from hence everyone running for administrative office in the university undergo the Phaido-crotch examination.

Now, this is a bit silly. Dogs too can err. They are only human. Yet it is certain, in the way that divine things are certain, that they are better judges of human character than either the Stranger or the Younger Socrates. Probably better than the older one too, who, in both *Timaeus* and *Statesman,* is as silent as Phaido himself. One might almost suspect that Plato is waiting for his readers—the women and men who study the dialogues in our own disordered time—to shout, "By the dog, Socrates! speak up!"

Notes

1. Translated by Benjamin Jowett, with changes. For a discussion of this passage from *Timaeus,* see Krell, "Female Parts in *Timaeus,*" *Arion: A Journal of Humanities and the Classics,* new series 2, 3 (1975): 400–421; *Of Memory, Reminiscence, and Writing: On the Verge* (Bloomington: Indiana University Press, 1990), 36–39; and *Archeticture: Ecstasies of Space, Time, and the Human Body* (Albany: State University of New York Press, 1997), chapter 1. Needless to say, the present essay is work-in-progress.

2. See especially 272b–d for what follows. I have used throughout the Insel edition of Platon, *Sämtliche Werke* (Frankfurt am Main: Insel Verlag, 1991), with the Greek text of Éditions Belles Lettres and translations by Friedrich Schleiermacher.

PART II
SOCRATES AS *MUŌPS* AND *NARKĒ*

3 American Gadfly
Plato and the Problem of Metaphor

Michael Naas

IT IS SURELY the best known of all of Plato's animals, even if it is by far the smallest and no doubt the strangest for a noble discipline like philosophy. It is the one that almost every philosophy student encounters at the beginning of his or her studies and the one by which many will remain smitten for a lifetime. Indeed it is the one that has come to characterize for many the very vocation of philosophy and the face of the philosopher. I am speaking, of course, of the famous image of Socrates as a *gadfly* in the *Apology*, an image that Socrates not only accepts but himself first advances, an odd image, to be sure, for the "father" of Western philosophy to have chosen to characterize himself and an even odder one, it would seem, for those of us who follow and imitate him to wish to endorse.

This image of Socrates as gadfly has, it appears, taken hold of the philosophical imagination like no other in Plato's dialogues and perhaps like no other in the history of philosophy. The name Socrates almost immediately calls up the image if not the name of the gadfly, and the gadfly is almost a synecdoche for Socrates. But in what follows I would like to argue that this image and this name have become particularly tenacious and have come to exercise a particular fascination for those of us who read Plato today not in the original Greek or some other language but, strangely, in English, and, perhaps especially, in American English. At the risk of outrageous provocation, I would like to suggest, at least in a first moment, that Plato's *Apology* might best be read today in English translation, as if Plato had introduced this curious little beast called the gadfly into his bestiary some two and a half millennia ago in the hopes that it would be understood and translated in precisely the way a contemporary American reader understands and translates it.

In what follows, then, I would like to demonstrate how this seemingly simple image of Socrates as gadfly works in Plato's text, how it works in Greek but then

43

also how it works—and works perhaps uniquely—in English, making it an ideal image or metaphor for understanding how images and metaphors work in general in Plato. As we will see, the metaphor of Socrates as gadfly will be in some sense the *ideal* of all metaphor in Plato insofar as it transforms a common Greek name into a word with, on the one hand, a unique meaning in contemporary American culture and, on the other—and perhaps in opposition to this first meaning—a very special philosophical meaning in the register and lexicon that Plato was trying to develop. Though Plato may have written in the hope that other terms, other metaphors, "Socrates the swan," for example, or "Socrates the torpedo fish," might function in a similar fashion, none of these has been as successful as the gadfly, though this is at once most evident and, as I will suggest to conclude, most obscured, in the American English translation of Plato.

Let me begin, then, by recalling the famous passage from the *Apology* in which this odd image of Socrates as gadfly occurs. Socrates has been arguing that he has spent much of his life obeying the Delphic injunction "Know Thyself!" and trying to get others to do the same, if only by getting them to recognize that they do not know what they think they do. Socrates says he has spent his entire life questioning citizens and foreigners to this end, and he tells the jury that if he is acquitted of the charges he is facing he has absolutely has no intention of stopping this practice: "This I shall do to whomever I meet, young and old, foreigner and citizen, but most to the citizens, inasmuch as you are more nearly related to me. For know that the god commands me to do this, and I believe that no greater good ever came to pass in the city than my service to the god. For I go about doing nothing else than urging you, young and old, not to care for your persons or your property more than for the perfection of your souls" (*Apology* 30a). Hence Socrates underscores that he has questioned people throughout his life as a "service" to the god—that is, to Apollo—and thus as a service to the city of Athens. A few lines later, he goes so far as to describe himself as a "gift" sent to the Athenians by Apollo, a claim that no doubt provoked—and was perhaps meant to provoke—the Athenian jurors: "And so, men of Athens, I am now making my defense not for my own sake, as one might imagine, but far more for yours, that you may not by condemning me err in your treatment of the gift God gave you" (*Apology* 30d).

A gift from the gods, that's what Socrates says he is, a godsend from Apollo to Athens. But Socrates then goes on in the lines immediately following this ennobling self-description to characterize himself in terms that, on first blush, appear far less noble and a lot less divine:

> For if you put me to death, you will not easily find another, who, to use a rather absurd figure, attaches himself to the city as a gadfly [μύωπός] to a horse, which, though large and well bred, is sluggish on account of his size and needs to be aroused by stinging. I think the god fastened me upon the city in some

such capacity, and I go about arousing, and urging and reproaching each one of you, constantly alighting upon you everywhere the whole day long. Such another is not likely to come to you, gentlemen; but if you take my advice, you will spare me. (*Apology* 30e)

Socrates thus compares himself, by means of an image that he himself admits to being rather absurd or laughable, to a "gadfly," that is, a sort of horsefly, sent by Apollo to arouse or provoke the sluggish horse that would be Athens. He is a gift from Apollo that urges, reproaches, reproves, prods, stings, needles, or bites. He is a gadfly who goads the city of Athens, or who, he says by shifting the analogy just slightly, awakens the men of Athens from their slumber. As such, he may well suffer the fate of many an irritating gadfly that awakens a slumbering man intent on remaining asleep:

> But you, perhaps, might be angry, like people awakened from a nap, and might slap me, as Anytus advises, and easily kill me; then you would pass the rest of your lives in slumber, unless God, in his care for you, should send someone else to sting you. And that I am, as I say, a kind of gift from the god, you might understand from this; for I have neglected all my own affairs and have been enduring the neglect of my concerns all these years, but I am always busy in your interest, coming to each one of you individually like a father or an elder brother and urging you to care for virtue. (*Apology* 30e–31b)

So there you have it, more or less as every Introduction to Philosophy student will have encountered it. The city of Athens is like a large horse prone to sluggishness, and Socrates is like a gadfly or horsefly that urges it on; he is the gadfly that keeps the inhabitants of the city from falling into a lifelong sleep by turning them through questioning away from the pursuit of material gain and toward the acquisition of virtue. Though he believes this stinging or goading to be a unique service to the city, he is well aware that the city may not see it the same way and so may swat him down in order to get back to its everyday business, that is, from Socrates's perspective, in order to fall back into its mindless slumber.

It all seems fairly straightforward and transparent, even if, upon reflection, it is a little bit odd. The image Socrates uses to describe his importance to the city that is bringing him to trial, the one he himself chooses with the apparent intention of commending himself and his philosophical activity, is not the courageous lion or the prophetic swan but the ignoble, uncelebrated, and rather absurd gadfly. Socrates compares himself to an insect that bites and pierces, needles and stings, and that does so repeatedly, since a gadfly, unlike a bee or venomous snake, can sting or bite multiple times, making it not just a one-time nuisance but a lifelong pest. The image is surely meant as a positive one insofar as keeping the city aroused and its citizens awake is understood to be a great service to the city, but the image itself is hardly ennobling.

In a dialogue that is very likely one of Plato's earliest and one with as good a claim as any to having included or captured some of the historical Socrates, the father of Western thought thus describes himself as a gadfly. More precisely, he compares himself to a *muōps* (μύωψ). But what exactly is a *muōps*? What kind of animal was this, or, more to the point, what did Plato and/or Plato's Socrates—what did Plato's audience—consider a *muōps* to be? With what images or values was it associated and what, if anything, within the history of this word would have made it a suitable image for the work of philosophy or the face of the philosopher?

Though neither etymology nor entomology will be decisive here, both can be helpful. According to the experts, the word *muōps*, typically translated as *horsefly* or *gadfly*, has a few possible etymologies. It might be related to the adjective *muōps*, meaning short- or near-sighted, that is, precisely, *myopic*; it might come from the verb *muō*, meaning closed or shut; or it might be a combination of two Greek words, *muia* (fly) and *ôps* (face).[1] There is thus no common agreement regarding the origin of the word, though from a philosophical point of view all these etymologies would be somewhat problematic insofar as the one thing Socrates would surely want to deny in the comparison or analogy he has constructed is the shortsighted or blind needling or goading of the *muōps*, the shut eyes or closed face of this ignoble beast—in short, the gadfly's animal blindness and lack of forethought or intelligence. For while Socrates denies having any determinate knowledge to impart to others, he is not at all blind or shortsighted. On the contrary, he stings or goads because he "knows" what is best for the sluggish beast he is stinging, because he sees better or sees further than Athens's slumbering inhabitants, who have a tendency to doze off and so avoid their true or genuine interest, that is, the acquisition of virtue rather than material goods.

From the philosophical perspective that would seem to be Plato's, Socrates the *muōps* would be the least shortsighted and the least closed up or closed off, the one most awake, the one always buzzing about with an eye and an art for keeping others awake. Indeed Socrates's philosophical vocation would seem to be much more in line with that other *muōps* or that other meaning of *muōps* in Greek, that is, not the horsefly or gadfly but "a certain type of goad for horses" (*GI* 161–62), a piece of equipment used by horsemen trained in the art of horsemanship to urge their horses forward or keep them moving in the right direction. Though it is very clear from Socrates's speech in the *Apology* that what he means by *muōps* is not goad but gadfly, this other meaning of *muōps* already seems to haunt this first one. Certain animals, like the sluggish horse, would require the application of a *muōps* in order to keep moving, just as the inhabitants of Athens would require the *muōps* or goad of questioning or cross-examination in order to keep them awake. Both, therefore, would require the application of a *muōps* that is being held in a decidedly human hand.

In the end, the Platonic Socrates would seem to be much more like a goad or a horseman armed with a goad than a fly. He would seem to be much more like a man or horseman with art and foresight than a blind and senseless gadfly intent simply on biting or stinging others. For if Plato had Socrates call himself a *muōps* in his *Apology*, it was surely with the intention of having his reader understand this *muōps* to be a distinctly human if not even a superhuman fly, a *muōps* unlike any other, perhaps even a *muōps* in the contemporary American sense of *gadfly*. But to demonstrate this, it is necessary to look not just at the term *muōps* but at all the terms with which it is associated.[2]

Curiously, the single use of the term *muōps* at *Apology* 30e is the only one in all of Plato's dialogues, a genuine *hapax legomenon*—one very small indication, though far from conclusive, that the image may in fact have originally come from Socrates's mouth and not Plato's imagination. For while Plato often uses a very similar image in his dialogues, he employs a related but different term, namely, *oistros* (ὁ οἶστρος), which is also often translated into English as *gadfly* and is often used more or less interchangeably with *muōps* in authors before and after Plato. In Aeschylus's *Suppliant Maidens*, for example, Io is said by Pelasgus, King of Argos, to have been pursued or urged on by a *muōps*, "a sting [μύωπα], torment of cattle," while the Chorus says in the following line that "those who dwell hard by the Nile" "call it . . . *oistros* [οἶστρον]" (307–308). In *Prometheus Bound* Io herself complains of being pursued by an *oistros*, that is, by "a gadfly [that] . . . stings me to my misery" (567). Hence the two words, *muōps* and *oistros*, were not only associated but sometimes used more or less synonymously, which is why they are often translated identically.[3] Aristotle too, in his *History of Animals*, associates the *muōps* with the *oistros*, calling them both "bloodsuckers" (596b15) that "can bore through the hides of quadrupeds" (528b32). Both, he says, are "two-winged" animals with a "sting [κέντρον] in front"—this word for sting, *kentron*, being yet another point of contact, as we shall see, between the two words in Plato (490a21).[4]

Since it is very likely, then, that Plato would have associated the *muōps* with the *oistros*, we are justified in looking at Plato's use of the term *oistros* in order to get a better sense of what he meant by *muōps*. "Cognate with the Greek nouns *oima* ('rush') and *oistros* ('arrow')," the word *oistros* names a large, buzzing fly that attacks, goads, bites, or pricks large animals like horses, bulls, and cattle (*GI* 161). It is because Io has been transformed into a cow by Zeus that she is pursued by an *oistros* from Greece to Egypt, persecuted and, in the end, driven mad by its pricks and goading. The *oistros* is thus, in Aeschylus and elsewhere, an insect that stings or bites and drives one mad, and the term is used in exactly this way, and pretty much without exception, throughout the dialogues. It suggests a kind of madness, an irrational drive or impulse, a blind tendency, even a rage, that would seem to be the very opposite of the kind of knowing or at least controlled goading that would have been practiced by Socrates.[5]

In the *Laws*, the impulse to temple-robbing, one of the most heinous offenses in the state, is described as a kind of inherited urge or goading, an *oistros* that drives men to evil-doing. "Neither of human origin nor of divine," says the Athenian, it is "some impulse [οἶστρος] bred of old in men from ancient wrongs unexpiated" (*Laws* 854b). The term *oistros* is thus identified with an impulse that is, if not blind, at least unthinking, unguided; inherited from of old, it stings or drives irrationally and spurs one on to commit irrational, impious deeds. In Book 9 of the *Republic*, Socrates speaks in a very similar vein of the tyrannical soul as a tyrannized soul, one that, contrary to what Thrasymachus had argued much earlier in the dialogue, "will least of all do what it wishes" insofar as it is "always perforce driven and drawn by the gadfly [οἴστρου] of desire" (*Republic* 577e). Such a tyrannized individual, as well as the city in which he is found, is, as a result, full of terrors, lamentations, and anguish, "maddened by its desires and passions" (*Republic* 578a). The word *oistros*—associated so closely with *muōps* and often translated, it too, as *gadfly*—seems to suggest to Plato a sort of madness, a far cry indeed from the kind of goading or stinging that Socrates would seem to have exercised for the good of the citizens and foreigners whom he questioned. When Socrates compares himself to a gadfly in the *Apology* he is quite clear that his intention was always to awaken the city and set it right, not persecute it or drive it mad, and that he was doing what he considered to be best for the city and its inhabitants, not acting unthinkingly or irrationally. The *oistros* is thus a beast that, like Socrates, pricks and goads, but unlike him it does so in a blind and beastly, uncontrolled and hardly human, way.

Often associated with the *oistros* in Plato's dialogues is, as suggested above, the word *kentron*, from which we get the English word *center*. The *kentron* is the midpoint, the point of a compass or of spear, the sting or stinger of a bee, though also a goad, which brings it too into proximity with *muōps*. More often than not, it is used in Plato to characterize the sting of a craving, the pricking or goading of desire. Again in Book 9 of the *Republic*, the tyrant is described as being besieged by "the sting [κέντρον] of unsatisfied yearnings" (*Republic* 573a). Though it might seem—and did seem to Thrasymachus—that the tyrant is the one most able to control, goad, and tyrannize others, Socrates argues that he is the one most tyrannized, his soul held in thrall by the "indwelling tyrant Eros." "Urged, as it were by goads [κέντρων], by the other desires, and especially by the ruling passion itself," such men "run wild [οἰστρᾶν] and look to see who has aught that can be taken from him by deceit or violence" (*Republic* 573d–e). Both *kentron* and *oistros* are thus often used in relation to men who are driven like beasts, or in relation to beasts driven by men. Hence it is said in the *Laws* that it is common for the "servant-class" to be struck with a *kentron*, that is, treated "like brute beasts, with goads and whips [κέντροις καὶ μάστιξιν]," a treatment that, the Athenian argues, causes the souls of these servants to become even more "enslaved" (*Laws* 777a).

Like the noun *oistros*, associated, as we have just seen, with *kentron*, the verb *oistrō* (οἰστρῶ) means to be mad or to be driven mad. It is used to describe those who obey no logic or who are perpetually and unreasonably changing their views or positions. Theodorus says in the *Theaetetus* that "it is no more possible ... to discuss the doctrines of Heraclitus ... with the Ephesians themselves ... than with madmen [τοῖς οἰστρῶσιν]. For they are, quite in accordance with their textbooks, in perpetual motion" (*Theaetetus* 179e). This passage brings together two of the ideas we have already seen associated in the story of Io, madness or frenzy on the one hand, and being set or driven into perpetual motion by the sting of the gadfly on the other. The sting or goad of the gadfly drives one ceaselessly forward, without respite, and so drives one to the point of madness, in short, drives one mad.

This same conjunction of ideas can again be seen in a passage from the *Laws* comparing the temperate to the intemperate life, the moderate to the "licentious life," this latter being "violent in all directions, affording both pains and pleasures that are extreme, appetites that are intense and maddening [οἰστρώδεις], and desires the most frenzied possible" (*Laws* 734a). Once again, the *oistros* goads irrationally, drives one mad and does so in a mad and frenzied way, precisely the opposite of what Socrates would like to do and the opposite of the effect he would like to have on others. For even if his sting initially makes one frenzied, or at the very least intensely dissatisfied with one's previous way of life (think of Alcibiades in the *Symposium*), Socrates sees ahead, it would seem, to a time when this frenzy, which is at first turned either inward (into melancholy) or outward (into aggression), is eventually transformed into a more dispassionate or at least more controlled self-interrogation or self-care, into a form of *eros*, even, that is no longer opposed to rationality but is in fact its highest form.

In the *Phaedrus*, the lover—that is, the as-yet nonphilosophical lover—is described as being "driven by the sting [οἴστρου] of necessity, which urges him on, always giving him pleasure in seeing, hearing, touching, and by all his senses perceiving his beloved, so that he is glad to serve him constantly" (*Phaedrus* 240d; see also 251d–e). What pricks or goads the lover is, again, a kind of power or necessity, an impulse that is not at all under the lover's control.[6] As with the tyrant, the lover is subject to a drive to see and possess his beloved. He is thus not at all like the trained horseman driving a horse, or like the Socratic *muōps* biting the horse for its own good, but, rather, like the horse itself, and an untrained or undisciplined horse at that, one that is driven mad by a mad or irrational horseman. This goading thus characterizes the tyrannical soul, the impassioned soul, and, in the *Laws*, the lustful or craving soul, for it is there argued that, insofar as "every creature has an instinctive lust [ἔρωτα], and is full of craving [οἴστρου]," it remains "quite deaf to any suggestion that they ought to do anything else than satisfy their tastes and desires for all such objects" (*Laws* 782e). Hence lust or desire, which is something natural and common to all animals, is not just blind in its pursuits but deaf to all good counsel or persuasion. It is what drives all animals, including the animal in man, toward the satisfaction of bodily desires and the pursuit of material possessions—the very things that Socrates in the *Apology* tried to prevent the inhabitants of Athens from blindly pursuing.

Finally, in the *Timaeus*, there is a passage where it is not the soul that is driven or pricked, that is mad or disobedient, but the genital organs themselves, a passage where the sexual connotations of *arousing*, *pricking*, and *penetrating* are as unmistakable in Greek as they are in English. Having described the nature of sexual intercourse in humans, that is, the receptive nature of women and the desire for emission in men, Timaeus argues that "in men the nature of the genital organs is disobedient and self-willed, like a creature that is deaf to reason [τοῦ λόγου]," a creature that thus "attempts to dominate all because of its frenzied lusts [δι' ἐπιθυμίας οἰστρώδεις]" (*Timaeus* 91b). Moved by passion, deaf to all reason or persuasion, the genital organs act of their own accord; driven to the point of frenzy, they come to drive or dominate the soul and body to which they are attached. Dominating and domineering, uncontrollable and self-willed, they sting, prick, and penetrate with no other object than the satisfaction of their own frenzied desires.

But let's now return to Socrates, who compares himself in Plato's *Apology* to a *muōps*, that is, to a gadfly, a quasi-synonym of *oistros*, a horsefly of sorts, but also an impulse, a stinging or a goading that is associated, as we have seen, with the prick or goading of a *kentron*. Socrates seems to have used, at least within Plato's lexicon, the most unlikely image imaginable for his provocation of foreigners and citizens. Following the semantic skein we have just seen, it is as if Socrates were to have compared himself to a stinging desire, an irresistible craving, or a tyrannical impulse, a goading that is deaf, blind, and unthinking, a relentless stinging that drives the one who undergoes it to madness. How, then, we must now ask, could anyone possibly recuperate this image according to what we would imagine to be Plato's intention? In other words, how could Plato have ever thought that this would be an appropriate image for Socrates?

First, we might point to the few places in Plato where the word *kentron*, at least, is used in the context of a goading that is indeed under the control or guidance of someone equipped with knowledge or art, someone who goads with the clear intent of disciplining or training the beast being goaded. In the famous passage from the *Phaedrus* where the soul is compared to a charioteer and a team of two horses, one good, one bad, *kentron* is used in the space of just a few lines to designate *both* the blind goading of a desire or impulse *and* the goading of a charioteer trying to train or tame his bad or unruly horse.

> Now when the charioteer beholds the love-inspiring vision, and his whole soul is warmed by the sight, and is full of the tickling and prickings [κέντρων] of yearning, the horse that is obedient to the charioteer, constrained then as always by modesty, controls himself and does not leap upon the beloved; but

the other no longer heeds the pricks [κέντρων] or the whip of the charioteer, but springs wildly forward, causing all possible trouble to his mate and to the charioteer, and forcing them to approach the beloved and propose the joys of love. (*Phaedrus* 253e–254a)

While the good horse is obedient to the goading or pricks of the charioteer and so is able to resist the pricks or goading of desire, the bad horse is not, or is not yet. The same word, *kentron*, is thus used to describe at once the uncontrolled, unguided, unoriented, indeed shortsighted or blind goading or pricks of desire or necessity and the artful pricks or goading of a skilled charioteer trying to train and make obey the two horses of the soul. Perhaps we could say, then, that Socrates goaded the young men with whom he came into contact in Athens in this latter way, that is, with some foresight and with the intention of keeping them awake and oriented toward virtue. He would have goaded them not blindly, like the *muōps* or the *oistros*, but with the intelligence and foresight of a charioteer equipped with a *kentron* (or a *muōps*, a goad) that stirs or provokes his interlocutor to seek virtue and care for himself rather than material possessions.

But if this emphasis on art or foresight was so important, we would then want to ask why Socrates, or Plato's Socrates, did not compare himself in the *Apology* to just such a charioteer, or else to the captain of a ship, a trainer, or a doctor—all very prominent Platonic metaphors and ways of characterizing the philosopher in the dialogues. Why, instead of all these more appropriately human analogies, did Socrates compare himself to a *muōps*, that is, to a common fly? Why use such a strange and, as we have seen, in so many ways inappropriate image for the kind of purposeful goading Socrates clearly thinks he has been providing the city of Athens?

Perhaps this is the moment to make explicit two points that are obvious to almost every reader of the *Apology*, even those encountering Socrates for the very first time. First, when Plato's Socrates speaks of himself as a lowly gadfly he does so with that famous Socratic irony for which he is known. While Socrates *calls* himself a lowly gadfly, we know that what he *means* is the opposite, that is, that he was and was considered by those who really knew him to be nothing less than a gift from the gods. As always in the dialogues, irony allows Plato, and particularly Plato's Socrates, to convert what appears to be lowest and least valuable into what is best and most worthy.

Second, and perhaps even more obviously, Socrates's use of the term *muōps* in the *Apology* is merely *metaphorical* or *analogical*. As such, it plays an important strategic and rhetorical role in Socrates's speech and so must be read in that context. As we have already seen, it allows Socrates to compare not only his activity to that of a gadfly but the likely reaction of those who hear him to the reaction of those who encounter such a fly: rather than being awakened so as to recognize and appreciate the service that has been rendered them, they may well be irritated to the point of wanting to rid themselves of the irritating pest. The image thus allows Socrates to envision the likely outcome of the trial or, better, Plato to explain the reason for what he already knows to have been the outcome.

But even more importantly, analogy or metaphor allows one to select out some common attributes of disparate things without having to affirm any kind of identity between those things. To state the obvious, when Socrates calls himself a gadfly he is not in any way suggesting that he *is* a gadfly, only that he is *like* one in some respects, for example, that he acts like a gadfly by keeping the sluggish horse that is the city of Athens moving and its inhabitants awake. As in all metaphors or analogies, some characteristics are being selected for comparison while others, indeed the vast majority of the others, are being ignored or bracketed. Hence Socrates is *like* a gadfly insofar as he stings individuals and arouses the sluggish city with his constant questioning, but he is decidedly *unlike* a gadfly insofar as he is not blind, not even shortsighted, insofar as he sees who needs goading when and for what purpose, and, most obviously and importantly, insofar as he is human and not at all a fly. By letting Socrates speak of himself as a *muōps*, Plato could count on his readers or hearers to help construct a new, metaphorical meaning of *muōps*, not the blind, ignorant, irritating horsefly but the vigilant, self-sacrificing, knowing human gadfly who pricks and goads the city and its citizens *for their own good*—the very meaning that I think most students grasp on even a first reading of the *Apology*.

To say that Socrates is *like* a *muōps* is thus to speak analogically; to say that he *is* a *muōps* is to speak metaphorically. This analogy or metaphor would then be transferred into other languages more or less intact when *muōps* is translated into French, for example, as *taon*, or into German as *Bremse*, or into English—for this would be a perfectly legitimate translation—as *horsefly*. But when *muōps* is translated into English not as *horsefly* but as *gadfly*, something else seems to happen, as I have been suggesting, something that seems to put the English translation into profound accord with what appears to be Plato's intention and yet also, perhaps, risks overdetermining and maybe even concealing that intention. For as far as I know, English is the only language in which the word commonly used to translate *muōps*, namely *gadfly*, has come to take on an additional meaning that is no longer simply metaphorical in the way Plato's *Apology* explicitly develops it. Indeed it is the only language that has given us what resembles a "dead metaphor," that is, a metaphor so widespread (e.g., the leg of a table) that it is no longer taken as a metaphor, a metaphor so common that it simply becomes the common name for the thing itself. In other words, *gadfly* is the only translation of *muōps* that came to be detached from the specific context of the *Apology* and, no doubt inspired in part by it, came to designate *before* or *beyond* any metaphorical transformation or transposition a human being who plays the role of a kind of provocateur. In this new sense of the word, Socrates would not simply *resemble* a gadfly but would actually *be* one; he would be not just a metaphorical or analogical gadfly but a literal one, a distinctly human gadfly—a metamorphosis that the English language alone, and perhaps the American brand of it in particular—will have facilitated.

It is thus not insignificant, I would like to argue, that the term Socrates uses in the *Apology* to characterize himself—the rather "absurd" term, as he admits, *muōps*—has been for the past few decades at least translated almost systematically into English as *gadfly*. Not only Fowler in the Loeb Classical Library Edition of the *Apology* but Allen, Grube, Jowett, and West all translate *muōps* as *gadfly*, as if it were obvious that this rather uncommon name of a fly suited Socrates particularly well.[7] But such a pervasive and seemingly self-evident translation for a Greek word that occurs only once in Plato should perhaps cause us to turn the question we posed earlier regarding the *muōps* in the direction of its English counterpart; that is, it should cause us to ask: just what exactly is a gadfly?

The *Oxford English Dictionary* traces the term *gadfly* back to *gad*, "from ON. *Gadd-r*, meaning spike, nail, and influenced by OE. *gad* Goad." A gadfly is thus, as we might have suspected, a goad-fly. The *OED* then offers two principal meanings or uses of the term, one literal, one figurative: "1. The popular name of a fly which bites and goads cattle, esp. a fly of the genus *Tabanus* or of the genus *Oestrus*; a bot-fly, breeze 2. *fig.* One who irritates, torments, or worries another. Also (after Latin *oestrus*), an irresistible impulse to some course of action."[8] Hence *gadfly*—which is related in both definitions, notice, through the Latin *oestrus*, to *oistros* and not *muōps*—names, just as we saw in Plato, at once a thing, an animal, and a human, that is, at once an irresistible drive or impulse, a kind of fly, and someone who irritates, torments, or worries others.

But something significant seems to be missing from this short list of definitions from the *OED*, which bills itself as "the definitive record of the English language." Moreover, what is missing is the definition of *gadfly* that would probably come to mind *first* for an American English speaker. Fortunately, there are other authorities, other records of the English language, that allow us to fill in this gap. The *American Heritage Dictionary*, for example, defines the gadfly, in addition to the above definitions, as someone who "acts as a constructively provocative stimulus" or who is "habitually engaged in provocative criticism of existing institutions, typically as an individual citizen." It is these two supplementary definitions, and not either of the definitions found in the *OED*, that seem to sanction calling Socrates a gadfly in the *Apology* and that seem to justify the English translation of *muōps* as *gadfly* rather than as, say, *horsefly*. In both of these supplementary and apparently quintessentially American definitions, the gadfly is a human being and not an animal, certainly not an animal as lowly as a fly, and in both the gadfly is someone who works constructively for some individual or collective good by offering a "provocative stimulus" or "provocative criticism."

Socrates would appear to be the spitting image of this kind of "provocative" gadfly, someone who might ironically characterize himself as an annoying pest but who, we all know, is working for the good of the *polis* and its citizens. While few English-speakers would ever really use the word *gadfly* to describe an actual fly, most, I wager, including the typical introductory student of philosophy, would not hesitate to use it to describe the kind of provocateur Socrates appears to be in Plato's *Apology* and other dialogues. This figurative meaning of *gadfly* is in fact so common that it is no longer even heard as a figure. No one would ever say that Socrates was *like* a gadfly in this more positive or ennobling sense of the term but that he truly *was* one. If the translation of *muōps* by *gadfly* in this more American sense of the term does not really seem justified by the semantic resources Plato puts at our disposal in his own use of the term *muōps* and his multiple uses of *oistros* and *kentron*, the notion of a gadfly-provocateur seems to fit our image of Socrates to a T.

Socrates would thus seem to have been the first example or first specimen of this uniquely American species of gadfly, an individual who might be considered a pest, an irritating horsefly, from the point of view of those being provoked, but who is considered to have a positive influence or to administer a positive stimulus by those who truly understand the role of a gadfly. In the contemporary American context, the gadfly is a nuisance or a blessing, depending on one's point of view, but not a criminal to be pursued or prosecuted. Indeed he or she (and I say *she* here, though it is perhaps not insignificant that there are so few—if any—women gadflies) is often the one who exposes the criminal activity of those in power and encourages the people to pursue them. While the powers that be thus usually do not like having such gadflies on their back and might even wish that they were gone, they usually do not have them arrested, prosecuted, or killed, at least not *as* gadflies. While they might thus try to rid themselves of such gadflies by calling them criminals, subversives, traitors, or terrorists, they cannot do so by *calling* them *gadflies*. The gadfly is instead typically tolerated as a quasi-marginal figure who prods and provokes, who snipes from the margins in an attempt to keep everyone honest. Even when the gadfly is considered an irritation, the nobility of his motives is usually recognized and his presence in the state appreciated as a check on the arrogance of individuals or the authority of institutions.

Though just about any institution might do well to have such a gadfly provoking or questioning it, it is no doubt significant that in the contemporary American use of the term it is almost always *political* institutions, structures, or regimes that are the targets of the gadfly. Hence many in the United States, on either the right or the left, would be willing to call Noam Chomsky or Ralph Nader or the editorial staff of the *Onion* a *gadfly*, that is, someone who tries, whether in a sensible or misguided way, depending on one's perspective, to keep the polis or the nation-state awake by acting as its social conscience. This notion of a gadfly is in fact perfectly in keeping, we would like to think, with a certain understanding of the American values of freedom of speech and expression, perhaps even with a certain notion of civil disobedience. A so-called free society would even pride itself on allowing gadflies to buzz about freely in order to pose irritating and sometimes inconvenient and embarrassing questions. And this is precisely, I would suggest, the image that many English-speaking readers of Plato—and particularly in the United States—get from their first introduction to Socrates in the *Apology*, an impression that, for good or ill, is likely to follow the student of ancient Greek philosophy well beyond that introductory course.

Socrates would appear to be the very essence of a *political* gadfly, an individual who stings, awakens, goads, and rouses, who is anything but blind and who knows what is best for the state and its inhabitants, or who at least knows that complacency and stupor are not in their best interest. He would be the epitome of the antiestablishment freethinker, the first and best and most admirable of all questioning gadflies, the first and best example of a distinctly American species of gadfly, a gadfly who was born and bred in Athens and in the Greek language but who would have truly come into his own only in an English language that will have spawned this other meaning of *gadfly*. For if Plato's original text *says* muōps and not *gadfly*, what Plato *meant*, it seems, is *gadfly* and not *muōps*. American English will have thus been the best language, a sort of *chosen* language, a unique and ideal "target language," so to speak, for the *Apology* to have been translated into. It is thus altogether fitting, it would seem, that today's philosophy students reading Plato's *Apology* in American English come away with the image of Socrates as the gadfly rather than simply the horsefly of Athens . . .

It's a fascinating hypothesis and I have done my best to try to support it here. But one might wonder whether this political interpretation of Socrates and, thus, this translation of *muōps* by *gadfly* really is as transparent or self-evident as I have been presenting it, so transparent or self-evident that it has seemed ineluctable for so many translators of the *Apology* into English.[9] Indeed one might wonder whether the English translation of *muōps* by *gadfly* does not, precisely by highlighting the political connotations we have just explored, conceal other possible meanings and interpretations, including, and perhaps especially, an even more insistent, significant, and original *philosophical* meaning. For it could be argued that Plato's Socrates is not just *a* gadfly in the political sense we have just seen, one political gadfly among others, but the gadfly par excellence, the Platonic form, as it were, of the gadfly, the only real or genuine gadfly, a gadfly that is neither animal nor even really human but, in heeding the call of philosophy, something quasi-divine, the only gadfly endowed with a sense of what is best for the city and its inhabitants. Such a portrait of Socrates would be consistent with the transition or the transformation for which Plato's dialogues so often aim, a transformation of all categories and values, from the merely animal to the human to the superhuman or divine, from the blind, irrational, self-absorbed, and desiring animal fly to the vigilant and Promethean gadfly that knows how to keep the city and its citizens awake in their pursuit of virtue. By comparing himself through irony and metaphor to the lowliest of creatures, to a mere horsefly, Socrates is able to raise himself up to the highest and most noble position; he is able to become not just the political gadfly that assures our political freedoms but the *philosophical* gadfly who turns us toward virtue and philosophy. And this, perhaps, is the sense that Plato would have wanted us to hear in addition to, *or perhaps even to the exclusion of,* those associations with free speech and democratic openness we just recalled.[10]

From the animal to the human or the quasi-divine, from the literal gadfly to the metaphorical or philosophical one, from blindness to insight or body to soul, from a natural impulse to philosophical foresight—that is the movement we see sketched out time and time again in Plato's dialogues. Socrates calls himself a gadfly, but the irony of the attribution lets the reader understand that he is not simply an irritating gadfly, not even the first and best of political gadflies, but the first and perhaps only truly philosophical gadfly. This is the kind of metaphorical transformation Plato seeks to establish in the dialogues through a whole variety of names and self-attributions. In the *Theaetetus*, for example, Socrates will call himself a *midwife*, but only so long as he is understood as a midwife who helps not mothers give birth to flesh and blood children but young boys to the ideas with which their souls are pregnant (149a–151d). In other words, he will accept and even appropriate such a term only so long as it is understood in a new, philosophical sense, that is, only so long as he is understood as a uniquely *philosophical* midwife, a midwife of the soul, a midwife unlike and superior to any other. One might thus imagine a world or a language in which this word *midwife (maia)* came to be a common term for a teacher or a philosopher, just as gadfly has come to mean someone who pricks the conscience of the state. Or else, to stick with Plato's animals, one might imagine a world or a language in which the name *swan* (from *Phaedo* 84e–85b) came to signify not simply and perhaps not even primarily a bird endowed with prophetic powers but a human gifted with philosophical foresight. But this is not what has happened—at least in not this world and not in the English language. Only *gadfly* has come to take on a supplementary meaning of this kind in English, one that, as we have seen, reveals and perhaps by the very same token conceals significant aspects of Plato's *Apology* and of Plato's method more generally.

From the insect to the human to the quasi-divine, from the literal gadfly to the metaphorical one: Plato's dialogues bring about what might be called a philosophical transformation or elevation of language whereby the lowliest of animals, the common gadfly, can become an appropriate image of the philosopher. With this one image, the blind, ignorant, frenzied, and artless animal is transformed into the knowing, controlled, and artful human philosopher. Indeed with this one image Plato is able to transform what is lowliest and lowest in value into what is highest and most noble, into the very source of all that is good, if not, in fact, into the Good itself.

To take this final step in my argument, I will turn briefly to Jacques Derrida's 1968 essay "Plato's Pharmacy," a great text on Plato in general and on Plato's animals in particular.[11] In this essay, Derrida evokes almost all of the animals to which Socrates is compared in the dialogues, from the gadfly to the bee to the torpedo fish, in order to argue that "this whole Socratic configuration composes a bestiary," one that runs from the lowliest insect right up to the demonic. And all this is done, Derrida argues, so as to sketch out "the contours of the *anthrōpos*," that is, so as to situate the human between the animal and the demonic or the divine ("PP" 119n52). Having thus advanced this argument, Derrida cites the very passage from the *Apology* that we have been looking at here, putting emphasis, however, on an analogy or a metaphor that I have up until now ignored or left in the shadows. It is the moment when Socrates, just after having called himself a gadfly, goes on to compare himself to a father for all those with whom he came in contact: "And that I am, as I say, a kind of gift from the god, you might understand from this; for I have neglected all my own affairs and have been enduring the neglect of my concerns all these years, but I am always busy in your interest, coming to each one of you individually like a father or an elder brother and urging you to care for virtue" (*Apology* 31b). The gadfly par excellence is thus not only a human gadfly but a father, a *gadfather,* as it were, a holy gadfather even, a father who is even more or better than what is usually called a father insofar as he is attentive to his sons' spiritual as well as material well-being.

Derrida will go on in "Plato's Pharmacy" to argue through a reading of the *Phaedrus* and other dialogues that this position of the father is always associated in Plato not only with speech—the father as the one who produces or fathers spoken discourse—but with a whole series of values associated with speech, from thought, intelligence, knowing repetition, and truth, to breath, life, legitimacy, spontaneity, fertility, and so on. In the end, Derrida claims, "the figure of the father . . . is also that of the good (*agathon*)": "chief, capital, and good(s). . . . *Patēr* in Greek means all that at once" ("PP" 81). The father thus stands always in the position of the Good, and the Good is always understood as a kind of father, as that which is productive of all things, visible as well as invisible, the things of becoming as well as those of being. It is thus highly significant that in the same passage where Plato's Socrates compares himself to a gadfly he also compares himself to a father, as if the two images actually reinforced one another in painting the portrait of a Socrates who is a genuine gift from the gods. In just a few lines of the *Apology,* that which is lowest on the rung of Plato's hierarchy of being, the lowly horsefly or gadfly, gets compared to and thereby raised up to the level of that which is at the top, the father and the Good, the father as the Good.

Analogy or metaphor is arguably Plato's most powerful and effective tool for sketching out "the contours of the *anthrōpos*" and for transforming what is lowest and of least value into what is highest and best. Anyone with ears to hear Plato's metaphor, whether in American English or any other language, knows straightaway that Socrates is anything but an irritating horsefly. Yes, Socrates calls himself a *muōps* because he irritates and bites and just might be swatted down by the state, but he is neither blind nor frenzied. He is that figurative or metaphorical gadfly who stings in order to keep others awake, a figurative father who knows what is best for his figurative offspring and who encourages them to pursue what is best and most divine. He is a gadfly who sees ahead like a charioteer, armed not with some determinate knowledge but with a kind of forethought or fore-vision that understands that virtue and the things of the soul are more to be prized than wealth or material goods. He sees that what is proper to being human, that the divinity that is proper to the human, resides in the soul and not the animal body, which, Socrates suggests in the *Phaedrus* and elsewhere, we must learn to domesticate or control like a beast under the goad of a human master.

From the gadfly to the "gadfly," then, from the animal gadfly to the human one, and then from the political gadfly to the philosophical one—that is the itinerary traced out in the few lines from the *Apology* that I have attempted to reread here, an itinerary that comes into relief in an exemplary fashion, for better or for worse, for better *and* for worse, in the American English translation of this dialogue. Socrates is indeed a *gadfly*, but Socrates the philosopher would have surely been the first to cause us to question whether we really do know what we think we do when it comes to this now common name.

Notes

1. For the various etymologies of *muōps*, see Malcolm Davies and Jeyaraney Kathirithamby, *Greek Insects* (New York: Oxford University Press, 1986), 160; hereafter abbreviated *GI*. According to some scholars, this association of *muōps* with shortsightedness or blindness is supported by the fact that in certain versions of blindman's buff in antiquity the one blindfolded was called the fly and those around him or her the cattle. Aristotle too seems to support this association when he writes in his *History of Animals*, "The horse-fly [μύωπες] dies when its eyes become dropsical" (551b21) (*History of Animals*, Books 1–6 trans. A. L. Peck, Books 7–10 trans. D. M. Balme [Cambridge, Mass.: Harvard University Press, 1970, 1991]; hereafter abbreviated as *HA*).

2. Art in antiquity was sometimes judged by its ability not only to *depict* animals but to *deceive* them, and the gadfly sometimes figures into this history. Hence "sparrows fed at the grapes painted by Zeuxis, a stallion tried to mate with a mare painted by Apelles," and "within the framework of this theme falls the epigram on Myron's bronze statue of a heifer ... which deceived a *muōps* into trying to sting its brazen hide" (Davies and Kathirithamby, *Greek Insects*, 161).

3. Aeschylus, *Suppliant Maidens, Prometheus Bound*, trans. Herbert Weir Smyth (Cambridge, Mass.: Harvard University Press, 1938).

4. According to Aristotle, *muōps* and *oistros* differ in terms of their origin. Whereas the former is "produced out of timber" (*HA* 552a30), the latter seems to come from "the small flat creatures that run about on the water of rivers" (*HA* 551b21).

5. On *oistros* as a metaphor for madness, see Davies and Jeyaraney Kathirithamby, *Greek Insects*, 164n144.

6. On the common metaphor in Greek literature of the *oistros* as the "sting of erotic passion," see ibid., 164.

7. R. E. Allen, *The Dialogues of Plato* (New Haven, Conn.: Yale University Press, 1984); G. M. A. Grube, in *The Complete Works of Plato,* ed. John M. Cooper (Indianapolis: Hackett Publishing, 1997); Benjamin Jowett, *The Apology* (Chicago: Encyclopedia Britannica, 1952); Thomas G. West, *Plato's Apology* (Ithaca: Cornell University Press, 1979). The only notable exception to this trend is Hugh Tredennick, who translates *muōps* simply as "some stinging fly" (in *Plato: Collected Dialogues,* ed. Edith Hamilton and Huntington Cairns [Princeton, N.J.: Princeton University Press, 1961]).

8. The OED actually gives four definitions, though neither of the remaining two is particularly relevant for our purposes here. One is with allusion to the verb *gad,* as in the phrase "to have a gad-fly," which means "to be fond of 'gadding about,'" so that a gadfly is someone who is "constantly 'gadding about'"; the other is used as an adjectival attribute, as in "gad-fly time" or "gad-fly haunted."

9. If, as I am trying to argue somewhat provocatively here, one would be better off reading the famous passage on Socrates as gadfly in English rather than Greek, the rest of the dialogue is surely better read in Greek than in English. Only in Greek, obviously, is one fully able to appreciate all the connotations, plays on words, jokes, and, especially for my argument here, the rich interplay between everyday language and the philosophical language Plato was trying to forge. This is true already in the title, of course, since *Apology* means not "apology" (Socrates apologizes for nothing, as we know, and even appears to provoke the jurors in several places) but *defense,* the argument or discourse (the *logos*) of the defense that follows upon the discourse of the prosecution. "Apology" is thus a good a translation insofar as it allows one to see that what Socrates is giving is a *logos,* and a misleading one to the extent that it suggests what we typically mean in English by "apology."

10. In *The Trial of Socrates* (New York: Doubleday, 1988), I. F. Stone argues against this image of Socrates as a liberal thinker and proponent of democracy. Stone gives us instead a Socrates who is unapologetically aristocratic and antidemocratic, a political Socrates who bears little resemblance to the American gadfly that I have tried to present here.

11. Jacques Derrida, "Plato's Pharmacy," in *Dissemination,* trans. Barbara Johnson (Chicago: University of Chicago Press, 1981), 61–171; hereafter abbreviated as "PP."

4 Till Human Voices Wake Us and We Drown

The Aporia-fish in the Meno

Thomas Thorp

We are at Stephanus page 80a, a third of the way into the dialogue, when Meno offers up what is certainly the most famous appearance by a fish in the history of philosophy. Except the fish does not actually appear.

Plato wants us to hear in Socrates's words—"Then answer me again from the beginning [πάλιν ἐξ ἀρχῆς]"—the insistence of an orchestra leader struggling to encourage his musicians to begin again, but to listen to themselves this time. Once more from the top: "what do both you and your associate [ἑταῖρός] say that virtue is?" (79e). This is followed by the manifest frustration of the young performer, who, despite having mastered the technique, and having been praised by others, has never really learned to listen to himself: "on countless occasions I have made abundant speeches on virtue to various people—and very good speeches they were, so I thought—but now . . ." (80b).

Meno is unable to listen to himself because when he turns to where his own voice and ear should be he finds only the words of his "associate," Gorgias, neatly packaged and ready to present. And so, now, having run through what he "knows" about virtue, which is what he can remember—namely, that virtue is, first, as Gorgias says, ruling others (73d), and then that it is, as a poet says, "to be able both to delight in and to have honorable things" (77b)—Meno is now empty and, unable to play, insists that Socrates is to blame for his perplexity: "Socrates, I used to hear, before I met you, that yours was a case of being in doubt yourself [ἀπορεῖς] and making others doubt also [ἄλλους ποιεῖς ἀπορεῖν]; and so now I find you are merely bewitching [κατεπᾴδεις] me with your spells and incantations, which have reduced me to utter perplexity [ἀπορίας]. And if I am indeed to have my jest, I consider that both in your appearance [εἶδος] and in other respects you are extremely like the flat *narkē* of the sea [τῇ πλατείᾳ νάρκῃ τῇ θαλαττίᾳ]" (79e–80a).¹

a bit obtuse

Despite this being the most famous fish in the history of philosophy, and having virtually no competition in this regard, the philosophers who study Plato have persistently mistaken our *narkē* for a fish it is not. It is not a stingray.² Lamb in the Loeb edition gets it right, as does Jowett. But Guthrie, in Hamilton and Cairnes's standard edition of Plato, has "the flat sting ray," a confused or indifferent identification that is more or less standard.³

Stingray is the common name of a family of fish (Mylobatidae) equipped with a stinger in its tail through which it can deliver venom. Our fish is an electric ray (Torpediniae). Its Linnaean name is *Torpedo torpedo*. Both are flat with the characteristic shape of a ray, but their ability to induce torpor or narcosis differs dramatically in both manner and purpose. The stingray's venom is delivered through direct contact and is entirely defensive, whereas our torpedo ray electrically infects a conductive medium, usually seawater, in order to stun and then thereby capture its prey. It will turn out that the power of our fish to inform the question of virtue is going to hinge upon this distinction between a venomous touch and action at a distance.

Indeed, for centuries our fish was studied precisely in order to dispel the idea of *actio in distans*. From the sixteenth through the eighteenth centuries, European scientists had simply denied the facts about our fish, insisting that for a shock or effect to be communicated there would have to be direct contact, and so they invented various proximate and material causes to account for the torpedo ray's power to stun at a distance: microscopic effluvia or corpuscles.⁴ It is, then, not surprising that in the modern period laboratory investigations of its mysterious powers did not merely overlap with the modern discovery of electricity but constituted one of its essential elements. Experiments by Benjamin Franklin, Joseph Priestley, and John Walsh that led to the "discovery" of electricity included a concerted effort to account for the torpedo ray's power to stun prey without contact, a power that appeared to be a mysterious violation of the law of proximate and material causality.⁵ The ancients, on the other hand, knew full well that the fish they called *narkē* was capable of inducing a narcotic effect in what merely "came near." Here is Aristotle in *History of Animals*: "And the torpedo by causing numbness [ἥ τε νάρκη ναρκᾶν ποιοῦσα] in whatever small fishes it intends to overcome, catching them by means which it possesses in its body, feeds on them; it hides itself in the sand and mud, and catches all the fishes that swim towards it and become numb as they are carried near."⁶ Notice that what is identified by Aristotle is precisely what will be most problematic for the Moderns. Namely, while there is nothing uniquely mysterious or problematic in the notion of a venomous sting, nor in the idea of hiding in order to ambush passing prey, characteristic of the fish called *narkē* is that it neither stings its prey nor speeds from hiding to capture it. Instead it infects the medium itself, seawater, the presumably neutral, ambient medium in which both hunter and prey are suspended and in which they live and breathe. In short, it is not the power to induce numbing, narcotic, torpor that is mysterious, but the power *of that power* to introduce its effect through what we may call an inflection of the apparently neutral medium of nautical life, a medium that due to its very ubiquity does not itself appear unless and until it is suddenly inflected with a stunning charge. And, to come full circle, this doubling gesture that focuses not on the power to stun but on the power *of that power* to alter and thus render manifest an otherwise opaque medium is reflected in the names the ancients gave our fish, names that by one measure fail to name the fish at all, allowing it to disappear into its effect.

When the Greeks referred to our fish as *narkē* their reference was less to the fish than to its effect; or, strictly speaking, its name, *narkē*, is the same as the word for its effect, *narkē* (ἥ τε νάρκη ναρκᾶν ποιοῦσα). And this withdrawal of the thing into its effect is retained in the Roman texts where the *narkē* is *torpedo* (later to be *Torpedo torpedo*), a name in the form of a repetition of a name. What sort of being is this whose defining virtue causes its identity to withdraw into its effect, such that its name is the repetition or doubling of that defining virtue? And what does the fact that this mysterious power acts through the inflection of the very medium of life, of being, have to do with the guiding question of the *Meno*?

Oh, do not ask, "What is it?"

Well, what is the guiding question of the *Meno*? "Can you tell me, Socrates, whether virtue can be taught, or is it acquired by practice, not teaching?" (70a) Doesn't Plato have Socrates immediately alter the opening question? "So far am I from knowing whether it can be taught or not, that I actually do not even know what the thing itself, virtue, is at all" (71a). Doesn't Socrates insist upon replacing Meno's question (How is virtue acquired?) with its double, the question "What is virtue?" And isn't this substitution justified by the suggestion that the latter is taken for granted by the former? Rather than acceding too quickly to this interpretation, I propose that we pause and allow the aporia-fish to do its work. We would notice, then, that Socrates goes to some length to resist the *ti esti* formulation and in fact introduces it only in the negative, contrasting the Thessalians (Meno and Gorgias) who have a ready answer for every question to those living "here" (*enthade*), in Athens, where "a drought of wisdom has come on." Here, we not only do not know how human excellence is attained, we go so far as to assert that we do not even know what it is.

Rather than insisting upon a definition—presumably in the form of a "what it is"—Socrates should be read as asserting that it might be a good idea to pause and reflect upon the very medium subtending and sustaining the question of the acquisition of virtue. And yet, in order to reflect upon that subtending and sustaining medium, it would have to be rendered present, and to be rendered present this prerequisite question (What is it?) would have to be articulated. So if we begin our reading by noticing that Socrates has insisted on this "What is it?" question, we must also recall that he has no intention of answering it. And this apparent paradox itself might justify a shift of focus from the much-discussed "what it is" of virtue to what we are calling the sustaining medium of the inquiry. This much at least is clear at the outset: Socrates cannot really resist the force of the logic of the *ti esti*—he must in fact himself introduce it—but he does so within a clear (one is tempted to say a "transparent") frame of reservations.

Our hypothesis, then, will be that in the *Meno* Socrates's insistence on the *ti esti* and his simultaneous reservations regarding it—the necessity of the question and the pause that accompanies and interrupts it—is personified by our fish. To test that thesis, we must ourselves be willing to shift our focus from the thing (the answer, the entity, the fish) to its effect, and in particular to the power of that effect to suspend the utter transparency of the medium itself. For is not Socrates about to electrify that medium to stunning and torporific effect?

that is not it, that is not what I meant at all

Plato has Meno invoke the *narkē* in the form of a common insult at the moment in the dialogue when Meno, embarrassed and having exhausted his crib sheet, is left with nothing more to say. Meno has recourse to an insult and invokes the *narkē* because he now sees no way out (*aporia*). Yet like its name and its mysterious power, our fish's aporetic power too is doubled. In other words, it is not that Meno is now willing and able to admit that he does not know. Having run through a set of stock answers is not the same as being on the verge of a Socratic insight, not the same as being willing to join Socrates in the exercise of the manifestation of previously unacknowledged presuppositions and in the work of rendering present the presuppositions of thought by rendering them questionable. But this is, finally, not really a question about Meno, is it? Allow me to suggest, rather, that the purpose of the initial doubling of the question about virtue ("How is it acquired?" becoming "What is it?") is that Meno's impasse (*aporia*) is now being turned back upon us, upon the readers, the true audience of the dialogue, we who up until this point will have likely satisfied ourselves by occupying our manifestly superior posture relative to the sad and embarrassed Meno. We who have been smugly disparaging the one who seems to believe that knowledge is simply reciting what one can remember are about to learn that all of us are Meno, that all knowing is a remembering and, finally, that remembering is not what we and our associates have presumed it to be.

Rather, the repetition characterizing the name of our fish, along with its attendant withdrawal of the thing (the fish) into its effect (aporetic narcosis), mirrors precisely the problem of the relation of virtue or excellence to knowledge, and of knowledge to repetition or recollection, as they are set forth in the *Meno*. Only because all knowing is doubled, because all knowing is a form of *anamnesis*, is it possible for Meno's particular form of remembering (mere memorization) to occupy, block, and distort his own fundamental capacity for comprehending or acquiring virtue. The alternative to Meno's recourse to mere recitation is not, as we shall see, the pure presence of the object—nor the presence of the pure form of the object—but, rather, an originary and transcendental repetition, a necessary but impossible re-presentation whose power is not presentation (knowledge) but the withdrawal of the grounding relation of the appearance to its form.

Instead of appearance and form, Socrates's insistent "What is it?" has the power to inflect the medium sustaining these bonds of knowing and being and to do so by effecting the suspension of beings. Look at it this way: the inevitable force of the question "What is it?" is to predetermine the logic of an answer, which will have to come in the form of a posited "it," an entity or the reified ground of an entity, its form (*eidos*). But while this positing of the "it is" is inevitable, it need not be self-satisfied, and so we are justified in suggesting that the purpose of the question and its effect may be a matter of highlighting the inevitability itself and of rendering it, thereby, questionable. This suspension of the presumption can leave one either in Meno's version of *aporia*—having simply run out of answers—or in a Socratic *aporia:* the shocking suspension of the very presumption that is the being-Being or appearance-Form binary. And what Socrates demonstrates in the opening exchanges of the dialogue, leading up to the invocation of the electrifying fish, is that this suspension of the presupposition of appearance takes the form of rendering it present, rendering Being, almost and for just an instant, present.

But just as the one who emerges into the light and, faced with the impossible necessity of suddenly seeing not things but the condition of the visibility of things, is blinded, so too here in our nautical analogy the sudden and shocking appurtenance of the medium or background, the sudden presentation of the condition of life, is inimical to life. The condition of sight is not itself visible, and the condition of life (*pneuma, thumos, psychē*) cannot support life, or in truth can support life but only so long as it remains withdrawn and presupposed. Were a being to come along with the power to render the medium "present," then the status of the medium as safely withdrawn would be violated, as would our status as safely suspended within it. If life itself, breathing itself, requires that the horizon or background of beings *not* appear, then we breathe only so long as we are suspended in a breathless medium of appearances. We cannot breathe Being, cannot breathe, that is to say, the medium itself that is the condition of breathing. And what this might suggest to us, as readers, is that Being is not in fact the condition or ground of beings, though its withdrawal would be. Our life—what Plato never tires of viewing as a sort of dream-life—requires that we are suspended in a home or medium in which we are decidedly not at home. In the shocking momentary presence of Being, in the reversal of its withdrawal, in the presence of the *aporia* itself, we are thus taken aback, we pause, struggling simply to catch our breath.

In any case, this is certainly the effect I want to investigate, this double effect whereby what appears to be the underlying form withdraws in the very act of being expressed, not because of any failure or weakness of expression but simply as the condition of the expression *of* any form. Or, plainly put, in order for virtue to be acquired, it will be first of all necessary to pursue the underlying question "What is it?" This is not because the question can be answered but because it cannot be answered, even though, if we are to acquire virtue, it must be asked. The exhaustion of the pursuit of the thing (the fish) will infect, or inflect, the medium of discourse, rendering it electric and stunning our normal ways of knowing, not in order to launch us into a world beyond this one but in order to make this world of appearances and of things withdraw in favor of that effect itself, perplexity. And if this use of the fish seems far-fetched, it is only necessary to recall that this pattern of necessary but impossible expression is already fully at play in the passage from the *Meno* where the fish first seems to appear but does not even appear insofar as the critical passage could properly be translated without positing the fish. A perfectly solid reading giving us no "thing," no "it is," no fish at all, but simply "the flat [πλατείᾳ] narcosis [νάρκη] of the sea [θαλαττίᾳ]."[7]

in patterns on a screen

This is an eccentric reading, and so I mean to test it. If the power of the aporia-fish is its habit of withdrawing into its own effect—if simply reading the name of the fish induces a double reading—then we ought to be able to recognize that power in and through its power (the power *of the power*) to reconstruct the network of philosophical problems actually raised in Plato's text.

Here, trusting that they are familiar, I will simply list them by name, as it were. Of the classic Platonic doctrines swimming about in the vicinity of our fish we can identify: First, the unmistakable appearance of the theory of Forms, where, in response to Meno's initial claim that there are many different kinds of virtue, Socrates insists in response, "And likewise with the virtues, however and many they may be, they all have one common character [εἶδος] whereby they are virtues" (72c). To say what virtue is, is to know its *eidos*, the Form itself. Second, in response to the second properly formulated definition Meno can remember—virtue is to be able both to delight in and to have honorable things—Plato has Socrates ask: "Do not all men, in your opinion, my dear sir, desire the good?" No one desires evil and so to truly know the good is to desire it. Third and fourth, and apparently in direct response to Meno's comparison of Socrates to an ugly electric fish, the well-known learner's paradox—"even supposing you were to hit upon it, how will you know it is the thing you did not know?" (80d)—along with what we are taught is Socrates's response to it: the doctrine of the immortality of the soul and the theory of knowledge as recollection (*anamnesis*).

This is quite a list, and it is remarkable that these fundamental teachings of Plato are to be found as densely schooling as they are here in the *Meno*. And yet, if we are able to follow the lead of the fish, with its shocking capacity to induce torpor and *aporia*, we are quickly going to arrive at a point where each and every one of these fundamental teachings is itself suspended.

Scuttling across the floors of silent seas

"I consider that both in your appearance [εἶδος] and in other respects you are extremely like the flat *narkē* of the sea" (80a). If it appears that Socrates may have purposely induced Meno to resort to his fish-insult[8] by his insistence on the form of the question "What is it?" Socrates's mysterious response justifies the claim that he presses the form of the question "What is it?" not because he thinks of *aporia* as the lack of an answer to that question, and not because he considers that we might come to understand the question of human excellence (virtue) by answering such a question, but in order, rather, to push us past a limit (*horos*) that we cannot in fact pass. We both must and cannot (*aporia*) pass beyond beings, beyond things and answers. We cannot because we are bound to representation through language and must consequently grasp anything "as" the sort of thing that it is, or fail to grasp it at all. We must pass beyond beings (*epekeina tēs ousias*) because to grasp anything "as" it is means to transcend the thing. We are limited to thinking through things, but we can think things only if we take them "as" the sort of things they are, and yet the "as-this" that we must posit in grasping the thing is not itself a thing and is, thus, something we cannot grasp.

The dizzying and narcotic effect does not stop there, for Socrates has no intention of allowing the moment of broad marine narcosis to be translated immediately into a word or a concept. He will instead immediately work to mark the moment of the suspension or withdrawal of language (*aporia*). Socrates is made to mark the moment twice, as is his habit: first and most famously, of course, by insisting that "as for me [ἐγὼ δέ] if the torpedo [ἡ νάρκη] is torpid itself [αὐτὴ ναρκῶσα] while causing others to be torpid, I am like it, but not otherwise" (80c). But, second, and most notably, Socrates marks the necessarily impossible feature of our capacity for knowing and naming things by himself pausing or stumbling—almost as if he were dizzy, out of breath—just at the moment when the word of wisdom might have been forthcoming.

I am referring, of course, to the moment when, as a response to Socrates's "I am like it, but not otherwise," Meno offers the *eristikon logon*, his famous "captious argument" that all knowing may be impossible since one can never come to know what one does not already know. In response, it seems, Socrates is just on the verge of offering a recollection of his own—"for I have heard from wise men and women who told of things divine that . . ."—only to be suddenly and rudely interrupted by Meno.

> MENO: Now does it seem to you to be a good argument, Socrates?
> SOCRATES: It does not.
> MENO: Can you explain how not?
> SOCRATES: I can; for I have heard from wise men and women who told of things divine that—
> MENO: What was it they said? (81a)

This moment of Socratic narcosis will serve as the test case for our analysis insofar as it appears to be a moment when Socrates is himself about to offer an answer, an "it is," only to pause or stumble. If there is a properly Socratic *aporia*, and if it is brought to light by the work of our *narkē*, then we should find its effects in that Socratic pause.

How to do justice to that Socratic pause or interruption? Try to think of it not as a withholding of the word, not as a failure or flaw, but as the interruption, or perhaps eruption, of a moment of *alogia into logos*, a resounding though wordless cry or howl at the very source of *logos*, a source that while essential to discourse exceeds saying; or perhaps, given our marine theme, why not imagine it to be a momentary pause for the soul to catch its breath, since if in fact Socrates is the *narkē* he admits to being, then he at least, and perhaps also we, must be breathing underwater.

Given the complexity of this need to grasp for images, we could do worse than to begin with the realization that our fish is an animal, maybe even the animal that we are. If this animal has the power to suspend the traditional readings of the three classic Platonic doctrines outlined above, then we might want to take seriously the fact that this Socratic pause results from the fact that the fish is an *alogon*. And yet Socrates has just allowed that he too has been infected by this temporary narcosis, this *alogoria*. So it seems that there are two ways to be deprived of words or speech. One is to be an animal for whom this condition is no deprivation at all, and the other is to be an animal having speech but being momentarily deprived of it.

I do not think they will sing to me

In *The Animal That Therefore I Am*, Derrida works to provoke a wholesale reorientation of philosophy both with respect to and in the form of different questions about animals. Now to a degree, Derrida is expressing his dissatisfaction with all the well-meaning work of philosophers wanting to rescue animals by showing that we are like them or they like us. Of exceedingly greater importance, both to

Derrida and to our reading of the *Meno*, is the suggestion that under the proper regard our animals can grant to thinking an opportunity that was lost to thinking when it turned to metaphysics. And when I say "when it turned" I mean precisely the moment we are now investigating, the traditional reading of the Platonic doctrines outlined above. But I also mean the moment of interruption of that traditional set of doctrines: the moment of the invocation in the *Meno* of the aporia-fish and the Socratic pause or gasp it induces.[9] It is no coincidence that the origin of the traditional reading would also be the moment of an alternative: the moment when, faced with the fact that language speaks to us of things and in terms of things, Plato appears to have his Socrates entertain another path or way (*poros*). But there is no other way, only a stumble, gasp, or pause that marks both the necessity and the impossibility of the form of the question. Why even entertain such an *aporia*, such an "impossible possibility?" We can learn something about Plato's invocation of the aporia-fish at this point of the breakdown of the question "What is it?" by drawing a few insights from Derrida, who knows our fish quite well.

In *The Animal That Therefore I Am*, Derrida advances his earlier analyses of the Heideggerian *Zusage*, the spiraling self-inflecting power of language to greet us in advance. Derrida is now willing to suggest that the power of animals to reorient philosophy hinges less on our willingness to care for them (an imperative certainly) than on our regard for their cries and howls.[10] Derrida follows the question of language into the question of the animal (the animal that I follow, or that I am: both translate *que je suis*) in order to suggest that the moment or the pause that constitutes signification in language—the "moment" of difference between what I *say* and what *is*, which difference is constitutive of signification—is not mute. What we have here, I propose, is a shift from the vocabulary of the paths of thought (new paths, new approaches, new answers) to the problem of the medium itself.

The focus of this new question is, however, familiar. It is the problem of the connection and thus the difference between speech and phenomena, except that the new formulation with its focus on the animal that I am/following generates a shift from what remains necessarily unthought to what sustains thought. Here in this late work devoted to animals, Derrida is willing to insist that this silent gap or pause is not mute: not because it has a voice but because it comprises the connection between voice and phenomena. There is, it seems, strong reason to believe that due to their exclusion from language animals may offer us the key to thinking in a new way about what remains unsayable in language. "But if one links the concept of the animal, as they all do from Descartes to Heidegger, from Kant to Levinas and Lacan, to the double im-possibility, the double incapacity of question and response, is it because the 'moment,' the instance and possibility of the *Zusage* belong to an 'experience' of language about which one could say, even if it is not in itself 'animal,' that it is not something that the 'animal' could be deprived of? That would be enough to destabilize the whole tradition, to deprive it of its fundamental argument."[11] We would not be overstepping in the least were we to add here that this impossible possibility for thinking anew about being and language was in fact already present and available at the very beginning, indeed at the precise "moment" that our little fish induces in Socrates a pause.

Evidence for that leap from Derrida's animals to our fish is offered just at the moment this thesis of "a bestiary at the origin of philosophy" is introduced. For just as Derrida is busy inventing a new word for "the" animal, namely, *animot*—a name that mimics precisely the relation of *narkē* to its name—Derrida finds himself recalling a moment from even farther back in his private bestiary: "I tried (in 1968, thirty years ago, therefore) to imagine what the program of a Socratic bestiary on the eve of philosophy might be." Derrida then proceeds to quote this famous passage from his text "Plato's Pharmacy": "Alternately and/or all at once, the Socratic *pharmakon* petrifies and vivifies, anesthetizes and sensitizes, appeases and anguishes. Socrates is a benumbing torpille (*narkē*)."[12] If the voice of an animal speaks through the same pause that makes language both possible and necessary, then could the cry or howl of an animal speak on behalf of the unsayable? Can the impossible be the condition of the possible in this way? Or isn't that precisely the gesture that is put into question by the double reading (Plato's or Derrida's), namely, that despite all the careful protestations to the contrary, every previous philosophical expression of regard for the animal, even Heidegger's, amounts to asking the unsayable to speak. This is not because they define the unsayable in the light of speech or saying but because they leave the animal wordless, thus deprived, thus voiceless. And of course every animal is voiceless if by speech (*logos*) we mean the power to ask, "What is it?" and the tendency to name things.

Like a patient, etherized upon a table

Because we owe it to our fish, and our thesis of the Socratic pause, to show that its influence can produce a set of recognizably contestable claims, we should, by way of concluding, return now to the traditional doctrines from the Plato archive.

Logos: Under the narcotizing influence of the aporia-fish, the doctrine of the theory of Forms turns out to be simply the most profound reflection possible on the fact that in order to grasp anything we have to take it "to be." To grasp something as *a* being is to conceptualize it "as" this or that. This posited "as-this" is the *eidos*.

It is important to insist that this apophantic gesture, this positing of the thing "as" the sort of thing it is, must not be viewed as some sort of subsequent philosophical development coming along after the fact in order to categorize the sensibly given object. It is, rather, the very condition of the possibility of there being things or objects of thought and perception in the first place. What occurs when we partake of appearances is an originary act of repetition, a pause or hiccup, if you will, as the *zōion logon echon* pauses to take in its world. The pause *appears* as temporal but *is* ontological. We must re-present the thing "as" this or that in order even to see it. Because it is itself the condition of any rational grasp or vision, this constitutive pause cannot itself be an object grasped, and so it is necessary to acknowledge it through analogy, through images, stories, or depictions. Hence the much-studied Forms are simply Plato's various efforts to account for the pause or hesitation that is the medium of the originary re-presentation of any thing "as" the sort of thing it is.

This is the basis of our capacity for truth through logos: a momentary pause or hesitation constitutes givenness itself.

Thumos: Whenever Plato does give in to the temptation to posit Being-beyond-beings, it is in the name of the Good.[13] Hence whenever we encounter, in Plato, something that might be taken for a posited Form, it is critical to note that the discourse has shifted from the presentation of beings to the problem of being and becoming. Consequently, the doctrine that no one desires evil turns on this shift, or reorientation, from the possibility of beings to the possibility of becoming, from knowledge to action. But on this new ground, we encounter the aporia-fish as well. The moment of originary repetition recurs. Just when we imagine we have caught him in a flagrant act of metaphysics (positing Being beyond beings), Plato repeats the same fundamental move. Just as perception or sensible knowledge requires an attending supplement that both conditions and escapes the function it makes possible, so too, here, in the case of the Good the condition of being good is the re-presentation of desire (a movement from *epithumein* to *boulesthai*).[14] In the *Meno*, that transformation from desiring to willing requires, Socrates suggests, an "addition," a prosthesis: "Very well; procuring gold and silver is virtue according to Meno, the ancestral friend of the Great King. Tell me, do you add [προστιθεῖς] to such procuring, Meno, that it is to be done justly and piously . . . ?" (78d). And what is the prosthesis that, by being added, would constitute virtue? It is, of course, virtue. Virtue would have to be added to any act that would be virtuous. This "addition" that must accompany "the power to desire and to have noble things" is itself neither a desire nor a noble thing. Nor is it their sum. Virtue *is* the addition of virtue. Originary repetition.

What constitutes the goodness of an action is not its power to procure the thing-desired, nor the desire itself, but the addition of what is, as we see, the re-presentation of the procuring act "as" virtuous. Just as the re-presentation of anything "as" the sort of thing it is constitutes the very possibility of the givenness of that thing, so too here, in the sphere of action, what looks like an addition is in fact the very condition itself. It is an aporetic moment, a narcotized pause. Simply put—and by now our fish ought to be familiar—the "addition" is the fact that, in order to act, human animals must re-present their desires "as" ends to be pursued. This means not that virtue can be added in the transition from mere *epithumein* to willful *boulsethai* but that such a transformation already attends the *thumos* (thus the *epi-*) in its originary form. The life of the soul (*thumos*) is the breath (*thumos*) of the soul. We are approaching a new medium, and it seems to have something to do with breathing when and where it is impossible to breathe.

This originary and radical supplement displaces the "act" of procuring, displaces it into a radical medium that suspends time (understood "as" causality) and sustains action (understood "as" freedom). In the sphere of what we cannot quite help calling epistemology, this shift to an account of the transcendental medium of originary re-presentation obviates any need to posit transcendent Forms. But here in the sphere of human action the same shift requires precisely that the Good actually be posited "as" such, posited not as a supreme being, of course, but as the most fundamental confirmation of the fact of originary repetition: namely, that the initial givenness of desire is, for humans, always and necessarily the re-presentation of desire. Plato presages Freud. A desire is a desire only when it represents an act or an end "as" worthy of enacting. The metaphysical status traditionally afforded the Good collapses into this originary moment, this pause or fold or fissure, through which desire becomes a desire in this originary moment of self-re-presentation. Ours is a thirsty soul.

This is the basis of our capacity for virtue: a momentary pause or hesitation does not come along after the fact in the form of some addition. Rather, what first appears to be an addition actually is the original condition, which is to say that the addition is itself virtue.

Eros: The addition (prosthesis) turns out to be a possibility only for a being whose soul is breathing, a condition of active repetition. With the help of our aporia-fish, we have the charioteer and one horse: we have recollected *logos* and now *thumos*. What would be left to be recollected were we to complete this aporetic account of a Platonic soul?

Given the close identification of re-presentation with originary repetition, we arrive at the third of the traditional Platonic doctrines: the learner's paradox and the theory of *anamnesis*, of learning as originary repetition. If Being is the medium rather than the logic or the ground of thought and action, then we are, it seems, suspended not in time but in a dream. The dream-report is the original form of the dream, and yet this only indicates that we are suspended in a medium of signification and action that is itself a repetition or re-presentation. The medium itself is the ether, if you will, of the difference between the event and its re-presentation. We live out our lives in that brief *espacement* of difference, but we are not really at home there. Like wind-blown whitecaps on a wave, we are suspended above the animal we are and we reassure ourselves only through the constructions that follow from that space of originary re-presentation.

The most trenchant and moving manifestation of the pause that sustains our being attaches neither to *logos* (reason) nor to *thumos* (desire) but occurs rather as the erotic medium, as touch. There is no finer and truer expression of the disenabling power of our aporia-fish than the pause that attends touch. If we are to complete our depiction of Plato's aporetic soul, then we need to account for Eros. We need to account for the aporetic pause in the case of touch.

Pause: In the face of Meno's rude and impudent insistence ("What was it they said?"), and on the verge of offering what will turn out to have been if not a dream then a poetic reverie, Socrates is forced to pause. When he resumes he repeats what he has heard from those who "told of things divine [περὶ τὰ θεῖα πράγματα]": "They were certain priests and priestesses who have studied so as to be able to give a reasoned account [λόγον . . . διδόναι] of their ministry: and Pindar also and many another poet of heavenly gifts. . . . They say that the soul of man is immortal, and at one time comes to an end, which is called dying, and at another is born again, but never perishes" (81a). Two consequences follow, according to Plato, from this reverential reverie that he is willing to recount. First, that "one ought to live all one's life in utmost holiness." Second, that since the soul is immortal, "she has acquired knowledge of all and everything; so that it is no wonder that she should be able to recollect all that she knew before about virtue and other things."

Now, in the tradition, Socrates's recourse here to divine and poetic images is taken to be a doctrine. And it is presumed to be an answer to Meno's challenge that it is impossible to learn anything, the infamous "learner's paradox." Taken in this way, the thesis that the soul is immortal could possibly address the challenge, assuming only that Socrates were too dense and Meno too weak a debater to notice that it would amount to saying that the soul can get around the fact that it is incapable of learning by instead simply remembering what it already learned. As if shifting the soul from this life to an earlier "this life" would address the challenge. But of course this is to miss the point entirely.

How is the Socratic repetition of what he has heard any different from what we have criticized in Meno, his obdurate recourse to repeating what he has heard from Gorgias? If our aporia-fish has his way, then we will have to accept that memory is not the recollection of something previously learned; learning is, rather, originally a re-collection.

Touch: How would that work exactly? How could the repetition precede the thing or event? What sort of distortion of space and time would allow for such an impossible possibility?

I know the voices dying with a dying fall

"So now, for my part, I have no idea what virtue is, whilst you, though perhaps you may have known before you came in touch [ἅψασθαι] with me, are now as good as ignorant of it also" (80d). It is perhaps not all that surprising that the readers and translators have so often mistaken the *narkē* for a stingray, since Plato comes very close to making the mistake himself. From a zoological perspective, there is a critical difference between a numbness induced by coming in touch (*haptomenon*, from *haptō*, to fasten to, cling to, undertake, to touch or effect) and numbness induced simply by approaching or coming near. From a philosophical perspective, the difference is exactly the same as the difference between Meno's and Socrates's acts of recollection. The former is venomous and defensive and characterizes the stingray. The latter is electrical and employs a medium so that it can be used for hunting. Indeed, where the *narkē* is discussed in the classical literature writers are occasionally inclined to crib a line from Aristotle, who remarks insightfully that one proof of the power of the *narkē* to act across a distance is the fact that "they are often caught with grey mullets inside, though they themselves are the slowest of fishes while the grey mullet is the swiftest."[15]

The earliest commentaries on *narkē* were concerned with its therapeutic powers.[16] They understood perfectly well that the same power that made our fish able to alter the order of time (it is the slowest fish but captures the swiftest) made it capable of acting across space. And before we decide the matter by giving it a name (electricity) we should at least consider the nature of this sort of contact over distance and its therapeutic effect.

For the soul to know or to learn it must cleave to the true and the Good. But to cleave is both "to cling to" and thus "to divide." I cannot grasp or touch anything unless I am divided from it. And this holds true for the animal I am as much as for anything I would grasp or touch. To touch is necessarily to cleave. Touch must, at one and the same time, "adhere closely, stick, or cling" to its object and "be divided" from that object. Touching is possible only because actually touching is impossible.

When he touches on this question, Derrida is willing to employ the same apparently hyperbolic rhetorical turn that he employed in his re-presentation of the *pharmakon* passage in *The Animal That Therefore I Am*, where he wrote of the pervasive tendency to speak in the general singular of "the" animal: "for the gesture seems to me to constitute philosophy as such."[17] In his book *On Touching, Jean-Luc Nancy*, Derrida invokes what he calls a "haptic intuitionism" and claims to have thereby touched upon the principle of philosophy itself: "But then, by touching on it by way of a figure, *psychē* really touches (*haptetai*) upon truth. It touches on it in giving up touching. Truth is not touched except where it is untouchable. In Plato's *Republic* the same 'haptic' figure describes the relation of the immortal soul with everything that it touches or attains (*hapestai*) in its love for truth—'philosophy' itself. . . . For, as the *Republic* spells it out, what is at issue here is philosophy itself and the desire of pure *psyche*."[18] It is no accident that Derrida is willing and able to identify these two gestures with the an-archē "itself" that constitutes philosophical desire: the desire to put the soul in touch with truth even at the price of touch itself ("it touches on it by giving up touching") and the desire to certify the soul through the pure transcendence of (animal) desire as posited in the neutralized sexuality, "not to say castrated" concept, of "the" animal.[19] The animal is no more an animal than pure touch is touch, and for exactly the same reason.

Though we cannot speak with them, and we are not like them in the critical sense of the question of the *Meno*, the question of justice and virtue, we touch our animals and are touched by them in turn. Here, (un)like the pause constitutive of *logos* and of *thumos*, the "being-touched" manifests its *aporia* literally on the surface, literally and actually thereby deconstructing the surface with every acknowledged touch. When I speak of a shift to the question of the medium of being, what I am suggesting is something like a field-theory of touch, whereby the linear phenomenon we call electricity is set aside in favor of its therapeutic power, the former having to conform to the latter and thus requiring that time and space be bent or warped in order to account for the truth of the contact that is touch. What passes through the narcotized medium is the animal's spirit, life, breath ("They say that the soul of a man is immortal"). And just as gravity can compel any object across the vacuum of space, and though we are dealing here only with the analogue of an analogy, so too does touch turn out to be a special case ("and at one time comes to an end"). The entire cosmos cleaves ("which is called dying"). Space and time are warped in order to reassure touch ("and at another is born again"). For our part we are homeless in our logocentric world ("but never perishes").

I am moved over impossible gaps of space and time by voices I remember. I grow old. A love song plays. In a dream I see you speak. (My organs shutting down). I hear, as if for the first time, your voice. (My lungs filling with fluids). My animal sits up and touches me. I am touched by the animal I am. I am hunting again. I am (*je suis*) following now. Collapsing into that cosmic pause (not now!), all being cleaves, now, to me. I am awakened by a voice I can no longer recognize, a human voice I suppose, and I drown.

Notes

The chapter title is from T. S. Eliot, *The Love Song of J. Alfred Prufrock*: "We have lingered in the chambers of the sea/By sea-girls wreathed with seaweed red and brown/Till human voices wake us, and we drown." All section subheads are also from this poem.

1. Plato, *Meno*, trans. W. R. M. Lamb (Cambridge, Mass.: Harvard University Press, 1924).
2. Stingrays comprise eight distinct families of the suborder Myliobatidae and are characterized by a barbed stinger that can deliver venom, but only on direct contact. Electric rays (Torpediniforms) and stingrays (Myliobatiformes) share class (Chondrichthyes) and subclass

(Elasmobranchii) but then differ at the level of superorder. On the history of competing efforts to taxonomize the Torpedinaidea and Narcinaidea (the two electric ray superfamilies) and their subfamilies, the interested reader is invited to consult the taxonomic section included in Leonard J. V. Compagno and Phillip C. Heemstra, "Electolux addisoni, a New Genus and Species of the Electric Ray from the East Coast of South Africa (Rajiformes: Topedinoidei: Narkidae), with a Review of the Torpedinoid Taxonomy," *Smithiana*, Bulletin 7 (May 2007): 15–49.

3. W. K. C. Guthrie, "Meno," in *Plato: The Collected Dialogues*, ed. Edith Hamilton and Huntington Cairnes (Princeton, N.J.: Princeton University Press, 1961), 363. Despite his "sting ray," Guthrie does a very nice job with the *thallatia*, giving us "that we meet in the sea." Derrida gets it right. In section 5 of *Plato's Pharmacy*, he gives us *la torpille* in the body of the text and *Socrate est la torpille narcotique* in the note. But his English translator then turns around and gets it wrong again: "Socrates is a benumbing stingray" (Jacques Derrida, *La Dissémination* [Paris: Éditions du Seuil, 1972], 135, 136; Derrida, *Dissemination*, trans. Barbara Johnson [Chicago: University of Chicago University Press, 1981], 119). John Sallis makes it "stingray" in his *Being and Logos* (Bloomington: Indiana University Press, 1996), 64, 78. Gareth Matthews, in a book ostensibly devoted to Socratic perplexity, gives one of his chapters the subtitle: "The Self-Stinging Stingray" (Gareth B. Matthews, *Socratic Perplexity and the Nature of Philosophy* [Oxford: Oxford University Press, 2006]). The conflation of these two fish is so embedded that it creeps out into the general culture. The British military named one of their weapons launched from combat helicopters (technically referred to as an LWT: light-weight torpedo) the "Sting Ray torpedo."

4. Chau H. Wu, "Electric Fish and the Discovery of Animal Electricity," *American Scientist* 72 (1984): 598–607.

5. Ibid., 601.

6. Aristotle, *History of Animals, Books VII-X*, trans. D. M. Balme (Cambridge, Mass.: Harvard University Press), 620b20.

7. I am indebted to Professor Nickolas Pappas, whose superior understanding of Plato and of Attic Greek occasionally saves me from excessively free translation.

8. "But when we deride, or rail at, stupid and ignorant people we call them 'fish'" (Plutarch, *Moralia XII* 413). Nothing rests on it, but that Plutarch just might have our passage in the back of his mind is suggested by the fact that he mentions Socrates a few lines above.

9. Michael Naas has offered—as he does—an invaluable recollection of the occasion, in 2002, when Derrida was asked to comment on an exhibit of photos documenting the history of the legendary conferences held over the years at Cerisy-la-Salle: "And then [Derrida] spoke of the exhibit itself. He said that when you enter the exhibit room and see all those photographs of the past you cannot help but gasp, you cannot help but have your breath taken away, and this feeling of being breathless, he said, this suspension of breath, this gasp before the past, is—and I will never forget these words because they were for me so striking and unexpected—'the very experience of the future'" (Michael Naas, *Derrida From Now On* [New York: Fordham University Press, 2008], 95).

10. See Leonard Lawlor, *This Is Not Sufficient* (New York: Columbia University Press, 2007), 73.

11. Jacques Derrida, *The Animal That Therefore I Am*, ed. Marie-Louise Mallet, trans. David Wills (New York: Fordham University Press, 2008), 166; *L'animal que donc je suis* (Paris: Éditions Galilée, 2006), 62.

12. Take your pick. The passage appears originally in Derrida, *La dissemination*, 135, and then again in a footnote on the following page, 136n47; *Dissemination* 118, 119n52. Derrida then cites the passage in *L'animal que donc je suis*, 64. The English translation in *The Animal That*

Therefore I Am repeats, simply through citation, the error: "Socrates is a benumbing stingray" (40).

13. Plato, *Republic*, trans. Paul Shorey (Cambridge, Mass.: Harvard University Press, 1935), 509a.

14. On this transformation from *epithumein* to *boulesthai*, see Jacob Klein, *A Commentary on Plato's Meno* (Chicago: University of Chicago Press, 1989), 75.

15. Aristotle, *History of Animals*, 620b20.

16. Wu, "Electric Fish and the Discovery of Animal Electricity."

17. Derrida, *The Animal That Therefore I Am*, 40; *L'animal que donc je suis*, 64.

18. Jacques Derrida, *On Touching, Jean-Luc Nancy*, trans. Christine Irizarry (Stanford, Calif.: Stanford University Press, 2005), 120–121.

19. Derrida speaks in *The Animal That Therefore I Am* of "the general singular of an animal whose sexuality is as a matter of principle left undifferentiated—or neutralized, not to say castrated" (ibid.).

PART III

The Socratic Animal as Truth-Teller and Provocateur

5   We the Bird-Catchers

Receiving the Truth in the Phaedo *and the* Apology

S. Montgomery Ewegen

THERE IS NO doubt that the *Apology* comes *before* the *Phaedo*. This sequence is obvious enough: the *Apology* presents the trial of Socrates, the *Phaedo* the final conversations that took place on the day of his death. Beyond the question of which of the two texts was written first—a matter of likely insoluble debate—the dramatic settings of the two dialogues make it clear that the *Apology* comes *before* the *Phaedo* and occurs dramatically prior to it.[1]

Suppose, however, that one wished to place the *Phaedo* before the *Apology*. Suppose that one imagined that the *Phaedo looks back* upon the *Apology* and communicates with it in certain provocative ways. Suppose that one wished to *turn back* from the *Phaedo* to the *Apology* while striving to carry over, if not everything from the former, then at least as much as would prove to be philosophically illuminating or provocative. At the risk of doing violence to a certain universally accepted chronology, this reading would place the *Phaedo* before the *Apology* in order to explore certain ways in which the *Phaedo* enriches and complicates the λόγος of the *Apology*, a λόγος that has much to do with λόγος.[2]

The authorization for such a retrograde reading appears in a comment made by Socrates in the *Phaedo*. Not long after Socrates has been released from his fetters into the Aesopian duality of pleasure and pain, Cebes asks Socrates why it was only after coming to prison that he composed poetry (60c–d). Socrates's response is that it was in order to test the meaning of certain dreams and "to make sure that I was neglecting no duty in case their repeated commands meant I must make music in this way [ταύτην τὴν μουσικήν μοι ἐπιτάττοι ποιεῖν]" (60e; trans. modified). Socrates then explains the reoccurring dream: "the same dream came to me often in my past life [ἐν τῷ παρελθόντι βίῳ], sometimes in one form

79

and sometimes in another, but always saying the same thing: '*make music and work at it* [μουσικὴν ποίει καὶ ἐργάζου]'" (60e). Socrates goes on to say that in his former life he interpreted the dreams as exhorting him to make "the greatest music [μεγίστης μουσικῆς]," that is, philosophy (61a).[3] It was only after having been tried and imprisoned that Socrates *looked back* upon this reoccurring dream and re-interpreted it as urging him to make demotic music (61a).

In this *looking back* we are told by Socrates that in his past life—that is, in the time before the *Phaedo*, the life before his death—he had a recurring dream. The precise scope of this "past life" is unclear, though we are told by Socrates that the dreams occurred "often." Given Socrates's former interpretation of the dream as urging him to continue practicing philosophy ("the greatest music"), the dream could extend to every occasion on which Socrates practiced philosophy. This would mean that *every* Platonic text that presents Socrates doing philosophy has Socrates *making music*, though, of course, music of a very peculiar sort. One can imagine, much more modestly, that Socrates's dreams extend at least to the *Apology*, whose events occurred some thirty days prior to those depicted in the *Phaedo*.[4] One could thus imagine that Socrates, as he delivers his ἀπολογία to the people of Athens and to the history of philosophy, *is making music*, that is, making the sort of music he believed his dreams to be urging him to make.[5]

The task, then, will be to determine the character of this music. Coming to any clarity on this point will require that we place the *Phaedo* before the *Apology* and listen to what Socrates has to say in the *Phaedo* about this music. More precisely, this will require that we listen to the swans of the *Phaedo*—the very swans to whom Socrates will liken himself—and to what they tell us about their own (and therefore Socrates's) way of speaking, a way that will be seen to bear a unique and peculiar relation to *the truth* (ἀλήθεια). After listening to the swans, we shall *turn back* to the *Apology* in order to hear this music at work within a discourse preeminently concerned with the truth. Through this *looking back* from the *Phaedo* to the *Apology*, our understanding of Socrates, his speaking, and the truth will undergo a transformation, one brought about by the joyful song of the swan.

Phaedo

It is, to begin with, a matter of *scope*. Within the *Phaedo* Socrates speaks of the swans, of their song and of their divinely given powers. In speaking of the swans, Socrates is speaking about an animal that, properly speaking, *cannot* speak, an animal that, for the Greeks, was without λόγος. I say "for the Greeks" and most readily mean those Greeks who *followed* Aristotle, who, in a formulation now dangerously familiar, took the human being to be the ζῷων λόγον ἔχων, the animal with λόγος, the animal who *speaks* (λέγειν).[6] The scope of λόγος for the history of philosophy has extended only to this human animal.[7]

However, in speaking about this animal who does not have λόγος, Socrates speaks about a being who nonetheless engages in an operation of signification that, though not "logical" (in the sense of being *of* λόγος), can tell us much about Socrates's own way of speaking: for Socrates, within the *Phaedo*, likens himself to the swans. Socrates compares himself to a bird in order, I shall argue, to better understand his own way of λόγος, a λόγος that precisely through this comparison shall prove to be beyond what is normally understood as λόγος. Further, it is through this likening of himself to the swan that Socrates will come to better understand *himself*, a likening that thus lets him live more in accord with the dictum "know thyself" that is attributed to the very god *of* the swans, Apollo.

We enter the *Phaedo* at the moment that λόγος has stopped and a silence has befallen the room. Having just heard Socrates's most pointed discourse on the immortality of the soul, and on the manner by which the soul of the philosopher must spurn emotion and purge itself from its attachment to the body, all those present fall into a contemplative silence (σιγή) (84b). This silence is finally broken by the mutterings of Cebes and Simmias, who come to voice a concern regarding the insufficiency of Socrates's account. Upon hearing this concern, Socrates, revealing a certain *joy* in the face of the somber proceedings, laughs (84d).

Speaking to Simmias in particular, Socrates attempts to assuage his fear, no doubt smiling as he does: "I should have hard work to persuade other people that I do not regard my present situation as a misfortune, when I cannot even make you believe it, but you are afraid I am more churlish [δυσκολώτερόν] now than I was in my life that came before [ἐν τῷ πρόσθεν βίῳ]" (84e; trans. modified). It is important to note the scope of Simmias's concern. It is not the case that Simmias, believing Socrates to have been churlish throughout his life, is now afraid that on the eve of his death he will be more so. Rather, the concern is that Socrates might now be churlish, in the face of his death, despite the fact that he was *never* churlish in his life that came before: for, as we learn in the *Crito*, Socrates was always of a happy disposition (εὐδαιμόνισα) throughout his life (πρότερον ἐν παντὶ τῷ βίῳ) (43b). Thus, even though Socrates's life had been a happy one, and his mood generally jovial, his comrades are nervous that his imminent death will have soured his otherwise joyful demeanor.

It is in an effort to allay this concern that Socrates speaks of the swans: "You seem to think I am inferior in prophetic power [τὴν μαντικήν] to the swans [τῶν κύκνων] who sing in the time that comes before [ἐν τῷ πρόσθεν χρόνῳ], but when they feel that they are to die, sing most and best [πλεῖστα καὶ μάλιστα ᾄδουσι] in their joy that they are to go to the god whose servants they are. But men, because of their own fear of death, tell lies against the swans and say that they sing for sorrow, in mourning for their own death" (84e; trans. modified). In other words, owing to a certain hermeneutic posture informed by their own fear of death, those human beings who interpret the swans as singing out of grief fail to truly hear the song of the swan *as it is given,* hearing instead only their own fear.[8]

Against those who would hear such lamentation, Socrates interprets the song of the swan as expressing not grief but joy, observing that "no bird sings when it is hungry or cold or has any other trouble. . . . I do not believe they sing for grief . . . but since they are *of Apollo* [τοῦ Ἀπόλλωνος ὄντες], I believe they have prophetic vision [μαντικοί], and because they have foreknowledge of the blessings in the other world they sing and rejoice on that day more than ever before" (85a; my emphasis). It is important to note that Socrates emphasizes the importance of interpretation, finding it necessary to re-interpret the song of the swan in order to free it from this incorrect interpretation. It is a matter, then, of *reception,* of how one is to receive the song of the swan. On the one hand, one may receive it as signifying grief and lamentation in the face of death.[9] On the other hand, one may receive the song as denoting joy and blessedness. It is by holding this latter interpretation that Socrates believes one would truly receive the song of the swan as it is *given.*

Here again we must attend to a matter of scope. It is not the case that the swans, who sang in grief throughout their lives, finally come to sing joyfully on the day of their death. Rather, it is that the swans sing *more* joyfully as their deaths approach, implying that their song is *always* joyful, even in the time that comes before their death. On Socrates's interpretation, the swan's song is *essentially* joyful.[10] Moreover, it is not just their foreknowledge of the blessings that await them after death that brings about their joyfulness. Rather, their joy is most of all owed to their belonging to Apollo, to their being *of* Apollo, even in the time before their deaths. The joy that Socrates hears in the song of the swan is owed to their intimate relation to Apollo.

We turn now to Socrates's account of the specific powers that the swans receive from this musical god. Socrates claims that the swans receive both foreknowledge (προειδότες) and prophetic vision (ἡ μαντική) and that he himself is a recipient of these powers (85b). Foreknowledge is, as Socrates tells us, the ability to apprehend the blessings that await them in Hades after death. Prophetic vision (μαντική), however, is a much broader conception of prophecy, one that we can learn much about by turning to certain other of Plato's texts. In the *Phaedrus*, for example, Socrates describes this divinely given mantic power, offering four phenomena where such mania is, far from evil, one of "the greatest goods" for human beings (244a). For our purposes, we shall address only two of these phenomena. First, Socrates mentions the oracle at Delphi, whose pronouncements are valuable only when they are offered from out of a mantic state (μαντική) (244b). Secondly, Socrates mentions the sort of mantic power characteristic of poets when inspired by the Muses, a power so valuable as to render the poems created without it worthless (245a). *Only* when the oracles and the poets are divinely inspired with this mantic power are their words worth receiving.

The Socrates of the *Ion* speaks similarly. The poets, Socrates here claims, are able to make worthwhile poetry only if they are "out of their minds" with divine inspiration. Just as "with prophets [χρησμῳδοῖς] and diviners [μάντεσι]," "the god takes [the poets'] intellect [νοῦς] away from them when he uses them as his servants" (534b–c). The beautiful poetry that results is owed not to technical mastery on the part of the poets but to this divine gift by which the god speaks through them (534c): and "as long as a human being has his intellect [νοῦς] in his possession he will always lack the power to make poetry [ποιεῖν] or sing prophecy [χρησμῳδεῖν]" (534b). Only by virtue of this mantic power can human beings *make music and work at it*.

According to Socrates in the *Meno*, those inspired with this mantic power not only speak beautifully—they speak the *truth* (99c). The divinely given power makes those inspired speak the truth, though in such a way as to lack knowledge of what they say. It is precisely by dislocating or disrupting the mind (νοῦς) of the speaker that the divinely given mantic power allows him or her to speak the truth.

With this broader understanding of μαντική, we can see that the swans of the *Phaedo*, as they sing joyfully from out of this mantic state given to them by Apollo, sing the truth beautifully. More precisely, the truth passes *through* Apollo's birds as they sing. This latter function of the swans can be understood more clearly if we attend to the role of birds in ancient Greek ornithomancy. For the Greeks, birds in general bore an intimate relationship to the gods, serving in many cases as their messengers.[11] As messengers, birds were signs *of* the gods, and in a double sense: they were signs used by the gods and, thereby, they signified the gods themselves.[12] It is important to note, however, that birds were not so much given signs from the gods as they *themselves* were given *by* the gods to others *as* signs.[13] In other words, the birds were not given signs—they were *given-signs*, signs that were given. As given-signs, birds were *gifts* from the gods intimating some truth. In the case of the swans in particular, this mantic ability of giving signs is connected to their musical ability: for it is precisely through their beautiful music that the swans offer signs of the gods to human beings. The *Homeric Hymn to Apollo* says just this, and with the dulcet elegance of the very bird of which it speaks: "Phoebus, *of you* [σέ] even the swan sings with clear voice to the beating of his wings, as he alights upon the bank of the eddying river Peneus" (*Homeric Hymn* 21; my emphasis).[14] The swans, possessing this mantic power, serve as signs of Apollo and his truth: they accomplish their belonging to Apollo through their very act of existing as his signs.[15]

In light of this sojourn into Greek ornithomancy, we can say that the swan, whose Greek name κύκνος came to be transliterated as "cygnet," *signifies* insofar as it points beyond itself toward the god. The significance of the cygnet—that is, the swan's function as signifier—can perhaps best be seen in the etymological history that the sign "cygnet" and the sign "sign" evidently share. Through a rich and tortuous history of onomastic development, and across differences of culture, tongue, and meaning, the sign "cygnet" has leaped from tree to tree, as it were, finding itself at times *in look* no different from the look of both "sign" and, more obviously, "signet" (a "little sign"). One can perhaps see this confusion most clearly if one simply lets these signs flutter, as if in some great flock, onto the page:

> *Cygnet:*[16] sygnett, signett, *signet,* cignet, cygnette, cygnet.
> *Signet: sygnett, signett, signet,* sygnet, syngnet.
> *Sign:* singne, signe, sygne, sygnne.

As the swan and the sign pass through times and tongues, their histories drift across one another, as two soaring birds in flight. As a result, when one looks for the κύκνος, one finds oneself chasing cygnets, signs, and signets; likewise, when one looks for a "sign," one stumbles into permutations of the "cygnet," variations of the swan. This onomastic intimacy, if not verifiable etymological connection, suggests philologically what has already been argued philosophically: that the swan was *significant,* both in its song and in its very look. Though perhaps without λόγος, the swans *spoke:* or, rather, the god spoke through the swan, using it as a sign. The swan sung in such a way as to intimate Apollo: through the bird, the god, just as through the mouth, the word. Owing to their mantic ability, these swans, as given-signs, bespoke the god to whom they belonged.

As seen above, it is precisely this mantic ability that Socrates claims to share with the swans: "And I think that I myself am a fellow-servant of the swans, and am consecrated to the same god and have received from our master a mantic gift [τὴν μαντικὴν] no whit inferior to theirs" (85b; trans. modified). Thus, it is not the ability to foresee the blessings that await him in the next life that Socrates shares with the swans but rather this prophetic art of receiving messages from the gods.[17] There are many moments within the Platonic corpus where Socrates's mantic ability is remarked upon. For example, Euclides of the *Theaetetus* comments upon how "prophetically [μαντικῶς]" Socrates spoke in predicting the eventual accomplishments of the then young Theaetetus (142c). In the *Phaedrus,* Socrates himself extolls his mantic ability, calling both himself and his soul a seer (μάντις / μαντικόν) (242c). In these passages, we see moments where Socrates, owing to this mantic ability, is able to divine something about the future. Yet, as we saw above, the mantic power is much broader in scope than this predictive ability.[18] More precisely, we saw the way in which the swans and poets, as mantic, speak truth without knowing the nature of that truth, thereby serving as given-signs to others.

Does Socrates share this aspect of the mantic power with the swans? Does Socrates, like the mantic swans, speak the truth? Is Socrates a sign? It is precisely in order to answer these questions that we turn to the *Apology,* which, I suggest, can show us concretely this aspect of Socrates's mantic, and swanlike, ability.

"Speaking Away" in Plato's *Apology*

From the beginning of the *Apology* it is a matter of *reception*, of how words are to be received. Having already received the speech from his accusers, Socrates prepares the audience to receive his own speech, his own way of speaking, his ἀπολογία.[19] It is a matter, too, of indecorous speech, of Socrates not wanting to make "speeches [λόγους]" unbefitting someone his age (17c). Rather, Socrates—as someone so close to death as to render the punitive efforts of the Athenians superfluous (38c)—will speak in a manner befitting himself. Indeed, Socrates will use his "customary speech [εἴωθα λέγειν]," "the same way of speaking [τῶν αὐτῶν λόγων]," he says, that he always uses (17c).[20] Just as the swans' joyful song does not change radically as they approach their death, Socrates's own way of speaking will not radically change here as he faces the trial that will render his verdict of death.

But what is this customary way of speaking? Whereas the previous speakers took the way of persuasion (πείθειν), Socrates will take the way of truth (ἀλήθεια) (*Apology* 17b). Of course, everything depends upon what "truth" (ἀλήθεια) would prove to mean in the *Apology*, of what it would mean for Socrates *to speak the truth*.[21] That truth cannot simply be opposed to persuasion, despite Socrates's juxtaposing of them in his opening words, becomes clear later when Socrates insists that his philosophical efforts have been a matter of trying to persuade (πείθειν) the people of Athens to care for themselves and the good (36c). Of course, it is equally clear that truth and persuasion cannot simply be aligned: for despite speaking nothing but the truth to the jury (34b)—or, perhaps precisely *because* he speaks nothing but the truth to the jury (see 24a)—Socrates fails to persuade them to acquit him (35e). However, whether or not the truth Socrates speaks also proves persuasive, either to the jury or to us, is immaterial here: what is of interest is the *fundamental structure of the truth* that Socrates speaks. In order to address this issue, we shall focus our attention on two moments in the *Apology* where truth *happens*. By attending to these two moments, we will come to some clarity regarding the nature of Socrates's way of true speaking, a way now lit up for us by our analysis of the signifying gestures of the cygnet.[22]

The first moment concerns the truth that flows through the oracle at Delphi, as reported by the impetuous Chaerephon, that claimed that no one is wiser than Socrates (21a). What is of interest here is the manner by which Socrates *receives* this oracle. Socrates's immediate reaction to the saying of the god is befuddlement: for, knowing himself not to be wise, Socrates is initially at a loss as to the god's meaning (21b). Yet, we learn that this befuddlement is rooted in a deeper certainty held by Socrates: namely, the certainty that the god cannot be lying (21b). Thus, Socrates first and foremost receives the oracular pronouncement as *true*, despite being at a loss to understand it.[23]

However, Socrates does not stop here. In the face of the conflict that arises between the purportedly true λόγος of the god (that Socrates is wise) and Socrates's own λόγος (that there is no one wiser than he), Socrates responds by interpreting the oracle in such a way as to seek to determine its truth.[24] More precisely, in hearing the god's oracle, Socrates *reinterprets* it by seeking to free it from its most obvious interpretation, namely, the one held by Chaerephon as he went and asked the oracle in the first place. Chaerephon, believing Socrates to be wise in the sense of knowledgeable, went to the oracle to have this belief confirmed or refuted. Socrates, upon hearing the god's answer, responds as one ought to respond to an oracle: by *interpreting* it, by testing it in order to determine its truth.[25] In this case, Socrates receives the oracle by reinterpreting the meaning of "wisdom." Socrates's re-ception of the oracle is a re-interpretation, one that grants the truth of the oracle *before* it works to test and determine it. Thus, in the face of the god's truthful riddling (see *Symposium* 192e), Socrates reinterprets the meaning of the oracle, just as in the *Phaedo* he will reinterpret the meaning of his reoccurring dream as well as the song of the swans. In each of these cases, Socrates is given a sign from some divine source—dream, god, swan—which he receives by reinterpreting (see *Apology* 33c).

The second moment of truth occurs in Socrates's discussion of the poets. In describing his elenctic interactions with them, Socrates claims that the poets "composed what they composed not by wisdom [σοφίᾳ] but by nature and because they were inspired, like the prophets [θεομάντεις] and givers of oracles [οἱ χρησμῳδοί]; for these also say many beautiful things, but know [ἴσασιν] none of the things they say" (22c). Notwithstanding Socrates's claim in the *Republic* that the poets (as imitators) stand at a third-remove from the truth (597e), one must observe that Socrates's complaint in the *Apology* is not that the poets do not speak the truth: rather, it is *precisely because they speak the truth* that the poets know not what they say. Owing to the mantic ability analyzed above, the poets speak the truth, but in a manner that is beyond their control. More precisely, the truth speaks through the poets, who know not what flows out of them. It is *only* because they are not in control of their speaking that the poets speak the truth. (Indeed, it is said here that the sort of truth the poets speak is the very same sort spoken by oracles—sayings, for example, like that offered by the Delphic oracle claiming that no one is wiser than Socrates, a divine pronouncement that Socrates *insists* must be true.) In his discussion of the poets, what is emphasized by Socrates is their ability to let the truthful sayings of the gods speak through them.

If one were to let the swan song of the *Phaedo* echo back into the *Apology*, one would begin to see a certain intimacy between Socrates and the poets here. We have seen that the poets, owing to their divine inspiration, speak the truth. We also saw that the swans of the *Phaedo*, owing to their mantic ability, speak the truth as a sign, and that Socrates claims to share precisely this mantic power. Both Socrates and the poets—and, indeed, the oracle—speak the truth as the swans do: or, more precisely, the truth speaks through these vessels as signs. The swans, the oracle, the poets, and Socrates all share the mantic ability to serve as *given-signs* of the gods. One recalls here that Socrates insists in the *Apology* that he was "given [δεδόσθαι]" to Athens by Apollo as a gift (31b).[26]

Socrates intimates the mantic-like character of his speech at the outset of his ἀπολογία. Immediately after insisting that he shall speak only the truth, Socrates states "not however . . . speeches finely tricked-out [κεκαλλιεπημένους γε λόγους] with words . . . nor carefully arranged [οὐδὲ κεκοσμημένους], but . . . said at random with the words that happen to occur to me [λεγόμενα τοῖς ἐπιτυχοῦσιν ὀνόμασιν]" (17a–c).[27] The truth that Socrates will speak will be "at random" and thus lacking in the rational arrangement (κόσμος) that λόγος, understood as "reason," would presumably provide.[28] Many scholars take Socrates's insistence on the disorder of his speaking to be ironic, claiming instead that a coherent and deliberate order is to be found in Socrates's speech, one characteristic of ancient forensic oratory.[29] However, any such structure belonging to the *Apology* would be more properly attributed to Plato, the author of this literary text, and not to the speeches of its main character.[30] Even if some such order pervades and arranges the Platonic text—something that can hardly be doubted—this order need not characterize or determine the *character* Socrates as he appears in this well-ordered Platonic text, or how he acts within that order. It is perfectly possible that Plato ordered the *Apology* in such a way as to emphasize the disorder, or even irrationality, of Socrates's speaking—just as, for example, the *Symposium* is ordered by Plato in such a way as to show, via Aristophanes's hiccups, the disorder of the evening's proceedings (185c). What Plato gives us in his *Apology* is a defense speech that follows a certain customary order in which the main speaker, Socrates, serves to work against that order, to call it into question, to destabilize it from the inside, and to bring a certain disorder to the court.[31]

Evidence of this disorder lies in Socrates's initial response: for, rather than beginning with a response to the indictment just articulated against him (as would be customary), Socrates begins by responding to certain rumors that had arisen against him over the years. In other words, rather than letting his accusers dictate the order of the proceedings, Socrates reorders the indictment, placing it behind a different set of accusations to which he himself gives voice. Additionally, on several occasions throughout his defense, Socrates's words are so out of order as to cause the jury themselves to fall into disorder, to make disturbances to the narrative flow (20e, 30c). From its very beginning, Socrates's way of speaking does not follow the order of the court, the court-order, that would, for example, expect him to employ ordered (κεκοσμημένους) phrases (17c) and later present his family as a ploy to beg for mercy, as many other defendants had done (34c).[32] It is precisely this disorder of Socrates's way that evokes the disorder of the courtroom and upsets the court-appointed order.

Thus, although it is surely true that Plato's *Apology* follows the determined dramatic order of what has been called "logographic necessity," it is through that very order that a resistance to order is announced by the character Socrates.[33]

This is most clearly seen in the fact that Socrates goes to great lengths in his *prooemium* and elsewhere to establish that *if* there is any order to his speaking—in or out of court—it is not an order that can be attributed to him. For Socrates has claimed that his way of speaking in court will follow his customary way, a way, we learn, ordered (κελεύει) by Apollo (30a). In following this way—in speaking the truth in elenctic exchanges in an effort *to order* (παρακελευόμενός) the people of Athens to philosophize (29d)—Socrates follows Apollo's order as if it were an order issued by a military general (28d–e), an order he believes he must *follow*, no matter how much disorder and disarray it brings to his life (31b). If there is an order to Socrates's way of speaking, it is one he claims is given to him by Apollo. It is thus not Socrates's reason that sets the order that he, even perhaps reasonably, claims he must follow. Socrates's way is one of *following* a *given* order, of giving himself over to it, not of setting or establishing it by way of rational exercise. This is made especially clear at the end when Socrates claims that it is only because his "divine sign [τὸ τοῦ θεοῦ σημεῖον]" has not opposed his speech that he knows that everything has preceded as it should (40b). Only because of his "customary mantic power [εἰωθυῖά μοι μαντικὴ ἡ τοῦ δαιμονίου]"—but certainly not his *reason*—does Socrates know that everything has followed the correct order (40a).[34]

What is at stake here, in these musings on the disorder of Socrates's words announced at the beginning of his ἀπολογία, is the relationship between λόγος, understood as reason, and the truth. It is often supposed by scholars that, in speaking the truth, Socrates would employ reason in such a way as to set or order the truth into a rational arrangement.[35] For example, this would be the sort of truth that comes about when Socrates reveals to Meletus, through rational argument, that belief in "spiritual things [τοὺς δαίμονας]" implies belief in "the gods [τοὺς θεούς]" (27c). Truth, understood in this way, would come about when speech (λόγος), following the order of reason (λόγος or νοῦς), shows the illogic at work in an accusation, or the logic at work in a defense. This would also be the sort of truth that would come to light when one, using λόγος, shows the way in which mind (νοῦς), in ordering all things, ordered them (κοσμεῖν) in the best way possible (*Phaedo* 97c).

However, as already shown, there is an additional sort of truth at play in the *Apology*, one that operates independently of, or at least antecedently to, reason: for, as was seen with the poets, it is precisely reason (νοῦς) that must recede into the background if the poet is to speak the truth. In this case, the reason of the poet *obscures* the truth precisely by seeking to rearrange or reorder it: for it is when the poets attempt to explicate this truth that speaks through them that they show themselves to be ignorant of its meaning (22b). It is when reason tries to reorder this pre-rational truth pouring out of its source (be it poet, oracle, or Socrates himself) that reason risks setting this truth into disarray. It is *this* sort of truth that Socrates claims to be speaking at the beginning of his speech when he reflects upon his way of λόγος. The speaking (λέγειν) that Socrates will offer in his ἀπο-λογία is concerned solely with bringing the truth to pass, yet in a way that is free from the strictures and imposed order that human reasoning would bring.³⁶ The speaking that is to come, the one wherein Socrates will give voice to the truth, is an ἄκοσμος λόγος, an unordered speaking. Insofar as λόγος can be understood as the sort of order that reason would bring to speech, Socrates's unordered way of speaking in his ἀπο-λογία can be understood as an ἄλογος λόγος, an unreasonable speaking, a λόγος that somehow falls beyond or above "rational" discourse and yet remains significant.³⁷

Yet how can this be? Does Socrates not make arguments in the *Apology*, thereby displaying his rational ability? Indeed, does he not at one point offer a primitive form of a deductive syllogism (27b–d), thereby demonstrating his logical prowess? Certainly this is so. Yet given Socrates's comments regarding the nature of his way of speaking in the *Apology*, and given our analysis of Socrates's swanlike mantic ability, we are invited to wonder in what ways Socrates's speaking might exceed its attachment to reason and logic narrowly construed.

In this register, we turn back to the dream from the *Phaedo*—Socrates's dream that, it was argued, refers back to his previous life, including of course the time of the *Apology*. In this reoccurring dream, Socrates was repeatedly told to "make music [μουσικὴν ποίει] and work at it" (60e), a command he interpreted as exhorting him to practice philosophy. Socrates's philosophizing, even in those days leading up to his death, was a kind of music, a philosophizing, therefore, done in relation to the very god *of* music, Apollo, the god to whom he belongs, the god who gave him and his fellow servants the swans the power of μαντική. Socrates's way of speaking, his *true* speaking, must be understood as a certain kind of music (60e)—a music not unlike that of the swans.³⁸

When the swans sing—when they signify—they point *away* from themselves, lending voice to the god to whom they belong. In speaking away from themselves, these messengers bring divine signs to human beings, signs that then need to be interpreted. Such *singing*, such *signing*, and such speaking-away, characterizes Socrates's way of λόγος.³⁹ In his elenctic encounters with others, Socrates, through no knowledge of his own, brings about a divinely given truth: namely, that no human being knows anything important or worthwhile. Such speaking, Socrates claims, is a speaking done in the service of Apollo (23c). Thus, in his ἀπο-λογία, Socrates speaks away (ἀπό) from himself, intimating a truth beyond himself that he, as ignorant, does not *know*, a truth that passes through him as a given-sign. Socrates's own command of his λόγος is displaced precisely to the degree that he speaks the truth—that is, precisely to the degree that the god speaks this truth through him.

What is accomplished in this speaking-away is the opening up of a space between the human and the divine in which the human is seen to abide.⁴⁰ By intimating the god in his speaking, Socrates reveals an essential truth about the human condition: namely, that it is characterized by finitude, ignorance, and radical concealment. The truth Socrates speaks as he speaks-away is the disclosure of the human as limited in its ability to know the truth: a truth he makes manifest by leading those with whom he speaks to see their own ignorance. When he speaks-away, Socrates thus discloses the essential attachment of the human being to concealment. This is accomplished through Apollo's use of Socrates as an example (παράδειγμα)—which is to say, as a *sign*—of a truth broad enough in scope to apply to the human condition as such (23a). Socrates *himself*, as Apollo's gift, signifies the truth of human finitude.

Thus, it is not only near the end of his ἀπο-λογία that Socrates utters prophecy (as he explicitly does at 39d) but rather throughout the whole *Apology*. This prophetic speaking—this giving of the gift of signs—is the character of Socratic music, which is to say Socratic philosophy as "the greatest music." The way of Socratic music is the way of signs, which is the way of the *cygnet*. Socrates's "philosophical music" is music precisely insofar as Socrates, being *of* Apollo, is a given-sign.

This state of being a given-sign (see *Apology* 31b) accounts for Socrates's joyful demeanor both in the face of his death and throughout the life that came before. Though we see this joy expressed in the *Phaedo* in the form of laughter (84d), it is most clearly seen in the *Crito*, where the eponymous character remarks upon Socrates's generally happy demeanor: "I have often thought throughout your life that you were of a happy disposition [εὐδαιμόνισα], and I think so more than ever in this present misfortune" (*Crito* 43b). It is not that Socrates, dour throughout his life, is happy only as he finally approaches death and the god to whom he belongs. Rather, Socrates is the *happiest* as he faces his death, a superlative condition that reveals the extent to which he was happy throughout the life that came before. It is precisely because he belongs to Apollo throughout his life that Socrates holds a happy—which is to say, a blessed (εὐ-δαιμόνισα)—disposition. Understanding himself to be a given-sign, Socrates, like the swans, "goes out of this life with as little sorrow as they" (*Phaedo* 85b). It is with joy that Socrates lives and dies.

Swan Song

In the end, then, it is a matter of reception, of how we are to receive the words of Socrates. To receive them simply as arguments, as λόγοι in the narrow sense of arguing for some particular philosophical position, is to miss a more basic function of Socrates's speaking. To receive them instead as *given-signs* is to receive them as utterances that are in need of interpretation, gifts that are best re-ceived by re-interpretation. In other words, we should receive Socrates's words in the same manner that Socrates himself receives the speaking of the oracle or, indeed, the song of the swan: as disclosive intimations, the specific meaning of which comes to light only through a process of interpretive engagement and self-examination. In speaking-away—that is, in speaking in a manner that, while bringing truths to the fore, disavows ownership or mastery of those truths—Socrates invites us to chase down these truths and strive to interpret their meanings. We are given, through his words, truths whose senses we ourselves must work to determine. Socrates, within the *Apology*, exemplifies both the process of delivering given-signs *and* the process of seeking to determine them through reinterpretation. Understanding himself to be a given-sign, Socrates understands himself as in need of interpretation. To live in accordance with the dictum Apollo had given—"Know Thyself"—the given-sign Socrates interprets himself.

In writing his Socratic dialogues, Plato gives us signs to be interpreted: not just by giving us Greek words that we must carry over into our own idioms, but by giving us a Socrates who, through his very way of λόγος, serves as a given-sign. Plato's words, in this way, are musical signs that require a certain type of reception. Plato's signs are like the swans: his signets are cygnets.

Olympiodorus, writing in the sixth century AD, claims the following about Plato: "When he was about to die, he saw in a dream that he became a swan moving from tree to tree and in this way caused much trouble to the bird-catchers. Simmias the Socratic judged from this that he would not be captured by those desiring to interpret him" (Olympiodorus, 2. 156–159). The multifaceted history of Plato scholarship attests to this power of the Platonic text to "leap" around from tree to tree, to engender many (and often conflicting) interpretations, even if this history itself has failed to draw sufficient attention to this power of the dialogue. We, the bird-catchers, all too often arrest the meaning and sense of the Platonic text, believing we have trapped the elusive truth. By attending to the swans, we have seen the manner in which Plato himself warns us of too hastily trying to trap that whose very nature is to fly away. By reading the *Phaedo* before the *Apology*, and by listening to the song of the swan, we can gain an appreciation of the oracular, musical, and enigmatic character of the Platonic dialogue: the gift of a riddle meant to be pondered, not necessarily solved.

To read Plato is to race after the swan. To read him *well* is to know that the swan can never be captured.

Notes

1. Catherine Zuckert comments upon the uncertainty, after all these years, of the order in which Plato wrote his texts: "The fact is, we do not know when or in what order Plato wrote the individual dialogues" (*Plato's Philosophers: The Coherence of the Dialogues* [Chicago: University of Chicago Press, 2009], 5).

2. I am not arguing that one should deny the obvious temporal and dramatic sequence that stands between the *Apology* and the *Phaedo*. However, as I will suggest forthwith, the

dramatic posteriority of the *Phaedo* with respect to the *Apology* should not prevent us from reading the *Phaedo* back into the *Apology*.

3. Francis M. Cornford notes the Pythagorean tone of the phrase "the greatest music" as a description of philosophy (*Plato's Theory of Knowledge* [London: Routledge, 1935], 300n1). Socrates's depiction of philosophy as a type of music harmonizes perfectly with the overt Pythagorean overtones of the *Phaedo*. In this register, Pythagoras's connection to Apollo (who is crucially important to Socrates) should not go unnoticed (see K. Guthrie, *The Pythagorean Sourcebook and Library* [Michigan: Phanes Press, 1987], 30, especially n26).

4. One knows, at least, that Socrates was dreaming in the *Crito* as he so peacefully awaited his death (44a).

5. In Socrates's response to Cebes's inquiry regarding the origin of his poetic compositions, it is easy to hear Socrates sharply dividing his current musical practice from the (nonmusical) philosophy that came before. Yet nothing could be further from the truth. It is not the case that Socrates, prior to his imprisonment, was simply speaking in a nonmusical way and that now, in the face of his impending death, his speaking is being transformed into song. Rather, as Socrates makes clear, his life before the trial was no less involved in making music, though perhaps music of a different sort. Both in his death and in the life that came before, Socrates's practice bears a relationship to music—and thus a relationship to the very god *of* music, Apollo. (For Apollo's connection to music, see *Odyssey* VIII, 488; see also *Cratylus* 405a.)

6. Cf. *Politics* 1253a9. Christopher P. Long has offered a wonderful and compelling analysis of the status of bird "speech" for Aristotle. Drawing mostly upon Aristotle's *Parts of Animals* and his *History of Animals*, Long observes that for Aristotle "[birds] in particular seem capable of a kind of articulated speech that rises to the level of dialect and, indeed, pushes toward the border of human λόγος itself" (Christopher P. Long, *Aristotle on the Nature of Truth* [Cambridge: Cambridge University Press, 2001], 80). But even where Aristotle observes the ability of birds to make "articulate literate sounds [γράμματα]" (*Parts of Animals* II.12, 504b1–3) or "significant expressions," it is arguably only to mark the degree to which such sounds differ from human *logos*, as Long's analysis of the opening pages of the *Politics* makes clear (90, 92). Thus, no matter how far birds push toward the border of human *logos*—and Long's analysis of Aristotle's texts makes it clear that it is much farther than we tend to think—they remain, for Aristotle, decisively on the other side of human *logos*.

7. It is perhaps telling in this regard that one of the Greek terms for *animal* is τὰ ἄλογα ("speechless" or "without reason") (see *Protagoras* 321c). Additionally, the extent to which λόγος is strictly a human phenomenon is seen in the fact that even the gods, at times, are supposed to be without λόγος (see *Cratylus* 391e).

8. Interestingly, one such person is Aristotle, who in his *History of Animals* offers just the sort of account against which Socrates is speaking: "[Swans] are musical, and sing chiefly at the approach of death; at this time they fly out to sea, and men, when sailing past the coast of Lybia, have fallen in with many of them out at sea singing in mournful strains" (615a30).

9. See, for example, Clytemnestra in Aeschylus's *Agamemnon* (1680).

10. This sentiment is nicely echoed millennia later by another birdwatcher, Immanuel Kant: "A bird's song proclaims his joyfulness and contentment with existence" (*Critique of Judgment*, trans. W. S. Pluhar [Indianapolis: Hackett Publishing, 1987], 302).

11. See, for example, R. Flacelière, *Greek Oracles* (New York: W. W. Norton, 1965), 8–9.

12. Cf. *Homeric Hymn* 4, 543–549.

13. See, for example, *Odyssey* XV, 525–534: "Even as he spoke a bird flew forth upon the right, a hawk, the swift messenger of Apollo. In his talons he held a dove, and was plucking her and shedding the feathers down on the ground midway between the ship and Telemachus

himself. Then Theoclymenus called him apart from his companions, and clasped his hand, and spoke, and addressed him: 'Telemachus, surely not without a god's warrant has this bird flown forth upon our right, for I knew, as I looked upon him, that he was a bird of omen. Than yours is no other house in the land of Ithaca more kingly; nay, ye are ever supreme.'"

14. The word σέ is in the accusative case. However, no matter how one translates it—"of you," "to you," or "for you"—it is clear that the swan's singing is *indictating* or *intimating* Apollo by pointing beyond itself toward him, as the context of the remainder of the hymn makes clear. See also Aristophanes's *Birds*, 769–784.

15. However, birds did not offer signs only in the form of their songs and their bodily movements, but also through their types and poise (Flacelière, *Greek Oracles*, 8). Thus, it was not just the movements and speech of birds that were significant of the gods but *the birds themselves* in their very look, that is, in their very being. Birds, merely by virtue of being birds, *signified* the gods: "The very word for bird (*öinos* or *ornis*) came to mean 'portent'" (ibid., 9). The very *look* of a swan would have signified Apollo, calling out to him in an indicative gesture.

16. I have placed in italics those words that are exactly the same in appearance, despite their differences in meaning. These etymological permutations have been drawn from the *Oxford English Dictionary*. For typographical reasons, I have not cited all of the variations of these words that appear in the *OED*.

17. That Socrates does not have foreknowledge of precisely what awaits him after death is clear from the *Apology*, where he entertains various possibilities (40c).

18. In the *Cratylus*, Hermogenes remarks upon Socrates's mantic ability as the latter begins his playful display concerning the knowledge of the correctness of words (396d). Here, the mantic power is in no way connected to predicting the future, but is instead seen to be a matter of divining the truth about names.

19. If one simply accepts the common translation of ἀπολογία as *defense*, one reads the *Apology* as a presentation of Socrates's defense against the charges brought against him by Meletus. Despite the rather obvious way in which this is true, one would do well to be more cautious: for, from the beginning of the Ἀπο-λογία, it is a matter of λόγος (see John Sallis, *Being and Logos* [Bloomington: Indiana University Press, 1975], 30–31). The *Apology* begins with a reflection upon λόγος, indeed, upon the very sort of λόγος that will occur within the *Apology*. To decide too quickly upon the meaning of ἀπο-λογία before encountering the text's own explicit consideration of λόγος is to close oneself off from one of the philosophical issues that the text wishes to open. For a similar warning regarding the translation of ἀπολογία as *defense*, see R. E. Allen, *Socrates and Legal Obligation* (Minneapolis: University of Minneapolis Press, 1980), 4.

20. On the foreignness and atopic nature of Socrates's customary speaking in the *Apology*, see Claudia Baracchi, "The 'Inconceivable Happiness' of 'Men and Women': Visions of an Other World in Plato's *Apology* of Socrates," in *Reexamining Socrates in the* Apology, ed. Patricia Fagan and John Russon (Chicago: Northwestern University Press, 2006), 276.

21. See Sallis, *Being and Logos*, 31.

22. There are many excellent scholarly works that comment upon the so-called *prooemium* of Socrates's speech, where Socrates differentiates his way of speaking from that of his accusers—indeed, far too many to list comprehensively. More often than not, the question of the truthfulness of Socrates's speech centers on the issue of Socratic rhetoric, and on the issue of how to reconcile Socrates's claims to speak truthfully and without rhetorical adornment with the obvious rhetorical flourishes of his speech itself (see, for example, James Barrett, "Plato's '*Apology*': Philosophy, Rhetoric, and the World of Myth," in *Classical Review* 95, no. 1 [2001]: 3–30). Others deal with the relationship between these pretentions to truth and Socratic irony. (See J. Burnet, *Plato's Euthyphro, Apology of Socrates, and Crito* [Oxford: Clarendon Press,

1924], 66–68; see also Allen, *Socrates and Legal Obligation*, 5–7.) In addition to the question of irony, still others explore the connection between the truth of Socrates's speech and its justice (see D. Leibowitz, *Ironic Defense of Socrates: Plato's* Apology [Cambridge: Cambridge University Press, 2010], 7–14). What is at issue in the present inquiry is the *meaning* of truth itself in Socrates's unique *way of speaking*—a way that, I contend, must be understood in light of the swans in the *Phaedo*.

23. See C. D. C. Reeve, *Socrates in the* Apology: *An Essay on* Plato's Apology of Socrates (Bloomington: Indiana University Press, 1989), 22.

24. See Sallis, *Being and Logos*, 47.

25. On this, see Reeve, *Socrates in the* Apology, 1989: "[Socrates] believed from the beginning that, properly interpreted, the oracle had to be true [. . .]. Hence his strategy of refutation is interpretative only. By showing that one proposition the oracle might be taken to have expressed is false, he can get closer [. . .] to the true propositions that is its real meaning" (23). As Reeve further observes, such testing of the oracle's meaning is in no way peculiar or impious.

26. It is this gift-like character of Socrates that accounts (or so he claims) for the inhuman nature of his work, that is, for the fact that he worked tirelessly and without compensation in exhorting people to attend to themselves (31b). There is something *not human* about these deeds of Socrates, something super-human, something suggestive of a god.

27. As Reeve puts this, Socrates will "extemporize, speaking as he pleases in the words that come to him and putting his trust in the truth and justice of what he says rather than in rhetorical niceties" (Reeve, *Socrates in the* Apology, 6).

28. For the connection between order and reason, see *Phaedo* 83e, where it is said that the philosopher, being ordered (κόσμιοί), must follow reason (ἑπομένη τῷ λογισμῷ).

29. See, for example, A. E. Taylor, *Plato: The Man and His Work* (New York: Dover Publications, 1926), 156; see also Allen, *Socrates and Legal Obligation*, 5–6. Against the notion that Socrates has spent any time preparing his defense, consider Xenophon's *Apology of Socrates to the Jury*, where Socrates tells Hermogenes, "I have tried twice already to meditate on my defense, but my divine sign interposes" (trans. O. J. Todd [Cambridge, Mass.: Harvard University Press], 4).

30. On the literary nature of the *Apology*, see James Riddell, *The Apology of Plato* (Oxford: Oxford University Press, 1877), xii, xix, who calls it "artistic to the core." See also Jacob Howland (*Kierkegaard and Socrates: A Study in Philosophy and Faith* [Cambridge: Cambridge University Press, 2008]), who argues that the *Apology* incorporates formal elements of tragic drama. For a less-than-compelling argument that Plato's *Apology* is meant as a more-or-less verbatim account of Socrates's trial, see Taylor, *Plato: The Man and His Work*, 156. The mere fact of the differences in order and arrangement between Plato's *Apology* and Xenophon's *Apology of Socrates to the Jury* ought to suggest to us that neither was *simply* producing historical facsimiles.

31. Furthermore, as many other scholars have noted, although Socrates's speech follows a certain rhetorical order, it does so precisely to *parody* and *criticize* that order, to mark its limits through a parodic performance (see, for example, Kenneth Seeskin, "Is the *Apology of Socrates* a Parody?" in *Philosophy and Literature* 6, nos. 1 and 2 [1982]: 94–105). One sees Socrates's criticism of the order of the court when he claims that such a short speech as he has time to offer has little or no chance of counteracting the rumors that had been growing against him for years (18c–19a).

32. On Socrates's refusal to employ the standard "tricks of the trade," see also Xenophon's *Memorabilia* IV. iv. 4.

33. On the law of logographic necessity, see Leo Strauss, *The City and Man* (Chicago: University of Chicago Press, 1964), 53. See also Sallis, who, drawing upon Strauss, claims that

"nothing is accidental in a Platonic dialogue" (*Being and Logos*, 17). See also Ronna Burger, *The Phaedo: A Platonic Labyrinth* (New Haven, Conn.: Yale University Press, 1984), 3. All three authors draw upon the idea of λόγος as a living being developed in the *Phaedrus* (264b). However, as just suggested, it would be perfectly in keeping with the law of logographic necessity—if indeed one can call this a law, based as it is on a single passage from a single Platonic text not without its own issues of order and arrangement (see Jacques Derrida, "Plato's Pharmacy," in *Dissemination*, trans. Barbara Johnson [Chicago: University of Chicago Press, 1981], 61)—for Plato to order his text in such a way as to emphasize the disordering conduct of Socrates.

34. On Socrates's irrationality in the *Apology*, see J. S. Hans, *Socrates and the Irrational* (Charlottesville: University of Virginia Press, 2006), 55.

35. For example, Reeve, even while emphasizing the extemporaneous character of Socrates's words, insists that they will follow "truth, justice, and rational persuasion" (Reeve, *Socrates in the* Apology, 6).

36. On a certain sort of disorder that belongs to Socratic *elenchus* as such, see Thomas Brickhouse and Nicholas Smith, *Plato's Socrates* (New York: Oxford University Press, 1994), 7.

37. If this reading proves to be tenable, it is only because of the breadth and scope of the word λόγος and the many different meaning that this word can sustain.

38. On the musical character of Socrates's speaking, see Alcibiades's speech in Plato's *Symposium*, 215b–222b.

39. See *Phaedo* 78a, where Cebes remarks upon Socrates's ability as a singer of incantations.

40. On this, see Hans, *Socrates and the Irrational*, 55.

6 The Dog on the Fly

H. Peter Steeves

> Plato had defined man as a biped and featherless animal, for which he was applauded. Diogenes plucked a chicken and brought it into the lecture hall, saying, "Behold Plato's Man!"
>
> —Diogenes Laertius

W<small>E READ PLATO</small> because Plato's texts are around to be read. This is, in the end, why anyone reads anything: because it's there. Whether or not the work is worthy of keeping around so that it can be read is often beside the point. Bad things remain and good things disappear for accidental reasons. Had history taken another turn—papyrus misplaced, turned to dust, and forgotten—we philosophers, thinkers, Westerners would be an unrecognizable lot, horses of a different color, impossibly plucked chickens, real toads swamping around imaginary gardens in praise of poetry rather than finding it suspect. Say Plato's work was lost, or another of Socrates's students' writings had gained more favor, or someone had studied with Diogenes long enough to want to write a series of books and dialogues about him after he died so that his thought could live on. Say we start with love of comedy over tragedy, with the superiority of the nonhuman animal, with a dogged commitment to perform our beliefs rather than talk about them. The subjunctive conditional does little logical work, but history is carried on the backs of counterfactual beasts; and it is thus that the contingencies of the past create the apparent necessities of the present.

This much is true of both intellectual and evolutionary history (if there is such a distinction). Move the asteroid that wiped out the dinosaurs a fraction of a degree in its ancient trajectory through our solar system, and the little mole-like creature hiding in the bushes that eventually survived and begat Socrates and Diogenes and you and me stays on its own humble course as nothing other than a mammal-snack for the lizard king. No species, no individual, no text *had* to be here, and this is the most important thing to remember when species and individuals and texts start speaking of necessity.

This could all have been different. That difference, no matter how one tries to suppress it, is the point at which meaning begins. Even in the dialectic, even between two characters in a dialogue, between two historical friendly enemies conversing, there is the prior difference that makes the dialectic differ from itself and thus possible. *We are featherless bipeds... with broad flat nails,* replies Plato. And this is all already different.

* * *

> The soul of the tyrant will be forever driven onward by the gadfly of desire.
> —Plato, *Republic* 577e

The philosopher desires wisdom, has a literal love for it, but what is it that drives the philosophic soul in such pursuit? Something small that nevertheless makes itself that to which we must continuously attend? Something without a mouth capable of speech yet nevertheless makes itself heard? Something insignificant that nevertheless will not be quieted, will not let us rest? It is not, perhaps, that different souls have different gadflies spurring them to action—some good, some bad, each turning us in a different direction. Rather, the same gadfly of desire comes to reside on different souls. That toward which the city of Athens will be driven forever onward will be determined not by the nature of the local gadfly but by the soul of the city.

Socrates is compared to a multitude of animals throughout Plato's writings, but it is the moniker of the gadfly that remains the most famous and the most enigmatic. How often an Introduction to Philosophy course begins with this metaphor in an attempt to explain all of Western philosophy: *Socrates is a fly that buzzes around the horse-like city of Athens, bothering and nipping at the civic body, but in the end doing good and stirring the people to action; so, too, must we philosophers ask the hard questions and make people think about important things even if they don't want to at first.* Socrates and all of philosophy are cast in the role of a pest, an annoyance, something at which one might understandably swat. But it is not just that Socrates is called a pest by others. To be sure, Plato has Socrates himself use the gadfly analogy in his *Apology*—proof that, at least in the mind of a man acting as his own lawyer, it is something positive and good to say. But what is it that Socrates thinks he is accomplishing by comparing himself to an animal—and a "low-level" animal, at that? Socrates, after all, does not *spur* his neighbors to action, as this would suggest that he is a human riding the horse that is the body of the *polis*. Rather, he compares himself to an insect, to a creature that can merely *annoy* the *polis* into movement. And he has, indeed, annoyed the citizens of the *polis*. They are moving to kill him. It is with this realization of the life-and-death stakes that Plato has Socrates announce:

> At this point, therefore, fellow Athenians, so far from pleading on my own behalf, as might be supposed, I am pleading on yours, in case by condemning me you should mistreat the gift which God has bestowed upon you—because if you put me to death, you will not easily find another like me. The fact is, if I may put the point in a somewhat comical way, that I have been literally attached by God to our city, as if to a horse—a large thoroughbred, which is a bit sluggish because of its size, and needs to be aroused by some sort of gadfly. Yes, in me, I believe, God has attached to our city just such a creature—the kind that is constantly alighting everywhere on you, all day long, arousing, cajoling, or reproaching each and every one of you. You will not easily acquire another such gadfly, gentlemen; rather, if you take my advice, you will spare my life. I dare say, though, that you will get angry, like people who are awakened from their doze. Perhaps you will heed Anytus, and give me a swat: you could happily finish me off, and then spend the rest of your life asleep—unless God, in his compassion for you, were to send you someone else. (*Apology* 30d-e)[1]

Why, specifically, are the people of Athens swatting at this fly? There are charges of impiety and corrupting the youth, of course, but Socrates's crimes are far greater. This insignificant insect has managed, with only the weapon of his mouth, to turn his fellow citizens into animals as well. It is not just that the state is a horse, but that the citizens with whom Socrates has interacted have typically become mute animals. And for this, they are striking him dead.

For the Greeks, as well as for most modern civilizations, *logos* understood as speech is thought to be a necessary part of our essential humanity. Simply to speak, though, is not enough according to Socrates. What is truly radical in Socrates's claim is that the most important element of our humanity is not merely that we speak, but that about which we speak.[2] Earlier in his *Apology*, before he compares himself to a gadfly, Socrates explains it to his accusers thus:

> Perhaps someone might say, "Socrates, can you not go away from us and live quietly, without talking?" Now this is the hardest thing to make some of you believe. For if I say that such conduct would be disobedience to the god and that therefore I cannot keep quiet, you will think I am jesting and will not believe me; and if again I say that to talk every day about virtue and the other things about which you hear me talking and examining myself and others is the greatest good to man, and that the unexamined life is not worth living, you will believe me still less. This is as I say, gentlemen, but it is not easy to convince you. (*Apology*, 37e-38a)[3]

To see just why this is so important—why it is not speech that makes us human, according to Plato, but philosophical speech in particular—we need to step back a bit and consider the sort of talk that will not get the job done.

The cicadas of the *Phaedrus* might be said to speak. They sing their words, and as such are like rhetoricians, lulling us to sleep with the beauty of how the words are said rather than the truth of what they mean. Socrates introduces the myth of the cicadas halfway through this dialogue, in fact, because it seems that Phaedrus himself has failed to be stirred appropriately by the words that have so far been spoken. They have moved him, but only as words. When Phaedrus worries about Lysias's speeches, for instance, what concerns him is not the philosophic truths at which Lysias might point but rather how he will appear as a competitor in the art of rhetoric.[4] And it is soon after that Socrates tells Phaedrus the myth: the cicadas used to be a race of men who, long ago, were bewitched by the beauty of the songs of the Muses; thus they were cursed, turned into short-lived insects that drone on all day in beautiful yet empty song, reporting back to the Muses the conversations of humans and never having anything to say themselves. To drone on—to speak of unimportant things—is to be less-than-human. One might as well not be speaking at all. The cicadas are animals that used to be men: by using their speech for nonphilosophic purposes, they have become animal. Socrates, however, is a man who emerges from the metaphor of the gadfly: by using his stinging mouth to incite others to become philosophers, he becomes fully human.

For better or for worse this is a major Platonic distinction between humans and nonhuman animals. The problem is that Socrates, if we are to be honest about it, has more or less failed at his task to care for the souls of the young men of Athens by this measure. Whenever he speaks with his fellow citizens about virtue and the examined life, it isn't long until everyone but Socrates is beaten into silence. The finest minds, excited early on to engage Socrates in conversation, are again and again reduced to the caricature of the Socratic interlocutor, spouting only the occasional, "Yes," or "Of course," or "It is as you say, Socrates." And it would be disingenuous to say that Socrates himself is not aware of this.

Consider the encounter with Thrasymachus—a dialogue that essentially is a contest to see who can silence whom. Socrates admits to being frightened of Thrasymachus at first, even saying: "if I had not looked at him before he looked at me I would have lost my voice" (*Republic* 336d). The allusion here is to a superstition that would have been well-known to Plato's audience. A wolf, it was thought, could steal a human's voice if the wolf saw the human before the human saw the wolf. Socrates thus casts Thrasymachus in the role of the wolf from the start; and by the end of their encounter in the *Republic*, Thrasymachus has, indeed, been reduced to animalistic silence. What makes this interaction all the more interesting is not merely that Socrates has reduced his interlocutor into bestial quiet, but that it is possible to see this animal allusion reflecting back on Socrates himself, thus casting *him* in the role of the wolf. There are, in fact, at least four possible readings of the wolf allusion.

The first and most obvious interpretation of Socrates's encounter with Thrasymachus is that they are two humans and Socrates eventually just gets the better of Thrasymachus, who is forced to be silent because his logic and arguments are the weaker. The wolf allusion is just a bit of poetry. A second, more metaphorical, reading is that Socrates thinks of Thrasymachus as an animal from the start—a dangerous wolf out to steal his *logos*—and fears losing his own humanity (his voice) to this beast if Thrasymachus should see him first. A third reading suggests that Socrates takes Thrasymachus to be an animal from the start and then, by means of stripping Thrasymachus of his voice, ensures that Thrasymachus is truly an animal at the end. But a fourth reading sees the metaphor doubling back on itself, questioning who has been the human and who has been the wolf all along. Here, we must acknowledge that after his encounter with Socrates, Thrasymachus has surely had his voice stolen. Socrates wins the day and Thrasymachus mumbles assent here and there. Thus it is Socrates who can be seen cast in the role of the wolf—the wolf that sees the man first and thus is able to take his voice by the end of the encounter. The people of Athens are putting Socrates to death based on the third reading. That is, they have noted and taken offense at the fact that Socrates regularly strips them of their humanity by reducing them to silence and thus animality. What they fail to realize, however, is what is anamorphically hidden in plain sight in the text: that Plato is turning Socrates into the animal, and perhaps thus even the villain, in order to accomplish this. Plato's Socrates is the wolf who steals men's voices, the blind gadfly who annoys the *polis,* the bull whose insatiable appetite threatens the youth of Athens. Plato's Socrates is not always what he seems, and is never wholly this or that.

So Socrates is swatted because he strips citizens of their humanity (though he is able to do this only by means of becoming animal himself). But why call Athens a horse? A horse can't actually kill a gadfly. A horse is, in reality, ineffective at ridding itself of its pests, yet the city of Athens will do an excellent job of this when Socrates is forced to drink the hemlock.

Perhaps we might say that Socrates rightly sees that he has bothered Athens and not merely the individual people of Athens. The metaphor of Athens as a single beast—a horse—thus makes sense because in stripping individual citizens of their humanity by stealing their voices it is truly the idea of the *polis* that is being attacked. Indeed, it is the Greek ideal that one is to be measured by one's public standing, by mere speech and not the content of that speech, that is under assault. As John Heath argues, in Ancient Greece "from Homer to Aristotle, the striving for public recognition, and the concomitant fear of public humiliation and reproach, remained undiminished. . . . There was little if anything to separate who a person was from what others thought of him."[5] It is thus the ideal of Athens at which Socrates nips, as he both humiliates individuals into stunned animal silence and calls into question whether such a sense of selfhood is truly constitutive of a proper citizen and thus a proper state.

The gadfly, after all, is not truly a pest, not something other and alien to the horse. The gadfly is part of the horse, part of what makes the horse a horse, part of what makes the horse act in a horselike way. In true Platonic fashion, we should be asking about the *eidos* of the horse. And in doing so we would have to admit that the head twitching from side to side, the ears flicking back and forth, the long, full, flowing tail that swishes from haunch to haunch—each is an important ingredient in Horse. But these qualities are, precisely and fully, the result of the work of the gadfly. It is the gadfly that circles the horse's head and makes it twitch. It is the gadfly that buzzes the horse's ears and makes them flick. It is the gadfly that, evolutionarily, caused the horse's tail to grow thick and coarse—the gadfly that keeps the horse's tail in perpetual motion. Without the gadfly, we would not recognize the horse as a horse. The gadfly, that is, is not an addition to the horse—parasitic and problematic. Athens *as it should be*—Athens if we could further capitalize the "A" in its name—is *constituted* by Socrates.

* * *

> Oh Ferryman of the Dead, receive Diogenes the Dog who laid bare the whole pretentiousness of life.
>
> —Diogenes's epitaph

Socrates, especially in large doses, can seem a bit pretentious in his supposed irony. If we return to his *Apology* speech we will recall that, perhaps with an eye toward spicing things up and connecting with his audience, he tells the jurors that he will now make a "somewhat comical" analogy. This is how he comes to call himself a gadfly—as a joke. But hemlock is easy; comedy is hard.

The true philosopher of comedy, the funniest philosopher of antiquity, was the dog, not the gadfly. Like Socrates the gadfly, Diogenes the dog strove to bother, annoy, and shock citizens from their complacency. Plato, however, and most of the history of philosophy that follows him, see the two projects as somehow radically different. Socrates, homegrown in the city that kills him, is the godfather of all Western thought. Diogenes is an adopted, foreign footnote—a dirty, lewd, nonphilosophical addendum that is rarely mentioned and certainly far less respected. Historical accident, of course, made this so.

It is clear that Plato and Diogenes knew each other well and disrespected each other intensely. Plato, the man who put the moniker of gadfly on Socrates by putting the funny word in his mouth, was also not afraid to call Diogenes's humanity into question. In fact, when Plato attempted to insult Diogenes by calling him a dog, Diogenes simply agreed, snapping back that the name "was correct because of his habit of staying close to those who had betrayed him."[6] Plato also reportedly said that Diogenes could be described as "a Socrates gone mad."[7] The gadfly, stripped of sanity, becomes a dog, and it is unclear—at least for Plato—who is nipping at whom.

Diogenes was a foreign beast to the Athenians, born in Sinope sometime around 412 BCE. He arrived to Athens after having been banished from his home for defacing the local currency—perhaps in collusion with his father, a minter of coins. Once in Athens, Diogenes took to heart the Delphic Oracle's proclamation to him to keep up the good work, and so he dedicated himself to defacing the local (cultural) currency by calling on the Athenians to question their customs and most foundational assumptions concerning the city, virtue, and the meaning of life. Like Socrates, that is, Diogenes saw his animalistic mission as one of questioning what the Athenians took to be constitutive of their very humanity.

Thucydides tells us that years before Diogenes arrived, Pericles had declared: "We maintain Athens open and accessible to everybody, and we do not turn away those who flee from danger or who come to us moved by curiosity or by a desire to improve themselves."[8] Athens during, and to a certain extent after, the thirty-year rule of Pericles was known as a place that actively welcomed strangers and curiosity. But only to a certain extent. It was curiosity, after all, that later killed the cat in this place—or at least the gadfly, which has only one life to give. And yet the dog was allowed to live. Given that the particularities of this place gave rise to both philosophers, we would be remiss to ignore the historical and political realities of the times when trying to undertake an Athenian zoology.

Diogenes lived in abject poverty, begging for all that he had, taking shelter in a barrel. He reported that the idea of tub-living had come to him after observing, and consequently wishing to emulate, snails.[9] And the idea of begging and living poorly yet contentedly had come from his praise of the mouse who scavenges for crumbs and lives a happy life no matter where he is.[10] Diogenes tended to look to animals in order to model himself after them. Plato, however, was part of the aristocracy. He begged for nothing and lived a life of privilege, preferring to look to animals in order to model his descriptive metaphors of *others* after them. It is this class distinction, which we might think of as being mapped onto a species distinction as well, that formed part of the tension between the two men. Diogenes, after all, once said that there is no place to spit in a rich man's home, so a visitor must find the dirtiest spot possible—that's why he always spat in the rich man's face.[11] Over the years, Plato would take much abuse from Diogenes— spittle-laden and otherwise, both inside and outside his home. But the closer one looks, the harder it is to find sympathy for Socrates's most famous student.

It was during the time of Socrates that Athenian democracy fell and the *polis* came to be ruled by precisely the sorts of people with whom Plato was related and friendly. The openness of Pericles's Athens was quickly gone under the regime of the Thirty Tyrants, and though the antidemocratic aristocrats held power for only eight or nine months, it would take many years for Athens to recover—if, in fact, it ever did. Plato's cousin, Critias, was perhaps the cruelest of the dictators among the Thirty, and Socrates had been Critias's teacher as well as Plato's. While it is true that Socrates's capital crime was, philosophically speaking, calling into question the public identity (and humanity) of his fellow citizens, there is good reason to believe that part of what his accusers meant by charging him with corrupting the youth was that Socrates had spoken out against democracy and had tutored many of the sons of the established bourgeoisie who had taken part in the dictatorship. Though Socrates reportedly refused to help the Thirty carry out an arrest and execution at one point during their reign, he was never punished by them, lived comfortably in the city during and after their regime, and never spoke out strongly against them while they were in power, murdering hundreds, banishing thousands, and denying rights to all but a select few in Athens. As I. F. Stone remarks, "*Socrates remained in the city all through the dictatorship of the Thirty Tyrants.* . . . [T]hat single fact must have accounted more than any other for the prejudice against Socrates when the democracy was restored. . . . Socrates, in Plato's *Apology,* calls himself 'the gadfly' of Athens, but it seems his sting was not much in evidence when Athens needed it most."[12]

Again, though, we are talking about *Plato's* Socrates—the version of the man our narrator chooses to offer us. We can admit that it is undoubtedly the case that "the true" Socrates is not only epistemologically inaccessible but ontologically suspect as well. That is, everything—even a person—is an enmeshed, hermeneutical set of interpretations. But Plato's particular version of Socrates is a strange sort of hybrid creature. Socrates, under the control of Plato's narrative pen, becomes something of a domesticated beast, forced to do the bidding of his master and defend the status quo. Perhaps it is precisely in part to hide this fact that Plato refers to Socrates as the contrary—as a series of wild animals (such as a gadfly, a wolf, and a stingray) rather than a domesticated animal (such as a dog). By describing his protagonist as wild, the author's intention to break and domesticate that protagonist is obscured. But Plato protests too much, and the obscuring cannot erase the trace of what we might see as a point of *différance*. Over the course of the dialogues, Plato attempts to mold Socrates into what is surely an incongruous mixture of, on the one hand, a radical revolutionary who constantly questions authority, and, on the other hand, someone who argues against the ability of the masses to rule themselves and who will thus always need a central authority figure to take charge of them. This tension, as we are beginning to see, finds its way to the surface in the animalistic metaphors with which Plato chooses to describe Socrates; and as such, the text betrays a distrust for Socrates's teachings and a simultaneous casting of Socrates as a villainous animal.

If so much of this tension, then, is class-driven and political, it is not surprising that many of the disparate fragments we have from Diogenes are direct attacks on Plato and the upper-class values for which Plato ultimately stood. "Plato winces when I track dust across his rugs," said Diogenes, "because he knows that I'm walking on his vanity. . . . Beg a cup of wine from Plato and he will send you a whole jar. He does not give as he is asked, nor answer as he is questioned.... Plato begs too, but like Telemakhos conversing with Athena, with lowered head so that others may not overhear.... Share a dish of dried figs with Plato and he will take them all."[13] Relentlessly, Diogenes goes after Plato's character like a dog catching scent of a squirrel. But it is Plato's philosophizing, too, that is the enemy—because, of course, one cannot so neatly separate the values of the author from the ends of the project. And so, Diogenes will reportedly declare, "Plato's philosophy is an endless conversation.... And his lectures are tedious."[14] While as for the theory of the Forms, after visiting Plato at his home Diogenes can only say, "I saw Plato's cups and his table, but not his cupness and tableness."[15]

Though there are accounts of various texts authored by Diogenes and lost to the vagaries of history, it is far more likely that we have nothing written by Diogenes because Diogenes refused to write. Sosicrates of Rhodes and Satyrus of Callias Pontica both reported that Diogenes not only maintained a strict oral tradition of teaching and consequently refused to write "like Plato," but that he often argued for "the futility and uselessness of reading and writing" in general.[16] The style of Diogenes's quips is thus key to their content as well. And like an animal, all we know about Diogenes is what humans have said about him. All of Diogenes's life was lived rather than spent recording it for others to read about how it was lived.

Much has been made of Diogenes's dogged style and catty remarks. He was, truly, doing philosophy as stand-up comedy or perhaps, better, as a sort of performance art. Caught up in an argument with a man who could not accept that Diogenes did not believe in the gods, for instance, Diogenes finally admitted that he would begin believing in them because how else could he explain someone who was so obviously godforsaken as his accuser? And another time, seeing a woman "who had flopped down before an altar with her butt in the air ... [Diogenes] remarked in passing that the god was also behind her."[17] In comedy there is much truth. But the truth, here, is even deeper, because such a style of philosophizing and living suggests that there is a strong parallel between the gadfly and the dog.

Socrates and Diogenes are closer to each other than are Socrates and Plato. Both Socrates and Diogenes refuse to write, instead choosing to perform their philosophy. And in this way they are both similar to animals as well. Animals, too, do not write. They act, embody, and carry out their identity, emotions, desires, and thoughts. They live what they believe rather than talk about it and transcribe it. For Socrates, this meant living the life of a conversationalist who discussed philosophy with friends, strangers, and anyone willing to engage with him in a search for answers to the big questions about life. And for Diogenes it was also about interacting with the public, though in a less dialectical manner. If Socrates was the first ironist, and his most ironic claim was his interpretation of what the Delphic oracle had announced—he was the wisest man in Athens simply because he knew how little he truly knew—Diogenes happily echoed this each time he was made fun of by the citizens of Athens. "If, as they say, I am only an ignorant man trying to be a philosopher," the dog declared, "then that may be what a philosopher is."[18]

Irony, too, is the domain of the animal. Because all language fails to refer—because all words fail to denote, never mirroring the world, but instead find meaning only by means of performance and usage and instantiation in a body doing, and thus a subject meaning, *this, here, now*—only humans seem capable of misunderstanding *logos* so deeply as to need a category of "irony" to separate it from "straight discourse." The animal lets meaning play. The animal is pre-ironized, never leashed to sense and reference, never demanding an impossible correspondence theory of truth, never separating *logos* from the community and from its communal performance. The animal *acts* as the truest philosopher.[19]

"I pissed on the man who called me a dog," explained Diogenes. "Why was he so surprised?"[20] Like the animal he was (called), Diogenes let his body be, and thus let his body philosophize. When Diogenes was caught "working with his hands" (i.e., masturbating) in the marketplace, rather than showing shame, the dog began begging and told the public, "If only I could rub my stomach in the same way so as to avoid hunger."[21] Here, then, is a deep philosophical claim about desire, satiation, generosity, charity, community, embodiment, and truth. When Plato lectured publically on such truth being found only in an abstract realm far away from our own material life, does it not make sense to say that a philosophic refutation might properly begin with Diogenes squatting down, lifting his toga, and evacuating his bowels?[22] What else could better pull us back to the real and the present—to the political and ethical commitments our metaphysics always have already made, to the complicated filth and materiality of our shared existence—than the excrement of the dog, the argument become carnal, the fecund fact of our public embodiment suddenly exposed and made impossible to ignore?

History insists on Socrates's and Diogenes's ugliness. Snub animal-noses, hair in inhuman places, animal features that distorted their humanity. Aesop, too, on trial for irony and satirization, was cynically said to be canine-ugly—"dog-headed" and "like a dog in basket."[23] But what is a human's conception of beauty to an animal? And what worth has beauty, then, at all, especially in a world in which one must watch one's step in the *agora*, careful not to walk in a refutation? Isn't the privileged human face of Plato—nose-upturned, perfumed, and judgmental—potentially more disturbing?

Like animals, Socrates and Diogenes did not court death, but neither did they obsessively fear it. Pondering the end of life, in fact, it seems the gadfly and the dog thought of each other.

Toward the conclusion of his comments to the jurors who had just condemned him to death, Socrates speaks of what is to come rather than what will pass away. He prophesizes:

> I say to you who have slain me, that punishment will come upon you soon after my death.... For you have done this to me because you hoped that you would be spared a rendered account of your lives, but you will find the result far different. Those who will force you to give an account will be more numerous than before. They will be men whom I restrained, though you did not know it; and they will be harsher, inasmuch as they will be younger, and you will be more annoyed. (*Apology* 39c–d)

Earlier, in the *Republic* (539b), Socrates had called the young people who imitate him puppies [σκυλάκιον] that "delight in pulling and tearing the words of all who approach." Socrates's curse to Athens is that upon his death the dogs will descend upon the city.

And let the humans and the gadflies be gone as a whole, without remorse or apology, said Diogenes the dog that descended on Athens: for "whoever trusts us [i.e., the Cynics] will remain single. Those who do not trust us will rear children. If the human species should one day cease to exist, there should be as much cause to regret as there should be if flies and wasps pass away."[24] The fly, the dog, the human—the ugly truth that Diogenes knew is that the world can get by fine without the whole lot.

After the execution of Socrates, on rare occasions an upper-class Athenian would approach Diogenes in conversation, looking for advice, looking to be persuaded, looking for a path toward virtue that would typically not include having to sacrifice anything. Diogenes's counsel was consistent and clear, harsher and more ruthlessly true than anything Socrates had predicted: "Hang yourself," barked the dog.[25]

* * *

> "And consider this also," I said. "If [the escaped prisoner] went back down again [into the cave] and took his old place, would he not get his eyes full of darkness, thus suddenly coming back out of the sunlight?"
>
> —Plato, *Republic* 516e

Before the hemlock shut his eyes permanently, the gadfly seemed to champion light. The sun, in fact, came to be associated with the Form of the Good itself. And a life in the cave, a life in shadows and darkness, was the ultimate life not worth living—one of unquestioned falsehood and illusion. Socrates, Plato tells us, could see what others could not, even if that meant that he could see just how little he truly saw clearly. But we must remember that the philosopher who escapes the cave is blinded twice: once on his assent as an explorer into the world to search for truth, and once on his descent as a revolutionary back into the cave to tell the others. Coming and going lead to blindness; the liminal spaces of transition cannot support open eyes.[26]

If we return to Socrates's gadfly speech with this in mind, then something amazing comes to light. Socrates calls himself a μύωψ, that is, a gadfly, and as such what he is literally saying is that he is *myopic*, that he has his eyes closed, that he cannot see. The word μύωψ stems from μύειν (to shut) and ὤψ (eye). One can imagine that the Greek etymology begins in a physical reaction to the actual animal: we close our eyes, or at the very least squint, when such an insect annoyingly buzzes around us. But even if we understand "gadfly" to mean "that which makes us close our eyes" rather than simply (and more literally) "eyes that are closed," it would mean that Socrates is saying he is someone who makes the people of Athens close their eyes—precisely the opposite of what he typically claims he is trying to do.

Perhaps Socrates is the one who cannot see. Or perhaps Socrates is making the people of Athens incapable of seeing. But in either case, why this particular animal metaphor, one with a meaning apparently contrary to Socrates's perennially declared intentions? A gadfly would, in fact, be incapable of theory [θεωρία]—literally "a seeing, a looking at." But of course this is all that Socrates seems to have an interest in when talking with others. He doesn't want examples of love or justice. He wants to know what Love and Justice are in general, abstractly, *theoretically*. Yet the gadfly, by definition, cannot see, cannot know theory, cannot do philosophy.

So, we must pause and wait for our eyes to adjust.

When Plato's Socrates speaks out against the written word, but Plato is writing to us to tell us about this, we pause and recognize something more complicated working itself out in the text. When Plato's Socrates warns us about poetry and the corrupting force of art, but Plato is describing all of this in a dramatic dialogue full of metaphor and beautiful language, we pause again. And when Plato's Socrates tells us that he champions seeing, light, and rousing people to visionary action and knowledge, but Plato puts the term "gadfly" into Socrates's mouth, we take a final pause. Plato and Socrates are distinct, but perhaps no more distinct than Shakespeare and Hamlet. And in the tension between the two, between how they necessarily differ and how one must always defer, there is the undermining of the text that is, at the same time, the force that inflates it to meaning.

Plato is in control of his protagonist, yet only to the extent that any author finds freedom by means of being constrained by a narrative, a history, and a goal. Plato wishes to tell the story of a free, brave, wild man who inspired the youth of Athens—himself included—and was martyred for a grand cause. This is Socrates the revolutionary, the questioner of authority, the nagger of nags, the anti-spelunker who knew he was the only one who had been up into the light. This is the Socrates who might have questioned democracy but never in the name of oligarchy; the Socrates whose notions of meritocracy and a life of the mind would call the bourgeois values of his home, and his students, into question. This is Socrates as the finest man, and thus the finest human, fully in control of *logos*. But when that story is told, when Plato begins to commit it to papyrus, all of the ways in which it conflicts with the rest of Plato's values and goals find a way of exposing themselves. Plato turns to the animal to describe this paradigm of humanity. And in so doing, he portrays Socrates as villain, as failed, as the antithesis of all he announces himself to be. Socrates thus becomes the wolf that steals Thrasymachus's voice by seeing him first, though Socrates—the gadfly in wolf's clothing—is paradoxically unable to see. The gadfly, too, is the seemingly insignificant pest that at the same time makes the larger animal what it is and what it should be. The gadfly, though he seems to be an annoyance to the horse, is what makes the horse into the horse—what makes the horse swish his tail and twitch his ears—and thus the work of the philosopher is co-opted: Athens is made Athens by having such men around—perhaps to vent the frustrations of the youth, perhaps to keep up the façade of welcoming creativity and difference, perhaps to have in stock in order to slaughter them when necessary. So the wild animal is no wild animal. Socrates is Plato's domesticated hybrid beast, like an ox, a bull-man, tugging the plow along rows of conformity, kicking against the prick and finding the spike driven further into his flesh. In the space between the wild and the tame, the revolutionary and the aristocrat, the man and the animal, the two eyelids just barely meeting to form a squint, there is the meaning of Socrates. There is what it means to be Socrates.

The gadfly, blinded, is on his way either out of the cave or back into it. Socrates—so says Athens, so says his author—is on his way out.

* * *

> At the same time, the man held out the cup [of hemlock] to Socrates. He took it, and very gently, Echecrates, without trembling or changing color or expression, but looking up at the man with wide open bull-like eyes, as was his custom, said: "What do you say about pouring a libation to some deity from this cup? May I, or not?"
>
> —Plato, *Phaedo* 117b

At the end of his life, Socrates is waiting for his execution. It has been delayed due to the late return of the annual embassy sent to Delos in commemoration of Theseus's killing of the Minotaur. Prior to Theseus's slaying of the beast, Athens had been sending fourteen young people to be sacrificed to the "Bull of Crete" each year. Through Phaedo, Plato tells us that Socrates, in his last moments of life, was surrounded by fourteen nameable friends. Phaedo points out, however, that the fourteen did not include Plato, who was ill that day. The dialogue thus attests to being a firsthand account of the death of Socrates ("I was there myself," says Phaedo), though it refers to its own author, the author of those very words, as not having been there. We pause. This should be the first indication that we are—once again and as always—not seeing everything that can be seen.

It is easy to see the *Phaedo* as an allegorical and philosophic reenactment of Theseus's victory: Socrates is the hero who slays the Minotaur, and the monstrous bull he destroys is the fear of death itself. Socrates saves his own fourteen gathered souls by arguing, in his customary conversational way, that the soul in general is immortal and there is no reason to fear the end of the life of the flesh. It is a slaying with *logos* rather than a sword, though the end result is said to be the same. The youth are once again safe.

But Plato's Socrates is no Theseus in this text. He is, instead, the bull. The victory of Theseus—the return of the celebration ship—will mark Socrates's death, not his triumph. The gathered friends, the youth of Athens, are the ones Socrates is said to have corrupted, not saved. And with bull-like eyes, Socrates drinks down the hemlock and dies in the end like the slain Minotaur. No, it is the city of Athens that is cast as the hero Theseus in this dialogue. And Socrates, his eyes finally wide open in his last moments, is no longer myopic, no longer the pest, but Plato's vanquished half-man, half-animal beast. Plato's final words speak of Socrates as "the best, the wisest, the most just." But his dialogue doubles back on itself, a labyrinth full of untrustworthy word monsters.

Socrates, the gadfly-become-the-bull, dies at the hand of Athens and of his narrator.

Diogenes, the dog, dies in a barrel outside a city wall, keeping silent by holding his muzzle shut and stopping his own breath.

Plato, the human, dies in luxury, unpersecuted, eventually a comfortable decade older than Socrates, in a warm bed, a young Thracian girl playing the flute for him—perhaps performing the tunes that Socrates himself composed in jail while putting Aesop's animal fables to music, waiting for his delayed execution finally to commence—the sensual melody rising and falling, ensuring no one, least of all the zookeeper, could hear a fly buzz when the old man died.

And all of this could have been different.

Notes

1. Plato, *The Apology*, in *Plato: Defence of Socrates, Euthyphro, Crito*, trans. David Gallop (Oxford: Oxford University Press, 1997), 45.

2. Cf. John Heath, who does an excellent job arguing just this point: "Socrates cannot be silent . . . because his divine mission is to spend each day conversing about and examining virtue: the unexamined life—that is, the life that neither inquires nor is inquired about—is not a human life (37e3–38a6). Speech is essential to lead a human life. Any Greek would agree with this, but Socrates means something rather different: this distinctly human possession must be used in philosophizing, and not for the temporal goals of politics and power. Speech in and of itself is of little use, and hardly makes one fully human." *The Talking Greeks: Speech, Animals,*

and the Other in Homer, Aeschylus, and Plato (Cambridge: Cambridge University Press, 2005), 305–306.

3. Plato, *The Apology*, in *Plato in Twelve Volumes*, trans. H. N. Fowler (Cambridge, Mass.: Harvard University Press, 1966).

4. For an interesting commentary in line with this same interpretation, see Daniel S. Werner, *Myth and Philosophy in Plato's Phaedrus* (Cambridge: Cambridge University Press, 2012), 139. Bruce Gottfried's interpretation of the myth as being key to Socrates's decision to continue talking at noontime even though he is aware he might incur the wrath of Pan (who sleeps at noon and punishes those who bother him) is also intriguing. In many ways, the Pan interpretation is not at odds with what I am suggesting here. Indeed, if *logos* is threatening to Pan, it is the content and not the form that will be the threat. The cicadas' drone, after all, doesn't disturb Pan. Only human speech—true human speech in service of philosophy—might. Cf. Bruce Gottfried, "Pan, the Cicadas, and Plato's Use of Myth in the *Phaedrus*," in *Plato's Dialogues*, ed. Gerald A. Press (New York: Roman and Littlefield, 1993), 179–182.

5. Heath, *The Talking Greeks*, 267.

6. Ibid., 45. Diogenes was not the first to be called a dog, however, nor was Plato the first to use that label for the Cynics. Diogenes initially studied under Antisthenes after coming to Athens, and Antisthenes referred to himself as "The Dog" and lectured at the Cynosarges: the park of the white-swift dog. The Cynosarges was not only a dog-place, but also a place where "outsiders" in Athens gathered—bastards, foreigners, non-citizens, etc.

7. Diogenes Laertius, "The Life of Diogenes of Sinope," in Navia, *Diogenes of Sinope*, 162.

8. Navia, *Diogenes of Sinope*, 13–14.

9. Ibid., 22. In a nice twist, this is also why the hermit crab's official Latin name today is *Diogenes*.

10. Diogenes Laertius, "The Life of Diogenes of Sinope," in Navia, *Diogenes of Sinope*, 154. Indeed, though I have above used the mouse as an example of a creature who is skittish and cowardly (in order to poke fun at Aristotle), Diogenes sees the mouse bravely moving through the darkness unafraid of whatever might lay ahead. Diogenes is, no doubt, the one who is correct here.

11. For a version of this story, see Diogenes Laertius, "The Life of Diogenes of Sinope," in Navia, *Diogenes of Sinope*, 156.

12. "I. F. Stone Breaks the Socrates Story: An old muckraker sheds fresh light on the 2,500-year-old mystery and reveals some Athenian political realities that Plato did his best to hide," *New York Times Magazine*, April 8, 1979.

13. *Herakleitos and Diogenes*, trans. Guy Davenport (San Francisco: Grey Fox Press, 1976), 41, 47, 59, 47.

14. Ibid., 46.

15. Ibid., 57.

16. Navia, *Diogenes of Sinope*, 5 and 21.

17. *Herakleitos and Diogenes*, 50, 56.

18. Ibid., 53.

19. Evolution, too, is an ironic maker. It is evolution that, by chance, made beings who began to think that by design something godly had made them, chosen them, and created all of the cosmos just for them. It is evolution that, with a chaotic twinkle in its eye, let dogs domesticate humans to do their bidding but also let humans think it was the other way around. It is evolution that let the chicken develop from the fiercest dinosaurs to walk the earth. Had Plato been somewhat better at comedy (and understood evolution), perhaps Socrates's final words should have been, "Crito, I owe Asclepius a contemporary Velociraptor. Be sure to pay the debt—carefully."

20. Ibid., 51.

21. Diogenes Laertius, "The Life of Diogenes of Sinope," in Navia, *Diogenes of Sinope*, 160.

22. Cf. Jeanne Gunner and Ed Frankel, *The Course of Ideas: College Writing and Reading* (New York: Harper & Row, 1986), 412. In many ways, too, Diogenes was acting in much the same way as Triumph the Insult Comic Dog, saying to Plato: "You have a wonderful theory... for me to poop on!"

23. Todd Compton, "The Trial of the Satirist: Poetic Vitae (Aesop, Archilochus, Homer) as Background for Plato's *Apology*," *American Journal of Philology* 111, no. 3 (1990): 344.

24. Navia, *Diogenes of Sinope*, 24.

25. Ibid., 27.

26. We soon learn that philosophers appear ridiculous when viewed by those still inside the cave (*Republic* 517a). Once back in the cave, philosophers aren't so good at telling one shadow from the next anymore. They seem laughable to others. The wise man feels pity for such a traveler in both cases (that is, both leaving and reentering the cave). And it is thus that Socrates might look ridiculous to Thracian maids—eliciting laughter and derision. But if it is true that once you get to know Socrates and understand what he is saying, you will stop laughing and will come to admire him, how is Diogenes not potentially in the same position?

PART IV
The Political Animal

7 Taming Horses and Desires
Plato's Politics of Care

Jeremy Bell

IN WHAT IS perhaps the most well-known (animal) image in Plato's corpus, Socrates likens himself to a μύωψ, a gadfly, that has been set upon Athens as if upon a large and well-bred horse. Because of its size, this horse has grown sluggish and complacent and is now at risk of sleeping its life away. Thus Socrates proclaims that it is in need of an analeptic, the sting of the gadfly, to rouse it from its torpor (*Apology* 30e). That this has become one of the most famous images not only in Plato's corpus but in the whole of the Western literary tradition is due, no doubt, to the remarkable aptness of the comparison between Socrates and an unsightly, unpleasant, and inexhaustible pest, rather than to the aptness of the comparison between Athens and a large, sleepy horse. Indeed, the nearly ubiquitous tendency of English translators to render μύωψ in the *Apology* as "gadfly" rather than "horsefly" reflects the equally pervasive tendency of scholars to overlook, dismiss, or downplay the other image that Socrates invokes in this passage, the image of the horse. We speak primarily and unhesitatingly of Socrates the gadfly not Socrates the horsefly, despite the fact that the latter translation is justified, if not recommended, both lexicographically and entomologically. Moreover, when speaking of this image we remain largely silent regarding its correlate. Yet, to overlook the likeness that Socrates draws between Athens and a horse is to overlook the analogical character of the image that he presents when he proclaims that his relation to the *polis* is *the same* as that of a gadfly to a horse. The complementarity of these terms—Socrates as a gadfly, the city as a horse—not only establishes a strict parallelism between Socrates's entomic qualities and the equine qualities of Athens; it also sets these qualities in a mutually reciprocal relation with one another so that Socrates's gadfly-ism is dependent upon and derived from Athens's equinity and vice versa. To be sure, Socrates is a gadfly, but only insofar as Athens is a horse. This fact takes on still greater significance when one recalls that Socrates offers this entomic image as a way of accounting for his philosophical practice: philosophy is the practice of waking up sleeping horses. If, therefore, one wishes to better grasp this understanding of philosophy, one must determine how the tracks of the horse have worked to form the landscape of Socrates's and Plato's thought.

Because the horse has forged an exceptionally broad path throughout Plato's corpus, one that cuts across nearly every text and terrain therein, a comprehensive account of the myriad connotations that it carries within his thought and writings would require a much longer study than what can be offered here.[1] I will therefore limit the scope of the present inquiry to a single issue, or complex of issues, brought to light by the dual image of Socrates's gadfly-ism and Athens's equinity. On the one hand, this image portrays *how* Socrates philosophizes: he bites, spurs, and annoys, he relentlessly disrupts and displaces—in a word, he rouses. On the other hand, it illustrates *why* he philosophizes: he converses with others in order to exercise care over both the *polis* and his fellow citizens, so that they, in turn, may care for themselves and each other. Moreover, in the portrayal of how and why Socrates philosophizes, this image demonstrates the unity of these two features: the activity of philosophizing is an exceptional instance of the practice of care (ἡ ἐπιμέλεια). Finally, this image proffers the horse as a privileged example of an object of philosophical care. In the first instance, care is concerned with wakefulness, with an almost insomniac vigilance against sleep, to which Socrates opposes the oversized and drowsy horse of state. However, if one examines the horse further, if one looks it in the mouth, as it were, one sees that it likewise bespeaks the idiosyncrasy of an animal that, like a human, is tame by nature yet wild by birth, and that, therefore, requires supplementary practices, practices of care, in order to return to its nature. In what follows, I will trace out the contours of this idiosyncrasy in order to map out the point of coincidence between horses and humans and to demonstrate that the persistent and recurring concern over the twin tropes of wakefulness and tameness reveals Socratic philosophy to be a politics of care.

Breaking the Youth

Just prior to introducing the image of himself as a gadfly biting at the horse of state, an image intended to define the nature of his relation to the *polis* and its citizenry in terms of his practice of philosophy, Socrates reveals that which has spurred this practice: "I go about doing nothing else than persuading [πείθων] you, young and old, not to care [ἐπιμελεῖσθαι] for your persons or your property more than for the perfection [ἀρίστη] of your soul" (30a–b).[2] This assertion explains both the irreducibly interpersonal character of Socratic philosophy and its stinging effect: Socrates is spurred by his care for the care that others exercise over themselves, and, being spurred in this way, he has become a spur, a μύωψ, himself. His gadfly-ism is nothing other than the practice of a philosophy that understands itself to be directed by and toward the care of oneself and others and that has identified wakefulness as the necessary precondition for the exercise of such care. That to which Socrates awakens his fellow citizens, that which he insists one must recognize in order to care for oneself, for others, or for one's *polis*, is the finitude of one's knowledge. Because the contours of this finitude are distorted, if not altogether covered over and concealed, by the supposition that one knows things of which one is in fact either partially or entirely ignorant, Socratic dialectic attempts to awaken its auditors to the ignorance and the *doxai* harbored within this claim to knowledge; by exposing the limits of human knowledge and possibility, the recognition of our epistemic finitude brings human virtue and the human good into relief. Thus, when he announces that the god has both sent him as a gift intended to awaken the city and made him a paradigm (παράδειγμα) upon which his fellow citizens are to model their lives (30d–e and 23a–b, respectively), Socrates proclaims that the way to live a good life, the way to care for oneself, is to live the sort of life that he himself has lived—a life dedicated to the wakefulness and vigilance demanded by that specifically human wisdom whereby one guards against supposing oneself to know that which one does not (21d).

It is noteworthy that Socrates does not oppose the image of himself as a gadfly to the image of the city as a horse *tout court*. As Justina Gregory has demonstrated, horses enjoyed a largely positive assessment in Attic culture, literature, and semiotics, conveying, among other qualities, "pent-up strength and vigor" (197).[3] It is for this reason that, when he likens the city to a large and sleepy horse, Socrates claims that his concern is over the city's lethargy, not its equinity. What comes to the fore in the image of Athens's equinity is not the horse in an unqualified sense but the horse as the embodiment of an animal whose endogenous vigor has been lost amid the myriad and unbridled values, beliefs, and desires structuring the daily life of the *polis*. Offered as a counter-image to the wakefulness and vigilance of the gadfly, the representation of Athens as a large, sleepy horse serves to define the city's as-yet unactualized potential for self-care in terms of its somnolence and lethargy, and, by this, to underscore the dangers of a life spent asleep: ignorant and unwise, unaware of one's ignorance and lack of wisdom, disposed by this lack of awareness to consider oneself knowledgeable and wise when one is in fact neither of these, one fails altogether to know oneself—indeed, one takes oneself to be one's opposite—and is thereby rendered incapable of caring for oneself.

This first, and admittedly cursory, account of care has a decidedly epistemic, or anepistemic, character: in order to care for oneself one must know oneself, one must be cognizant of one's ignorance, one must not suppose oneself to know that which one does not. Yet Socrates's activities, his way of life, suggest that the (an) epistemic character of care has immediate and unavoidable ethical and political implications. Because Socrates's concern over his own and others' epistemic finitude is motivated by his concern with the care that he and others exercise over themselves, his daily attempt to expose the ignorance of his fellow citizens, his daily attempt to wake them up, is likewise revealed to be motivated by care. Moreover, because such care is concerned with how one lives one's life and relates to one's *polis*, the practice of exploring and exposing the finitude of knowledge, that is, the practice of philosophy, is found to have always already been the practice of ethics and politics. Thus we see that Socrates is offered as a paradigm for human existence precisely because his way of life (his *ethos*) has been determined by the desire to abide in and by the finitude of his knowledge, and because his attempt to live such a life has turned him toward the care that his fellow citizens exercise over both themselves and the *polis*.[4]

This concern over the way that his fellow citizens conduct themselves, this attempt to direct or redirect their conduct, is clearly reflected in the image of Socrates as a gadfly relentlessly spurring on the horse of state: he tries to wake up his fellow citizens, to get them moving, to get them to care for themselves and their *polis*, and to prize virtue over vice and complacency. Less clearly reflected in this image, however, is the end or *telos* toward which the gadfly sought to conduct the city and its citizens. Thus, even as Socrates avers that he is a gift sent by the god, that his gift consists of examining his fellow citizens, that the unexamined life is not worth living because it fails to perceive and abide by the finitude of human knowledge, and that this failure simultaneously conceals the properly human good and effects the impious transcendence of the boundary separating the human from the divine (for one supposes oneself to know that which only a god may know)—even as he avers all of this, the majority of his jurors see only that, in attempting to (re)direct the conduct of his fellow citizens, Socrates threatened to undermine the predominate values of the *polis*, and, thereby, to corrupt both the city and its citizens. Indeed, despite his protestations regarding a number of other issues leading to and arising in his trial, Socrates in fact confirms the jurors' suspicion that he is a threat to their way of life and to the way of life characteristic of the *polis* itself. But because this threat is directed against a way of life that he understands to fall short of the good, Socrates does not extend his agreement to the further suspicion that his activities amount to the threat of corruption.

It is true that Socrates attempts to *de-educate* his fellow citizens, both young and old, in the predominate "knowledge," values, and desires of the *polis*, but this, he suggests, is to be likened to one who trains an otherwise wild or unruly horse to be tame and good. When, earlier in the *Apology*, Socrates responded to Meletus's claim that all Athenian citizens improve the youth with the exception of himself, who alone makes them vicious, he induced Meletus to agree that things are just the opposite with horses and all other animals (including, presumably, the human animal); whereas the many (*hoi polloi*) are likely to have a negligible, if not a negative, effect on horses, "he who is able to make them better is some one person, or very few, the horse-trainers" (25b). Likening his philosophical practice to the training of horses rather than to the bite of the gadfly, Socrates here suggests that what sets him apart from his fellow citizens is the care that he exercises over them. With this, Socrates explicitly links his philosophical practice to the process of education or training: by challenging those who claim a knowledge beyond what they in fact possess, Socrates educates his interlocutors in the limits of their knowledge and trains them to care for themselves.[5]

This comparison between the youth and unbroken horses recurs throughout Plato's corpus and is concerned, in each instance, with the issue of education. Earlier in the *Apology*, for instance, Socrates had likened Evenus's two sons to colts, πῶλοι, and their educator to a horse-trainer (20a); in the *Republic*, Socrates claims that the guardians of the city must be brought up from youth like colts whose temperaments are regularly tested (413d); and, in the *Laws*, the Athenian Stranger remarks that the Spartans raise their young in common "like a herd of colts at grass" (666e).[6] Later in the *Laws*, we are given a still clearer sense of the stakes involved in the comparison of the youth to unbroken horses. Echoing Socrates's insistence that his fellow citizens exercise wakefulness, vigilance, and self-care, the Athenian Stranger proclaims that if the second-best city (that is, the city whose constitution he is currently describing in speech) is to come into existence, the law must impose upon its citizens "the weightiest task of all": to practice "the care [ἐπιμέλειαν] of bodily and spiritual excellence [ἀρετὴν]" (807c–d). Because this task is so great that "every night and day is not sufficient for the one who is occupied therein to win from them their fruit in full and ample measure" (807d), one must sleep as little as possible if, like Socrates, one has dedicated one's life to self-care: "For when asleep no man is worth anything, any more than if he were dead: on the contrary, every one of us who cares most greatly for life and thought keeps awake as long as possible, only reserving so much time for sleep as health requires" (808b–c). Here, as in the *Apology*, sleep is something to be managed and minimized; though it has been transformed from metaphor into flesh, though it has metamorphosed from an image of ignorance into the life-sustaining process of rest and repose, sleep nevertheless remains opposed to the care of the self. Just as the unexamined life is not worth living, so too is a life occupied with too much sleep likened to death.[7] And, again as in the *Apology*, the good of the city—indeed, the possibility of a good city—depends upon the care that its citizens exercise over themselves. If, like Socrates, they dedicate their lives to self-care, if they allow such care to determine their way of life, then the second-best city may succeed; if, however, they neglect themselves, then it will fail.

Yet even this, as demanding as it may be, is not sufficient; in order for the second-best city to succeed, its citizens must care not only for themselves but for the youth of the city as well, so that they, in turn, will grow up to be virtuous and capable of caring for themselves and their progeny. Here, once again as in the *Apology*, equinity serves as the privileged model for the care of the youth. The Stranger proclaims: "But of all wild beasts [θηρίων], the child is the most unruly; for, insofar as it, more than all others, possesses an undisciplined source of *phronēsis*, it is a treacherous, guileful, and most impudent creature. Therefore the child is such that it must be bound with many bridles [χαλινοῖς]" (808d–e).[8] Possessing an as-yet unactualized potential for *phronēsis*, human children are the wildest of all creatures and the least capable of caring for themselves. Plato thus employs language intended to call to mind the process of breaking an untamed foal or colt, which, because of its excessive wildness, requires many bridles or trainers—the child's mother and nurse to begin with, his or her tutors and teachers, and, finally, "any free man" (808e).[9] The second-best city is, as it were, teeming with trainers.[10]

With this discussion of bridling the youth, one begins to see more clearly why equine images served as a touchstone for Plato's articulation of the philosophical practice of care and training. Both humans and horses are understood to be naturally tame animals that are nevertheless born wild and unbroken.[11] By nature, each is born at a remove from its nature. It was in recognition of this that the wildness of human children was attributed to an as-yet unactualized potential for *phronēsis*. And yet, though they are wild by birth and tame by nature, though they are, as it were, congenitally *denatured,* both horses and humans may be drawn closer to their nature and their virtue through training, attention, and care.[12] Both, that is to say, may be broken. It is this insight that spurs Plato's many appeals to the image of human equinity as a way of expressing the failure to care for oneself; these references give voice to a concern over the duality of our natures and highlight the paramount importance of philosophical training for living a life of care.[13]

The centrality of the opposition between tameness and wildness to Socrates's philosophical practice is underscored in the closing lines of the *Theaetetus*. Here, only moments before reporting to the king archon to learn what charges have been brought against him, Socrates assures the dialogue's namesake that, as a result of their conversation, "you will be less harsh and gentler [ἡμερώτερος] to your associates, for you will have the wisdom not to think you know that which you do not know" (210c). Such wisdom—what Socrates in the *Apology* had called human wisdom—is here marked as a, if not *the,* possibility of human tameness. With this, Socrates aligns such tameness with the wakefulness to which he had appealed in the *Apology,* and sets it forth as the end toward which a philosophical education is directed. In a similar gesture, the Athenian Stranger claims that a philosophical education is the pivot upon which our dual natures turn: "Man [ἄνθρωπος], as we affirm, is a tame [ἥμερον] creature: none the less, while he is wont to become an animal most godlike and tame when he happens to possess a happy nature combined with right education, if his training be deficient or bad, he turns out the wildest [ἀγριώτατον] of all earth's creatures" (766a).¹⁴ In these passages, and there are many more like them, we see that Plato expresses the duality of human nature alternatively as the opposition between a life of wakefulness and a life of sleep, and as the opposition between tameness and wildness. Accordingly, he divides human life into two *ethē*: a life of wakefulness and vigilance in which one engages in various practices—most notably the practice of philosophy—in order to work on and improve, that is, tame and care for, oneself; and a life of lethargy in which one neglects oneself and remains wild. Thus, the remarkable similarity that Plato finds between humans and horses is that each bears a nature that requires supplementary practices in order to attain the good unique to that nature.

The Tame and the Wild

While it may be tempting to see Plato's invocation of the duality of humanity as a prefiguration of the savagery and brutishness of the state of nature that would become so prominent in the social contractarian philosophies of the seventeenth and eighteenth centuries, we should guard against anachronistically interpolating this later concept into Plato's thought. Plato's discussion of human wildness does not make reference, even as a hypothesis, to a primeval, pre-political state that was, for better or worse, overcome with the birth of the *polis*; nor does it bespeak the vestige of such primevality within the otherwise tame milieu of the *polis*.¹⁵ Moreover, human wildness is not synonymous with human animality, as this equivalency would assume that Plato unproblematically aligns animality with wildness, which our discussion of horses has already shown not to be the case; horses may, after all, be tamed. Rather, human wildness is a way of relating to oneself and others that is, at least in part, made possible by living with others; it is a way of conducting oneself that is not antithetical to one's political life but is in fact dependent upon it. Such wildness names that way of life, or those ways of life, in which one fails to care for oneself; it names, therefore, the life in which one takes no care over one's pleasures and desires, the life in which one merely values and believes what others value and believe, and the life in which one supposes oneself to know things that one does not. Thus it is clear that, while Plato may understand juvenescence to bear the ubiquitous mark of wildness, this mark is by no means limited to the youth but extends rather to all those who fail to care for themselves. It was this recognition that led Socrates to liken his fellow citizens, en masse, to a large, sleepy horse. For Socrates had found the failure of self-knowledge to be pervasive throughout Athens and so concluded that in the absence of this knowledge his fellow citizens were incapable of caring for themselves, each other, or the city.

In the *Republic*, the most extreme manifestation of human wildness, the most extreme manifestation of the failure to care for either oneself or others, is identified with the figure of the tyrant, who, in this and so many other ways, is portrayed as the antithesis of the philosopher. Having earlier asserted that the success of the ideal city depends upon the care (*epimeleia*) that its rulers exercise over themselves, the citizenry, and the *polis* (499b, 543c), Socrates claims that once the nuptial number has been incorrectly calculated the city's decline into tyranny is precipitated by the rulers' failure to care (*amelein*) either for themselves or for their fellow citizens (546d). Set loose from the reins of care, the city and its citizenry become increasingly feral, vicious, and lustful, until, at last, this increase begets the tyrant, who is altogether feral and vicious and whose desires know only increase. Ruled only by this increase, the tyrant emerges as the one who fails altogether to care for himself and who possesses sufficient power to drown the entire *polis* in this self-neglect. Bordered on one side by the radical care of the guardians, and, on the other by the radical carelessness of the tyrant, the decline and fall of the city outlined in Books 8 and 9 may be read as a narrative portraying the unsustainable extremes of care.

The logic structuring this decline is one that runs throughout the *Republic*. As in the earlier books, it is here assumed that there is a formative and reciprocal relation between individuals or groups and political regimes. This is expressed most conspicuously by the fact that the ideal city was allowed to succeed only for so long as it was able to sustain the fragile symbiosis whereby it continued to produce citizens capable of supporting it.[16] Yet this reciprocal relation is also expressed in the succession of regimes, as well as individuals corresponding to those regimes, that is initiated by the collapse of the ideal city. As improbable and problematic as this succession may be, one should not lose sight of the larger methodological assertion underlying it, namely, that individuals and regimes do not develop autochthonously but emerge, in large part, from out of a given sociopolitical milieu.[17]

It is in this light that Plato claims democracy to be the necessary forbearer of tyranny and the "democratic man" to be the father of the tyrant. Portraying it in a rather dim light, Plato here casts democracy as an anarchist libertarianism in which laws are devalued and debased in the name of freedom (562c-e, 563d-e) and the common good is supplanted by the pleasure of the individual (561a-d). By unifying lawlessness and hedonism, democracy provides the sociopolitical conditions necessary for the production of tyranny and the tyrant. Speaking from the perspective of this narrow understanding of democracy, Socrates proclaims that "tyranny develops out of no other constitution than democracy—from the height of liberty, I take it, the fiercest [ἀγριωτάτη] extreme of servitude" (564a). The ferocity or wildness of tyranny and the tyrant develops as an extension of the lack of self-care identified in democracy and the democratic man. Socrates describes the last of these in the following manner: "he establishes and maintains all his pleasures on a footing of equality, and so lives turning over the guardhouse of his soul to each as it happens along until it is sated, as if it had drawn the lot for that office, and then in turn to another, disdaining not but fostering them all equally" (561a–b). Translating onto the level of the soul the Athenian practice of allocating administrative positions by lot, Plato envisions the inner life of the democratic man to be a democracy of pleasures that has no ruling principle other than a commitment to the satisfaction of whatever desire has, temporarily, acceded to a position of rule.

Like the democratic man, the tyrant, too, has abdicated self-governance to the rule of desire. The tyrant, however, radicalizes the democratic/libertarian hostility toward law to such an extent that the law is altogether expunged—with the exception, of course, of whatever law, however capricious or arbitrary, the tyrant may institute. Politically, this translates into the repression, expulsion, or execution of anyone other than the emerging tyrant who possesses wealth or enforces either law or custom (563d–569c). Psychologically, it translates into the expulsion of all that is lawful within the soul in favor of certain lawless (*anomos*) desires that rule over and determine the ethos of the tyrant.[18] Speaking as if the political and the ethical were joined at the head, Socrates proclaims that the tyrant who successfully rises to power will be the one "who has the greatest and mightiest tyrant in his own soul" (575c–d). The outward expression of tyranny, that is, the domination of the *polis* and the reduction of all others to functionaries of one's passions, reflects the inner subservience of the tyrant to the ferocity and lawlessness of those desires that have rendered him nothing more than a means to their own gratification. The tyrant is lawless, wild, and incapable of caring either for others or for the city because he is ruled by desires that are lawless and wild, and because he is incapable of practicing self-care.

The desires to which the tyrant succumbs—the desire for sexual intercourse with humans, gods, and beasts alike, the desire for blood, food, wealth, and every extravagance (571c–575a)—are said to exist within us all (571b). These are the desires "that are awakened in sleep when the rest of the soul, the rational, gentle, and dominant part [λογιστικὸν καὶ ἥμερον καὶ ἄρχον], slumbers, but the beastly and savage part [τὸ δὲ θηριῶδές τε καὶ ἄγριον] . . . repelling sleep, endeavors to sally forth and satisfy its own instincts. . . . In such cases there is nothing it will not venture to undertake as being released from all sense of shame and all reason [φρονήσεως]" (571c). Sleep is understood to be a state in which our tame faculties—*logos, phronēsis,* and our sense of shame—are suspended, and our wilder, less lawful desires are awakened and allowed to feast without restraint. As in the *Laws*, sleep, the physiological state of repose, is here too presented as a danger and a threat and thus as something to be managed.[19] In the soul of the tyrant, however, this danger spills over into the apparently metaphorical understanding of sleep evoked in the *Apology*. Finding within the despot only vice, excess, and the violation of every limit, Plato proclaims that the tyrant erases even the boundary separating waking life from the wild repose of sleep. Indulging daily those desires that others know only in dreams, the tyrant "is continuously and in waking hours what he rarely became in sleep" (574e–575a).²⁰

This overturning of the boundary between sleep and wakefulness, this erasure of the difference between the literal and the metaphorical conceptions of sleep, is due, Plato avers, to the tyrant's failure to exercise care over himself. Imagining the tripartite soul as the fantastical unity of a human (*logos*), a lion (spirit), and a many-headed beast (the desires), Socrates claims that the last of these "has a ring of heads of tame and wild beasts [ἡμέρων δὲ θηρίων ἔχοντος κεφαλὰς κύκλῳ καὶ ἀγρίων] and can change them and cause to spring forth from itself all such growths" (588c). Unjust individuals are said to feed the lion and the polycephal beast within themselves while starving the human, thereby affecting the thoroughgoing wildness of their souls (588e–589a). In the tyrant, this carnival of the desires reaches its culmination when the wildest heads of the beast all but devour the rest of the soul. Turning against and preying upon itself, the tyrant's soul is factious and self-devouring. It is for this reason that, as early as the first book of the *Republic*, injustice was said both to cause faction within the city and the soul and to make one an enemy to oneself (351e–352a). This, in turn, was attributed to the fact that "a bad soul governs and cares for things badly [κακῇ ψυχῇ κακῶς ἄρχειν καὶ ἐπιμελεῖσθαι]" (353e). The wildness, factiousness, and autophagy of the unjust soul are the result of a lack of care and governance.

The opposite of the tyrant's carelessness is not the ascetic rejection of one's desires but the practice of exercising care over these desires. Thus Socrates claims that "the one who says the just things are profitable affirms that it is necessary to do and say those things from which the human being [ἄνθρωπος] within will most be in control of the human being and take charge [ἐπιμελήσεται] of the many-headed beast—like a farmer, nourishing and cultivating the tame heads [τὰ μὲν ἥμερα], while hindering the growth of the savage ones [τὰ δὲ ἄγρια]" (589a–b).²¹ The ruling part of a just soul, the part with *logos*, resists the factious, wild, and autophagic tendencies that characterize the unjust soul; it alone does not care for itself alone but for the entirety of the soul. As such, it does not exile or eradicate the desires but cares for and cultivates them. To be sure, such care does not amount to the indiscriminate propagation of or indulgence in one's desires, for Plato has already argued that this failure to discriminate, this indifference to the differences within oneself, results from a failure to care for oneself. Rather, in contrast to the "democratic man," who indulges all desires equally, and the tyrant, who indulges primarily wild and unruly desires, the one who cares for him- or herself fosters only those desires that are tame, that is, those that do not oppose wakefulness understood either literally or metaphorically. This is to say that the exercise of care weeds out those desires that are antithetical to *phronēsis* and cultivates those that are aligned with it or that, at the very least, are not opposed to it. Because he understands human tameness to be that state which is conducive to and coincident with the development of *sōphrosunē, dikaiosunē,* and *phronēsis,* and because he understands humans to be naturally moderate, just, and prudent animals, Plato identifies this tameness as the return to one's nature. Speaking of those who care for themselves, Socrates concludes that when "the brutish part is lulled and tamed and the gentle part liberated, the entire soul, returning to its nature at the best [καὶ ὅλη ἡ ψυχὴ εἰς τὴν βελτίστην φύσιν καθισταμένη], attains to a much more precious condition in acquiring sobriety [σωφροσύνην] and righteousness [δικαιοσύνην] together with wisdom [φρονήσεως]" (591b).

If we turn briefly to the *Phaedrus,* a dialogue that is in part framed by Socrates's concern over his own tameness (230a), we find that this return to one's own nature is imagined as the soul regrowing the wings that it possessed prior to falling to earth, that is, those wings that had enabled its vision of noetic beauty (246a–256b). As in the *Republic,* the possibility of this return is here attributed to the practice of philosophy; for it is through this practice that one orders one's soul and tames one's wild and unruly desires (256a–b).[22] In the *Phaedrus,* this process of ordering and taming oneself is portrayed as a struggle between a wild, dark horse (the unruly desires) and a charioteer (that part of the soul with *logos*) who is assisted by a tame, light horse.[23] Elizabeth Belfiore notes that this struggle "results not only in the taming of the black horse but also in a permanent—or at least semi-permanent—agreement of all three parts of the soul. The charioteer is in command, and the two horses obey willingly. . . . The motion toward the beloved that the black horse once forced upon the others has now been imparted to the whole soul so that it follows the beloved in orderly fashion" (193–194).[24] The *Phaedrus* suggests, in terms perhaps still more clear than those of the *Republic,* that the highest form of the care of the self consists in an agreement between the various parts of the soul regarding which will rule and which will be ruled. Moreover, despite the initially violent confrontation between the charioteer and the dark horse (254d–e), the trilateral nature of this agreement prevents such rule from resulting in the unidirectional domination of the ruled by the ruler. Thus, not only are the desires of the dark horse not eliminated, these desires in fact serve to motivate and mobilize the soul as a whole. Indeed, it is only by following the dark horse's desire for the beauty of the beloved that the soul is able to return to its own nature and regrow its lost wings (254c–256b).[25]

And yet, because this return cannot occur so long as the dark horse's desires remain wild and intemperate, Plato portrays the charioteer as both pilot and trainer. With this gesture, he situates the relation between horse and trainer within the locale of the soul. Thus, in contrast to the *Apology,* where Socrates had compared himself to a gadfly or trainer taming his fellow citizens, the relationship has here been internalized: one now stands in relation to *oneself* as a trainer stands in relation to a horse. One must tame oneself, one must become moderate (*sōphrōn*), in order to live a good life. Moreover, the necessity of training, taming, and ruling oneself extends beyond one's own good; it is also necessary in order to be of any benefit to another. If, unlike the lovers of Lysias's speech and Socrates's first speech, the lover of Socrates's palinode has a salubrious relationship with his beloved, this is because his love has become *sōphrōn* (256a–b). Here, then, Plato underscores the importance of training, ruling, or governing oneself before taking up such a relation with another. In the context of the *Phaedrus*, this means that the lover must first tame him- or herself in order to benefit the beloved. In the context of the *Republic*, this means that one must first rule oneself before ruling others.

Because the possibility of governing others well depends upon the rule that one exercises over oneself, the importance of self-rule becomes paramount in the *Republic*. Having established through his conversation with Glaucon that care is concerned with and directed toward the good of the soul in its entirety, Socrates argues "that it is better for everyone to be governed by the divine and the intelligent [φρονίμου], preferably indwelling and his own, but in default of that imposed from without" (*Republic* 590d–e). Recognizing the best form of governance to be that which one exercises over oneself in the careful practice of *phronēsis*, Socrates concludes that external ruling structures, such as political and educational institutions, are, in the best of cases, subordinated to and enacted for the sake of developing the careful self-governance of those governed: "This is the purpose of the law, which is the ally of all classes in the state, and this is the aim of our control [ἀρχή] of children, our not leaving them free before we have established, so to speak, a constitutional government within them and, by fostering [θεραπεύσαντες] the best element in them with the aide of the like in ourselves, have set up in its place a similar guardian and ruler in the child, and then, and then only, we leave them free [ἐλεύθερον]" (590e–591a). Both the law and the education of the youth, if they are to perform their functions well, have one and the same concern: to care for the care that the citizenry exercises over itself and, in this way, to promote the freedom and self-governance of the citizenry. The concern over self-care is thus revealed to be a concern over freedom (ἡ ἐλευθερία). To care for oneself is to take over the governance of oneself. *The exercise of care is the exercise of freedom.* If, then, the existence of the best, or the second best, city demands that its citizens exercise care over themselves and each other, this is because it is conceived of as a *polis* of free citizens, where such freedom is identified with self-governance rather than with, for instance, the libertarian anarchy that Plato, in the *Republic*, found to be central to democracy.

Understanding the true *telos* of politics to be the liberation of the citizenry for the sake of their own self-governance, Socrates denies Glaucon's assertion that one who cares for him- or herself "will not willingly take part in politics." He responds to Glaucon with the following: "Yes, by the dog . . . in his own city he certainly will, yet perhaps not in the city of his birth, except in some providential conjuncture. . . . The politics of this city only will be his and of none other" (592a–

b). In these brief lines, we witness the complete unfolding of a Socratic *aporia*. Whereas in the *Apology* he had denounced his involvement in politics (30d), in the *Gorgias* Socrates claims to be "one of the few, not to say the only one, in Athens who attempts the true art of statesmanship, and the only man of the present time who manages affairs of state" (521d).[26] The apparent tension between these two positions—Socrates both is and is not engaged in politics—is resolved in the previous quote from the *Republic*, where politics is conceived of as operating on two structurally different levels. On the one hand, politics is identified with the administration and operation of the concrete mechanisms and institutions of the state or *polis*, such as the Assembly, Council, and courts. On the other hand, it is identified with the care and governance of souls. While Socrates does not practice the former, he does practice the latter, and this, that is to say, the care and governance of souls, he proclaims to be the true art of statesmanship.

And yet, if this passage from the *Republic* resolves the tension between Socrates's claim that he both does and does not practice politics, it has the opposite effect on our understanding of politics itself. Socrates inserts himself into the sphere of the political in such a way that he causes it to fracture. Moreover, this fracturing effects an internal hierarchization within the political: whereas the care of souls is understood to be the true form of politics, the administration and operation of the concrete mechanisms of state is, or at least tends to be, seen as a degraded form of politics. While the full implications of this schism cannot be addressed here, its most immediate and profound effect is to provide Socrates with a measure by which he is able to evaluate statesmanship and the statesman: because true statesmanship is concerned with souls rather than with institutions, the good statesman is identified not as the one who most effectively institutes laws and prosecutes wars but as the one who best conveys others to the good. This is to say that the true statesman is identified as the one who practices a politics of care.

In the *Gorgias*, Socrates articulates this politics of care by reference to an equine image wherein the bad statesman is likened to a herdsman or horse trainer who turns tame animals wild.

> SOCRATES: Well, at any rate a herdsman in charge of [ἐπιμελητὴς] asses or horses or oxen would be considered a bad one for being like that—if he took over animals that did not kick him or butt or bite, and in the result they were found to be doing all these things out of sheer wildness. Or do you not consider any keeper [ἐπιμελητὴς] of any animal whatever a bad one, if he turns out the creature he received tame [ἡμερώτερα] so much wilder [ἀγριώτερα] than he found it?
>
> CALLICLES: Certainly I do, to oblige you.
>
> SOCRATES: Then oblige me still further by answering this: is man [ὁ ἄνθρωπος] also one of the animals, or not?
>
> CALLICLES: Of course he is. (516a–b)

Contrary to the bad statesman, the good statestman, or, let us say, the good gadfly, like the good herdsman, cares for others by conducting them toward their own good, which, for horses and humans, entails that they be conducted toward tameness. This, of course, is not to say that the character and *telos* of such care is the same for both of these animals. Rather, the care of each is directed toward that which is appropriate to each as the animal that it is. Thus, the true art of statesmanship consists in caring for oneself and others, where such care has as its *telos* tameness and liberation understood as self-governance. As we have seen, it is philosophy, understood as the practice whereby one both preserves oneself within and awakens others to the finitude of human knowledge, that Plato marks out as the practice par excellence of conducting others toward that tameness which, far from being a state of docility, enables one to care for and govern oneself. This is to say that the politics of care is not a second- or third-tier concern appended to Socrates's practice of philosophy; it is rather that which organizes and motivates this practice.

Notes

1. Horses appear in no fewer than twenty of the dialogues—twenty-one if the *Hippias Major* is considered to be authentic—and are invoked in order to illustrate issues as varied as rhetoric (*Phaedrus* 260b–c), recollection (*Phaedo* 73e), eugenics (*Republic* 459b), education (*Republic* 413d; *Apology* 20a), ontological difference (*Phaedo* 78e), military training (*Republic* 467e, 537a), hedonism (*Philebus* 67b), and eroticism (*Phaedrus* 253d–254e).

2. Plato, *Apology*, trans. H. N. Fowler (Cambridge, Mass.: Harvard University Press, 1999). Socrates reiterates this assertion at *Apology* 36c and again at *Phaedo* 115b, where, in response to Crito asking if Socrates has any final directions for how his friends might serve him once he is dead, Socrates replies: "What I always say, Crito . . . nothing new. If you take care of yourselves [ἐπιμελούμενοι ὑμεῖς] you will serve me and mine and yourselves whatever you do" (Plato, *Phaedo*, trans. H. N. Fowler [Cambridge, Mass.: Harvard University Press, 1999]).

3. Justina Gregory, "Donkeys and the Equine Hierarchy in Archaic Greek Literature," *Classical Journal* 102, no. 3 (2007): 193–212.

4. Indeed, the use of the singular in the image of Athens as *a* horse reflects a subtle, yet significant, ambiguity running throughout Socrates's *apologia*, which vacillates almost imperceptibly between an account of his relation to the *polis* itself and his relation to its citizens. Even as he constructs the image of himself as a gadfly spurring on the horse of state, he underscores the fact that his bite is in fact always directed at each citizen individually: "I go about arousing, and persuading, and reproaching each one of you" (30e–31a). This movement between city and citizen, between *polis* and *politēs*, serves as an important counterpoint to Socrates's denial, only a few lines later, that he practices politics (31d), for it suggests not only that this denial is not tantamount to a rejection of philosophy's care for the *politeia* but that such care need not be practiced—indeed, that it is perhaps not even best practiced—through involvement in such political institutions as the Council, Assembly, and courts. See, also, *Apology* 36c.

5. At least this is what he attempts to do, though it must be admitted that texts such as the *Alcibiades*, *Meno*, and *Charmides* stand as testaments to Socrates's failure.

6. Plato, *Laws*, trans. R. G. Bury (Cambridge, Mass.: Harvard University Press, 2004).

7. It should be noted, however, that, owing to the apparently literal character of the reference in the *Laws*, Plato here includes a qualification that was not present in the *Apology*'s nearly insomniac vision of wakefulness; because care is of the body as well as of the soul, the salubriousness of wakefulness finds its limit point at the health of the body, which, Plato here concedes, requires sleep.

8. The translation is my own.

9. An examination of both ancient and modern texts dealing with the issue of horsemanship has revealed no evidence that multiple bridles would ever be used on one horse, regardless of how wild it may be. It is clear, however, from the context that the bridles referred to in this passage in the *Laws* represent all of those people within the city who care for and educate the youth. The definitive ancient source on the subject of horsemanship, Xenophon's *The Art of Horsemanship* (trans. Morris H. Morgan [New York: Dover, 2006]), limits its discussion of breaking horses to the sagacious recommendation that one leave it to a professional.

10. Here one sees that the city described in the *Laws* in fact resembles the image of Athens that Meletus offered when he claimed that all of its citizens, with the exception of Socrates, improved the youth, whereas Socrates alone corrupted them (*Apology* 24c–25c). With the description of the second-best city in the *Laws*, Plato affirms the utmost desirability of such a city as Meletus envisioned Athens to be, that is, one in which the average citizen would have a beneficial rather than deleterious effect on the youth. However, in affirming this, Plato simultaneously affirms that such a city is possible only if, as Socrates advocated, each citizen cares for him/herself and others. Hence the practice of the care of the self and others that Socrates's accusers perceived to be a threat to the very lifeblood of the *polis* was in fact that which would have fulfilled the promise that these accusers believed Athens to hold.

11. In the *Statesman* (trans. H. N. Fowler [Cambridge, Mass.: Harvard University Press, 1995]), tameness (ἡμερότης) is identified as being a potentiality or faculty of the soul; thus any animal whose "nature admits of domestication [may be] called tame" (264a).

12. For instance, when discussing care (θεραπεία) in the *Euthyphro* (trans. H. N. Fowler [Cambridge, Mass.: Harvard University Press, 1999]), Socrates claims that "it aims at some good or benefit to the one to who it is given, as you see that horses, when attended to by the horseman's art are benefited and made better" (13b).

13. This is not to say that human duality accounts for all of Plato's references to horses. As I noted previously, Plato makes reference to horses in order to express a remarkably broad range of philosophical issues, and it would, as such, be impossible to address them all in this essay; I have limited my analysis to those instances of human equinity pertaining to the confrontation between our wildness and tameness.

14. Aristotle makes a claim strikingly similar to Plato's: "For as man [ἄνθρωπος] is the best of the animals when perfected, so he is the worst of all when sundered from law and justice. For unrighteousness is most pernicious when possessed of weapons, and man is born possessing weapons for the use of wisdom and virtue [φρονήσει καὶ ἀρετῇ], which it is possible to employ for the opposite ends. Hence when devoid of virtue man is the most unscrupulous and savage of animals" (*Politics*, trans. H. Rackham [Cambridge, Mass.: Harvard University Press, 1998], 1235a33–39).

15. According to the *Statesman*, in the Age of Cronos, an age that preceded the advent of the *polis*, "no creature was wild" (271e).

16. Indeed, the anxiety brought about by this unrelenting imperative accounts for the *Republic*'s unbridled concern with the development and implementation of a multitude of techniques intended both to effect the formation of certain types of individuals and prevent the development of others.

17. In the *Statesman*, for instance, Plato replaces the timocratic regime of the *Republic* with an aristocracy and divides democracy into two regimes, the worst form of which borders on oligarchy, not tyranny (*Statesman* 291d–292a).

18. While defining the democratic man, Socrates had divided desires into those that are necessary (i.e., implanted within us by nature), such as the desire for foods conducive to health, and those that are unnecessary (i.e., developed through habituation), such as relishes, which are eaten irrespective of their nutritional value (558d–559c). By way of introducing the tyrant, Socrates further divides the unnecessary desires into those that are lawful and those that are lawless (571a–b).

19. At the beginning of Book 9, Socrates provides detailed instructions for remaining temperate and avoiding, to the greatest extent possible, the presence of unlawful desires even when asleep (571d–572b).

20. Socrates repeats this sentiment at 576b, saying that the tyrant "is, I presume, the man who, in his waking hours, has the qualities we found in his dream state."

21. This is Allan Bloom's translation (New York: BasicBooks, 1986). Shorey consistently and problematically translates ἄνθρωπος as "man," thereby insinuating into this passage a gendering of humanity that does not appear in the Greek.

22. This is not to say that there are not important differences between the two accounts. For instance, the *Phaedrus* places a far greater emphasis on the role of *eros* than does the *Republic*, whereas the *Republic* places a greater emphasis on the factious and multifarious nature of the desires than does the *Phaedrus*.

23. While the white horse is never identified as such, it is generally assumed that, in light of the tripartition of the soul in the *Republic*, this is a representation of spirit or *thumos*.

24. Elizabeth Belfiore, "Dancing with the Gods: The Myth of the Chariot in Plato's 'Phaedrus,'" *American Journal of Philology* 127, no. 2 (2006): 185–217.

25. For a further discussion of the important role that the dark horse plays in the soul's recollection of beauty, see Jill Gordon, *Plato's Erotic World: From Cosmic Origins to Human Death* (New York: Cambridge University Press, 2012), 103–104.

26. Plato, *Gorgias*, trans. W. R. M. Lamb (Cambridge, Mass.: Harvard University Press, 2001).

8 Who Let the Dogs Out?
Tracking the Philosophical Life among the Wolves and Dogs of the Republic

Christopher P. Long

> The wolf exerts a powerful influence on the human imagination. It takes your stare and turns it back on you.
> —Barry Lopez, *Of Wolves and Men*

> Philosophies diffuse odors.
> —George Santayana, *Dialogues in Limbo*

THE COMPLEX OLFACTORY communication practices of wolf scent-marking remain in many ways a mystery to us. But for the wolves themselves, who make or inspect a scent mark once every two minutes, olfactory communication must play a rather important role in their relations with one another and the wider world they inhabit.[1] Although scent-marking in wolves is thought to be in part an attempt to warn off intruders, some research suggests that it is used as a kind of "cognitive map" for members of the pack to find their way through the home territory by locating sources of water and standard hunting trails.[2] Of course, for the breed of philosophers who seek meaningful pathways through the territory of our most ancient and familiar textual homes, the eyes, ears, and even the sense of taste have long been faithful guides, while the nose has remained always ancillary.[3] Perhaps it is a species problem, for as Aristotle notes in the *De Anima* with respect to smell, "we do not have precision in this power of perceiving, but are inferior to many animals."[4] And yet, the wolves, and their more domesticated descendants, the dogs, may be onto something.[5]

In his rich and engaging *Dialogues in Limbo*, George Santayana imagines himself entering into conversation with immortal dead philosophical figures, the first of whom, Democritus, insists that "a philosophy can be smelt."[6] In discussion with Alcibiades, Democritus claims: "Hence, though it be a delicate matter and not accomplished without training, it is possible for a practiced nose to distinguish the precise quality of a philosopher by his peculiar odor, just as a hound by the mere scent can tell a fox from a boar."[7] However comical, Santayana's Democritus, like our wolves and dogs, may be on to something. Perhaps the nose knows something of philosophy, if only we would attend to it as we navigate the territory of our most familiar textual homes. There is arguably no home more familiar and no text more odiferous than Plato's *Republic*. So perhaps something of Plato's quality as a philosopher and of Socrates's attempt in the dialogue to sniff out the longer road toward a philosophical life may be discerned by tracking the scent of wolves and dogs in the *Republic*.[8]

Despite its rather peculiar absence of any thematization of smell or smelling as a mode of perceiving, Plato's *Republic* reeks of various animals, but the smell of wolves and dogs permeates the text with striking pungency. The scent-markings of the canines in the *Republic* leave a trail that might itself be used as a kind of cognitive map leading us to one of the central teachings of the text itself: that the philosophical life is situated precariously between the tyrannical tendencies of the wolf and the blind obedience of the well-trained dog.

The Scent of the Wolf

The first hint of the presence of wolves in the *Republic* can be discerned even before one attacks Socrates in the form of the "wild beast" that is Thrasymachus. Autolykos, Odysseus's cunning maternal grandfather, appears at a turning point of the discussion Socrates has with Polemarchus about the nature of justice.[9] The appearance of Autolykos, the "lone wolf," marks the moment when Polemarchus, having so eagerly taken up the question of justice inherited from his father, Cephalus, begins to wonder if he himself understands what he meant when he insisted that "justice is helping friends and harming enemies" (334a–b). Socrates brings him to this recognition by insisting that Autolykos would be the embodiment of justice on the account Polemarchus had been defending. Citing Homer, Socrates emphasizes that Autolykos is said "to excel all human-beings in stealing and swearing oaths" (334b).[10] The appeal to Autolykos has a strong effect on Polemarchus, for he would rather relinquish his previous position than endorse a conception of justice that would elevate the "wolf itself" as a paragon. In Homer, Autolykos is said to have learned his skills of lying and thievery from Hermes, the trickster god, so well versed in using verbal equivocation to gain advantage. His name, Autolykos, the "lone wolf" or the "wolf itself," like the name he gave Odysseus, is rife with significance. Homer tells us that Autolykos named Odysseus after his own nature; since he himself was hated (ὀδυσσάμενος) by many men and women throughout the land, his grandson should have the name Odysseus.[11]

This hatred is one side of the rather equivocal attitude the Greek mythical tradition has toward the figure of the wolf. On the one hand, the wolf, as Richard Buxton suggests, "stands for one who by his behavior has set himself beyond humanity."[12] This is particularly true of the "lone wolf," a figure isolated from human and lupine community alike. Connected to this, of course, is the idea, embodied by Odysseus's grandfather, of cunning criminality. In *Pythian 2*, Pindar emphasizes this cunning in a passage that resonates deeply with the conception of justice for which Polemarchus advocates: "May I love my friend; but against my enemy I shall make a secret attack, like a wolf, treading now here now there on my crooked paths."[13] This dimension of the lupine character is what drives Polemarchus to recognize the limits of his own position. On the other hand, however, because of its cooperative nature, its social life together with others in a pack, and its practices of collaborative hunting and of the equitable sharing of quarry, the wolf also stood in the Greek mythological tradition as a symbol of community and even as an analogue for human social life.[14] This strand of the tradition finds further expression in the treatment of domesticated dogs; and Socrates himself draws upon it during his discussion of the second wave in *Republic* 5 when he suggests that the guardians, men and women alike, should share all pursuits in common, "like dogs" (466d).[15]

These two dimensions of the wolf, its connection with the early phases of domesticated civilization and its recalcitrant segregation from communal life, can be discerned in the very ancient story of Lycaon in Arcadia. Lycaon's father, Pelasgus, was said to be the first to settle the land, building shelter and clothing the people in sheepskins. These civilizing efforts were continued by Lycaon, who founded a city and established games in honor of Zeus. "But," as Pausanias reports, "Lycaon brought a human baby to the altar of Lycaean Zeus, and sacrificed it, pouring out its blood upon the altar, and according to legend immediately after the sacrifice he was changed from a man to a wolf [λύκον]."[16] Civilization is not established without cost; and although the figure of the wolf here appears only at the moment of exile, a hint of its civilizing effect can be discerned already in the sheepskins Pelasgus used to clothe his people against the cold.[17]

If the wolf signifies the emergence and possible dissolution of community in the logic of Greek mythology, then it is perhaps no surprise that the scent of Autolykos marks the moment Polemarchus recognizes the limitations of his own understanding of justice and agrees ultimately to join Socrates "to do battle then as partners" (*Republic* 335e).[18] We might, then, discern something sweet in the scent left by this first mark of the wolf in the *Republic*; yet something more malodorous remains, for the final mark of the wolf in the *Republic* is found in Book 8, when Socrates appeals to the story of Lycaon to articulate the manner in which the just leader metabolizes into the tyrant (565d). The wolf then marks the moment of the emergence of the possibility of community in Book 1 and a decisive point in its dissolution in Book 8; between these markings of the wolf, however, the scent of its more domesticated cousin, the dog, emerges as dominant. Following the canine scent that permeates the text between the first and last appearances of the wolf will put us on the trail of the philosopher and the just life that is possible when a desire for the Good is cultivated in an excellent soul set upon the trail of dialectic.

A Whiff of the Dog, the Savagery of the Wolf

The first appearance of the dog in the *Republic* points in this direction. Its distinct scent marks the first appearance of *aretē*—excellence or virtue—in the dialogue, although the smell of horses is also in the air. Socrates first touches upon the question of excellence by appealing to the virtue of dogs (335b). At the end of his discussion with Polemarchus, having convinced him that "it is just to do good to a friend, if the friend is good, and harm to an enemy, if bad," Socrates turns his attention to the impact unjust actions have on other living things. Here he solicits agreement from Polemarchus that when a horse is harmed, it is made worse, not better. Socrates then asks Polemarchus if harming a horse makes it worse "with respect to the virtue of dogs or to that of horses" (335b). In agreeing that what it means to be an excellent dog is different from what it means to be an excellent horse or human being, and that harming and doing good to each can ruin or cultivate the virtue of each, Polemarchus is led ultimately to the conclusion that "it is never just to harm anyone" (335e). This preliminary conclusion about the nature of justice is the basis upon which Socrates and Polemarchus agree "to do battle as partners" against those who claim otherwise; and sure enough, it is also the moment when they are attacked by Thrasymachus, a wolf among those gathered.

Although Socrates does not explicitly call Thrasymachus a wolf, he says that as they were talking Thrasymachus was "restrained by the men sitting near him" and then, "hunched up like a wild beast [θηρίον], he came at us as if to tear us to pieces" (336b). That Socrates has a wolf in mind, however, is made clear when, after Thrasymachus attacks him for speaking nonsense, he says: "I was thoroughly amazed hearing these things and, seeing him, I was terrified; and it seemed to me that if I had not seen him before he'd seen me, I would have become voiceless. But as it was, just when he first was made savage [ἐξαγριαίνεσθαι] by the argument, I looked at him first, so that I was able to answer" (336d–e). This seems to be the first articulation in literature of the ancient proverbial belief that being seen first by a wolf renders a person speechless.[19] It is perhaps not unreasonable to think that the first appearance of the "lone wolf" in the argument with Polemarchus was what set Thrasymachus back on his haunches. Socrates would perhaps have noticed then that Thrasymachus was being "made savage" just as Polemarchus was being tamed. Indeed, the stance Thrasymachus takes—that justice is the advantage of the stronger—is itself simply a more extreme and savage stance than the position Polemarchus defended and then relinquished (338c). Thrasymachus's harsh position dovetails with his harsh disposition, which becomes yet more savage the closer Socrates comes to establishing among those gathered a community oriented by a concern for the question of justice. This vacillation between the savage and the tame, the wild and the domesticated, is a trope running through the entire dialogue, though it is most poignant here in Socrates's encounter with Thrasymachus. It is no surprise, then, to catch the scent of tyranny in the things Thrasymachus says, and to find the distinction between tyranny and democracy emerging as a central concern of a discussion that increasingly focuses on the question of just rule and the nature of the just human being.[20] Thus the entire question of the nature of a just ruler and, by extension, of what it is to embody the excellence of justice emerges in an atmosphere thick with the savage scent of the wolf, even if it is also already marked by the virtue of the more domesticated dog.

Thrasymachus himself seems particularly resistant to domestication throughout the dialogue, though this initial encounter is a powerful demonstration of Socrates's ability to tame the wolf.[21] Although his resistance has already been suggested by the vicious response Thrasymachus has to the emerging community between Socrates and Polemarchus, it is reinforced again when, just as Socrates has those gathered convinced that the good ruler cares about the advantage of the ruled, Thrasymachus lashes out again in a particularly demeaning manner, asking Socrates if he has a wet nurse and insisting that his nose needs a wiping because he does not recognize the dynamics of the relationship between sheep and shepherd (334a). Here Thrasymachus draws on a long tradition, one heard already in Homer's standard epithet for Agamemnon as "shepherd of the people," which identifies political leadership with shepherding.[22] The analogy is introduced, however, in order to argue that tyranny, "the most perfect injustice," makes one the happiest (344a). Immediately upon articulating this position, Thrasymachus sought to leave, but, as Socrates reports, "he was forced to remain by those present" (344d). With Thrasymachus so restrained, Socrates identifies the central concern of the entire dialogue, which is not really justice per se but rather "the course of a whole life, on the basis of which each of us would live a most profitable [λυσιτελεστάτην] life" (344e). By putting it in terms of profitability here, Socrates intends to shift the very meaning of what is valuable. If Thrasymachus understands justice and the good life it enables in terms of the self-interest of the stronger, Socrates will lead those gathered at the home of Cephalus to recognize as most profitable and stronger the life of justice and virtue. Thus, already in the first book, Socrates confronts Glaucon with the central choice of the dialogue: Thrasymachus "'claims that the life of the unjust person is stronger than that of the just person. Which do you choose, Glaucon,' I said, 'and which of the two things said seems to you to be truer?'" To this Glaucon replied: "I, indeed, say that the life of the just person is the more profitable [λυσιτελέστερον]" (347e).

The question is directed to Glaucon, who emerges in the middle of the discussion with Thrasymachus to become the central figure of the dialogue. Glaucon is the one with whom the main teachings of the dialogue find articulation and the one toward whom Socrates directs his most poignant questions. The community Socrates establishes with Glaucon in the *Republic* is the only city founded in deed rather than merely in speech.²³ Here, in fact, is the moment when Socrates appeals to the image of jurors in a court of law, and it is Glaucon who agrees that it will be best if they proceed as judges and speakers both (348b).²⁴ On the basis of this procedure, Socrates seeks to found a community animated by a concern for justice among those gathered. But before that community can be established, Thrasymachus has to be tamed by being shown the dysfunctional nature of injustice and tyrannical rule. This Socrates does in part by appealing to the training of animals, and specifically horses, to illustrate first, that each being has a particular work [ἔργον] proper to it in which it can excel and second, that the proper work of human being is to live well. Such a life, however, requires an orientation toward justice (352d–354a).²⁵

The smell of horses here draws our attention back to the argument with Polemarchus and the possible community that emerged there. Indeed, these passages are braided tightly into that discussion with Polemarchus in three discernible strands. First, there is a structural parallel between the shifting positions of Polemarchus and Thrasymachus: the former moves from his original position that justice is harming enemies and benefiting friends to the view that "it is never just to harm anyone," while the latter moves from the claim that justice is "the advantage of the stronger" toward the begrudging recognition that justice is a certain way of life.²⁶ Second, an appeal to animal training generally and to the training of horses in particular punctuates Socrates's introduction of the question of virtue with Polemarchus and his introduction of the proper work of a being in his discussion with Thrasymachus (352d). Finally, if the virulence of the wolf is provoked the moment Socrates appeals to Autolykos and begins to establish a philosophical friendship with Polemarchus, by the end of Socrates's discussion with Thrasymachus the wolf himself has ultimately "grown gentle [πρᾶος ἐγένου]" and has "ceased being hard [χαλεπαίνων ἐπαύσω]" (354a).

With these words—πρᾶος and χαλεπός, gentle and hard—the pungent scent of the wolf disperses, giving way to the discernable smell of the dog. The words themselves point to what is perhaps the most famous reference to dogs in the *Republic*, the moment when Socrates compares the guardians of his more luxurious city in speech to "noble puppies." There he goes so far as to suggest to Glaucon that such dogs are "truly philosophic" (375e, 376b). Let us follow the scent.

Philosopher Dogs and Kings

Like a dog with a stick, Socrates plays with words. Having turned Glaucon's attention to the unhealthy, "feverish" city, Socrates insists that there will be a need for guardians who will be fierce to enemies and yet gentle to citizens. He puts it this way: "Don't you think . . . that for guarding [εἰς φυλακὴν] there is any difference between the nature of a noble puppy [γενναίου σκύλακος] and that of a well-bred young man?" (375a). The words put Glaucon—and us—on alert: this analogy is playful; but as with all Socratic playfulness, something important is at play.

What Socrates says here with respect to the analogy between dogs and boys points at once back to his discussion with Polemarchus and Thrasymachus and forward to his account of the philosopher king. Linguistically, Socrates situates the nature of the dog and thus of its analogue, the guardian, between gentleness and savagery. In this way, he gestures back to the appearance of Thrasymachus, now tamed. The language is striking. Socrates asks Glaucon about the spirited nature of dogs, wondering "how will they not be savage [ἄγριοι] with one another and the other citizens?" And he continues: "But, indeed, it is necessary for them to be gentle [πράους] toward their own but hard [χαλεπούς] on their enemies" (375b–c). The words recall the position Polemarchus originally defended, namely, that "justice is helping friends and harming enemies," and they echo those that mark the taming of the wolf at the end of Book 1 (334a–b, 354a). Thrasymachus, who first appeared having been "made savage"—ἐξαγριαίνεσθαι—by the discussion with Polemarchus, is ultimately "made gentle" by the words Socrates speaks. The entire encounter with Thrasymachus is thus woven deeply into the texture of this passage about guardians and dogs.

If, however, the bark of the wolf can still be heard among the guardian dogs, we catch here too the first scent of the philosopher. Socrates evokes the "image [εἰκών]" of the noble dog in order to suggest that there are, in nature, animals who are at once gentle and great-spirited, but he goes on to insist that a guardian will, like a noble dog, "need, in addition to spiritedness [θυμοειδεῖ], also to be a philosopher [φιλόσοφος] according to nature" (375c–e). This marks the first appearance of the word φιλόσοφος in the dialogue.[27] The analogy is further fleshed out by the suggestion that both the philosopher and the dog "distinguish friendly from hostile looks by nothing other than by having learned the one and by being ignorant of the other" (376b). Here again the passage is Janus-faced, pointing back to Polemarchus's original articulation of justice and forward to the laughable suggestion in Book 5 that unless philosophers rule like kings, the city they have founded in speech will never "come forth by nature" (473e).[28] The scent of the noble dog, embodying at once the opposing characteristics of moderate gentleness and spirited ferocity, marks the site at which the connection between spiritedness and philosophy is first introduced into the dialogue. This scent-marking points already to the discussion of the philosopher king in Book 5, and, even beyond it, to the "longer road" that leads to the heart of Socrates's teaching about the power of dialectic and the philosophical life animated by a desire for wisdom.[29]

The appeal to noble puppies here in Book 2 points more immediately, however, to the question of the proper education of the guardians; although in their natures they are "philosophic, spirited, swift and strong," they must nevertheless be "reared and educated" in order to become gentle to their own and fierce to their enemies (376c).³⁰ In Book 3, we encounter a series of markers leading to the heart of Socrates's proposed education for the guardians; but the further we follow, the more the education of humans is reduced to the training of dogs, with the virtue of moderation emerging as primary. Music, in this context, becomes central to the proposed training, for music is capable of cultivating moderation in the soul.³¹ The scent of the "wild beast [θηρίον]" that is Thrasymachus reasserts itself in this context; for Socrates insists that a person who is "not trained [τρεφόμενον] and whose abilities to perceive are not purified" is the sort of person who "becomes a misologist and unmusical. For he no longer uses persuasion through words, but brings things about through force and savageness [ἀγριότητι], like a wild beast [θηρίον], and he lives in ignorance and awkwardly without rhythm and grace" (411d–e). A terrifying picture of this awkward life without rhythm was presented in the encounter with Thrasymachus, when he appeared to threaten the community that was emerging between Socrates and Polemarchus. In that context, Thrasymachus himself introduced the traditional image of the shepherd and sheep to characterize the proper relationship between a ruler and the ruled. Here, however, that image reappears, but Socrates has now shifted the focus to the proper training of dogs to protect the flock: "For indeed, the most terrible and shameful thing of all is for a shepherd to train [τρέφειν] dogs as assistants with the result that by intemperance or hunger or some other bad habit, the dogs themselves attempt to do harm to the sheep and instead of dogs become like wolves."³² The language of "training" is here amplified and the concern that the guardians not become "like wolves" made explicit.

Socrates develops this image yet further at the end of Book 4 as he introduces the spirited dimension of the soul between the logistical aspect and the part without *logos*.³³ There the tripartite soul is thought not in terms of the metaphor of shepherd and sheep but in terms of the relationship between the shepherd and his well-trained dogs. Socrates appeals to this image to illustrate how a just person will endure injustice. Such a person, when treated unjustly, will doggedly continue to attempt to do noble deeds, "having been called by the words in him like [a dog] called by a herdsman" (440d). Glaucon grasps the image immediately and makes it explicit: "we posited the guardians in our city like dogs obedient to the rulers, who are like the shepherds of the city" (440d). The imagery here of the guardians trained like dogs anticipates the bestiary that is Book 5 of the *Republic*.³⁴ The scent of the dog thus leads us directly into Book 5, where it mingles with all three of the waves Socrates identifies as crashing down upon him.³⁵

Playing in the Waves

If, as we have discerned, wolves have long stood as an analogue for the more cooperative dimensions of human life, even as they also often signify isolation and the breakdown of community, the scent of dogs that marks the first two waves Socrates encounters in Book 5 punctuates the more cooperative aspects of their character. Socrates introduces the first wave—that the male and female guardians should share all pursuits in common—by appealing explicitly to the behavior of dogs (451c–e). Female and male dogs guard the same things, they hunt together, indeed do "everything in common [κοινῇ πάντα]" (451e). As a result, according to Socrates, they must be given "the same rearing and education [τὴν τροφήν τε καὶ παιδείαν]" (451e). Here, where education is reduced to a kind of training, the analogy between guardians and dogs begins to stink. The stench emanates not from the fragrant idea that women and men ought to be treated equally but from the fetid suggestion that education is conditioning. The second wave Socrates seeks to navigate renders the analogy yet more rank; for with it comes not simply the notion that women and children should be shared in common, but also that the guardians must be pure-bred like animals (457c–461e). Socrates here proposes to Glaucon, who, perhaps because he is both erotic and musical, is well versed in the breeding of noble animals, that the guardians will need to be bred in a manner much like he breeds his own hunting dogs (459a–466d).[36]

The scent of the dog has thus led us to the third, "biggest and most difficult [χαλεπώτατον]" wave—that philosophers should rule as kings (472a, 473e). Indeed, already with the earlier suggestion that dogs were the most philosophical of animals, the trail had been established. That trail, however, is an upward road that does not end with the introduction of the philosopher king; rather, the appeal to the philosopher king is articulated within a generally comic context in which human beings are understood in bestial terms. And yet, here, with the suggestion that the ruler must be erotic, we have already been moved beyond the image of the philosophical dog; for earlier, Socrates had emphasized the importance of a love of learning, and of the need to learn—albeit perhaps by training—the difference between what is one's own and what is hostile. Here, however, this love of learning is pushed further toward a love of the whole; for Socrates insists that love is not of a part but of the whole and that "a philosopher desires [ἐπιθυμεῖν] wisdom, not a part of it, but all of it" (475b). Thus, however comical the introduction of the philosopher king may be, it marks an important moment along a longer path toward a deeper understanding of what it is to live a philosophical life. Indeed, if we reinscribe this discussion here back into Socrates's original suggestion that we might discern something of the nature of justice in the soul by writing it large into the city, and if we recall that the entire discussion of dogs and wolves concerns the proper role of the thumotic dimension of the soul in relation to the logistic and a-logical aspects, we might pick up the scent of the philosophical life itself. That life, to be sure, requires more than a certain training concerning the friendly and the hostile; it involves more than breeding a community of noble animals by well-intentioned, calculative shepherds; it also requires some familiarity with what is proper and a desire to integrate a sense of the good into the whole in which we together live. We thus catch something of the scent of the life to which Socrates calls Glaucon in the things said about philosophical dogs and kings.

Toward a Philosophical Life

The canine scent-markings we have thus far been following seem here to point to the central teachings of the dialogue and, indeed, even to territory that lies beyond the *Republic* itself along the longer road Socrates suggests that he and Glaucon would need to follow in order to discern the nature of justice. Socrates first mentions this longer road when he and Glaucon turn from their attempt to seek justice in the city to an attempt to locate it in the "single person" (434d–e).[37] Socrates points to the inadequacy of the road on which their current argument has progressed at precisely the moment they begin to consider the tripartite soul and the proper role spiritedness plays in orienting a person toward the Good. This too is the general context marked by the scent of wolves and dogs; for the image of noble dogs trained by caring shepherds seems to be the analogue of a well-bred soul whose spirited dimension has been properly trained to heed the commands of its logistical side. The longer road is, however, mentioned a second time in the dialogue, in Book 6, where the concern has become a proper philosophical education. There Socrates rehearses with Adeimantus the path they have traversed, dividing the soul into three forms and seeking justice, moderation, courage, and wisdom; but he insists that a finer look at these things would require "another and longer road" (504a–b).[38] The formulation suggests not simply that the course they have thus far traversed needs to be pursued yet further, but that there may be another road altogether that would afford "the finest possible" look at these things. There is, of course, controversy concerning the nature of this other, longer road, and, specifically, whether the road on which Socrates is compelled by Glaucon to embark is the beginning of that longer road or a longer way down the path of an inadequate trail.[39] Glaucon forces Socrates further down a path he is hesitant to take, a path that requires him to articulate the nature of the Good Itself and education in gymnastics, mathematics, and ultimately dialectic. Along this road Socrates is reticent to take, the scent of dogs is in the air, pointing in the direction of the longer road to which Socrates gestures. For in the final step of his account of the education that would be necessary for the guardians to become philosophers, Socrates comes to the highest study: dialectic. He describes how one engaged in dialectic attempts "by argument without the use of any of the senses—to attain each thing itself that *is* and doesn't give up before he grasps by intellection itself that which is good itself" (532a–b). When Glaucon presses Socrates to proceed to the dialectic itself, which he describes as a "haven from the road," Socrates refuses, insisting instead: "You will no longer be able to follow, my dear Glaucon . . . although there would not be any lack of eagerness on my part. But you would no longer be seeing an image of what we are saying, but rather, the truth itself, at least as it looks to me. Whether it is really so or not can no longer be properly insisted upon. But that there is some such thing to see must be insisted on" (533a). Socrates denies Glaucon's desire for a haven from the road only to redirect his thumotic energy toward the posited ideal of the Good. His insistence that there is such an ideal is rooted in his recognition that the Good Itself is "beyond being" and thus beyond even the power of the intellect to discern. By positing the Good Itself as an erotic ideal, however, Socrates encourages Glaucon to orient his life toward the Good, and challenges him to weave this love of the Good into community with others (509b).[40] That Glaucon might choose such a life was already suggested at the end of Socrates's encounter with Thrasymachus, when he expressed a willingness to embrace the life of a just person as more profitable.

In giving Glaucon a taste of dialectic, Socrates treats him like a well-bred dog. Indeed, Socrates appeals twice at the end of Book 7 to the analogy between dogs and the children they have been educating in speech. First, in order to discern who might demonstrate a readiness for war, he suggests that children be led to war as spectators and permitted, when it is safe, to experience and "taste blood, like puppies" (537a). Second, however, Socrates warns that although a similar dynamic is at play with regard to speeches, they must take great care not to allow young people to be exposed too soon, for "when young boys get their first taste of them, they misuse them as though it were play, always using them to contradict; and imitating those men by whom they are refuted, they themselves refute others, like puppies enjoying pulling and tearing with argument at those who happen to be near" (539b). Glaucon emerged from the encounter with the tamed wolf, Thrasymachus, as the readiest of the young men there present to receive a taste of dialectic; and when Socrates has finally made Glaucon eager for the path of dialectic itself, he transfers his desire for a haven from the road toward another, longer road: a life of questioning oriented by a concern for the good and a desire for justice.

If the scent of dogs in the *Republic* has led to the beginning of this longer road, the final appearance of the wolf in the dialogue reinforces the danger endemic to those who develop a taste for injustice and allow it to guide their lives. As he charts the transition from democratic leadership to tyrannical rule, Socrates appeals to the story of Lycaon. There he suggests that just as Lycaon was turned into a wolf the moment he tasted human innards mixed with other sacrificial victims, so too does the leader become a tyrant as soon as he sheds the blood of his tribe and acts unjustly against the citizens. After such injustices, Socrates suggests, such a man will either be killed by the people "or be a tyrant and turn from a human being into a wolf" (565d–566a). This last mark of the wolf in the dialogue evokes the memory of the first appearance of the "wolf itself," Autolykos, that odious figure who turned Polemarchus away from his own misguided sense for the nature of justice and toward a friendship with Socrates that was inherited ultimately by Glaucon. The scent of dogs marks important moments of Glaucon's developing friendship with Socrates, the philosopher, and points to a philosophical life oriented by a desire for the good and animated by the attempt to put justice into words. The scent-markings of the canines in the *Republic* seem thus to have led us to the longer road that charts a new territory beyond the text, toward a philosophical life in which a desire for the Good is permitted to inform our relationships with one another.

Notes

1. Barry Holstun Lopez, *Of Wolves and Men* (New York: Scribner Classics, 2004), 48.
2. One sign that the complex function of wolf scent-marking remains something of a mystery is a slight disagreement among researchers as to its primary function. Some, like L. David Mech and Luigi Biotani, argue that "one of its most important functions is to deter neighbors from intruding." See "Wolf Social Ecology," in *Wolves: Behavior, Ecology, and Conservation* (Chicago: University of Chicago Press, 2003), 26. Roger Peters, however, argues that the primary function of wolf scent-marking is to establish cognitive maps for the pack to successfully navigate its territory; see Roger P. Peters, "Mental Maps in Wolves," in *The Behavior and Ecology of Wolves: Proceedings of the Symposium on the Behavior and Ecology of Wolves Held on May 23–24, 1975 at the Annual Meeting of the Animal Behavior Society in Wilmington, N.C.*, ed. Erich Klinghammer, Garland Series in Ethology (New York: Garland STPM Press, 1979), 119–152.
3. A hint of this is discernable in *Truth and Method*, Gadamer's seminal articulation of hermeneutics. There we see the "fusion of horizons" and "insight" as "part of the vocation of man." See Hans-Georg Gadamer, *Truth and Method*, 2nd ed. (New York: Continuum Press, 1994), 306–307 and 356. We hear further that the openness of understanding is a kind of "hearing," and we sense that "taste undoubtedly implies a *mode of knowing*." See ibid., 361 and 36, respectively.
4. Aristotle, *De Anima* (Oxford: Oxford University Press, 1988), 2.9, 421a9–10. Translations from the Greek of Aristotle and Plato are my own.
5. The fossil record, anatomy, behavior, and genetics of the modern dog suggest that its origins may be found in the wolf. See Douglas J. Brewer, "The Evolution of the Modern Dog," in *Dogs in Antiquity: Anubis to Cerberus: The Origins of the Domestic Dog*, ed. Douglas J. Brewer, Sir Terence Clark, and Adrian Phillips (Warminster, England: Aris & Phillips, 2002), 5–20.
6. George Santayana, *Dialogues in Limbo: With Three New Dialogues* (Ann Arbor, Mich.: University of Michigan Press, 1957), 1.
7. Ibid., 4.
8. If Xenophon's *Symposium* is to be believed, Socrates himself anticipated the suggestion that smell might be a sense of philosophical discernment. That dialogue takes place at the house of Callias, where Socrates and others gathered to celebrate the victory of Autolycus at the pancratium. Autolycus, a young man with whom Callias was in love, was accompanied by his father, Lycon. Their names evoke the Greek, λύκος, *wolf*. Surrounded in this way by *wolves*, they turn their attention to beautiful odors, and Lycon asks Socrates: "What should our dis-

tinguishing scent be?" To which Socrates replies: "of the beautiful and good [καλοκἀγαθίας], by god." See Xenophon, *Opera Omnia*, vol. 2, 2nd ed. (Oxford: Clarendon Press, 1921), *Symposium*, 2.4.

9. Plato, *Opera*, vol. 4 (Oxford: Oxford University Press, 1992), *Republic*, 336b.

10. See, too, Homer, *Odyssea*, ed. Peter von der Mühll (Basel: Helbing and Lichenthahn, 1993), 19. 395–396.

11. *Odyssey*, 19. 407–409. For a discussion of the etymological origins of Odysseus's name and of whether or not the word ὀδυσσάμενος should be translated in an active or passive sense, Odysseus being "the man who suffers or inflicts pain, the Hated or Hater," see Norman Austin, "Name Magic in the 'Odyssey,'" *California Studies in Classical Antiquity* 5 (1972): 2–3.

12. Richard Buxton, "Wolves and Werewolves in Ancient Greek Thought," in *Interpretations of Greek Mythology*, ed. Jan N. Bremmer (London: Croom Helm, 1987), 69.

13. See Pindar, *Carmina Cum Fragmentis*, ed. Herwig Maehler and Bruno Snell, Bibliotheca Scriptorum Graecorum Et Romanorum Teubneriana (Leipzig: Teubner, 1987), 2:83–85. This translation is from Buxton, "Wolves and Werewolves in Ancient Greek Thought," 64.

14. Buxton, "Wolves and Werewolves in Ancient Greek Thought," 62–67. Buxton eloquently articulates these two dimensions of the figure of the wolf in the Greek mythical tradition. He reminds us too that "the origins of Rome were perceived as lying with a renegade band of young men, led by the foster-children of the she-wolf—outsiders in co-operation" (ibid., 76n14).

15. The second wave is introduced at 457b–c.

16. Pausanias, *Description of Greece* (Cambridge, Mass.: Harvard University Press), 8.2. Elements of this retelling of the myth have been informed by the account offered in Buxton, "Wolves and Werewolves in Ancient Greek Thought," 72–73.

17. Pausanias, *Description of Greece*, 8.1.5.

18. There Socrates says μαχούμεθα—"we will do battle." The word itself is used to refer to battles between humans and beasts alike. For an example of its use in relation to beasts, see Homer, *Ilias*, ed. Thomas W. Allen (Oxonii: e typographeo Clarendoniano, 1931), 16.824.

19. For a discussion of the origins and later articulations of the proverb, see Alexandra Pappas, "Remember to Cry Wolf: Visual and Verbal Declarations of Lykos Kalos," in *Orality, Literacy, Memory in the Ancient Greek and Roman World*, ed. E. A. Mackay (Leiden, Netherlands: Brill, 2008), 98–100.

20. This issue is introduced at *Republic* 338d.

21. Thrasymachus is portrayed not only as a wolf but also as a lion to be shaved (341c) and as a snake to be charmed (358b). Each reference is calibrated to the question of the subduing and taming of something wild and dangerous. Saxonhouse suggests that when these animals reappear in the dialogue, it is to recall "the earlier role of Thrasymachus as the potential (though far from complete) tyrant whose soul is now laid bare to reveal the internal condition of what was previously seen only as a savage and bestial exterior. Cf. 566a; 588c and 590b." See Arlene W. Saxonhouse, "Comedy in Callipolis: Animal Imagery in the Republic," *American Political Science Review* 72, no. 3 (1978): 892n10.

22. See, for example, Homer, *Ilias*, ed. Allen, 2.243, 54, and 772, 4.413, 7.230. For a discussion of the limits of this analogy between ruler and shepherd, see Christopher P. Long, "Socrates and the Politics of Music: Preludes of the *Republic*," *Polis* 24, no. 1 (2007): 75–76.

23. For a more detailed discussion of the role of Glaucon, see Long, "Socrates and the Politics of Music: Preludes of the *Republic*." John Sallis and Eva Brann both recognize that Socrates's relationship with Glaucon is central and in fact is the only actual community founded in the *Republic*. See John Sallis, *Being and Logos: Reading the Platonic Dialogues* (Bloomington: Indiana University Press, 1996), 454; Eva T. H. Brann, with Peter Kalkavage and Eric Salem, *The*

Music of the Republic: Essays on Socrates' Conversations and Plato's Writings (Philadelphia: Paul Dry Books, 2004), 141–142.

24. The Greek for *speakers* is ῥήτορες, suggesting perhaps that there is a certain way of speaking rhetorically that remains also capable of judging the value of what is said. This seems to anticipate the philosophical rhetoric developed in the *Gorgias*. See Christopher P. Long, "Attempting the Political Art," *Proceedings of the Boston Area Colloquium in Ancient Philosophy* 27 (2012): 153–174.

25. There is, of course, much debate about the contours of Socrates's argument against Thrasymachus and the nature of Thrasymachus's fluctuating position. The point here, however, is not to unpack the details of those arguments but to identify the direction toward which the dogs and wolves of the *Republic* point.

26. Polemarchus's original conception of justice is articulated at 332d, the agreed-upon understanding at 335e; Thrasymachus articulates his original conception of justice at 338c, and Socrates emphasizes that the argument about justice is ultimately "about the way it is necessary for someone to live" at 352d.

27. Commentators generally recognize the importance of these passages in which the philosopher appears first in close proximity to the dog. Some, like Reeve, find it strange, but see it as signifying an important moment along a path to a deeper understanding of the philosopher. See C. D. C. Reeve, *Philosopher-Kings: The Argument of Plato's Republic* (Princeton, N.J.: Princeton University Press, 1988), 179. Julia Annas argues that "the analogy is meant seriously," in Julia Annas, *An Introduction to Plato's Republic* (New York: Oxford University Press, 1981), 80. Many, however, argue that the connection is not to be taken seriously. As Bloom suggests: "This identification of dog-like affection of acquaintances with philosophy is, of course, not serious. It only serves to prepare the way for the true emergence of philosophy in Book 5 and to heighten the difference between philosopher and warrior." See Plato, *The Republic of Plato*, trans. Allan Bloom (New York: BasicBooks, 1991), 350. Peterson takes some issue with Bloom's position: "My reaction, rather than to take this as a nonserious preparation for a better account of philosophers later, is to take the unacceptable comparison here as a suggestion that the later description of philosophers is also unacceptable." See Sandra Peterson, *Socrates and Philosophy in the Dialogues of Plato* (New York: Cambridge University Press, 2011), 122n5. Rosen, for his part, insists that "this analogy cannot possibly be taken literally." Stanley Rosen, *Plato's Republic: A Study* (New Haven, Conn.: Yale University Press, 2005), 83. Most commentators, however, recognize that the passage draws the earlier discussion Socrates has with Polemarchus into relation to the discussion of the philosopher king later in the dialogue.

28. This suggestion about philosopher kings is the biggest wave Socrates must face, a wave that he calls "uproarious" and that he worries will "likely drown [him] in laughter" (473c).

29. In discussion with Glaucon, Socrates suggests in Book 5 that the method they have been pursuing in the hunt for justice in the soul was inadequate and that a "longer road" would be required (435d). For the significance of the appearance of spiritedness and philosophy in these passages related to the guardians and dogs, see Jacob Howland, *The Republic: The Odyssey of Philosophy* (New York: Twayne Publishers, 1993), 95.

30. Socrates sets the word θρέψονται next to παιδευθήσονται to deepen the connection between the rearing of animals and the education of guardians. In Homer, iterations of τρέφω are used in relation to dogs in particular (*Iliad* 22.69; *Odyssey* 14.22).

31. For a detailed discussion of the trope of music that runs through the *Republic*, see Long, "Socrates and the Politics of Music: Preludes of the *Republic*."

32. *Republic* 416a. Saxonhouse suggests that Socrates shifts the traditional focus of the shepherd/sheep model of political leadership when he focuses his attention on the shepherd's ability to cultivate restraint in his dogs to prevent them from harming the sheep. Saxonhouse, "Comedy in Callipolis: Animal Imagery in the *Republic*," 892.

33. In order to avoid the connotations of common English translations of λογισμός as "calculation" or "reason," both of which carry the weight of too much philosophical baggage, the term is translated as "logistical" so that the close connection with the Greek λόγος can be heard.

34. Saxonhouse recognizes the importance of the animal imagery of Book 5: "Though animal imagery of this sort persists throughout, it appears most frequently in Book 5. Book 5 also contains the most frequent laughter. On almost every page Socrates's suggestions are seen as laughable. Whereas previously the animal imagery may have been merely curious or mildly disturbing, in Book 5 we find that it is meant to be funny." See Saxonhouse, "Comedy in Callipolis: Animal Imagery in the Republic," 895. Rankin, on the other hand, posits a strict difference between "Plato, the poet," who was "capable of being led further by the spell of his own images than was always convenient for Plato the philosopher." See H. D. Rankin, *Plato and the Individual* (New York: Barnes & Noble, 1964), 54–55. Of course, Plato the poet is also Plato the philosopher, which is the entire point of writing dialogues as a mode of poetic philosophical expression. To describe the animal images as something tangential to the philosophical teaching articulated in the dialogue is to underestimate Plato and close off an avenue of interpretation rich in philosophical significance.

35. Wood calls our attention to the mythological context in which the three waves crash into the dialogue. Drawing on Eva Brann's notion that one of the central literary tropes of dialogue is "a re-enactment of the Labors of Heracles," Wood argues that the three waves symbolize Heracles's attempt to swim the river Styx to rescue Theseus and Peirethous. See Brann, with Kalkavage and Salem, *The Music of the Republic: Essays on Socrates' Conversations and Plato's Writings*, 4, and Robert E. Wood, "Image, Structure and Content: On a Passage in Plato's Republic," in *Review of Metaphysics* 40, no. 3 (1987): 506. Wood emphasizes the connection between the waves and dogs on a mythological level when he writes: "But before Heracles was even able to swim the river, he had first to tame the three-headed dog Cerberus who guarded the gate to and from the underworld" (507).

36. Socrates develops most of the important teachings in the dialogue with Glaucon precisely because of his erotic and musical nature (see 398e–403c). For a discussion of this, see Long, "Socrates and the Politics of Music: Preludes of the *Republic*," 79n27.

37. See also *Republic* 368d–e, where Socrates suggests that they seek justice writ large in the city before turning to justice in the soul of a single person.

38. Glaucon interrupts the discussion with Adeimantus and compels Socrates to speak about the Good at 506d–e.

39. Hyland argues that Glaucon compels Socrates further down an inadequate path. See Drew A. Hyland, "Aporia, the Longer Road, and the Good," *Graduate Faculty Philosophy Journal* 32, no. 1 (2011): 150. Miller, on the other hand, argues that it is the beginning of the longer road itself; Mitchell Miller, "Beginning the 'Longer Way,'" in *Cambridge Companion to Philosophy* (New York: Cambridge University Press), 310–344. Eva Brann agrees with Miller that Socrates is already on the longer road when he comes to this point in the dialogue. See Brann, with Kalkavage and Salem, *The Music of the Republic: Essays on Socrates' Conversations and Plato's Writings*, 170.

40. Hyland underscores just how apt this analogy between the Good and the sun is; just as the Sun is beyond the power of vision to look directly upon, so is the Good Itself beyond the power of intellection. See Hyland, "Aporia, the Longer Road, and the Good," 157.

PART V

The (En)gendered Animal

9 The City of Sows and Sexual Differentiation in the *Republic*

Marina McCoy

IN PLATO'S REPUBLIC, Socrates creates a city that Glaucon rejects as a "city of sows" (369d–371d).[1] As interpreters, we might take for granted that, in its animality, *sow* simply stands for this city's being not yet fully human.[2] Indeed, Glaucon rejects Socrates's city for its simplicity. The first city in speech is built upon basic human needs. Farmers, weavers, cobblers, and other artisans exist with specialized crafts for the more efficient and expert production of goods (370b–d). Merchants, traders, and a marketplace in which trade exists must also be developed, along with a common system of currency (371a–b). Together, these various craftsmen and merchants will form a community designed to meet human needs. Socrates emphasizes most of all the production of bread, wine, clothing, and shoes. Glaucon objects to the relative paucity of its material goods. At the same time, this initial city also allows for relaxation, singing, the enjoyment of sex and children, worship of the gods, and being together with one another in community (372b–d). Perhaps such a city could even allow for time for philosophy, insofar as its citizens would not be distracted by the enterprises of political assemblies, the accumulation of material goods, or the necessity to fight in wars that greater luxury entails.[3] Thus, it is not immediately obvious what is "inhuman" about such a city that values craft, music, religion, and community.

Socrates's first vision of civic life is thus asserted but never fully explored. Once Glaucon raises his objection, and Socrates's counteroffer of adding salt, olives, cheese, figs, and furniture is rejected, the *Republic* moves into a discussion of a larger, class-stratified city that includes added luxury but also war. This first city in speech is left behind, and while Socrates attempts to purify the second, more "feverish," city of its excesses, no return is made to the "city of sows."

Yet the very presence of a city of *sows* in the dialogue, and the heated anger with which Glaucon rejects such a vision of the political, reveals a deeper Platonic movement of discourse than that of mere rejection. The "city of sows" rejected by Glaucon is not discarded because it is a city of animals rather than one composed of sophisticated human beings. Socrates's inclusion of singing, religious worship, technical crafts, care for the family, especially children, and verbal discussion all point to uniquely human dimensions to this first city. Instead, we must look to the gendered dimension inherent in the Greek sensibility of the sow, as well as the sow's religious signification. I shall argue that Glaucon rejects this city because it is built upon feminine practice; it is a city that lacks the masculinity of politics, war, and the honors that accompany war. Taken together with Socrates's later suggestion for a city that includes women as equals while eliminating much traditional feminine *praxis*, the city of sows raises questions for the *Republic's* audience as to what constitutes the genuinely "political" and the ways in which sexual differentiation informs the Athenian understanding of the "political."

Socrates's use of feminine imagery to describe himself and his philosophical practice is familiar to readers of the Platonic dialogues: in the *Theaetetus*, he is the midwife who serves as a matchmaker and helps others to give birth to ideas. In the *Symposium*, he describes his philosophical education as taking place through the "cross-examination" of the prophetess Diotima, whose own vision of philosophy emphasizes giving birth to beautiful ideas and practices in the pursuit of the Beautiful. Socrates's use of the imagery of the feminine *sow* here continues his active engagement with the feminine. For the sow played a prominent role in the religious celebration of the Thesmophoria, a festival celebrated exclusively by women. Socrates's description of the "city of pigs" includes many elements similar to practices found in the Thesmophoria.

The Thesmophoria was a gynocentric festival at the heart of the cult of Demeter: Athenian women, normally confined to the home and excluded from the public sphere, gathered together overnight in the sanctuary without men or children present.[4] The festival centered on the loss of Demeter's daughter, Persephone, also known as Korē, to Hades, and it preceded the autumn sowing of crops. The festival began with an ascending procession to the Thesmophorian on the hill of the Pnyx and so bore the name "Road up" (*Anhodos*).[5] The center of the festival involved the sacrifice of a pig or piglets in the evening, with the remains of the sacrifice being thrown into a snake-filled "chasm of Demeter and Korē," the so-called megara.[6] Such sacrifices took place either during the Thesmophoria or perhaps even earlier in midsummer (on scholars' assumption that the piglets needed time to rot in order to be brought up as remains, and women could not afford to remain many days away from home). Symbols of fertility were also present, such as dough models of male and female genitalia, snakes, and other "sacred things."[7] On the second day, women fasted and abstained from sex, sleeping on simple mats. Such a period of fasting was followed by the retrieval of the remainder of the unconsumed remains of the sacrifice, which were brought up from the chasm and placed on an altar. This remainder (the *thesmos*) was thought to guarantee fertile crops when mixed with the seeds scattered for the new harvest. However, the name of this day, *Kalligeneia*, also focuses on the women's hope of bearing beautiful and healthy children.[8] Fasting was replaced with feasting, and destruction with a hope that what remained would lead to new plenty at harvest time. As Burkert notes, there is a pattern of descent into the underworld and death, coupled with signs of fertility and renewal.[9]

Nearly every particular in Socrates's description of the first city closely mimics some of the features of the Thesmophoria. In Socrates's city, its citizens build small houses for themselves but feast while sitting on rushes covered with myrtle and yew (372a–b). At the Thesmophoria, women erected small temporary tents to serve as simple shelters and slept on mats. Socrates's first city evokes the primitivism retained in the celebrations of the Thesmophoria, one of the few Greek festivals to retain the ancient practice of sleeping on mats.[10] No beds or furniture were allowed in the religious festival; instead, women slept on the ground on the leaves of plants (such as a willow-like tree called the *lugos*) said to dull the libido.[11] Socrates's city likewise features its couples sleeping on beds of yew and myrtle (371b). Socrates's city centrally features cakes of wheat and barley, just the Thesmophoria featured wheat and barley cakes in the shape of the female pudenda, and dough creations in the shape of phalluses.[12] Socrates describes the city's wheat and barley cakes as *gennaias*, suggesting a kind of nobility to their function (372b).[13] The Thesmophoria featured fasting preceding a large banquet meal honoring Kalligenia, the goddess of beautiful births. At this banquet, women indulged in *aischrologia* (shameful speech), offering mocking poems, telling dirty jokes, and trading barbs at one another.[14] Socrates, too, speaks of a city in which those lying on the mats enjoy food and offer hymns to the gods while "taking pleasure in being with one another [ἡδέως ξυνόντες ἀλλήλοις]" (372b). Socrates's city in speech evokes the central features of the Thesmophoria.

However, even more important than whether Socrates himself intended to refer to the Thesmophoria is Glaucon's angry dismissal of Socrates's first city as akin to a "city of sows." Plato as author constructs for us, his audience, a dialogue in which Socrates creates a first city that Glaucon rejects as being too feminine. The term "sow," *hus* (ὗς), is a Greek slang term for female genitalia. Henderson in the *Maculate Muse* shows that both the terms *delphax*, pig, and *hus*, sow, refer to the female genitalia of a mature woman, while the term *xoiros*, piggie, was used to refer to the genitalia of a hairless younger woman or girl.[15] Jokes centering on the double entendre of the term "sows" or "pigs" abound in Greek comedy, for example, in the Megarian scene of the *Acharnians* (e.g., 729–817) and at several points in the *Lysistrata*.[16] Thus, Glaucon's dismissal of the "city of pigs" could even be translated more aggressively: "If you were providing for a city of cunts, Socrates, on what else would you fatten them than this?" (372d).

The sacrifice of the pig at the Thesmophoria served as a reminder of the rape of Korē by Hades and her descent into the underworld, for accounts of the rape suggested that pigs of the shepherd Eubuleus were pulled into the earth along with Demeter.[17] Such signification carries over into the concept of the grain of wheat that must go beneath the earth before rising again in the form of new plants and sustenance.[18] This reference to the cycle of death and rebirth is also connected to the physical dependencies of human beings, insofar as human life itself depends on the sacrifice and eating of other life forms, whether grain or animal. The sacrifice of a pregnant sow and her fetuses in particular was connected to the fecundity of women as well as crops.[19] Although life inevitably ends in death, death is also the condition for the generation of new life.

Of course, the most significant difference in Socrates's city is the presence of men, women, and children, while the Thesmophoria was the sole province of women alone—although only adult female citizens who had participated in sexual union with their husbands were permitted to participate in the Thesmophoria, thus suggesting one's relation to men informed even this female-centered ritual.[20] Glaucon's objection to the city, however, seems to lie not in its inclusion of women along with men but in its placing feminine practices at the heart of civic practice. While many commentators focus more narrowly on Glaucon's desire for more material luxury—and this motivation cannot entirely be excluded—Glaucon's reference to "a city of sows" offers us clues into the deeper nature of his objection as one that is defined by the female and not the male.

Indeed, arguably, the Thesmophoria-like city proposed by Socrates is unrecognizable as a Greek city. The Athens in which Glaucon, Adeimantus, and Socrates reside is defined by war, honor, and a political assembly that centered not on the cycle of birth and death or the generative capacity of womb and soil but rather on economic, judicial, and interpolitical matters. But what makes the political practices of Athens recognizably "political" is their exclusion of the feminine in favor of masculine undertakings (i.e., masculine according to the Athenian cultural understanding). The politics of Athens is defined by its exclusion of feminine practices. Even the language of Glaucon's exclamation—"No relishes for the men [*andras*] you say are feasting!"—uses the gender-specific *anēr* rather than gender inclusive *anthrōpos* (372c). Glaucon's objection is that this city is not fit for men as men. It is a city of women or, more disparagingly, cunts.

Here, I do not wish to reify the category of the "feminine" or "female" but rather want to claim that, within the cultural vision of Socrates's Athens, those practices undertaken by women are excluded from being *understood* or *claimed* as political.[21] The things that women do—birthing, acting as caretakers, being sexual partners, weaving, managing the household, sacrificing to the gods for a good harvest, and tending to the graves of the dead—are construed as private matters. However, each of these actions could be claimed as "political," insofar as the *polis* depends upon such activities for its sustenance and thriving. Weaving, no less than shoemaking, is a necessary *technē* for the city's wellbeing. Birthing and caretaking, even more than the protection of the city by men in wartime, provide for its very existence. Sex, song, harvest, and religious feast are all activities that ground and sustain the city's being in community. But these "feminine" activities share a peculiar relationship to the temporal: while many "political" actions mark time in a way that is then named as unrepeatable (for example, the Battle of Salamis or the Peace of Nicias), Greek women's activities mark time cyclically. Each year the Thesmophoria is celebrated, each year sacrifices and feasting are repeated, each year the harvest is hoped for anew. But the significance of each individual action within the Thesmophoria lies within a greater temporal narrative, a narrative that values the continuity of the cycle of life and death and locates individual action within this larger cyclical framework.

Moreover, the pig sacrifice in the Demeter cult serves not only more specifically as a commemoration of the rape of Korē and the agricultural cycle of death and rebirth but also more broadly as a festival that differentiates the role of women and men in the productivity of the *polis*. In the Thesmophoria, the boundary between nature and city is overcome. That which belongs to the countryside, the *chōrē*, normally seen as "outside" the polis and demarcated from it, is brought into the boundaries of the *polis* and serves as a reminder of the dependency of the masculine activities of politics and warfare on the practices of farmers and the reproductive capacities of women. Indeed, the topography of the Demeter sanctuary vis-à-vis the polis suggests the importance of the Demeter cult as that which exists on the boundaries. As Susan Cole has shown, the Demeter sanctuaries often existed *pro poleōs* ("in front of the polis").[22] For example, Herodotus describes the sanctuary at Paros as on a hill just in front of the city (6.134). While a few sanctuaries existed inside the city, such as the one located near the people's assembly in Athens, a great number of sanctuaries in cities such as Olbia, Teos, and Thasos, along with other Greek colonial cities, placed the sanctuary just outside the city walls. An inscription in Smyrna even describes the sanctuary directly as *pro poleōs*.[23] This seems especially to have been true of colonial cities, where the placement of the sanctuary was deliberate rather than inherited from the archaic period. Thus, the Demeter sanctuary exists "for" the good of the city, without actually being included in it. As with the activities of childbirth and agriculture, the city is dependent upon women's religious activities, and yet it marginalizes them. They exist for the *polis* without yet fully constituting the political. (Fascinatingly, in a few cases, a sanctuary was built, both outside and inside the city, as in the cases of Gela, Akragas, and Heloros, where double sanctuaries, located on either side of the city walls, further emphasized the sanctuary's existence on the border both topographically and symbolically.[24])

Detienne has argued that the normal hierarchy of religious sacrifice reflected the political order of Athens as well: "Just as women are without the political rights reserved for male citizens, they are kept apart from altars, meat, and blood."²⁵ Men are central to the enactment of the sacrifice, and while married women (*gunaikes*) may distribute the portions of the sacrifice in accordance with tightly fixed rules, their privilege stems from their relation to male citizens.²⁶ Meat, and its handling, is ordinarily restricted to men. Detienne even notes that the term *mageiros* (butcher/sacrificer) possessed no feminine form, so that the comic poet Pherecrates claimed that a new word would have to be invented for such practice; it could not be adapted to the feminine.²⁷ At the Thesmophoria, women themselves "sacrificed" pigs by dropping them to the snakes in the chasm, but a male *mageiros* was likely hired to slit the throat of a pig upon the altar before again departing. The pig may then have been prepared as meat for roasting and feasting by the women.²⁸ Thus the wielding of the knife to take the life of an animal is viewed as of essentially male provenance even when it takes place in a female context.²⁹

Socrates's proposal of the "city of sows" subverts this usual Greek division of public and private, political and familial, masculine and feminine. In this first city of the *Republic*, men, women, and children alike share in all enterprises. Its citizens do better than subsist, as Socrates's insistence on wine and a few dainty foods makes clear. They do not suffer from want of food, shelter, or companionship. Even a basic market economy is present. But there are no wars or courtrooms, no political structures, no major architectural or artistic projects, and no science. There is also no meat, which arises only in the feverish city, along with cosmetics and prostitutes, and therefore no distinct role of men as priests or slaughterers. Activities from which Athenian women were ordinarily excluded are simply absent from the first city.

It is only with the development of the luxurious city that the city possesses musicians, poets, and courtesans (*heterai*). Indeed, the class divisions between the educated *heterai* and other women exist only in the feverish city, insofar as married women's tasks then change with the division of labor that requires more servants (and so a household to be run), weaving for more elaborate and extensive clothing, cooking, and other extensions of the household and perceived "necessities." Even the specific development of a class of educated *heterai* rests upon the notion that ordinary women, being concerned exclusively with the private, are not proper companions in the public sphere. Although Socrates will later in Book 5 "correct" this division of labor according to sex, the assumption of the luxurious city seems to be that men alone will be its guardians and rulers (see e.g., 376a).

Most importantly, in the city of sows, there is no political rule. There is no distinction between the government and those governed, no separation between ruler and citizen. Such idealism has often led commentators to be puzzled by the purpose of the first city and to ask whether it can be functional.³⁰ McKeen suggests that such a city could be functional for a limited time but that it too will eventually become subject to the contingencies of events that can lead to inequalities and the divergence of self-interest in the city.³¹ Others argue that the first city is indeed the healthiest but that it does not take account of unhealthy desires and their regulation. Devereux, for example, explains the absence of rulers in terms of the modest desires of this first city. He argues that its inhabitants have only "necessary" (*ta anagkaia*) desires but no "unnecessary" ones, borrowing from Socrates's language in Book 8 (558d–e).³² That is, the first city contains only inhabitants who seek and fulfill desires that are compelled by nature, none that exceed nature or that could be harmful. The key question is whether keeping to "necessary" desires is realistic for human beings.

However, we must still always ask the question: "necessary" for whom? As McKeen argues, there is no reason simply to assume that all human desires or appetites are inherently insatiable, or that all persons will have bottomless desires once exposed to luxury.³³ Perhaps the objection arises not from human nature as such but from Glaucon's own character and desires. For Glaucon, the city of sows does not "rise" to the political, that is, the world of men and honor among men. While we might name this desire for honor as an "unnecessary" desire, it is not simply a desire that indicates some excess on the part of the appetitive part of the soul, or even the *thumotic* part. Rather, Glaucon's desires are for goods that transcend the merely cyclical and atemporal. In war and politics, men make a mark on human history, and so define what comes to be understood as historical time. In ancient Athens, women mostly do not. Men also define themselves as men, in part through contrast to the lives of women. The city of sows provides neither for honor nor for the masculinity associated with political and military honor.

That this objection is Glaucon's and not Socrates's (or Plato's, in any simple sense) is clear from the contrast in Socrates's and Glaucon's attitudes toward the city of sows. Socrates describes the first city as both "healthy" and "true" (371e–372e), while Glaucon will object vigorously. In this first and feminine city, home and the state are not separate entities, nor is there a strong social division between men and women, or even one of social class akin to the later tripartite division of the city. The *oikos* and the *polis* are one. Perhaps this first city reflects something of Socrates's own priorities and values. Socrates's own political practice of questioning others in Athens also subverts this public and private distinction to an extent: Socrates calls his own private cross-examination of others a political gift to the city, despite others' charge that he is "useless" because he appears to be apolitical (*Apology* 30e).³⁴ He acts as midwife to the ideas of others, preferring to participate in the social practice of philosophy rather than to develop a written doctrine or attain a famous name. Despite his later identification as the father of Western philosophy, Socrates suggests that his most important legacy lies in passing along the practice of philosophy and care of the soul to a subsequent generation (*Apology* 29d–30b). His own death, he notes, will not eliminate philosophy from the city. The city of sows is in keeping with Socrates's own refusal to differentiate between the masculine/political and feminine/cyclical. It is not Socrates but Glaucon who resists this city.

We know from other sections of the *Republic* of Glaucon's great love of honor. Socrates especially highlights the poetry that was written by a lover to extol Glaucon's courage in the battle of Megara: "Sons of Ariston, divine offspring of a famous man" (368a). Glaucon agrees with Socrates's criticism of poetry as removed from the truth with reference to the claim that it would be better to leave behind many deeds worthy of honor when one dies, not mere imitations (599b). Moreover, Socrates calls Glaucon an erotic man who loves young men of all dispositions and appearances: "You praise the boy with a snub nose by calling him 'cute'; the hook-nose of another you say is 'kingly'; and the boy between these two is 'well-proportioned'; the dark look 'manly' and the white are 'children of gods'" (474d–e). When Socrates suggests that in the best city the bravest of men might kiss others upon his return from war, Glaucon adds: "And I add to the law that as long as they are on campaign no one whom he wants to kiss be permitted to refuse, so that if a man happens to love someone, either male or female, he would be more eager to win the rewards of valor" (468c). Thus we see that Glaucon is not only an erotic and *thumotic* man but one whose *thumos* and *eros* are specifically directed toward other men and masculine enterprises, especially deeds of honor performed in war.

In contrast, Socrates's first city is not feverish, but it is fecund. In his city, men and women alike enjoy the fruits of labor and benefits of intercourse with one another; their lives of simplicity are hardly lives of privation. The *eros* of this city still remains directed at objects that are largely concerned with the body: food, feasts, sex, sleep, protection from the elements. Some of the activities of this first, simple city are also goods of the soul: enjoyment of one's children, talk during feasts, and perhaps even the practice of natural philosophy or ethical concerns that arise in such a society. However, the "city of sows" lacks an *eros* directed at the honor of the exceptional man, whether we understand him to exist in contrast to the vulgar person or, as the city later develops him, as the philosopher in contrast to the nonphilosopher. If the philosopher can even exist in the first city, she or he is not a product of specialized training in mathematics, science, or study of the forms but someone who philosophizes from ordinary human experience. Such a city would hold little appeal to Glaucon, who is concerned with war-centered honor as well as *eros* directed at men and masculine enterprises.

The most developed city in speech of the *Republic* is modeled on just such a masculine approach to love, honor, and war. While women are included, they are included only insofar as they take up the activities of men and do so in a masculine way. All distinctively feminine activities, except childbearing itself, are eliminated: indeed, the public realm accommodates women through the elimination of the private. Men and women alike partake in gymnastics, war training, political speech, and all other civic enterprises. But as Saxonhouse long ago argued, this city can be achieved only by desexing women.[35] The city in speech that equalizes men and women produces a kind of paradox: to be a woman in this city means to give up all activities that make one distinctively a woman, with the exception of childbearing itself. Women must become like men, somehow able to coexist with them in the gym and on the battlefield without either group being overpowered by *eros*, even though the city is dependent on *eros* for its growth. Versnel notes the paradox of the Thesmophoria in the juxtaposition of sexual abstinence and fasting with the presence of phallic symbols and prayers for fecundity of both children and crops.[36] In Book 5, the city in speech gives us a similar paradox, but reversed: women and men may eat and engage in sexual activity, but their *eros* and other appetites must always remain moderate.

This city of Book 5 has reversed the situation of the city of sows. Here, in the later *polis*, women are full participants in the life of the city, but only by the city's abandonment of family life and all distinctively feminine practices. Where the first city asked men to live like women of the Thesmophoria, the later city demands of women that they give up their children to the "pen" and participate in civic marriages arranged by the state in order to procreate the right kind and number of children. This second city's approach to communal rearing of children is the reversal of the Thesmophoria, which mourns the loss of Demeter's child and grieves mother-daughter separation. As Rachel Barney notes, the city in speech that replaces the city of sows is not especially luxurious materially; the guardians must live without wealth.[37] Hence, the distinction between the first city and second one is not primarily one of material wealth. Rather, the differences lie in their social structures, especially in the contrast between the classless simplicity of the first city and the hierarchy of the second. Both cities achieve harmony through the elimination of sexual differentiation: the first through exclusive attention to feminine practice and the second through exclusive attention to the masculine.

This "city of sows," of course, also lacks the realism of an ordinary city. Religious festivals themselves have a peculiar relationship to temporality. Even a festival like the Thesmophoria, which is explicitly attentive to the temporal dynamics of birth and death, harvest and destruction, the cycles of the seasons, also stands "outside" time. For the participants in such a religious festival, ordinary time is left behind, and everyday activities are set aside. The activities of fasting, praying, and even residing in tents rather than in homes remove the festival's participants from the ordinary cycle of the day. For a short while, those activities that mark the day, especially those concerned with sex, food, and sleep, are set aside or fundamentally altered. In their conscious alteration, the very experience of the everyday is also disrupted.[38] Indeed, the self-regulated appetites of the women in the Thesmophoria can exist only because they are time-limited: the absence of men and presence of anti-aphrodisiac plants leads to limited abstinence. Extended periods of rest make fasting possible. But fasting is followed by feasting, and the women return to their homes and husbands. A city based upon the Thesmophoria would not be a city in which one can permanently reside. But Socrates's city, too, seems less to be a political plan than a mytho-poetic account of a distinctively feminine arrangement. It, too, can exist only with the construction of an elaborate system of eugenics and a nuptial number, as well with the perpetuation of the "noble lie" that is its grounding myth. *Eros* is carefully regulated, and women and men exercise together and participate equally in civic life, but only at the expense of removing the private and familial realm. While in the Thesmophoria piglets are sacrificed, in the city in speech of the *Republic* it is the family as such that is sacrificed, so that we are left only with its "remainder." And even this cannot last. The arranged marriages eventually must fail as the mathematical account that guides the production of the best citizens in proper proportions eventually falls apart (546b). Erotics overpowers mathematics.

Even in this carefully constructed city in which women's sexuality and familial roles are restricted, the city degenerates from aristocracy into tyranny. The cause of its degeneration is not only the breakdown of the nuptial calculus but also wives who object that their husbands do not care enough about honor and money and sons who listen to similar public evaluations of their fathers' honor (549c–550b). Rather than reading such degeneration as Platonic misogyny, I suggest that the problem lies in part with a city in which feminine practice has been subsumed to masculine value and practice, and in which wives/mothers have subscribed to the masculine ideology of competition for honor.

Interestingly enough, the sacrifice of a pig during secret rituals is explicitly referred to in the *Republic,* just following Socrates's discussion of the overthrowing of Ouranos by Cronos as one of the poetic stories that must be banned as a lie (378a). Thus we can see that, while the second city is purified of unhealthy competition and desire early on in its construction, the masculine competition for honor and being "better" than other men, especially one's own father, eventually causes the city to degenerate. Women also participate in this competition, but through their relationships to men, again indicating some kind of demise of the equality of women, or the subordination of feminine to masculine practices.

Thus the *Republic* raises the problems of both a masculine city that eliminates all feminine values and a "city of sows" in which the feminine exists at expense of the masculine. Where is philosophy in all of this? I suggest that Platonic philosophy exists precisely in living in the tensions and paradoxes posed by the oppositions of masculine-feminine, political-private, and marked history–cyclical history. For Socrates, philosophy is primarily about not a teaching but rather a way of being in the world. In the *Republic,* Socrates crosses between the countryside and the city and moves across the feminine and masculine cities. By integrating these into his understanding and discourse without entirely eliminating their tension, Socrates succeeds in maintaining a philosophical stance. The language of the *Republic* as a whole in some ways mirrors the mytho-poetic orientation of all of its "cities in speech": the *Republic* begins with a descent to the Piraeus and the religious festival of Bendis, and it ends with an ascent as Socrates finally makes his own return to Athens. Perhaps, in this ascent, he is walking in the footsteps of the women of the city whose journey carried them from the countryside to the city.[39]

Notes

1. Unless otherwise indicated, all translations of the *Republic* are from the Bloom translation; Plato, *Republic*, trans. Allan Bloom (New York: Basic Books, 1991).
2. See, for example, Christopher Berry, "Of Pigs and Men: Luxury in Plato's *Republic*," *Polis* 8 (1989): 2–24.
3. Commentators often take the absence of the mention of philosophy to be proof of its absence. Rachel Barney, for example, notes that since the military and philosopher-king are introduced in Socrates's later cities, they must be absent before their introduction. See Rachel Barney, "Platonism, Moral Nostalgia, and the City of Pigs," *Proceedings of the Boston Area Colloquium in Ancient Philosophy* 17 (2001): 213. However, while the sort of philosophy practiced in the city developed later in the *Republic* has not yet been introduced, that is, one that aims for rule of the city according to the good, there is nothing to suggest that those in this first city could not practice natural philosophy or even moral and political philosophy of a different sort, one that is appropriate to the simpler family structures of their own civic community.
4. Walter Burkert, *Greek Religion* (Cambridge, Mass.: Harvard University Press, 1985), 242.
5. H. S. Versnel, "The Festival for Bona Dea and the Thesmophoria," *Greece and Rome* 39 (1991): 34.
6. Walter Burkert, "The Myth of Korē and Pig-Sacrifice," in *Homo Necans: Interpretationen Altgriechischer Opferriten Und Mythen* (New York: De Gruyter 1997), 257.
7. Burkert, *Greek Religion*, 242.
8. Versnel, "The Festival for Bona Dea and the Thesmophoria," 34.
9. Burkert, *Greek Religion*, 242.
10. For more on the nature of such primitivism in the festival itself, see Versnel, "The Festival for Bona Dea and the Thesmophoria," 37–38.
11. Ibid., 35.
12. Burkert, *Greek Religion*, 244.
13. Catherine McKeen, "Swillsburg City Limits (the 'City of Pigs': 'Republic' 370C–372D)," *Polis: The Journal of the Society for the Study of Greek Political Thought* 21 (2004): 70–92.
14. Burkert, *Greek Religion*, 244.
15. Jeffrey Henderson, *The Maculate Muse: Obscene Language In Attic Comedy* (Oxford: Oxford University Press, 1991), 131–132.
16. Ibid.
17. Walter Burkert, *Homo Necans: The Anthropology of Ancient Greek Sacrificial Ritual and Myth* (Berkeley: University of California Press, 1983), 259.
18. Ibid., 260.
19. Susan Guettel Cole, "Demeter in the Ancient Greek City and Its Countryside," in *Oxford Readings in Greek Religion*, ed. R. G. A. Buxton (Oxford: Oxford University Press, 2000), 139.

20. Ibid., 137.

21. For example, Robin Osborne protests against Detienne's emphasis on the political. He argues, "Far from being highly 'political,' the cults from which women are expressly excluded seem more often to be marginal to the city" (403). See Robin Osborne, "Women and Sacrifice in Classical Greece," *Classical Quarterly* 43, no. 2 (1993): 392–405. However, the point is that, for any society, what "constitutes" the political realm is itself already partly defined by those who hold power. Glaucon's objection emphasizes the significance of gender: being men, and especially being men in contrast to women, is part of what forms an Athenian understanding of politics.

22. Cole, "Demeter in the Ancient Greek City and Its Countryside," 147–149.

23. Ibid.

24. Ibid., 152. Cole argues for the greater importance of water and the privacy of women in choosing a countryside site. But the very fact that women's private space is seen as "outside" the city belies the significance of gender in reading what constitutes the political.

25. Marcel Detienne, "The Violence of Wellborn Ladies: Women in the Thesmophoria," in *The Cuisine of Sacrifice among the Greeks*, ed. by Jean Pierre Vernant (Chicago: University of Chicago Press, 1989), 131.

26. Ibid., 131, 135–138.

27. Ibid., 143.

28. See Detienne, "The Violence of Wellborn Ladies," 134–135, 143–144. Whether and why women could participate in or be excluded from a sacrificial cult is a point of controversy. See, for example, in contrast to Detienne, Osborne's argument that while women were often excluded from cult sacrifice, there is insufficient evidence to attribute this exclusion to their menstruation, as Detienne suggests. See Obsorne, "Women and Sacrifice," 397–399.

29. Detienne attributes this to women's menstruation, noting the existence of several mytho-poetic accounts of women who, once given the knife to slaughter an animal, then wield the knife to emasculate or slaughter men. See Detienne, "The Violence of Wellborn Ladies," 144–147, and Versnel, "The Festival for Bona Dea and the Thesmophoria," 41–43.

30. For example, Julia Annas sees it as adding little of philosophical value. Julia Annas, *An Introduction to Plato's Republic* (Oxford: Oxford University Press, 1981), 78–79.

31. See McKeen, "Swillsburg City Limits."

32. Daniel Devereux, "Socrates' First City in the *Republic*," *Apeiron* 13, no. 1 (1979): 36–40.

33. McKeen, "Swillsburg City Limits," 80–81.

34. See also my argument for the collapse of the public-private distinction in this section of the *Apology* in Marina Berzins McCoy, *Plato on the Rhetoric of Philosophers and Sophists* (Cambridge: Cambridge University Press, 2008), 44–49.

35. Arlene Saxonhouse, "The Philosopher and the Female in the Political Thought of Plato," *Political Theory* 4, no. 2 (1976): 195–212.

36. Versnel, "The Festival for Bona Dea and the Thesmophoria," 40–43.

37. Barney, "Platonism, Moral Nostalgia, and the City of Pigs," 216.

38. Thus Barney takes Socrates to be teasing Glaucon in offering this city, which she sees as being akin to a pseudo-idyllic Hesiodic golden age. See ibid., 216.

39. Thanks to Tyler Viale, who worked as a research assistant and contributed valuable work to this project.

10 Animality and Sexual Difference in the *Timaeus*

Sara Brill

PLATO MADE MUCH of the connection between vitality and vividness that is at work in the Greek verb ζάω, as is evident by the variety and significance of phenomena explicated in the dialogues by means of an appeal to life [ζωή] and living beings [ζῷα] of various sorts: λόγος is characterized as a living being (*Phaedrus* 264c), the κόσμος as being alive (*Timaeus* 30b–c), and the πόλις as a living body (*Republic* 462c–d, 464b).[1] Throughout the dialogues, flocks and swarms of animals are treated as revelatory of human political and intellectual life, and particular animals as illuminating conditions of souls, forms of life, and kinds of character, from the virtuous to the vicious. The lion and boar, for instance, are lauded for their courage (*Laches* 196e–197c), the bee and ant for their social natures (*Phaedrus* 82b), noble puppies for their melding of spirit and gentleness (*Republic* 375e), the swan for its loyal service (*Phaedrus* 84e), while the wolf is castigated for its wildness (*Republic* 566a, *Sophist* 231a, *Laws* 906d–e), the cow for its slavishness (*Republic* 586a–b), and the donkey for its gluttony (*Phaedo* 81e). Occasionally, in the context of telling a mythos about the afterlife, Socrates will speak about animals as animated by souls that had formerly resided in human bodies, treating animal embodiment as punishment for or, as in the myth of Er, liberation from a human life.[2] In both metaphorical and mythical references, living beings are discursively useful because their lives are taken to be signifying entities; that is, they mean something beyond the fact of their existence. This is to say, animal life is treated less as an object of analysis than an event calling for interpretation (and thereby as useful for didactic purposes). What is, for Plato, philosophically significant about the lion or the wolf, for instance, is its illumination of the nature of courage or ferocity. That life as such tends toward signification is itself a noteworthy assertion, but it also invites the question: *What* do the lives of living beings signify?

In one sense, the *Timaeus*'s relevance to this question, and to a study of Plato's thinking about animals, is obvious. The bulk of this dialogue, at once a cosmogony and a zoogony, is taken up by an account of the origin of the cosmos that characterizes the cosmos as a living being and includes an account of the origin of mortal animals. But there is a more subtle and troubling line of relevance. Timaeus's answer to the question of how mortal animals come to be also purports to answer why they come to be; that is, the dialogue claims to discern the workings of mind not only in the behavior of certain animals but also in the diversity of animal life and in the processes of its generation. Thus, the *Timaeus*'s answer to the question of what life signifies is that, in the motions that engender it and actions that comprise it, life makes manifest to philosophic thought the workings of mind and mindlessness. But this vision of ζωή and ζῷα is accomplished only by granting a very peculiar generative capacity to human action and life. To be sure, such anthropocentrism is in part a function of the task that Timaeus accepts—to offer, as a prelude, an account of the origins of human beings in order to hand these beings to Critias, who will, in turn, display them in that action which, it is claimed, is most illuminating of the character of the city that nurtures them: war.[3] But, I argue, it is precisely in its attempt to separate an account of human nature from an account of political life that the cosmogony fails with respect to the task Socrates has set out for Timaeus. More specifically, this cosmogony posits a masculine human prototype whose actions generate the need for sexually differentiated bodies, thereby enshrining masculinity as a fecund generative force in the cosmos. However, its attempt to offer an account of human nature divorced from an account of the city renders it incapable of engaging in the kind of analysis that would permit probing inquiry into the question of human generation. The result is a vision of human nature with which Socrates could have hardly been satisfied. This, in turn, invites exploration of just what Plato is doing with his construction of Timaeus's cosmogony. Thus, an investigation into the emergence of sexual difference in the *Timaeus* not only provides insight into Plato's thinking about animals but also allows us to explore the status of Timaeus's cosmogony vis-à-vis philosophic thought.

In order to make good on these claims, it is necessary to give some consideration to what kind of investigation Timaeus undertakes and to sketch out the hermeneutic horizon within which his account of the origin of the cosmos unfolds. I will then turn to examine more closely Timaeus's account of the origin of the human prototype and the generation of women and other mortal animals, concluding with a consideration of what possibilities for critique this play with cosmogony opens up.

Cosmogony

Timaeus's cosmogony is the account of the origin of the cosmos that results from accepting three broad stipulations that are asserted and put to work but that are never argued for and that mark out the interpretive parameters of the dialogue.[4] The first is the intertwining of necessity and mind that is achieved by mind's persuasion of necessity: "For, in truth, this Cosmos in its origin was generated as a compound, from the combination of Necessity and Mind. And inasmuch as Mind was controlling Necessity by persuading her to conduct to the best end the most part of the things coming into existence, thus and thereby it came about, through Necessity yielding to intelligent [ἔμφρονος] persuasion, that this All of ours was being in this wise constructed at the beginning" (48a).[5] The nature of this persuasion and its causes are not described; that is, how, exactly, mind persuades necessity is left underdetermined, save perhaps for the action of chōra, which shifts like to like, giving the demiurge elements with a sufficient tendency toward stability as to be used in the making of an ordered cosmos. Perhaps we are to read persuasion as inserting a gentleness into the development of the cosmos, that is, read it as persuasion *instead of* force, although force does indeed creep in with the creation of cosmic soul, for which the demiurge must use βία to conjoin the Same with the Other (35b). Nevertheless, when compared to the principles of creation in Hesiod's *Theogony*, for example, Timaeus's cosmogony is an anesthetized cosmogony. Whereas in Hesiod the cosmos is arrayed through the violent and bloody conflict between divine forces, here we find a demiurge who, out of ungrudging generosity, creates a cosmos that will resemble himself insofar is it is as good as is possible for such a created thing to be, a principle of creation that Timaeus calls most sovereign (29e). Absent from this account is the matricide, patricide, incest, and general erotic mingling of Hesiod's tale. While the details of mind's domestication of necessity remain obscure in the dialogue, this domestication nevertheless forms one of the bases of the entire cosmogony and is decisive for the accord, appropriateness, and proportion between soul and body that enable the motion of the cosmos. More specifically, it makes possible the elision of technical production and sexual reproduction that is figured by a demiurge called both poet and father. It also undergirds the claims that the diversity of living beings serves a rational purpose and that their generation answers to the call of mind as well as to the demands of necessity.

A second parameter of this cosmogony is its dual character as a hymn of praise and a performance of justice. Critias's characterization of the purpose of his own contribution to their discussion—"as a payment of our debt of thanks to [Socrates] and also as a tribute of praise, chanted as it were duly and truly, in honor of the Goddess on this her day of Festival" (21a)—carries over to Timaeus, whose contribution opens up with the insistence that the cosmos is "the fairest of all that has come into existence, and [the demiurge] the best of all the causes" (29a). This assertion, which is clear, claims Timaeus, to everyone, demonstrates that it is not right (θέμις) to say that the cosmos was constructed by looking to what is generated rather than what is everlasting. Timaeus's invocation of θέμις serves to remind us of the borders of this intellectual pursuit, that is, its commitment to remain within the bounds of duty (to a host) and piety (as an offering to the goddess).[6]

This discursive specification is connected to the claim that *logos* resembles that of which it is a *logos* (29b–c), and it gives Timaeus some anxiety about whether his praise is adequately beautiful, requiring the caveat that proves decisive for his account, namely, that because it is given by a human to humans it can only be a likeness of the truest account (29d).[7] We might ask how Timaeus's account is like the cosmos he describes; that is, we might attempt to specify the motion of the account itself; if we did so we would have to observe that this is an account of perpetual beginnings, one that steps out before itself and must circle around back on itself, one that finds itself several times in need of beginning again.[8]

Timaeus's praise of the cosmos proceeds by appropriating those culturally specific terms of value and honorifics that convey superiority and nobility. Here, these are coded by age: the young should never rule the old (34c); gender/sex: the masculine is the most noble (42a); and domestication: the tame is superior to the wild (70e–71a).[9] Thus the enactment of justice that we find here is a very traditional one: it is a matter of "giving back what is owed." That is, Timaeus's cosmogony finds itself answerable to demands other than those of critical inquiry, and it has an irreducibly conservative element at odds with the more radical modes of thought and account that can be found in other dialogues, an element that requires us to ask about the limits of the thinking that is at work in it. As we follow the many beginnings of the *Timaeus*, we will thus also have the opportunity to compare them with that other return to beginning described in the *Republic* as a return to the beginning of thought, namely, dialectic (*Republic* 511c–d, 533c–d).

Most immediately, Timaeus's praise takes the form of calling attention to the beauty of the cosmos, an attribute that brings with it three specifications: 1. copies of eternal beings are more beautiful than copies of things that become (29a); 2. what has mind is more beautiful than what does not have mind (30b); 3. what is whole and complete is more beautiful than what is partial and incomplete (30c). Insofar as soul is the only entity through which mind comes to be present "in" anything (30b, 46d), and insofar as soul is that by merit of which any living thing comes to be alive, it follows that the cosmos must be a living being embracing all other living beings. Moreover, living beings provide a vehicle for the expression of mindfulness and its opposite. And, in most cases, mindfulness and its opposite are made visible in living beings by the movements that are appropriate to their bodies (e.g., the circling rotation of the heavenly bodies, the crawling of land-dwelling animals, etc.), save for plants, whose mindlessness is evinced precisely by their lack of motion (77b–c).

Indeed, the third parameter concerns the status of motion in the dialogue. The phenomenal world, as Timaeus describes it, cannot be understood without an account of the motions that define it. This is true not only for the passions and actions of particular beings but also for the thinking that permeates the cosmos and for time itself, all of which are presented as epiphenomena of a set of primeval movements described and documented in some detail.[10] Throughout these descriptions, the way something moves is treated as essential to what it is. An investigation of certain beings, then, must include an investigation of movement; the dialogue's ontology requires kinesiology, even if only as a way to mark the limits of its own inquiry into Being.[11]

As the cosmogony develops, its inquiry into the bodily and psychical aspects of living being takes the form of a phenomenology of motion, describing in detail the movements that belong to soul and to the elements.[12] One way to gain access to the relationship between the living cosmos as a whole and the various other forms of animals it embraces is, thus, to look at the relationship between the movements that belong to the three kinds as they are instantiated in the cosmos: Being (approximated by the circular motion of the cosmos itself and, to a lesser extent, by the heavenly bodies), Becoming (manifest in the streaming inflow and outflow to which bodies are subject), and Chōra (whose shaking produces the conditions in which like adheres to like and provides the demiurge with rudimentary elements to array and to use in his creation of the cosmos). To follow the development of Timaeus's description of these three cosmic motions would exceed the scope of a single essay. However, Timaeus's account of the origins of the human animal, in whom these three motions converge and intermingle, offers us some insight into the circling, streaming, and shaking that populate the cosmos, as well as the motions that belong to the demiurge—his begetting, and the actions that go along with this, namely, modeling, mixing, pouring, infusing, interweaving, and veiling of the cosmos with psychē, all actions that are faintly echoed in the work of human beings.

Anthropogony

As the first created mortal animal not guaranteed everlasting life (that is, whose living entails dying), the human prototype consists of a collision of circular and linear motions.[13] The embrace within which the living sphere of the cosmos holds all other animals—the *peri- labon*, *-echein*, and *-eilephein* of this animal—is reiterated in the *periodos* and *periphora* of the heavenly bodies and echoed in the circuits of thought housed in the immortal soul. These circuits are handed over by the demiurge to his children for the purpose of creating other mortal animals, and it is these circuits that connect human life to the "thinkings and coursings of the all."[14] The created gods take this immortal soul and, borrowing portions of fire, water, earth, and air, shape these portions into bodies, adding to the *peri-* of the circuits of the soul the *epi-* and *apo-* of the flowings of the body: "and within bodies subject to inflow and outflow they bound the revolutions of the immortal soul [τὰς τῆς ἀθανάτου ψυχῆς περιόδους ἐνέδουν εἰς ἐπίρρυτον σῶμα καὶ ἀπόρρυτον]" (43a). Timaeus continues: "The souls, then, being thus bound within a mighty river neither mastered it nor were mastered, but with violence they rolled along and were rolled along themselves [βίᾳ δὲ ἐφέροντο καὶ ἔφερον], so that the whole of the living creature was moved, but in such a random way that its progress was disorderly and irrational [ἀλόγως]" (43b).[15] The antidote for this streaming and irrational movement is to mimic the shaking motion of chōra itself (88d–e), accomplishing accord between soul and body by balancing their motions, thereby enabling human beings to regulate their chaotic internal streamings and return the circuits of the soul to the harmonious cyclical motion of thought. Thus, like the cosmos itself, the human animal is permeated and constituted by the interaction between circular, linear, and shaking motions.

Because it does not *necessarily* circle back around to itself, mortal life is capable of being estranged from itself, an estrangement that, eventually, comes to expression in human life by its capacities for pleasure and pain, decisive for the character of this life (64c–65b). But this estrangement is also expressed through the existential principles or "laws of destiny" that the demiurge reveals to the immortal souls destined for mortal bodies: "namely, how that the first birth should be one and the same ordained for all, in order that none might be slighted by him; and how it was needful that they, when sown each into his own proper organ of time, should grow into the most god-fearing of living creatures; and that, since human nature is twofold, the superior [part] is that which hereafter should be designated 'man' [ἀνήρ]" (42a).[16]

These three "laws"—common originary natality, separate growth toward a shared goal, and division into superior and inferior—inscribe equality, separation, and difference as fundamental features of human mortality. In so doing, they mark out three distinct dimensions of the estrangement to which human life is subject by reason of the linear motion by which it is, in part, constituted: the temporal estrangement by means of which the human is alienated from its original nature; the quantitative estrangement by means of which individual human souls are separated out from a common source; and the qualitative estrangement according to which human nature is double, consisting of superior and inferior kinds. They also determine a specific trajectory or tenor to the activities of human life. Because mortal life has a primordial equality granted by its shared original natality, birth takes on the character of an exile from the most amenable life, and successful completion of a human life will have the character of a return.[17] Because mortal life includes separation but must tend toward the same end, the successful completion of a human life must also include the achievement of community. The specific basis of this community as it is given here is the shared striving toward and enactment of fear of the gods. That is, it is the shared task of a particular vision of piety that provides the basis for the community necessary for a complete human life. Because human nature is double, it will have better and worse accomplishments of itself.

Timaeus goes on to stipulate that justice is the mastering of these streamings, and injustice is the failure to master them. In order to describe the various reincarnations that result from this failure, Timaeus says the following:

> And he that has lived his appointed time well shall return again to his abode in his native star, and shall gain a life that is blessed and congenial; but whoso has failed therein shall be changed into a woman's nature at the second birth; and if, in that shape, he still refraineth not from wickedness he shall be changed every time, according to the nature of his wickedness, into some bestial form after the similitude of his own nature; nor in his changings shall he cease from woes until he yields himself to the revolution of the Same and Similar that is within him, and dominating by force of reason that burdensome mass which afterwards adhered to him of fire and water and earth and air, a mass tumultuous and irrational, returns again to the semblance of his first and best state. (42b–d)

Thus, while humans do not have the same kind of set orbit or circuit as their heavenly kin, they do have a path of life, one that is determined by the quality of their actions. Nevertheless, the "orbit" of the human life is not unwandering. The mortal animal for whom death is a reality has a course of life that could go well or poorly depending on how well its actions navigate the various streamings to which this life is subject.

What are we to make of what amounts to the assertion of an originary masculinity of the human kind, and the emergence of sexual difference as a secondary expression of the moral status of an individual soul? Here we can see a tension emerging from what appears to be the polymorphosity of the immortal soul that will be placed into human bodies: the prototype human is masculine, yet his soul must be capable of being born into a woman as well as into other forms of mortal animal, all the while retaining some semblance of its original masculine nature.[18] Contending with this question will take us to the heart of Timaeus's account of the origin of nonhuman animals, an origin that, because of the curious potency granted to human action, must be located within Timaeus's account of the task of human life.

Zoogony

From the perspective of the human, the successful completion of the human life consists in returning the circuits of the immortal soul to a condition of accord with the celestial orbits to which they are akin, using perception as a resource for aligning the circuits of thought with those of the cosmic bodies, "thereby making the part that thinks like unto the object of its thought, in accordance with its original nature" (90c–d).[19] Timaeus observes that doing so achieves the goal of life set before humans by the gods (90d). However, the failure of this task has its own generative possibilities; that is, as we have seen, it is from prototypes who have been unsuccessful during the course of their lives that women and then eventually the other mortal animals arise.[20] An exploration of the strangeness of this generative role, its usurping of sexual reproduction and privileging of masculinity within the realm of mortal life, will occupy much of this section. For now, I note that the human prototype disrupts the categorization of mortal animals into winged, water-dwelling, and land-dwelling; humans are footed but also the cause of the footed, dwell on land but are also the source of land-dwellers (as well as the winged and the water-dwellers). I suspect that we are to think of the human prototype not as a land-dweller but as a city-dweller; nevertheless, in his possession of feet and his founding of cities on land that he will be willing to fight to defend, the human prototype stands both inside and outside the categorization of mortal animals, muddying the clarity of the system and unsettling the ease with which these living beings are allocated into kinds.

Human residence in cities also marks a limit to the task to which Timaeus's cosmology responds; it is not Timaeus but Critias who is to describe the best city and its citizens. Timaeus's speech does gesture toward the city, however, drawing in outline the work of the city and its role in the production of other mortal animals: it is in the absence of a good regime, upbringing, and education that human viciousness, figured at one point as a form of disease (86e–87b), flourishes (44b–c). Humans must compensate for this absence by fleeing from the city's deleterious elements and seeking the best upbringing, pursuits, and studies. Timaeus breaks off from any discussion of what these best practices might be, observing that such considerations belong to a different mode of speech [τρόπος ἄλλος λόγων] (87b). Thus, as we pursue what it is that human life is to accomplish and what the results of its failure are, we will also encounter a limit to Timaeus's tale, one that will return our attention to the interpretive parameters we outlined at the start of this essay.

The generative character of human action is connected to the third "law of destiny" we discussed above, that is, the double nature of the human, a nature that introduces difference as a fundamental aspect of human being and, more than this, specifies it as the difference that pertains to men and women. But how are we to take this difference? While Timaeus makes clear that the human prototype is a man (ἀνήρ), sexual difference, in the sense of biological difference, emerges only with the failure of the prototype to live a just and courageous life (90e). When Timaeus specifies that the more noble human kind will be called "man," we are to think of this as indicating that the prototype is masculine, using masculine in the culturally coded sense of noble, rather than thinking that it indicates anything about it being male (in the sense in which we indicate a kind of sexed body). That is, in more contemporary terms, he is speaking of gender, not sex, and in this case gendered difference precedes sexual difference, since it is the actions of the human prototype, animated by a masculine soul, that produce the need for sexed bodies.[21] The bodies of women and other animals serve as signs and symptoms of the souls that animate them, offering yet another expression of the "appropriateness" between body and soul that is presented as being of the utmost importance to the health of human beings (87d) and that is a function of mind's persuasion of necessity.

While Timaeus's cosmogony claims masculinity as an aspect of the nobility of mortal animals, we must ask whether this is the case for all living things. Specifically, what about that living thing that is the cosmos itself? Timaeus does not seem to give it a gender, and in perpetually sustaining itself, perpetually producing itself, it does not need to reproduce itself. Perhaps we are to take this as suggesting that being gendered and sexed enter into the cosmos with the human animal and that this subsequently characterizes those other animals that emerge from human failings (as distinct from the cosmos itself, which is a one, complete and without remainder). Will the successful completion of human life, as Timaeus conceives it, include the overcoming of both gendered and sexual difference?[22] There is some reason to think so. First, the return offered to those who have lived well is a return to a condition before the emergence of sexual difference. Second, we should note the differing of difference here: equality and separation (the first two "laws of destiny") are originary, as, it would seem, is the double nature of the human. But that this double nature will be a difference of gender is a function of naming—the "superior" human will come to be called [κεκλήσοιτο] "man" (42a). That is, gendered difference emerges under the auspices of logos and the labile social construction of identity it makes possible.

However, the difference between men and women is not only a matter that is "explained" in Timaeus's cosmology. It also supplies terms to aid in the evaluation of differing forms of soul, since it is the image of differing domiciles for men and women that provides illustration of the differing locations of two forms of mortal soul (70a). Even if we are to think of thought and immortal soul as sexless and genderless in the sense that their actions are not circumscribed by or reducible to the actions of male or female and masculine or feminine, the overall description and celebration of soul and its actions keeps to the traditional allocation of the male and masculine as superior to the female and feminine—its praise is conservative, making use of the value terms of the time and place of its composition.[23] At the least, this assertion of the double nature of human life that marks a qualitative distinction (between superior and inferior) and that will come to be demarcated by names that signify gendered difference requires us to ask how the parameters of the dialogue, especially its character as a form of praise, shape this discussion. In addition, while the cosmos itself may not act according to sexual difference, the work of the demiurge and the character of chōra are explicitly figured along sexual lines—he is the begetter (34b) and father (37c), she is the mother (50d, 51a) and wet-nurse (49b).[24] Sexual difference is thus both an effect of the human prototype and yet also treated as an indispensable figure of the creative potency of the demiurge. It is both form and function, both product and process.

Moreover, it is necessary to keep in mind that, regardless of the status of the possibility of a sexless and genderless cosmos, human failure, that is, the unsuccessful completion of human life, not only is woven into the fabric of the cosmos but is required by it, since without this failure the cosmos would be incomplete. This is the case because human failing (or, at least, the failing of the human prototype) is generative of the other forms of animal life the cosmos must embrace in order to be complete. Thus, humans will mirror the generative activities of the demiurge, and will do so in more than one way. There is, first, the ethical zoogony productive of animal life by the quality of the actions committed and the life lived by the human prototype. In this mode of creation, an unsuccessful human life (Timaeus specifies this as a life that was cowardly and unjust, 90e) results first in the rebirth of the soul of that human prototype into a woman and, from there, if further degradation occurs, into birds, land-dwellers, and in the most depraved of cases, sea-dwellers (91d–92c).[25] This generation of animal life according to the character of the human prototypes' actions precedes and competes with the generative power of sexual reproduction.[26] Timaeus's description of a mortal-life-generating process prior to that of sexual reproduction may be required by the relationship between Mind and Necessity that Timaeus imagines. But it also makes of sexual reproduction a third generative kind (the first two being divine creation and the creation of animals via vicious human action), thereby establishing a connection between it and that other third kind, chōra.[27]

Timaeus's description of this third kind of generation is conspicuous for many reasons. Not the least of these is his description of human sexual organs as animals themselves that are productive of other animals housed within the human (91b–d). Thus, both in its possession of animal organs and in its housing and cultivation of animals like itself, in its being an animal that embraces within itself other animals, the human again echoes the cosmos.[28] Moreover, the description of the creation of the human prototype uses animal imagery to aid the evaluative, praise-giving dimension of the account (with the primary distinction being between wild animal and tame). This dual valence of the animal, as object to be described and as instrument of the description, runs parallel to the duplication of the division of the sexes we observed above, whereby sexual difference is both an object to be explained and an image used in the explaining, in this case the bodily domains of the different aspects of mortal soul (70a).

In its treatment of the "race of women" as somehow distinct from that of men, its assumption that the male is the more quintessentially human, and its alignment of the female with other animals, Timaeus's cosmogony invites the same critique Froma Zeitlin develops of Hesiod's Pandora tale (and of the broader misogynist vein in archaic and classical Greek literature she catalogues).[29] Its unquestioning employment and conservation of the evaluations of its time makes of this cosmogony something quite less than a revaluation of all values. But we do not need to leave the realm of ancient Greek thought and go as far, historically speaking, as Nietzsche to see its failings of inquiry. As scholars have noted, it fails to offer an account of human nature that includes the possibility of women who are capable of being, to follow Socrates's description at the dialogue's start, harmoniously tuned and similar to men (18c).[30] In its unquestioning reliance on an established tradition of praise and blame, it makes use of "hypotheses" that are themselves never questioned; it is not, then, a dialectical cosmogony, if such a thing is even possible. In this sense it fails to be a fully philosophic investigation, under the terms for such a course of inquiry asserted in Plato's *Republic* (a standard that the *Republic* itself also quite self-consciously fails to attain). It may be inappropriate to ascribe to Plato a lively interest in defending the integrity of women, but it is not inappropriate to ascribe to Plato a vision of philosophy as unflinching inquiry. And yet here Plato's Timaeus flinches.

The *Timaeus* shares with other dialogues the attempt to cast generation as an activity of mind. It offers us some sense for why Plato would feel compelled to construct, in the voice of Timaeus, a cosmogony that is also a zoogony. Animality is treated as that mode of becoming in which mindfulness and mindlessness are made manifest by means of motion. Living being is philosophically indispensable because its motion provides a means through which mind and the lack thereof can be made available to observation and thought; it is this capacity that recommends and governs many of the appeals to animal life throughout the dialogues. Thus, while the spectacle of both mindfulness and mindlessness provided by animal motion accounts for the ambivalence infusing Plato's discussions of animal life, this is a fecund ambivalence, as life provides the basis by means of which mind presents itself to thought.

But the cost of this endeavor is high, and Timaeus's cosmogony lacks the depth of inquiry such an effort requires. In the *Republic*, for instance, this approach to generation was attempted only by means of a sustained meditation on politically relevant differences with respect to nature, a complex refiguration of the relationship between physis and technē, a radical legislative agenda in which elaborate conventions were designed in order to curb and channel erōs, and a clear sense of the inevitable failure of this agenda. The *Timaeus* includes none of these considerations, and instead simply displaces sexual reproduction, first by eliding it with technical production and second by attributing the existence of women and nonhuman mortal animals to the actions of a masculine human prototype. In this absence of thinking, Timaeus's cosmogony produces a vision of human nature whose impoverishment is made apparent by the terms of the very task with which Timaeus had been charged. This, in turn, invites some consideration of whether a philosophical cosmogony is possible, or whether Plato is experimenting with the limits of its inquiry into origins and exploring the point at which it must give way to dialectic.

At the very least, his construction of Timaeus's cosmogony invites a critical eye. The model of human flourishing Timaeus offers—the regulation of bodily appetites and the contemplation of motion—proves to be an impoverished vision when compared with other presentations of human excellence in the dialogues. Where in this is the exercise of dialectic, the serious play of dialogue, the critical gaze upon the city? Where, in other words, in this portrait of human nature, is there room for the uncanny, critical, gadfly Socrates, neither fully at home in the city nor able to live without it?[31] And where is the well-educated philosophic ruler, compelled to give up contemplation of the Forms for a time in order to govern the city, looking off toward *both* the eternal Forms and "what is in human nature" (*Republic* 501b)?

From this broader perspective, Timaeus's account of the origin of the cosmos suffers from the absence of political analysis and from Timaeus's reticence to address the city other than obliquely. It also suffers from Timaeus's unwillingness to posit any kind of positive political or legislative agenda beyond advocating flight from deleterious political elements (87b). But this reticence is in part a function of the allocation of tasks and ordering of speeches by Socrates's interlocutors, whereby Timaeus, the statesman philosopher, the most astronomical, the one who has most busied himself with matters of the all (27a), is to give an account of the origin of the cosmos terminating in the nature of the human, while Critias is to give an account of how those humans who have received the kind of education Socrates outlined the previous day wage war. Timaeus's cosmogony opens up, then, a critique of the very attempt to offer an anthropogony without an account of the city and to align the emergence of the human with an account that represents itself as cosmological *rather than* political.[32] Thus, it is a critique not only of the cosmos as it is envisioned by Timaeus but also of the cosmos that is the *Timaeus*.

Notes

1. See Pierre Chantraine's entry on zōō on the connection between zōion and zōgraphos, that is, between living being and image. This connection is specifically at work in the *Timaeus*, as Remi Brague notes. "The Body of Speech: A New Hypothesis in the Compositional Structure of Timaeus' Monologue," in *Platonic Investigations*, ed. Dominic O'Meara (Washington, D.C.: Catholic University Press, 1985), 54.

2. See the eschatological myths in the *Phaedo* 113d–114c, *Phaedrus* 245c–249d, and *Republic* 614b–621d.

3. As Carlos Steel puts it, the *Timaeus* is an attempt "to understand the universe in the context of the ethical finality of human life" ("The Moral Purpose of the Human Body: A Reading of *Timaeus* 69–72," *Phronesis* 46, no. 2 [2001]: 107). Timaeus himself specifically notes

the borders of his contribution to the day's discussion in a manner that gestures toward the "coming" political analysis in very revealing ways (44b–c, 87a–b).

4. On the peculiar features of the *Timaeus* in the context of other Greek cosmogonies, see J. B. Skemp, *The Theory of Motion in Plato's Later Dialogues* (Las Palmas, Spain: Adolf M. Hakkert, 1967); Andrew Gregory, *Ancient Greek Cosmogony* (London: Duckworth Press, 2007); Gordon Campbell, "Zoogony and Evolution in Plato's *Timaeus*," in *Reason and Necessity: Essays on Plato's* Timaeus, ed. M. R. Wright (London: Duckworth Press, 2000), 145–180; and Charles Kahn, "The Place of Cosmology in Plato's Later Dialogues," in *One Book, the Whole Universe: Plato's* Timaeus *Today*, ed. Richard Mohr and Barbara Sattler (Las Vegas: Parmenides Publishing, 2010).

5. All citations are drawn from Bury's Loeb translation, although I have consistently translated nous as "mind," removed many of the honorific capitalizations, and replaced Bury's translation of to pan as "Universe" with "the All." All Greek citations are taken from Burnet's OCT edition.

6. See also 17b where justice requires a return of speeches; at 19d Socrates speaks of the need for proper praise of "our" men and city (see also 20b–c and 26d–e). On the persistence of the standard of the beautiful, see 53b–54b.

7. For a probing study of the nuances of this phrase, see Miles Burnyeat, "Eikos Mythos," *Rizai* 2, no. 2 (2005): 143–165; Gabor Betegh, "What Makes a Muthos Eikos?" in *One Book, the Whole Universe: Plato's* Timaeus *Today*, ed. Richard Mohr and Barbara Sattler (Las Vegas: Parmenides Publishing, 2010), 213–224; and, in the same volume, Alexander Mourelatos, "The Epistemological Section (29b–d) of the Proem in Timaeus' Speech: M. F. Burnyeat on eikôs Mythos, and Comparison with Xenophanes B34 and B35," 225–248.

8. I am indebted to John Sallis for his thorough study of the trope of beginning in the *Timaeus* (*Chorology: On Beginning in Plato's* Timaeus [Bloomington: Indiana University Press, 1999]).

9. This conservatism marks a difference between Timaeus's performance of justice and other accounts in the dialogues characterized as giving back what is due, as, for instance, that found in *Republic* Book 10.

10. Hence Timaeus's emphasis on shape as the most vivid bodily expression of motion; for example, the head is said to be round in imitation of the circuits of the heavens (44d). The special status of motion in the dialogue is hinted at early on, in Socrates's desire to see the city in motion (19b–c). Further intimation of the primacy of motion for Timaeus's cosmogony can be found in his description of the creation of the cosmic soul, where the paths the celestial bodies are to travel, their orbits, are created before the bodies that will travel them (36b–d, 38c–d), and in his description of earth, which aligns its immobility with its malleability (55e).

11. In his introduction to the creation of time, Timaeus also marks a limit of motion: Being is unmoving, while "was" and "will be" imply motion (37e).

12. Fire ignites and melts, water liquefies, earth and air receive these motions (see especially 58d–61c); thought is a function of the circuits of the soul (90c–d); passion and perception are streams to which mortal soul is subject (43b–c), following the inflowing and outflowing that is characteristic of mortal life.

13. The linear motion that so powerfully determines human life is first intimated by Timaeus's description of the created heavenly animals. Unlike the animal that is the cosmos itself, which has one motion, the heavenly animals are allotted two: uniform motion in the same place, and forward motion. The linear motion of which these gods are capable is made harmonious with their self-same cosmic motion by their being placed in orbits, traveling a forward path that also circles back upon itself. The association asserted here between linearity and mortality is obscured somewhat by the fact that the demiurge grants to these created gods

everlasting life; however, their linear motion introduces other possibilities for movement, possibilities that are realized in the "products" of the work with which these gods are charged.

14. 90d, my translation; see also 47b–c: the orbits of thinking in us are akin to the circuits of intellect in the heavens. That Timaeus treats thinking as a motion of a particular kind is perhaps most clearly seen in his description of plants: as living things, plants must possess soul, but their passivity and lack of self-motion indicate that they have only the lowest form of mortal soul and are bereft of "opinion and reasoning and mind [ᾧ δόξης μὲν λογισμοῦ τε καὶ νοῦ]" (77b). See also J. B. Skemp, "Plants in Plato's Timaeus," *Classical Quarterly* 41, no. 1 (1947): 53–60.

15. This is followed by a passage that marks out the soul's confusion and what must happen in order to return to a state of giving correct accounts: the stream of increase and nutriment must abate, the circuits return to their calm, and their orbits reclaim their proper path; this requires a good upbringing and education (see 44b–d). On possible Parmenidean resonances in Timaeus's treatment of circular and linear motion, see Lynne Ballew, "Straight and Circular in Parmenides and the *Timaeus*," *Phronesis* 19, no. 3 (1974): 189–209.

16. My emendation to Bury's "superior sex," which muddies the distinction at stake here. The Greek text is τὸ κρεῖττον τοιοῦτον εἴη ὃ καὶ ἔπειτα κεκλήσοιτο ἀνήρ.

17. Timaeus makes this explicit when he observes that, if successful, human life will be lived attempting to return to its "first and best state" (42d). On the character of human striving as a striving to return, see also 42a–c and 44b–c. For a study of this dimension of nostalgia in multiple dialogues, including the *Timaeus*, see Jill Gordon, *Plato's Erotic World: From Cosmic Origins to Human Death* (Cambridge: Cambridge University Press, 2012).

18. For further examples of this conception of masculinity as an enduring quality of psychē and/or personhood, see Brooke Holmes, *Gender: Antiquity and Its Legacy* (Oxford: Oxford University Press, 2012).

19. On perception as an aid to thought, see 47a–e.

20. 42c–d; 90e begins as a description of "how women and the whole female sex have come into existence [γυναῖκες μὲν οὖν καὶ τὸ θῆλυ πᾶν οὕτω γέγονεν]" (91d). Comparison with Hesiod on Pandora and the birth of the "race" of women is invited.

21. As Stella Sandford puts it: "The categories of 'man' and 'woman' are conceptually distinct from those of 'male' and 'female' in Timaeus' discussion of human beings" (*Plato and Sex* [London: Polity Press, 2010], 151). While male and female are categories that roughly correspond to differing functions in sexual reproduction, "the difference between man and women, on the other hand, is not sexual but moral" (152). I accept Sandford's argument about the difference between differences here; I only diverge from her reading insofar as what she sees as a function of Timaeus's use of myth I see as a function of the character of the cosmology as an act of praise.

22. On the question of whether Plato sees sexual difference as a sign of human failing and thus as something to be overcome, see Marguerite DesLauries, "Plato on Sexual Difference and Sexual Reproduction," in *Platonic Inspirations*, ed. J. Opsomer and M. Beck (Leuven, Belgium: Leuven University Press, 2013); Sara Brill, "Plato's Critical Theory," *Epoché* 17, no. 2 (2013): 233–248; and Sandford, *Plato and Sex*. On the difficulties of mapping a sex/gender distinction onto ancient Greek cultural attitudes toward male and female, see Holmes, *Gender: Antiquity and Its Legacy*.

23. As Mitchell Miller rather generously puts it, the zoogony reveals this cosmology's "provincialism" ("The Timaeus and the 'Longer Way': 'God-given' Method and the Constitution of Elements and Animals," in *Plato's Timaeus as Cultural Icon*, ed. Gretchen Reydam-Schills [South Bend, Ind.: University of Notre Dame Press, 2003]). Morag Buchan argues that Plato does indeed conceive of the immortal soul as essentially masculine (see *Women in Plato's Po-*

litical Theory [New York: Palgrave, 1998]); I am more interested in the polymorphosity that the *Timaeus* attributes to soul.

24. On the language of procreation in Timaeus's description of the demiurge's work, see Stella Sandford (*Plato and Sex*, 154–155). For an overview of the engagements with the Timaean chōra in contemporary feminist thought, see Luce Irigaray, *Speculum of the Other Woman*, trans. G. C. Gill (Ithaca, N.Y.: Cornell University Press, 1985); Julia Kristeva, "Revolution in Poetic Language," in *The Portable Kristeva*, ed. K. Oliver (New York: Columbia University Press, 2002); Judith Butler, *Bodies That Matter* (New York: Routledge, 1993); Elizabeth Grosz, *Space, Time and Perversion* (New York: Routledge, 1995); and Emanuela Bianchi, "Receptacle/Chora: Figuring the Errant Feminine in Plato's *Timaeus*," *Hypatia* 24, no. 4 (2006): 124–146. On Plato's appropriation of the language of sexual reproduction in his depictions of Socrates and his accounts of philosophy, see Paige du Boise's "The Platonic Appropriation of Reproduction," in *Feminist Interpretations of Plato*, ed. Nancy Tuana (State College: Penn State Press University Press, 1994), 139–156; and Kristin Sampson's "Identity and Gender in Plato," in *Feminist Reflections on the History of Philosophy*, ed. Charlotte Witt and Lilli Alanen (Boston: Kluwer Academic Publishers, 2006), 17–32.

25. The kinship between women and these other animals is expressed grammatically as well as substantively: the clause in which Timaeus speaks of the birth of "women and the whole female sex" is a "men ... de" clause whose "de" is the "tribe of birds" (91d).

26. The attempt to deny female agency in the act of reproduction has a long history; see Hesiod on Pandora and Zeitlin's commentary on this myth.

27. Sarah Broadie, in *Nature and Divinity in Plato's* Timaeus (Cambridge: Cambridge University Press, 2011), reads erōs as the third kind here and views it as intimating Aristotle's radical refiguring of nutrition and the nutritive soul.

28. This imagery of animals within the animal occurred earlier in the description of the domain of the lowest form of mortal soul (70e–71a).

29. See J-P. Vernant, "The Myth of Prometheus in Hesiod," in *Myth and Society in Ancient Greece*, trans. Janet Lloyd (New York: Zone Books, 1990), 183–202, and Froma Zeitlin, "Signifying Difference: The Case of Hesiod's Pandora," in *Playing the Other: Gender and Society in Classical Greek Literature* (Chicago: University of Chicago Press, 1995), 53–86.

30. See David Krell's "Female Parts in *Timaeus*," in *Arion* 2, no. 3 (1975): 400–421; Catherine Zuckert's *Plato's Philosophers: The Coherence of the Dialogues* (Chicago: University of Chicago Press, 2012); and Cynthia Freeland's "Schemes and Scene of Reading the *Timaeus*," in *Feminist Reflections on the History of Philosophy*, ed. Charlotte Witt and Lilli Alanen (Boston: Kluwer Academic Publishers, 2004), 33–50.

31. At the very least, Timaean piety is not the same as Socratic piety. For an extended analysis of the divergence between Timaeus's philosophizing and Socrates's philosophic practice, see Catherine Zuckert's *Plato's Philosophers*, Part 2. For Zuckert, this difference is fundamentally a matter of two different approaches to erōs and desire. See also H. G. Gadamer's "Idea and Reality in Plato's *Timaeus*," in *Dialogue and Dialectic: Eight Hermeneutical Studies on Plato*, trans. P. Christopher Smith (New Haven, Conn.: Yale University Press, 1983), 156–193.

32. See Timaeus's explicit separation of his discourse from one that would address the way that humans are to live in the city and what character the city is to have (87b). Here we can mark another difference between Timaeus and Hesiod, as the latter treats cosmology as politics writ large. Nevertheless, for all of Timaeus's efforts to avoid discussion of the city, he cannot keep political language from infecting his account of the cosmos, as for instance, in his characterization of the interaction between elements as a kind of polemos (57a–c).

PART VI

The Philosophical Animal

11 Animal Sacrifice in Plato's Later Methodology

Holly Moore

> ... knowledge is not made for understanding, it is made for cutting.
> —Michel Foucault, "Nietzsche, Genealogy, History"

In several of his later dialogues, Plato's characters take up dialectical inquiries that oscillate between collecting particulars into their broader kinds and articulating those kinds into their subspecies according to a "natural line of cleavage [διαφυὴν]" (*Statesman* 259d).[1] In both the *Statesman* and the earlier *Phaedrus*, this second aspect of the dialectical method, the division of kinds, is likened to the everyday practice of animal sacrifice and butchery. In what follows, I address two ways that this analogy can be used to interpret Plato's later methodology. First, I argue that if we examine this analogy with respect to the details of its cultural practice, we discover evidence that Plato prioritizes the method of collection insofar as division is impossible without it. In addition, however, I also argue that since collection participates in constructing the subject of division *as divisible,* it, like division, fails to grasp the oneness central to the being of any class it produces. I conclude from this that both of these methods are inadequate and that the image of the sacrificable animal reveals the thoroughly mimetic nature of discursive reasoning.

In order to understand the significance of the appeal to animal sacrifice within Plato's later methodology, we must begin with a study of the *Phaedrus,* where, in addition to its many allusions to animals, we find the first reference to the method of division as a kind of butchery. We also find there a more complete account of the method of collection, an important aspect of Platonic methodology, which remains, for the most part, only implicit within later dialogues.

The Bestiary of the *Phaedrus*

The *Phaedrus* is full of allusions to animals and humans' relationship to them. From the singing cicadas (230c, 259a–d) to the straining winged horses of the soul (246a, 253d–e), which is later likened to an oyster trapped in its shell, the body (250c), the *Phaedrus* is one of Plato's most zoologically animated dialogues. Of the many creatures that populate Plato's bestiary, Socrates paints himself as the first. Walking with Phaedrus in the path of the Ilissus river, Socrates is reminded of the myth told of Oreithyia's abduction by Boreas, but he dismisses discussion of mythological happenings in favor of inquiring into himself, "to know whether I am a monster [θηρίον] more complicated and furious than Typhon or a gentler and simpler creature [ζῷον], to whom a divine and quiet [ἀτύφου] lot is given by nature" (230a).[2] Just a short time later, Socrates again underscores his "animal" nature: "For as people lead hungry animals by shaking in front of them a branch of leaves or some fruit, just so, I think, you [Phaedrus], by holding before me discourses [λόγους] in books, will lead me all over Attica and wherever you please" (230d–e).[3] As in other dialogues, Socrates is portrayed as strange, and here he becomes an image of the half-breed nature of the human, at once divine and bestial.

Not only does Socrates himself appear as an animal in the *Phaedrus*, he goes on throughout the dialogue to offer a variety of depictions of *logoi* as animal-like, making this relationship one of the more powerful tropes of the *Phaedrus*. Having listened to Phaedrus's recitation of Lysias's speech and offered his own speeches on erotic madness, Socrates turns to reflect upon the art of speechmaking itself, using Lysias's speech as an example for critique.[4] As Socrates famously claims, a good speech "must be organized, like a living being [ζῷον], with a body of its own, as it were, so as not to be headless or footless, but to have a middle and members, composed in fitting relation to each other and to the whole" (264c). Despite its display of many rhetorical techniques, Socrates faults Lysias's speech for lacking a unifying principle. According to his critique, Lysias's speech is a monster, having no head and far too many limbs, some of which appear not even to be attached. In contrast, the good speech, like an animal's body, must have all the right parts in all the right places along with sound relations, or joints, between them. The good *logos* and the animal's body share a similarly *articulate* nature. Moreover, the articulateness of the good speech is derived from the already articulate nature of the subject of the *logos*, which also reflects the symmetry of the animal body: "Just as the body, which is one, is naturally divisible into two, right and left, with parts called by the same names, so our two discourses conceived of madness as naturally one principle within us, and one discourse, cutting off the left-hand part, continued to divide this until it found among its parts a sort of left-handed love, which it very justly reviled, but the other discourse, leading us to the right-hand part of madness, found a love having the same name as the first, but divine" (265e–266b).⁵ Thus, the articulate nature characteristic of a good speech simply mirrors the already articulate nature of its subject.⁶

In addition to likening, in his discussion of rhetoric, the proper structure of speeches to that of an animate body, Socrates appeals to the liveliness of an animal in order to value spoken over written *logoi*. Lauding the vital responsiveness of spoken *logoi* in their ability to relate to an interlocutor, Socrates contrasts these with written *logoi*, characterized as lifeless and repetitive, rendered dumb by the static permanence of their inscription (275d–277a). Also within the portion of the dialogue devoted to rhetoric, Socrates introduces the *zōion* once more as he accounts for the relationship between the dialectician and *logos* in his discussion of the methods of collection and division.

The Methods of Collection and Division

In the midst of his critique of Lysias's speech, Socrates outlines the features of a good speech, saying that his own speeches on *eros* had demonstrated "two principles [δυοῖν εἰδοῖν], the essence of which it would be gratifying to learn, if art could teach it" (265d). As Socrates explains it, an initial collection produced a formal definition of love, affording his speech the "clearness and consistency" that was conspicuously lacking in Lysias's speech (265d).⁷ In addition, Socrates identifies the second *eidos* of speech as that of "dividing things again by classes [κατ' εἴδη], where the natural joints are, and not trying to break any part, after the manner of a bad carver [μαγείρου]" (265e). These "natural joints" appear to be echoed in the *Statesman* (quoted earlier) where division is said to cut along a "natural line of cleavage." Let us consider each of these methods in turn.

Socrates describes collection as a "perceiving and bringing together in one idea the scattered particulars, that one may make clear by definition the particular thing which he wishes to explain" (265d), and he characterizes the "divine" dialectician as one who can "see things that can naturally be collected into one" (266b). Nevertheless, collection is not simply reserved for the dialectician, as it is even invoked as the quintessential feature of the human soul in the elaborate myth describing the transmigration of souls: "For a human being must understand a general conception [εἶδος] formed by collecting into a unity by means of reason the many perceptions of the senses" (249b). In sum, collection marks the defining nature of the human soul, distinguishing it from that of the nonhuman animal soul: the ability to move from multiplicity toward unity and from sensible particularity to formal abstraction.

Humans are again distinguished as superior to nonhuman animals with Socrates's description of the second *eidos* of speech. Likening the method of division to the butcher's ability to dismember an animal by its joints invokes humans' domination over animals as food. That is, certain nonhuman animals are subordinated to humans as vehicles for maintaining our own animate existence. In addition, note the similar claim of the *Statesman* that the dialectician must divide classes "like an animal that is sacrificed, by joints" (287b–c). This reference to sacrifice also serves to elevate the human, since the nonhuman animal functions to preserve our relationship with the divine.

Throughout the *Phaedrus*, the trope of the animal appears ambiguous. On the one hand, the human is likened to the animal: Socrates is an animal hungry for *logoi*, and *logoi* are themselves articulate and animate. On the other hand, the human transcends the animal: collection produces abstractions purified of sensible nature, and division carves up a feast of *logoi*. This ambiguity appears to be grounded in human nature itself as simultaneously ruled by divine and animal natures. Because the methods of collection and division together negotiate the relation between similarity and difference, they serve as a key site for investigating the puzzling ambiguity of human nature. By looking more closely at these methods in light of the details of ancient Greek sacrificial practices, we will be able to investigate more deeply the way the nonhuman animal serves to highlight the human's peculiar relationship to *logos*.

The Insufficiency of the Method of Division

Most modern commentators agree that although the method of division is prominent in the *Sophist* and *Statesman*, this does not suggest that Plato was praising its use.[8] Even the Great Divider himself, the Eleatic Stranger, critiques the overzealous use of division: "the attempt to separate everything from everything else is not only not in good taste but also shows that a man is utterly uncultivated and unphilosophical" (*Sophist* 259d–e).[9] To divide simply for the sake of dividing is a mark of eristic disputation. In addition to this textual admonition against the excessive use of division, Mitchell Miller and Kenneth Dorter both assert that the performative failures of the bifurcatory divisions of the first half of the *Statesman* indicate Plato's reserve with respect to the exclusive use of division.[10]

Nevertheless, these same authors also argue that the shift to the sacrificial model serves as an attempt at rehabilitating the method of division, from its rigidly quantitative application in the early bisectional divisions toward divisions based on qualitative assessments in the latter half of the dialogue.[11] Thus, although division as strict quantitative bifurcation does seem to be under scrutiny in the dialogue, the invocation of sacrifice comes at precisely the point at which division is recast as founded on qualitative, eidetic judgments. In addition, the fact that sacrifice is a sacred ritual practice central to the daily life of the Greeks suggests not only that Plato is not critiquing "sacrificial" division but that he may even be embracing it.

In spite of these indications, I would like to argue that Plato is in fact offering a deeper critique of division than is recognized by those interpretations that offer a view of division as rehabilitated within the *Statesman*. In particular, I find that *especially* when division is compared to the practice of animal sacrifice, it is seen as insufficient on its own, as it must be accompanied both by a primary and by ongoing acts of collection.

Butchery and Sacrifice in Ancient Greece

To a modern reader, the *Phaedrus*'s appeal to butchery and the *Statesman*'s appeal to sacrifice might appear entirely unrelated, but in the context of ancient Greek language, the practice of sacrifice is not in fact separable from the butchery of animals for food. Whereas most contemporary industrialized cultures have a distinct term for butchery (profane dismemberment) as opposed to sacrifice (sacred dismemberment), by the fifth century BCE the Greek *mageiros* meant simultaneously butcher, sacrificer, and cook.[12] Jean-Pierre Vernant summarizes the term's ambiguous significance in this way: "For us, sacrifice and butchering belong to different semantic zones, [but] . . . among the Greeks matters were completely different. The same vocabulary encompasses two domains, from Homer to the end of the classical age. Ancient Greek has no other terms to convey the idea of slaughtering an animal to butcher it than those referring to sacrifice or killing for the gods."[13] Thus, even though division is at times related to the butcher's craft and at others to the sacrificer's, given the semantic overlap between *mageiros* as butcher and as sacrificer, we can safely assert that all these references invoke the ritual of animal sacrifice. We will find in what follows that insofar as sacrificial practice is constituted by an extensive series of cuts, it was for Plato an appropriate analogue for the method of division.

In his treatment of ancient Greek sacrifice, *Homo Necans*, Walter Burkert notes that, in addition to sources in ancient literature, the central acts of sacrificial ritual are attested to in many classical-era vase paintings.[14] According to these sources, upon arriving at the sacrificial site, the space of the ritual must first be sanctified: "the sacrificial basket [containing the sacrificial knife] and water jug are carried around the assembly, thus marking off the sacred realm from the profane."[15] The first (symbolic) sacrifice is that of the animal's hair. After this comes the killing blow, a deep cut at the neck, from which the animal's blood is carefully captured, so that it too may be offered at the altar. Drained of blood, the animal's body is stretched and cut lengthwise, dividing the left- and right-hand sides of the abdomen in order to expose both the upper and lower organs. We may note that these organs are double in two ways. First, the upper, "noble" organs, or *splankhna*, are opposed to the lower organs, which are undesirable for eating. That is, the organs are divided into the good and the bad, a sacrificial practice that corresponds directly to Socrates's account in the *Phaedrus*. Second, the upper organs each demonstrate a kind of double nature in themselves: the kidneys are paired, the lungs and liver each have discernable lobes, and even the heart has distinct chambers.[16]

In addition to this division between upper and lower viscera, the viscera as a whole are extracted first and are divided from the flesh and bone of the animal. After this is complete, yet another separation is made, this time between the upper and lower halves of the animal's body. Indeed, in many scenes of the "Ricci Vase," we see half a goat's carcass hanging like a festoon in the background.[17] All that is left is to separate the bones from the flesh and the flesh from the fat, each division corresponding to the distinction between the Promethean offering to the gods and the meat left for the ritual's participants to enjoy in common.

In all, since the ritual of sacrifice entails an elaborate series of cuts, it makes for a fitting analogue for the manifold divisions necessary in the search for some class, whether the divine madness of *eros,* the wily craft of the sophist, or the prudent wisdom of the statesman. But since it has been suggested that the analogy to sacrificial practice acts to elevate not only the human but also the method of division itself, let us consider in more detail the significance of this analogy for determining the relative value of this method.

Division as a Violation of Unity

Recall that when the method of division is first discussed in the *Phaedrus* Socrates warns against chopping up classes "in the manner of a bad carver." Whereas a "hack job" would likely leave behind splintered bones, a clean cut would preserve the integrity of each member that has been divided. As the master carver of the *Zhuang-zi* puts it:

> A good cook changes his blade once a year: he slices. An ordinary cook changes his blade once a month: he hacks. I have been using this same blade for nineteen years, cutting up thousands of oxen, and yet it is still as sharp as the day it came off the whetstone. For the joints have spaces within them, and the very edge of the blade has no thickness at all. When what has no thickness enters into an empty space, it is vast and open, with more than enough room for the play of the blade. (3:4)[18]

That is, the failure of the bad butcher consists in the fact that he *does* cut what is separated, harming the integrity of the parts that are separated. The excellent butcher, on the other hand, merely renders visible those perforations that are present but invisible within the animal's body.[19] In addition, proper butchery makes good on the original wholeness of the animal by preserving and revealing the unity of each part that is separated. Thus a successful division must reconstitute unity in the production of two wholes from an original one. From this perspective, division might appear to be quite productive. Just as butchery produces useful food, division produces useful concepts, which may in turn be divided in order to produce even more.

In spite of its productive quality, we are unable to overlook the fact that the virtuous *mageiros* cannot cut meat well without having first killed an animal.

Similarly, though the virtuous dialectician may divide adeptly, merely following the "natural joints," the practice of division requires that the unity of what is divided be somehow violated in the process. This would seem to suggest that the method of division, like animal sacrifice, may be productive only by means of a violation of the vital integrity of the original subject.[20]

But what, exactly, is violated by the method of division? Scrutinizing this original unity, we encounter an apparent divergence between the practice of sacrifice and that of division. It seems inaccurate to consider the sacrificial animal analogous with what is articulated through the method of division, for the class that is divided in each case is always something *other* than the target of division's inquiry. In order to pursue a definition by means of division, the Stranger in each case must *assume* the first class to be divided, and this class is not itself the subject of the inquiry. For example, the divisions of both the *Sophist* and the *Statesman* begin from the assertion of a class that is not itself produced on the basis of a prior division: the *Sophist*'s divisions begin from the assumption that sophistry is a form of *technē* (221d), and the Stranger begins his divisions with the agreement that the statesman will be found among those who have *epistēmē* (258b). Every time the method of division is employed to sketch the path toward a definition, some class must first be posited, a class that cannot itself be accounted for by means of the method of division.[21]

This apparent divergence is resolved, however, if we reconsider the transformation of the animal within the sacrificial rite. The animal that is sacrificed is, in at least one sense, decidedly different from that which is dismembered. That is, the life of the living animal, its *zōē*, must be sacrificed before the dead animal can be eviscerated and dismembered in a second sacrifice, which is made as an offering to the god(s). This living unity, then, is the sine qua non of ritual sacrifice, but it is different from the nonliving unity of the carcass that is dismembered.

In division, the correlate to the living animal of sacrifice is the class originally posited for analysis, as it must be different from the sought-after class at the same time as it also somehow harbors it. Notice, however, that division cannot provide this original class on its own. Before division may begin, there must be something for it to divide. The single class that begins the search by division is not something achieved by division but instead something posited by collection, which identifies a unified set of features shared by all members of the larger genus that is proposed as containing the division's target class.[22] In all, the fact that division should require the fundamental assumption of a class to be divided strongly suggests that division is viewed in the later dialogues as a method dependent upon a prior use of collection.

Not only is collection necessary in advance of any division, it also appears to be responsible for identifying the distinctions among subsequently divided classes. That is, since collection isolates traits common to a class, it thereby also illuminates their distinction from others. Thus, just as Zhuang-zi's butcher suggested that the space between the joints is more significant than the width of the blade, it would seem that collection's identification of classes paves the way for division's subsequent articulation. According to this model, then, every division is sketched in advance by the method of collection. As a result, the majority of what appears to be accomplished through division is in fact the work of multiple, ongoing collections, taking place, as it were, behind the scenes, unnoticeably tracing the line along which each cut is to be made.

On this interpretation, rather than demonstrating Plato's rehabilitation and innovation of the method of division, the analogy made between division and animal sacrifice shows division's utter dependence upon collection as logically primary. In so doing, Plato implicitly posits collection as the philosophical method more closely bound to the original unity of what is articulated through division, giving it the duty of identifying the natural joints, such that division may separate them appropriately. But insofar as collection acts as the preparation for division, it is also thereby implicated in the logic of sacrifice. In my final section, I will investigate the role of collection as a kind of "domestication" of forms from natural, "wild" wholes to constructed, and thus "tamed," unities.

Collection as the Domestication of Classes

I have argued above that, in the later dialogues, the method of division is shown as subordinate to the method of collection because of its dependence upon prior (and subsequent) unities that must be posited in order for it to conduct its characteristic articulation and analysis. I would now like to return to the method of collection in order to probe its role within the logic of sacrifice already uncovered in our analysis of the method of division. Let us look again to the practice of sacrifice in order to discuss a specific aspect of its "logic," as I have called it.

We have posited that the method of collection is presupposed by the method of division for the same reason that a living, whole animal must already be available for sacrifice before it can be butchered. Focusing on this living, whole animal, we can quickly see that much must already have been accomplished to have an animal "available" and "ready" for sacrifice. Most importantly, animals must be docile enough to be handled by human participants during a sacrifice. Indeed, the willing victim was the highest ideal in ancient Greek sacrifice—to such an extent, in fact, that evidence of this quality became embedded within the ritual itself. By pouring water over the animal's head, the participants encouraged the animal to extend its neck, lifting its head as if in noble assent to its coming death.[23] In addition to this ritual evidence, the geographer and anthropologist Erich Isaac has argued that this need for a stock of docile animals for sacrifice acted as the catalyst for extensive domestic breeding of herd animals, beginning in ancient Babylon and Egypt.[24]

Given these relationships between domestication and sacrifice, it is clear that the prior unity of the animal that is established before the sacrifice is not simply the animal given in nature but one already inscribed with social forms via domestication. In order to make a sacrifice, a sacrificial animal must be available, but insofar as the properties befitting a sacrificial animal are not immediately abundant without human imposition, specific domesticated animals must be bred *as sacrificable*.[25] Although the idea of an animal as sacrificable implies both the relationship between animal and human and that between human and divine, the notion of "animal-as-sacrificable" is exclusively indexed to human aims. If this is the case, then the living unity that precedes the sacrificial rite is necessarily a human construction. That is, the introduction of "sacrificable" into the very meaning of "animal" is something that does not occur simply by nature, although the natural vulnerability and tractability of certain animals is compatible with this meaning. I will now argue for an interpretation of the method of collection as performing a similar kind of constructive mediation of the classes it renders up for division.

On the face of it, depicting collection as a kind of "domestication" of concepts is problematic, for it seems to deny the claims throughout the dialogues that division occurs *diaphuēn*, according to "natural joints," which, as I have already argued, are marked out by prior collections. Furthermore, domestication suggests a technicity normally absent from discussions of dialectical inquiry and present, instead, in discussions of sophistry. Surely the dialogues suggest that the breaks between classes are *ontologically* grounded, with collection gesturing directly at this nature. But a gesture is not the same as that to which it points. The method of collection generates a class, a definition, perhaps even simply a single term, and each of these serves as a *sign* of the distinctiveness of that kind in nature, while not being that nature itself. This gap is sufficient to introduce what I see to be the similarity between the collection of divisible classes and the domestication of sacrificable animals: the production of a novel kind whose nature is inherently double because of its relation to the human.

We may begin by noting that domestication and collection both produce a "tame" version of their subject. Domestication begins with the animal "in nature" and then renders it behaviorally docile by conditioning and selective breeding, ultimately making the animal a being *relative to the human*, a being whose nature is not simply its own but is also *for the human*. Thus domestication introduces a duplicity into the nature of the animal, a nature that is self-same and yet oriented toward another, the human. This ontological and semantic doubling of the animal is necessary so that its material multiplicity may be exploited in the act of sacred dismemberment. This is not to say that the animal in nature is not sacrificed, only that this sacrifice occurs within the domestication that necessarily precedes the sacrificial ritual.

Similarly, collection also begins from a natural class, for instance "animal," which is itself whole "in nature," that is, with respect to being. As an ontological kind, "animal" is one, whole, unmediated, and uncomplicated. Though there are many different kinds of animals, they are all one in *being* animals. Collection "domesticates" the class for human understanding by identifying the common features within a variety of instances and stitching that sensible many into a coherent unity. But where there are stitches a seam remains, and collection's fabricated unity can never be other than the image of that whole. That is, thought's synthetic movement toward abstraction is discursively related to being, and, however faithful it may be, it remains an image of being rather than being itself. Though collection is responsive to the immediate oneness of the being of a class, it nonetheless mediates that singular nature, rendering each class composite and, thus, implicitly divisible. The "natural" class with which collection begins is tamed by *logos*, which produces a discursively intelligible kind. Thus, just as domestication is not directly responsible for sacrifice, though it produces the animal as sacrificable, so collection does not actively divide classes, though it constructs them *as* divisible.

As "taming" disciplines, collection and domestication actively produce natural subjects as relative to the human. In the case of domestication, an animal's disposition as either wild or tame is legible only within the context of human fear and need, and only by reflecting this relation does it become coherent as sacrificable. Similarly, ontological kinds have no inherent relationship to human knowledge, but when that relation is performed through *logos*, the kind produced includes a multiplicity reflective of that relation. Thus, in each case, what is sacrificed/articulated is not a natural being *tout court;* it is nature as relative to the human, nature as a reflection of itself.

If we take these considerations back to the context of the *Phaedrus*, a few things become clear. First, Socrates's early introspective turn to consider his own nature becomes more suggestive: is he a beast wilder than Typhon or a tamer, gentler animal? Though Socrates may be alluding to the fact that he is often confused with a sophist (and here we must be reminded of the Stranger's admonition about the wolf and the dog in the *Sophist*[26]), we must also notice that to ask the question of *whether* one is a wild or a tame animal is to have already decided in favor of the latter. For "tame" and "wild" both imply the animal's relationship to humans. In addition, the relation of collection to discursive knowledge clarifies the significance of the *Phaedrus*'s sharply drawn distinction between written and spoken *logos*. Spoken *logos*, like the natural class, is wholly oriented by proximity to its source, whereas written *logos* is an image abandoned by its origin, rigidly repetitive of its script, unable to be responsive to new inquiry. Perhaps the anxiety immediately following the discussion of dialectic arises in response to the fact that the sacrificial metaphor accurately depicts the dialectician's craft as endemically *mimetic* and thus divorced from direct contact with its origin in being.

The foregoing discussion has established at least one clear problem: there is a hidden insufficiency not only in division but in the method of collection as well.

On account of its implication in a logic of sacrifice, we determined that the unity identified by collection has a constructed rather than a natural coherence, revealing its distance from the singularity of the forms. Thus, although the priority of the method of collection ahead of division remains, the ontological integrity of the classes it produces has been undermined. By presenting a class as prepared for division, collection has to have already marked the joints so that they may be severed, and to have marked those joints is to have also already intimated a multiplicity of forms within a given class rather than its natural wholeness. Though it is constructive rather than destructive, and thus occupies the first position in the order of dialectic, the method of collection is nonetheless a sort of midwife of being rather than its direct heir. Since both collection and division are central to dialectical inquiry and both are represented in the analogy to sacrificial practices, we must now consider the possible implications of our analysis for our understanding of the "free man's science," that is, dialectic (*Sophist* 234b, 253c–d).

Reflections on the Mediated Nature of Dialectic

I have argued here that the invocation of sacrifice to describe the method of division serves to unsettle division's position within dialectic, thereby placing the method of collection as a requisite first step. However, by extending the metaphor of the sacrificial rite to consider the role collection plays, I have shown that, similar to the domestication that makes an animal sacrificable, collection also "tames" being, producing classes that are divisible because they are already complicated through their mediated relationship to being. But if collection is implicated in the logic of sacrifice in the way I have argued, then dialectic would be thoroughly mediated in its approach to being and the forms, something many of the dialogues would seem to dispute outright. We are forced to wonder: did Plato believe dialectic to be ultimately insufficient?

Perhaps it is simply too difficult to convince ourselves that Plato could be deeply skeptical regarding the philosopher's ability to achieve direct knowledge of the forms, so let us propose one possibility. In the *Statesman*, the Stranger presents not only the statesman's activity but also implicitly the philosopher's in terms of two kinds of weaving. This would mean that while dialectic is *composed* of collection and division, it is *conducted* by means of a third, and *this*, not collection or division or their combination, is the beating heart of dialectic. The *Statesman* reveals that this knowledge lies in the recognition and implementation of the principle of the mean. That is, the *phronēsis* of both the philosopher and the statesman rests with the adequate negotiation of the *propriety* of their application of the available methods.

According to this approach, we might have an explanation for why, in the later dialogues, Plato seems to ignore the question of the way direct knowledge of the forms is achieved, focusing instead on the dialectician's grounds for judging the use of images of the forms. In fact, rather than offering an account of how we might have direct access to the forms, Plato appears to presuppose that this is the case. Skepticism about the intellect's capacity to know the forms is as incoherent to Plato as skepticism regarding the existence of substances is to Aristotle.[27] Following from this, we might, then, claim that the goal of philosophy is not simply to achieve direct *intuition* of the forms, which is perhaps always already possible and present even within the experiences of perception. Instead, philosophy's aim must be to acquire the ability to adequately and effectively *judge the relationship* between the forms and our representations of them within thought. That philosophy is far more concerned with its relationship to what it thinks than with its content is a theme not limited to the critical dialogues of Plato's later period but is deeply embedded within both the aporetic early dialogues and the middle dialogues, which focus on the practice of philosophy as a way of life.

The careful reader of Plato's later dialogues would be justified in concluding that they reflect a sober position with regard to our ultimate access to the ideas. The ambiguity and inconclusiveness of some of the later dialogues' searches alone might point in this direction. But we are also rightly drawn to the triumphant claims the Stranger makes regarding the "free man's science," and the description of the statesman as a weaver suggests a fruitful analogy that offers the possibility of reclaiming even deeply imagistic and mediated thinking. Given this, we are justified in asserting that the later dialogues show Plato coming to terms in a deeper sense with his own need as a philosopher to think through images and with the fact that these images infiltrate the philosophical concepts they would illuminate. It is perhaps mediated knowledge itself that Plato aims to honor in these dialogues, even as that honor is bestowed by means of the sacrifice of images on the altar of dialectical thought. For these reasons, then, the sacrificial animal remains the ultimate analogue for the relationship between images and dialectic.

Notes

1. Plato, *Statesman*, trans. W. R. M. Lamb (Cambridge, Mass.: Harvard University Press, 1925).

2. Plato, *Phaedrus*, trans. Harold North Fowler (Cambridge, Mass.: Harvard University Press, 1914).

3. The intoxicating effects of *logos* as a *pharmakon* reappear throughout the *Phaedrus*. These moments are traced in detail in Jacques Derrida's landmark essay, "Plato's Pharmacy," in *Dissemination*, trans. Barbara Johnson (Chicago: University of Chicago Press, 1981), 61–171.

4. In the introduction to their translation of the *Phaedrus*, Alexander Nehamas and Paul Woodruff (Indianapolis: Hackett Publishing, 1995) make a compelling case for considering the *Phaedrus* itself to be unified by the theme of the relationship between rhetoric and philosophical dialectic. They argue that "the three speeches that form its first part turn out to be examples Plato puts forward in order to support the conclusion he reaches in the second" (xxviii).

5. This claim follows the Pythagorean table of opposites by aligning "good" with "right-handed" and "bad" with "left-handed."
6. This conforms to the principle described in the *Timaeus* that a "likely speech [εἰκὼς λόγος]" must formally reflect its subject matter (48d).
7. On collection as a method of definition, see Marguerite Deslauriers, "Plato and Aristotle on Division and Definition," *Ancient Philosophy* 10 (1990): 203–219. See also Deborah De Chiara-Quenzer's refutation of this claim in "The Purpose of the Philosophical Method in Plato's *Statesman*," *Apeiron* 31 (1998): 98–99.
8. Against Julius Stenzel, J. B. Skemp is an early proponent of the position that the *Statesman* is "a gentle satire on the over-enthusiastic use of the method of Division by some of the members of the Academy itself." Introductory essay, in Plato, *Statesman*, trans. J. B. Skemp (London: Routledge, 1952), 67.
9. Plato, *Sophist*, trans. Harold North Fowler (Cambridge, Mass.: Harvard University Press, 1961).
10. Mitchell Miller, *The Philosopher in Plato's "Statesman"* (Las Vegas, Nev.: Parmenides Publishing, 2004), 27; Kenneth Dorter, "The Clash of Methodologies in Plato's *Statesman*," in *Plato and Platonism*, ed. M. Van Ophuijsen (Washington, D.C.: Catholic University Press, 1999), 200.
11. In "Clash of Methodologies," Dorter specifically links this concern with qualitative judgment to the discussion of the mean in the latter part of the *Statesman*. See also Dorter's "Justice and Method in the *Statesman*," in *Justice, Law and Method in Plato and Aristotle*, ed. Spiro Panagiotou (Edmonton, Canada: Academic Printing and Publishing, 1987), 105–122, esp. sect. II.
12. See Guy Berthiaume's treatment of these three related roles in *Les roles du mágeiros: Étude sur la boucherie, la cuisine et le sacrifice dans la Grèce ancienne* (Leiden, Netherlands: E. J. Brill, 1982).
13. Jean-Pierre Vernant, "At Man's Table," in *The Cuisine of Sacrifice*, ed. Marcel Detienne and Jean-Pierre Vernant, trans. Paula Wissing (Chicago: University of Chicago Press, 1989), 25. Vernant is here summarizing Jean Casabona's view presented in *Recherches sur le vocabulaire du sacrifice en grec, des origines à la fin de l'époque classique* (Aix-en-Provence: Annales de la Faculté des Lettres, Éditions Ophrys, no. 56, 1966).
14. Walter Burkert, *Homo Necans*, trans. Peter Bing (Berkeley: University of California Press, 1983), 3, figs. 1–2. The following description closely follows Burkert's account in *Homo Necans* as well as in his *Greek Religion*, trans. John Raffan (Cambridge, Mass.: Harvard University Press, 1985).
15. Burkert, *Homo Necans*, 4.
16. Aristotle remarks on this in *On the Parts of Animals* 669b13–21.
17. The "Ricci Vase" is the name given to a fifth-century Ionic hydria from Caere by Jean-Louis Durand in his "Greek Animals: Toward a Topology of Edible Bodies," in *The Cuisine of Sacrifice*, 87–117; see figs. 1, 3–4, 11–12.
18. *Zhuang-zi: The Essential Writings*, trans. Brook Ziporyn (Indianapolis: Hackett Publishing, 2009), 3:4.
19. On *Zhuang-zi's* invention of the term *tianli*, that is, "divine/natural perforations," see Ziporyn's discussion in *Zhuang-zi: The Essential Writings*, 22n6.
20. This reasoning is similar to that of Georges Bataille in *L'Érotisme* (Paris: Les Éditions de Minuit, 1957).
21. In the *Phaedrus*, Socrates simply adopts one of the implicit claims of Lysias's speech, namely, that love is a kind of madness, as a guiding definition for his own speeches.
22. In his *Metaphysics and Method in Plato's "Statesman"* (New York: Cambridge University Press, 2006), Kenneth Sayre argues that recollection is similar to the method of collection,

both presupposing "prior knowledge" (39). Sayre references Charles Griswold's helpful account of the relation between collection and recollection in *Self-Knowledge in Plato's* Phaedrus (University Park: Pennsylvania State University Press, 1986), 116, 173–186.

23. Burkert, *Homo Necans,* 3–4, and *Greek Religion,* 56.

24. Erich Isaac, "Myths, Cults, and Livestock Breeding," *Diogenes* 41 (1963): 70–93. That the Athenians had a similar "need" for the prodigious sacrifices of the Babylonian kings is hinted at in Book 8 of *The Laws,* where the Athenian Stranger states his aspiration that, according to their proposed constitution, "there shall be not less than 365 feasts" (828b). Taking this along with W. S. Ferguson's calculation of the sacrificial animals slaughtered for two festivals in 324/3 BCE as 240 for the Dionysia and 75 for the Asklepieia, it would appear that the Athenians had a significant appetite for sacrificial victims (*Hesperia* 17, no. 2 [1948]: 134n7).

25. This is not to say, of course, that all domestication is for the purpose of sacrifice, nor that all domestic animals would be considered appropriate for sacrifice. In *Miasma: Pollution and Purification in Early Greek Religion* (Oxford: Clarendon Press, 1983), Robert Parker, referring to the structuralist ethnographers Halveson and Leach, writes: "in some societies, it has been argued, there is a correlation between an animal's edibility and its 'social distance' in relation to man" (363–364).

26. At 231a, the Stranger hesitates to grant the sophist any honor, saying that "a wolf is very like a dog, the wildest like the tamest."

27. *Metaphysics* VII, ch. 17.

12 The Animals That Therefore We Were?

Aristophanes's Double-Creatures and the Question of Origins

Drew A. Hyland

THE QUESTION OF animals in Plato will be, as almost always in Plato, the *question* of animals. Or rather, *questions,* many and in multiple registers, regarding animals—this animal or that animal, animals altogether, above all, perhaps, animals in their relation to that most curious and complicated of animals, human being. It must be emphasized: the *question* of animals, not "the Platonic theory of animals," not "Plato's doctrine of animals in the early (middle, late) dialogues," not even "Plato on animals." The presence of animals in the Platonic dialogues is always, then, question-worthy, an issue, one might say, of the *problematic* of animals and animality.

One instance of this problematic status of animals—and this one precisely in relation to the being of human being—occurs in Plato's *Symposium,* in the famous and often hilarious account of eros, love, by the comic poet, Aristophanes.[1] The announced intention of each of the speeches of the *Symposium,* with the apparent exception of the last one by Alcibiades, is to praise eros, to give an encomium to that phenomenon, whether god or daimon. Aristophanes emphasizes at the very beginning of his speech that he intends to give a very different one from the ones that have occurred so far, different, his opening lines suggest, because he intends to set forth a fundamentally religious account of eros. This begins by chastising humans for their failure so far to appreciate that eros is not only a god but "the most philanthropic" of the gods, literally the god who loves humans the most, and that as a result we should be much more pious toward the god than we have been (189c). So a pious praise of the god, eros, is forthcoming, or so Aristophanes tells us.

And yet, immediately after this introduction, Aristophanes seems—but only seems—to change the subject: "It is necessary for you first to understand human nature and its sufferings" (189d). Aristophanes is now going to give an account of human nature and its sufferings. Yet it does, indeed, prove to be an account both of human nature and of eros; for the two, we soon learn, are so intimately connected as to be virtually the same. Or rather, human nature *as it is now* is virtually the same as human eros, that is to say, now, in our incomplete state, as split beings, recognizing our incompleteness, striving after wholeness. But, we are told, it has not always been so. This striving for wholeness is in fact a striving for a *return* to a more original state, when we were whole beings, before we were split by the gods and rendered as we are now, incomplete, striving for wholeness, erotic. To know human beings and to understand eros, we must understand our origins; Aristophanes now tells us of our original, very different status, when we were whole beings. He tells us, now, of our origins as a race of most peculiar animals, the famous double-creatures of Aristophanes's myth.

The story is well known and highly comical. We were once beings who were each the double of what we are now, with two heads, four arms, four legs, two sets of genitals, and so on. We came in three versions: a double-male, a double-female, and a male-female combination, called "androgynous" (189e–190a). We are told presently that in our original state we procreated in the ground, "like cicadas" (191b–c), indicating not just an original animality but even a certain likeness to insects.² Nevertheless, in this double state, we were extremely powerful, capable of rolling along on the ground on our eight limbs at great speeds, of seeing in all directions, of moving in whatever direction we chose.

We can pause to note that Plato is already having Aristophanes portray an account of human origins that is in accord with many traditional religious accounts. Our original natures were different from and in ways superior to our present natures. Something happened that caused us to "fall" to our present state. We shall see in a moment what that was. But the difference between our original state and our present natures is perhaps even more pronounced than in traditional accounts—say, that of the Book of Genesis. For we were of superior form *and* of superior abilities. That is to say, we were a different sort of *animal*. The question is: Of what sort?

Despite the evident superiority of our original natures as double creatures, all, we learn, was not well. Aristophanes puts it bluntly: "They had terrible strength and power, as well as great ambitions [τά φρονήματα μεγάλα: literally 'great thoughts'], and they attacked the gods" (190b). Which is to say, still in accord with traditional religious accounts, our original condition, though superior, nevertheless contained a fatal flaw, an "original sin." We attacked the gods, and, presumably thanks to our great strength, we were apparently a serious threat to them. We had great strength, to be sure, and "great thoughts," but we were apparently not good, and certainly not pious. Nor, we soon see, were we erotic; eros will arise only when we are split and desire to come together again (191d). For this is precisely what, in Aristophanes's account, eros will turn out to be: the *human* desire, once we are rendered incomplete, to overcome our incompleteness and return to our original wholeness. So we were powerful but neither good nor pious, nor yet characterized by eros: strange animals, but animals indeed.

We need to ask: Whence our "great thoughts," if not yet from our eros? A speculative but I think not implausible hypothesis would be that we were animals fundamentally characterized not yet by eros but by *desire*, by ἐπιθυμία, that is, by desire *without reason* (ἄνευ λόγου; *Phaedrus* 238b–c), whereas, as we learn eventually from Socrates/Diotima's speech, eros is characterized by desire, to be sure, but also and decisively by an element of reason.³ To the extent, then, that, for Aristophanes, to be human (as we are now) is to be erotic, and for Plato (followed more explicitly by Aristotle) to be human is to have the possibility of λόγος, these double creatures, without eros or reason, characterized entirely by desire, are not yet human at all. They were animals. Or were they not rather *monsters*? Surely the gods would have thought so! Could Aristophanes be intimating, then, that we are descendent from the monstrous, and that our desire to return to that state is, perhaps ironically, the desire to return to the monstrous? Assuming, that is, that we ever entirely leave it.

Why were these double creatures not pious toward the gods? Aristophanes gives us the answer: because they had no natural kinship with the gods but were descendants, as their circular shape exhibits, from cosmic beings, the double-males from the sun, the double-females from the earth, and the androgynous beings from the moon (190b). Aristophanes's opening claims to piety are already becoming destabilized. The animals (or monsters) that were the progenitors of humans had no natural kinship with the Olympian gods, surely were not created by them, and so were not pious toward them. There is no natural foundation for (Greek) religion, unless it be some sort of cosmic pantheism. Little wonder that the Olympians should feel threatened by these animal/monsters! Something had to be done.

Aristophanes's comic myth now shifts significantly so that it is the gods who become the subjects of the comedy, who broach becoming comic fools themselves. For at first, Aristophanes tells us, the gods were literally in *aporia* about what to do with these creatures (190c)! They did not want to destroy us, as they had the giants, since then they would have to give up the honors and sacrifices they received from us. Nor could they continue to tolerate our outrageous behavior (190c). It should be noted immediately: Aristophanes misspoke at the beginning when he called eros the "most philanthropic" of the gods. The gods do not love us at all! They tolerate us only because they want our honors and sacrifices. Otherwise, we must surmise, they would have killed us, as they did the giants. Eros is the *only* god who loves humans. Moreover, the alienation deriving from our lack of natural kinship with the gods is mutual: the gods do not love us any more than we love them. As "natural" beings, the kin of the sun, earth, and moon, we have no natural basis for our piety toward the gods or their love for us. Contrary to Aristophanes's pious opening words, "religion," at least in the orthodox Greek sense, is *alienation*.

But let us return to Aristophanes's story. The gods were in *aporia* about what to do with these creatures. Finally, "with difficulty [μόγις δὴ]" (190c), Zeus comes up with an idea: split us in two, so that we would have to move around on two legs instead of four, and so would be at once weaker and more numerous. The gods get two for one! Since we are weaker, we will be at least less of a threat, and our greater numbers will increase the sacrifices and honors that the gods love so much. Moreover, Zeus issues a threat familiar to us, the typical religious threat for misbehavior: if we continue to act outrageously, the god will punish us, in this case by splitting us again, so that we will have to hop around on one leg. Zeus is hardly omniscient here; why did he not immediately cut us in four parts, thus weakening us even more and increasing still further the number of sacrifices? In any case, Zeus splits us in two and has Apollo pull our skin around in the front and tie it in the middle, as a sign when we look down that will remind us of our former condition and so cause us to be humble. Problem solved! Nice work, Zeus!

Not quite! In archetypically Aristophanic comic fashion, Zeus's original plan, offered with the best of intentions (from the self-interested standpoint of the gods), threatens to be disastrous! For our reaction to our punishment was to run around seeking our original other half and, caring neither for food, drink, nor anything else, we were throwing ourselves together and dying out (191b). Zeus has to think again! So he does, and comes up with a second scheme. He moves our genitals around to the front (they had been, Aristophanes tells us, still on the side), so that, at least when the formerly male-female pairings joined together, they would procreate and the race would be continued. As for the formerly double-males (Aristophanes says nothing here about the double-females, but presumably the same will be the case for them), when they come together, "at least they would be satiated, and stop, and return to their work and the other cares of life" (191c).

Much is at stake in this passage. First, and remarkably, Aristophanes presents what is at least a very early version (if not the earliest) of the view that sexual orientation is *by nature*. It should be noted that anything like sexual orientation arises in any functional sense only with our being split. Aristophanes indicates no functional sexual differences among the double creatures. All are alike extremely powerful, hubristic, impious. Our "sexuality," if one may even call it that, was like those of certain insects—we spilled our seed in the ground. Sexual orientation in the relevant sense arises only with our being split, and it is a function in each case of our original double status. That is to say, sexual orientation, once we are split beings, is not a "lifestyle choice," not "sexual preference," but a function of our original natures as double-males, double-females, or the male-female combination. We are thus now *born* homosexual, lesbian, or heterosexual (for as is obvious, after the first generation of split people, we are *born* split) and our sexual orientation is therefore not a choice but by nature.

Moreover, perhaps even more importantly, and despite Aristophanes's subsequent (and in my opinion demonstrably ironic) praise of the formerly double-males now homosexuals (191e–192b), it is the formerly male-female couples who, when they join together now with genitals in the front, will procreate and therefore save the race. Aristophanes is actually quite abrupt with the now homosexuals: when they join together, at least they will "be satiated and *stop*," and get on with the rest of their lives.[4] In tension with his apparent praise of the male homosexual pairs but very much in keeping with the historical Aristophanes's praise of heterosexual couples and suspicion of homosexuals in his plays, this passage affirms that it is the heterosexual couples that will literally save the race. Evidently, the relationship—and possible tension—between Aristophanes's affirmation of the natural basis of all three basic sexual orientations and his preference for one or the other (the heterosexual pairs in his plays, the male homosexuals in his speech here in the *Symposium*) is a complicated one that deserves further consideration.[5]

Third, Aristophanes now informs us of the most crucial implication of all this: "It is from this situation, then, that our natural love [ὁ ἔρως ἔμφυτος] for one another developed in human beings, collecting the halves of our original nature, trying to make one out of the two parts, so as to restore our human nature" (191d). Only now, once we are split, incomplete beings, does eros arise, and it arises as *our nature*, that is, our nature as incomplete beings, experiencing that incompleteness, and striving for wholeness. Aristophanes's initial claims and exhortations to religious piety are made to tremble once again. Not only is eros not the *most* philanthropic of the gods, not only is he not the *only* god who loves humans: eros is *not a god at all!* Eros is *human* nature as it is now, rendered incomplete and striving for wholeness. The inner core of his speech confutes the piety of his opening and closing words. On the other hand, Aristophanes was not at all wrong in beginning his account of eros with an account of "human nature and its sufferings," for by his account the two, eros and human nature, have turned out to be virtually the same. The "becoming human" of those strange animals, of those double-creatures who were our origins, is identical with our becoming erotic. Eros makes us human.

But this again raises a host of questions about Aristophanes's position. First, if it is eros that distinguishes us as humans from the animals—or monsters—that we were, what is it about eros that "humanizes" us? Aristophanes keeps his account of eros very simple—intentionally so in my opinion. By his analysis, eros has three "moments." The first is an ontological moment: we now *are* as incomplete, our very being is our incompleteness. But second, we manifestly *experience* that incompleteness, are troubled by it. Third, we strive to overcome it, strive to become whole again. However, Aristophanes intentionally keeps the manifestations of this eros at the sexual level. Now we understand why we take all those funny sexual positions! We are trying to become whole again! Aristophanes's comedy reaches its ribald peak here, and we should get a good laugh from it. To be sure, Aristophanes soon will acknowledge that this erotic striving for wholeness is not *limited* to physical sex (192c), but even in so doing he limits its range to a deeper personal love between two human beings. When two lovers come together, he says, "No one would think that this is a mere union of sexual passion [ἀφροδισίων συνουσία] as though that were the reason for which each so enjoys being with the other with such great seriousness" (192c). What Aristophanes does *not* here acknowledge is that this very same erotic structure—incompleteness, recognition thereof, striving for wholeness—also in principle goes far beyond personal love. I may experience an incompleteness of wealth and strive for a fortune; that is eros. I may experience an incompleteness of political power and run for public office; that too is erotic. Or, decisively, I may experience an incompleteness of wisdom and strive to overcome it; this experience is virtually definitive of Socrates's conception of philosophy. Eros, we may say, is potentially the source and explanation of all human aspiration. The latter two examples are pointed and serve to indicate why Aristophanes does try to limit the range of the eros he discusses. Manifestly, political and philosophical aspirations are instantiations of eros that, in his plays, Aristophanes finds highly suspicious! One need only consider that virtually every politician portrayed in the Aristophanic corpus is a scoundrel and that the most notorious and virulent attack on Socrates in Greek literature occurs in Aristophanes's most famous play, the *Clouds*. Which is to say, eros, on Aristophanes's account, may be our present nature, but it is very much a double-edged sword. He emphasizes how, in its manifestation as personal love between two lovers, it may "restore our nature." What he remains silent about, in this encomium to love, is that eros is also the source of the very human aspirations, for example, to political power and to wisdom, which he regards with deep suspicion. Eros may be our nature and may, as personal love, be the best that we can hope for, but it can also be the source of the worst of human nature. To be human may mean to be erotic, but for Aristophanes at least, that does not make us *good*. But then, once again, the question arises: how does eros transform us from the animals we were into humans?

But if the animals that we were were characterized by desire (ἐπιθυμία), whereas we humans in our present condition are characterized by eros, then what is the difference? It is by no means clear from Aristophanes's speech—or, I would speculate, from his plays—whether there is a difference and, if there is, what that difference might be. It is Plato who has his Socrates articulate the decisive difference between desire and eros, though, as we shall see, the difference that Socrates develops is one that Aristophanes would likely not accept, indeed, one that the rest of his speech implicitly rejects. Let us take a brief detour, then, and look into the difference that Socrates, under the tutelage of Diotima, will develop between eros and desire, the difference, that is, that might distinguish us from the animals that, according to Aristophanes, we were.

The beginning of Socrates's distinction is made during the brief dialogue with Agathon that opens his speech (199c–201d), before the introduction of his teacher on eros, Diotima. In that dialogue, Socrates makes two major points by way of refuting Agathon's claim that eros both is beautiful and loves the beautiful. First, that love (eros) is *of* something, and, second, that it is of something that it *lacks*. "Come then," Socrates said, "Let's agree about what's being said. First, is love the love of something, and, second, is that something some thing that at the moment it lacks?" (200e) The second of these points is of particular importance for our purposes, since it constitutes Socrates's proto-*Aufhebung* of Aristophanes's own central point, namely, that human eros always manifests a *lack*, an incompleteness of some sort. This is Socrates's "logical" version of the mythical point that Aristophanes has made. But in making these very points, Socrates begins to draw the distinction between desire and eros that Aristophanes had failed to make. After making the first central point, that is, eros is always eros *of* something (199c–200a), Socrates turns to the making of the second decisive point, and his precise words are crucial: "With regard to that which eros is an eros of, does he *desire* [ἐπιθυμεῖ] it or not?" "Altogether so, he said." "Is it while he has this thing he desires and loves [ἐπιθυμεῖ τε καὶ ἐρᾷ] that he desires and loves it, or is it when he does not have it?" "It seems likely that it's when he doesn't have it, Agathon said" (200a).

We see immediately that the relation between love and desire is complicated. For love *desires and loves*. Since the conjunction is repeated several times in the passage, it is clear that, if love "desires and loves," then it must be two different things that it does. So there *is* a difference between love and desire. That is the first point. But this point is immediately complicated by the fact that *one of the things that eros does is desire*. Eros desires and loves. Hence desire is part of the structure of eros, part of its makeup. We cannot *simply* and radically separate love and desire; they interact, insofar as one of the things that love does (along with the fact that it "loves") is desire. Socrates has now established that eros and desire are two different things but that their relation is intimate, in that one of the capacities of love is to desire. What they *share* is the very point that Aristophanes made, namely, that eros and desire both manifest a lack. What, then, is the difference?

We begin to learn this only later, when Socrates recounts his tutelage on eros under the woman, Diotima. There are two decisive moments in the differentiation of eros and desire, both with almost direct bearing on Aristophanes's position. The first occurs when Socrates asks Diotima the rather strange question, "who are eros' parents?" and Diotima responds with her own counter-myth to Aristophanes's of eros's origins (203b–204c). Diotima responds to Socrates's question by telling him that eros's mother was Penia, "Poverty," "Lack," and its father was Poros, "Resourcefulness," "Plenty." Significantly, Diotima adds that Poros's own mother was Metis, "Wisdom," "Craft." Poros, clearly, gets his primary qualities from his own mother. The feminine is decisive here, and not just in regard to lack or incompleteness.[6] Eros, relates Diotima, takes after both its parents, as most children do. It does indeed contain an element of incompleteness and lack from its mother. So far, so Aristophanic! But the Diotiman point is that Aristophanes was literally half-right—as was Agathon in the opposite direction, when he interpreted eros as entirely a phenomenon of fullness and completeness. What Aristophanes misses in his speech is the element of fullness, of overflowing resourcefulness, which is *also* part of eros's make-up. Eros cannot be characterized *just* in terms of incompleteness, as Aristophanes tried to do. In addition, it contains that element of fullness, of resourcefulness, that Diotima will go on to show is the source of its creative capacity, its "pregnancy" (206c). Desire, Diotima implies (but does not explicitly assert), may be entirely lack or incompleteness, but the same is not true of eros. In addition to the incompleteness that indeed characterizes it, eros also exhibits that wide range of qualities associated with Poros/Metis: overflowing fullness, resourcefulness, wisdom, invention, creativity. But there is one quality that prepares the way for eros to be the source of philosophy itself, so much so that philosophy can be the highest manifestation of eros, a quality that does not emerge fully until the famous "ascent passage" that begins at 210a. That quality is reason or, more broadly, something like "rational insight," adumbrated perhaps in grandmother Metis's wisdom.

The gist of the ascent passage is well known. Diotima will *try* (she emphasizes her skepticism here) to introduce the young Socrates into the "higher mysteries" of love. She begins in a most curious way for a supposedly intellectual ascent to an insight into "beauty itself," the form beauty. "It is necessary [δεῖ]," she begins, to begin with the love of a beautiful body (210a). From there, she tries to take Socrates from the love of a single beautiful body to the recognition of the beauty of all beautiful bodies, then on to the beauty of souls, thence to the beauty of "laws and institutions," penultimately to the love of all knowledge in "unencumbered philosophy," and, finally, suddenly (210e), to an insight into "beauty itself," after which, Diotima tells us instructively, we will "nearly" be at the end (211b). What is important for our purposes is the force that drives each step along the way of this erotic ascent. For the enabling force, at each step along the way, is some form or other of *insight*, of *reasoning*. The young aspirant must "realize [κατανοῆσαι]" that the beauty of one body is akin to the beauty of all bodies (210a), that it would be "mindless [ἄνοια]" (210b) not to believe that the beauty of all bodies is the same. When he "comprehends [ἐννοήσαντα]" this, he will literally "think down on [καταφρονήσαντα]" the love of a single body as "something small" (210b). After that, he will "believe [ἡγήσασθαι]" (210b) that the beauty of souls is more honorable than that of bodies and, from there, will "see [θεάσασθαι: clearly an *intellectual* 'seeing']" (210c) the beauty of laws and institutions. Next he will be led to the beauty of all knowledge, and "seeing [βλέπων: clearly, again, an intellectual 'seeing']" (210c) this wide sea of beauty, he will engage in "unencumbered philosophy" (210d). Finally, and "suddenly," he will "see [κατόψεταί: once more an intellectual 'seeing']" (210e) the source of all this beauty, "beauty itself."

I take the time to emphasize the verbs employed by Plato to articulate the movement of this ascent in order to bring out that the "engine" of this erotic movement is shot through with various forms of thinking, reasoning, insight. That would not be possible unless *eros itself*—after all, this is an ascent of *eros*—contained that element of reason as part of its structural makeup. Which is to say that, for Diotima and Socrates, eros is *not* "irrational"; *desire is!* The foundational difference, then, as Socrates understands it at least, between eros and desire is that eros is *rational*, it has *reason* as part of its nature. Only thus could it be the foundational motivation for philosophy.

This difference can be confirmed, incidentally, by a brief look at a crucial moment of Plato's other dialogue on eros, the *Phaedrus*. There, in Socrates's first speech, where he is "one-upping" Lysias by showing that he could give a better speech arguing that the beloved should gratify the non-lover, and where eros is being treated—temporarily and wrongly—as *mere* desire, eros is explicitly characterized there as "some sort of desire [ἐπιθυμία τις]" (237d) and then explicitly as desire "without reason [ἄνευ λόγου]" (238b).

For the Platonic Socrates, then, there is a clear if complicated difference between desire and eros. We are not *merely* desiring creatures and therefore not merely animals, though we do desire and so do participate in animality; we are *erotic* beings, and that means beings with the capacity for (in the broadest sense) reason. The question is whether there is anything like this qualifiedly optimistic view of human possibility present in or even implied by Aristophanes's position. Let us return to Aristophanes's speech.

At the point where we suspended our consideration of Aristophanes's speech, we were left with the question of whether he too, like, as we have now seen, Socrates and Diotima, has in mind a coherent distinction between the desire that characterized us as double-creatures and the eros that now characterizes us as incomplete beings striving for wholeness. The rest of his speech expresses great skepticism in this regard, especially in regard to the difference that we have seen developed in Socrates's speech, namely, that eros is characterized by a certain rational capacity for intellectual vision. Aristophanes now turns to an account of the experience of two lovers who come together in what looks like a "love at first sight" experience. The two, he says, spend their entire lives with each other, "though they are not able to say what it is that they want from each other" (192c). On the contrary, he continues, "it is clear that there is something else that the soul of each wants, something it cannot say, but speaks prophetically and in riddles" (192d). The implication is clear: human beings cannot know themselves, we cannot articulate our deepest desires. We lack the capacity for self-knowledge. Aristophanes immediately offers a substitute for this inability: religion. If the god Hephaestus should come along, he continues, and offer to meld us together into one so that we spent our entire lives joined together and even died as one, we would say that this is what we desired all along but could not articulate (192d–e). Humans need religion as a substitute for their lack of a capacity to know themselves. Aristophanes's real justification for religion is not that it is true but that humans *need* religion to make sense of themselves.

Aristophanes concludes, strikingly, "So the name 'love' [ἔρως] is given to the *desire* [ἐπιθυμία] for wholeness" (192e). Eros, alas, *is* desire and is apparently *only* desire, simply a desire with a specific object, a return to wholeness. Is there, then, in the end, a relevant difference, other than a lesser power, between our status as double-creatures and our human status? Are we still simply animals—or monsters—but just weaker ones?

Aristophanes's profound pessimism about our situation is supported by a curious but, once recognized, striking fact. Of all the speeches in the *Symposium,* Aristophanes's is the only one that does not even so much as refer to the issue of what, for the Greeks, was the same word for beauty or nobility, namely, τὸ κάλλος. The word or its cognates does not appear once in his speech. All the previous speeches referred to the issue of beauty and nobility and, in Agathon's and Socrates's speeches, it becomes utterly central to an understanding of eros. Indeed, it is not exaggeration to say that there is nothing of beauty in Aristophanes's speech. Which is to say, from the Aristophanic standpoint, there is nothing beautiful about eros, about "human nature and its sufferings." The reason why, I suggest, is clearly implied: there is no *essential* difference between the animal/monsters that we were and what we are now as humans. As creatures fundamentally of desire, we remain the animal/monsters that we were, and there is nothing beautiful or noble about that. At best, perhaps, we are fools, comic fools.

Aristophanes's pessimism about the human condition is confirmed and deepened by a subtle but decisive episode in his closing peroration. There, returning to the exhortation to religious piety toward the supposed god eros with which he began his speech, Aristophanes urges us—apparently optimistically—to "perfect love, and everyone must find one's own beloved, thereby returning to our original natures" (193c). But to this he adds, ominously, "If this is what is best, then the nearest thing to that is necessarily what is best in the present circumstances, and that is to happen upon a beloved who is according to one's own nature" (193c). To what is Aristophanes referring in this rather sobering qualification? As is empirically obvious, after the first generation of split beings, we are *born* split. But that means that we no longer *have* an original half with which to join. And without that "natural" other half, we cannot *in principle* "return to our original natures," since we now have no original nature to which to return. What humans most of all desire, Aristophanes here quietly teaches, we cannot have. We are destined to be disappointed. Our consolation "under the present circumstances" will be to try to "happen upon [τύχοι]" (193c)—and the element of chance in this should not be ignored—a compatible beloved, presumably one with the same sexual orientation as our own. Despite his encouraging rhetoric, Aristophanes presents a depressing view of the human situation. We cannot have what we most of all desire, to return to our original wholeness, and ironically, even if we could, that original condition was the very one for which we were punished in the first place. So the best we can do is "settle" for a sexually compatible mate and try to behave, avoiding the hubris for which we were originally punished and for which, if we continue to engage in it, we will be split yet again.

We may then draw quite different conclusions regarding Aristophanes's position in the *Symposium* and what we may surmise is the position toward which Plato points in the rest of the dialogue. Regarding Aristophanes, we may summarize his position as follows. In our "original position" as double-creatures, we were extremely powerful indeed, but we were characterized most fundamentally by desire. At the forefront of those desires, apparently, was the desire to overthrow the gods. The gods eventually punished us by splitting us in two, thus rendering us less powerful, therefore less of a threat, but more numerous, and so capable of sending more gifts to the gods. We indeed suffered a "fall," then, though hardly a fall from grace. Out of our fallen, incomplete status, we gained eros, the desire among split humans to become whole again. But from Aristophanes's speech we must conclude that this change was less a change in our *natures* than an intensified focus of the desire that always already characterized us in our "animal" natures. Now, our desire is fundamentally the "desire for wholeness," and this focused desire is given the name *eros* (193a). But that is what it is, a focused *desire*, and so, for Aristophanes, we are still the animals that we were, even if weakened ones. As such, the best we can do is try to limit or control that desire by practicing religion, by becoming pious, by "happening upon" a compatible beloved and living a pious life.

The position of the Platonic Socrates and his supposed teacher, Diotima, is qualifiedly more optimistic. The optimism derives from the implied critique of Aristophanes's own position, a "critique" in the proto-Kantian sense. For, by this critique, Aristophanes was *right* to say that eros, human love, is characterized by a fundamental incompleteness, by an experience of that incompleteness and a striving for wholeness, that is to say, by a certain *desire*. But he was literally only *half* right: what Aristophanes missed was the contribution to the nature of eros by its mythical father Poros (and his own mother Metis). That contribution was the gift of a certain overfullness, resourcefulness, inventiveness, and capacity for a certain rational insight into the nature of things, including ourselves. This capacity—and it must be remembered that it is *only* a capacity, a possibility—makes eros fundamentally different from *mere* desire, though it must be emphasized yet again that eros, which is also the mythical child of Penia, *does* desire. It enables, therefore, the potential for a certain transcendence, a finite transcendence, of our animal natures as merely desiring creatures. But it is a *finite* transcendence in at least two decisive ways. First, it is finite in the sense that as erotic we remain creatures of desire, though no longer *just* creatures of desire. There will therefore be no decisive "leaving behind" of our former animal natures, no "becoming no longer animal," though we *might* become no longer *merely* animal. And so, second, it is a finite transcendence because it is always and only a *possibility* of transcendence, one that will be realized only if we put into play, as it were, our Poros/Metis natures, our capacity for a certain rational insight and rational living.

We would go too far, then, to say that Plato joins Aristotle in *defining* human beings, and therefore differentiating us from animals, by reason, by *logos*. Yet we can say that one difference, a potentially decisive one, is the possible presence of *logos*, of reason, in human beings. But as the famous image of the soul/eros as a charioteer and horses (yet other "Platonic" animals) in the *Phaedrus* makes clear enough, this is a precarious presence, and so a precarious difference, indeed. The black horse of desire in our souls—and in our eros—can always take over, can always dominate the "charioteer" of our reason. Then we will be ἄνευ λόγου, without *logos;* then we will be the creatures of desire, the animals—or monsters—that we were. Then we will be the animals that therefore we are.

A final word about the title of this contribution and the previous line, both of which manifestly are indebted to Jacques Derrida's important work on animals, especially his *The Animal That Therefore I Am*.[7] Does the gist of my presentation confirm Derrida's reading of the history of philosophy's treatment of animals, especially his guiding theme that "we" humans regularly distinguish ourselves from "animals"—taken as a (falsely) homogeneous whole—and do so precisely by reference to our "having reason" as Aristotle long ago put it? Yes and no. Yes, insofar as my contribution suggests that in Plato's *Symposium* we see this distinction raised *as a possibility*. No, insofar as it is *not* presented by Plato in that dialogue (nor in any other dialogue, or so I would argue) as something *essential*, the "essence" of human being as opposed to the (homogeneous) "essence" of animality. On the contrary, and I think very much in the spirit of Derrida's own thinking, it is raised in the dialogues *in its full question-worthiness*, that is, as a *question, a problem,* and not an *assertion*. The latter claim remains, perhaps—and this is I think by no means as obvious as it seems to many—to be made by Aristotle. The issue for Plato, in any case, and as I suggested in my opening paragraph, is very much the question and the questionability of animals and their relation to the peculiar animals—and are not *all* animals, each in their own way, peculiar?—that we therefore are.

Notes

1. Plato, *Symposium*, 189c–193e. Translations are my own, but will often follow, with modifications, that of William S. Cobb, *The Symposium and the Phaedrus: Plato's Erotic Dialogues* (Albany: State University of New York Press, 1993).

2. That cicadas do not, in fact, procreate on the ground raises further questions. Did Plato not know this? Did he know it but is intentionally putting this mistaken view into the mouth of the comic poet Aristophanes? One way or the other, what implications might the mistake have?

3. *Symposium*, 210a. I will say more about this shortly. For a longer justification of this difference, see my "Eros, Epithumia, and Philia in Plato," *Phronesis* 13, no. 1 (1968): 32–46.

4. The Greek is emphatic here: διαπαύοιντο, "to stop utterly."

5. For my own take on this issue, see my "The Whole Comedy and Tragedy of Philosophy: Aristophanes' Speech in Plato's *Symposium*," *Norwegian Journal of Philosophy*, forthcoming.

6. An important issue indeed, but the subject of another paper.

7. Jacques Derrida, *The Animal That Therefore I Am*, ed. Marie-Louise Mallet, trans. David Wills (New York: Fordham University Press, 2008).

PART VII

ANIMALS AND THE AFTERLIFE

13 Animals and Angels

The Myth of Life as a Whole in Republic 10

Claudia Baracchi

> Once they say he was passing by when a puppy was being beaten, and he took pity and said: Stop, do not harm it; for it is the soul of a friend, I know it because I heard its voice.
>
> —Xenophanes, fr. 7

IN BEGINNING WITH the end of a text, one would act in a way not dissimilar to that of Lysias—at least if we are to heed Socrates's statement in the *Phaedrus*, which emphasizes the structural disorder of the speech on love by the celebrated Attic orator: "He's trying to swim through the speech on his back in reverse, starting from the end rather than from the beginning" (*Phaedrus* 264a).[1] The fact that the text at stake might be Plato's *Republic* only makes the predicament more severe, especially since the *Republic* ends with a myth: its conclusion is an opening; it presents the characteristic indefiniteness and infinity of myths. In this way, the text interminably defers its own end. It fails to reach a closure and abides unending.[2] Like *eros* (*Symposium* 203e), language (*logos*) is an animal that is fittingly arranged as a living organism (*Phaedrus* 264c, 265d–266b).[3] It is presumably just as mad.

Here, however, in this disorderly beginning, the problem seems to be not so much the lack of adequately clarified definitions, whose implications one would organically unfold, proceeding then to the necessary consequences (*Phaedrus* 263d–e). Rather, the difficulty in beginning, as we are, from the end, lies in starting from the outcome as if it were statically given: taking what is given, while neglecting the tortuous, laborious path of inquiry and exchange that allowed for such a giving.

As the barest gesture toward an archeology (or etiology) of the mythical gesture at the end of the *Republic*, let us simply note that this open conclusion in many ways echoes the beginning. Indeed, we should not forget two decisive elements in Book I: (1) the "theoretical" desire of Socrates, who descends to the Piraeus in order to satisfy his curiosity to "see" (327a), and (2) the evanescent figure of Cephalus, who seems an altogether negligible ornament placed at the entrance of the text, but who actually orients the entire dialogue and dictates its thematic focus. Recall those initial moments: Socrates addresses the father at "the threshold of old age": "For my part, Cephalus . . . I am really delighted to discuss with the very old. Since they are like men who have proceeded on a certain path that perhaps we too will have to take, one ought, in my opinion, to learn from them what sort of road it is—whether it is rough and hard or easy and smooth" (328d–e).[4] He then solicits from Cephalus a report (*exangello*) about his experience in that liminal position. For, near the end of his journey, the old patriarch stands before the gaping mouth of another world and is called to venture the most extreme transition into that chasm. Before long, however, Cephalus proves unable to sustain that conversation and be the *angelos* Socrates longs to hear, the messenger conveying something of the other world into this one. The dialogue then continues in Cephalus's absence, after he has withdrawn in order to perform ritual sacrifices to the gods, so as to secure a safe crossing of the threshold and assuage his fears.

With the myth bringing the nocturnal conversation to a close, Socrates will return to this question and show that it was never left aside, let alone forgotten. The question of such a crossing, and above all the *manner* of such a transition between worlds ("from this world to the other and back again," whether "by the underground, rough road" or "by the smooth one, through the heavens" [619e]), will be shown in its essential connection with the theme of justice on which the dialogue as a whole hinges. For indeed the issue of justice is cast from the start in terms of life (358a–d). Justice is to be investigated in its enactment within the *psychē*, as it informs the living in its becoming. In fact, as will become increasingly clear, justice designates a particular arrangement of life, life unfolding in a certain way and cherishing in this its own delight and fulfillment—whether seen or unseen, becoming the object of honor and public acknowledgment or encountering misrecognition and adversity.

Thus the investigation of justice develops through an investigation of life and its movements from one side to the other of the surface of appearances, between invisibility and visibility, interiority and exteriority, the private and the public—the actualization of the *psychē* and action in the *polis*. At the limit, the question of justice will be situated in the most extreme hovering between appearing and disappearing: the dance of life as a whole, in its broad, choral movements, and above all in its abysmal unity with its submerged other—death.[5] It will have taken a myth to give word to this embrace across the most unspeakable discontinuity. How one lives, how one dies, how life itself is thereby inflected, how a trace is retained and will inexorably reemerge, how life bears the marks and inscriptions, layer after layer, even immemorially, of every singular act, action, and enactment—these are the problems and materials of justice. At the end of the trajectory of this discussion, when *logos* is one last time (and necessarily) on the verge of reverting into *mythos*, Socrates remarks on the ultimate, if mysterious, unity of communally shared appearing (the luminosity of reputation) and what *in it* remains withheld. This is, at once, a remark on the unity of life and *its* beyond: "it must be assumed in the case of the just man that, if he falls into poverty, diseases, or any other of the things that seem bad, for him it will end in some good, either in life or even in death. For, surely, the gods at least will never neglect the man who is eagerly willing to become just and, practicing excellence, likens himself, so far as is possible for a human being, to a god" (613a–b).

In the ending myth, then, we discern, however transfigured, the lineaments of the inception of the dialogue. While Er the warrior was lying dead on the battlefield, the *psychē* that lived as Er was called to witness the movements on the other side of life—the movements of life after life, of life withdrawn into the mysterious labor of its creativity, preparing its own return. The wandering soul is then ordered to come back to this side of the living and report what it saw in life's invisible workshop. In the figure of Er are gathered the motifs of vision and communication. He is, first of all, someone who sees and, in seeing (*theorein*), retains, keeps safe. In him are reverberated both Socrates's desire to see (the "theoretical" longing that keeps Socrates in movement between the city and the port) and the amplification of it in the psycho-political function of the guardian: witnessing, contemplating, holding in view, are at once a matter of preserving and saving (621b). Consequently, then, Er is someone who, having seen and retained, recounts and shares, so that his individual vicissitudes and the stories he heard may circulate and become collective memory. He takes up the task Cephalus could not sustain and becomes a messenger from that other place, the *angelos* relating that world to this one, keeping worlds together even in their unfathomable irreducibility. He is the voyager bringing his vision of that world as a whole into this world, establishing a passageway, a connection, and an exchange.

The dialogue that has pursued the question of justice (of what it may mean to live and die as a just human being, as a well-ordered, harmoniously articulated *psychē*, having become one with itself, leaving in its wake a trace of the harmony once achieved) culminates with a contemplation of life as a whole. Only with this all-encompassing visionary evocation may Socrates attempt to do justice to the question of justice: his *logos*, turning into a *mythos*, endeavors to give back "the full measure" of what it owes the just (614a). In the *Symposium*, Socrates expounds Diotima's teachings on the erotic ascent, the desirous movement leading to higher and progressively more comprehensive visions, in which life comes to transcend its own narrow locality and understand itself as belonging in that which exceeds it. In the final myth of the *Republic*, such a movement of self-transcendence is *performed:* not unlike the rapture of transcendence in the ascent, the vision at the end (the vision of the unending) sees all of life, comprehends life's vast gestures in a glance holding them together.

In the broadest sense, *psychē* is that whose work is to live (*Republic* 353d). Speaking of soul, of *psychē*, then, means raising the question concerning the modes of aliveness, the shapes of life, of animation. The concluding myth addresses the question of the animate, of the animal, of animality as a whole—of life caught in its exuberant dynamism, stirred by the relentless fecundity of its self-differing, emerging and lingering in ever-differing guises, and letting them then sink back into invisibility.

The myth of Er opens with the barrenness of a battlefield after the antagonism and agony of war. This is the scene of a momentary suspension of becoming (*agony* literally means "privation of generation"), of a lapse, an interruption of motility. At the consummation of war, emptiness prevails, all life seems exhausted. On the battlefield everything is still. The theater of warfare is now a place of withdrawal.

And yet, within this arresting moment, the incubation of another movement is underway. Carried within the motionless landscape, protected by the dismal screen of what appears after the war, invisibly, movement is already beginning to unfold anew. This seems to be so, at least, according to the words Er is said to have uttered when he came back again into life. For, indeed, after ten days the uncorrupted body that once lived as Er was brought away from the battlefield and, on the twelfth day, "as he was lying on the pyre, he came back up to life and . . . told what he saw in the other place" (614b).

While dead to this world, Er traveled to another world—to a world other than the one in which he fought, albeit not necessarily *elsewhere*. This journey unfolded in the shadow of his corpse, sheltered from the glow of images that light up in this world and are shared, apprehended in common. Dying means: remaining as a corpse and otherwise disappearing. It means, precisely in the conspicuity of the lifeless remains, entering Hades the invisible, the one without shape or contour, a fold of the unseen within the seen. Er went away (undetected, his journey unshared), all the while remaining there, exposed as a corpse. He went away, invisible especially to those who saw his dead body lying there and mournfully prepared it for the funeral rite. Only an unreadable sign was left behind: the body still intact—well preserved and healthy, says the text (614b). Such, then, was Er's crossing: between manifestation and latency, connecting places altogether discontinuous, and realizing their inseparability.

Thus, for the warrior the battlefield is the gateway to other-worldly places (whether other worlds or places other than worldly). The ravaged land after the war secretly bears life returning, insuppressible. The scene of the battlefield, then, is that of a beginning, or even an initiation. From the battlefield the warrior is translated to the places of rebirth.

It should be emphasized, however, that this journey across the imageless domain of death, this crossing itself invisible and concealed from the visibility shared in this world, is still a matter of images: at once taking place *beyond* the images of this world and enveloped *within* images. After the brilliance of this world has faded out, absorbed into the dissolving obscurity of death, still other images arise. The departure from this world does not involve a departure from imaginal shining, a transcendence of images, but rather the magnification of their ineluctability. Mythical narration intimates precisely that radical discontinuity between visible and invisible can be hinted at only through the articulation of more images and so appears always inscribed within an imaginal or imaginative continuum.

It is said that, upon his return, Er reported what he saw beyond the threshold (614b). His narration begins with the evocation of the cyclical movement of life, ever beginning, ending, and returning:

> He said that when his soul departed it made a journey in the company of many, and they came to a certain daimonic place, where there were two chasms in the earth next to one another, and, again, two in the heaven, above and opposite the others. Between them sat judges who, when they had passed judgment, ordered the just to continue the journey to the right and upward, through the heaven; and they attached signs of the judgments in front of them. The unjust they told to continue the journey to the left and down, and they had behind them signs of everything they had done. And when he himself came forward, they said that he had to become a messenger to human beings of the things in that place, and they exhorted him to listen and to look at everything in that place. He saw there, at one of the chasms of both heaven and earth, souls going away when judgment had been passed on them. As to the other two chasms, souls out of the earth, full of dirt and dust, came up from one of them; and from the other came down other souls, pure from heaven. And the souls that were ever arriving looked as though they had come from a long journey: and they went away with delight to the meadow, and set up camp there as at a public festival. (614c–d)

Life is seized in its vast circulatory character. Having completed their mortal life, the *psychai* continue their journey to the "daimonic place" and, from there, upward or downward.[6] In turn, having completed their journey through the earth or through the sky, other *psychai* gather once more to prepare their return to mortal life. While most of the literature on the myth concluding the *Republic* focuses on its cosmological account, engaging in a kind of cartography of the souls' venture, the genuinely metabolic tenor of this discourse is seldom noticed.[7] Yet there it is, in all its prominence—a depiction of the endless circulation and regeneration of life, in its transitions, exchanges, and transpositions.[8] To be sure, such a metabolism is irreducible to purely mechanical or even physiological parameters. It is perturbed and in the end made somewhat unpredictable by an ethical variable. Indeed, the unfolding and continuation of life's movement, whether in its heavenly or earthly trajectories, is determined by the comportment in life: according to the assessment of one's way of life, life goes on living, deflected in this or that direction, readjusting its own course. We should underscore, however succinctly, this superb circularity: life draws its orientation from out of itself, is guided by no transcendent principle.

It should likewise not escape us that this upward and downward motility, this movement constantly drawing the regions above and below at once together and apart, echoes the alternation of ascents and descents rhythmically pervading the dialogue. Suffice it to recall the very inception ("I went down, yesterday . . .") and, most decisively, the vicissitudes of the prisoner mysteriously dragged out of the cave and then forced back down (514a–517a). We who entertain stories and recount them to each other have always already gone down and resurfaced ("up to [our] birth, shooting like stars" [621b]), and our life, this life here, unfolds in constant exchange and interpenetration with its beyond—never unmoving, never simply (stably and ultimately) situated. Life is crucially seized in its nomadic character, and it is perhaps not by chance that the *psychai* convening again in the "daimonic place," after their respective travels through dust or light, are portrayed very much like refugees: whether exhausted or relieved, all too humanly setting up camp in a meadow, sharing their stories of what they have seen in their restlessness. Exile is not primarily a matter of dwelling far from the motherland. It is, rather, a condition more deeply, enigmatically inscribed in life: not knowing whence one comes, not knowing one's proper place and belonging, circulating from time immemorial and presumably without end, all the while yearning for something missing, neither owned nor known, nor reached. Exile should be understood in relation to such a basic, uncontrollable experience of incompleteness and lack, most notably to the irreducibility of life (of any life, in any mortal guise) to a single place and proper position. However rooted and topographically situated, (a) life is *always also* elsewhere, open to that which is indeterminately ulterior. In and out of place at once, the animal appears to be essentially characterized by nonbelonging, extraneity, and strangeness with respect to any one place. At the same time, such a reach toward ulteriority marks the belonging of the animal together in and with its other.

Er's tale, however, is not simply a story of rewards and retributions after this life. It is a story concerned with the ethical question in its most encompassing implications. In this connection, we should observe the twofold work of death.

On the one hand, death names radical discontinuity. In its dissemination within life, death signals life's intermittence, the fragmentary, unstable character of the living, life flowing into a myriad of more or less accomplished registers, more or less wakeful modes. The interpenetration of life and death in many ways points to the ubiquity of the unconscious: far from vanquished in mixing with death, life descends into varying proportions of plenitude and exiguity, or, more precisely, manifests itself in its fullest range, from intellectual agility and contemplative saturation to the archaic layers of silent metabolic operations, physiological functions, and the crowded absence in sleep and dreams. On the other hand, and simultaneously, death points to a traversal of the abysmal rift it names. The exploration of death in the myth leads indeed to the question of choice, and how a connection with life may be drawn again—how, literally, rebirth may occur, not altogether disconnected from the lives that were before. In the passage from death to life renewed, as well as in the passage from moment to moment, in the choices one is called to make at any point in the course of one's life, what is at stake is the temporal nexus between past conditions and future developments and the fact that this linkage may nevertheless be anything but linear and predictable. The text is striving somehow to cast light on the always delicate, always surprising, issue of temporal articulations. Choice is that which, in and as the juncture between the prior and the posterior, directs the transition. It may or may not effect radical reorientations. However, it always *can* do so. In the juncture that choice names lies the discernment of possibility, the exploration of *dynamis*, and hence the always possible interruption of any given course. We note the intimate intertwinement of death, the labor of choice, and the regeneration of life: once again, an issue of *ethos*, and thus of justice, at the very heart of physical/cosmological vision.

Thus, the myth at the end of the *Republic* undertakes to address animation, animality in its dynamism, the embrace of death and life out of which life unfolds in many ways. Myth is the *logos* (the *eikos logos*, Timaeus would say) of life.

Not unlike choice, then, death indicates a pause, a rift, a withdrawal from immediate involvement in action: a reserve with respect to the course of worldly things, which may entail a redirection of them. This noncoincidence need not amount to separation, as if it were a matter of occurring before or after, this side or that side of worldly circumstances, somewhere else.

In the withdrawal of death, according to the letter of the myth, the *psychai* first undergo or enjoy the direct consequences of their enactment in the world: the journey above or below follows upon previous comportment. All comportment has repercussions, leaves effects often latent and prolonged in its wake. Every gesture unleashes concatenations of events at once uncontrollable and resulting with geometrical precision from certain acts. Death is a figure of this region of unheeded echoes—of the suffering or enjoyment of penalties or prizes, often below the threshold of consciousness, with no causal awareness (612e–613a).

After their underground or heavenly cycle, however, the *psychai* are called to return to the visibility of life. They are led away from the meadow where they gathered, taken across the expanse of the cosmos that hinges on the axis of light, and finally brought into the vicinity of Necessity and her daughters.[9] The mathematical/musical tenor of the description of the cosmic structure (the spindle of Necessity and its whorls, the harmony of the Sirens, the singing of the Fates) confirms our earlier hypothesis regarding the convergence, if not the identity, of necessity and justice: both are in fact evoked in terms of harmonization and balanced relationality (443d–e, 616c–617c).[10] The dialogue, which had been inaugurated with the question of justice and had positioned this question at the heart of life, culminates with a figuration of necessity at the center of the cosmic organism.[11] At this juncture, the *psychai*, preparing for yet another mortal ("death-bearing") cycle, are asked to choose how they will live, what kind of life they will inhabit, what shapes they will take on next. The passage to the life to come is not automatically determined, let alone left to the evaluation of judges. Here the mixture of necessity and revolutionizing possibilities becomes manifest. For, indeed, choice, the ethical variable, can always revolutionize the articulation of action. It always retains the potential for reconfiguring life's trajectory in unexpected ways. Of course, we need to look more closely into choice and its dynamics. The *psychai* are instructed on the procedure by the spokesman of one of the *Moirai*:

> This is the speech of Necessity's maiden daughter, Lachesis. Souls that live a day, this is the beginning of another death-bringing cycle for the mortal race. A *daimon* will not select you, but you will choose a *daimon*. Let him who gets the first lot make the first choice of a life to which he will be bound by necessity. Virtue is without a master; in honoring or dishonoring her, each will have more or less of her. The blame is of the one who chooses; the god is blameless. (617d–e)

As the procession of the psychai carrying out their task unfolds, the myth conjures up the magnificent vision of the recursive movement of life constantly connecting and, at once, overwhelming the singular lives. In the overall flow of becoming, all living beings come to be out of each other and, after their brief hesitation, fade into each other. Even more remarkably, the collective forms of life and modes of animality and animation are shown in their exchange with each other, in their plasticity, community, and communication. A life that once was human chooses to continue (to return) as a lion, or as a "musical animal," and vice versa, according to physiognomic resonance and ethical/ethological correspondences. The same life enters all forms and guises (kinds? species?) and flows away from each one: filling and emptying, surging and abandoning:

> After this, in turn, [the spokesman] set the patterns of the lives on the ground before them; there were far more than there were souls present. There were all sorts; lives of all animals and, in particular, all the varieties of human lives. There were tyrannies among them, some lasting to the end, others ruined midway, ending both in poverty and exile and in beggary. And there were lives of men of repute—some for their forms and beauty and for strength in general as well as capacity in contests; others for their birth and the virtues of their ancestors—and there were some for men without repute in these things; and the same was the case for women too. An ordering of the soul was not in them, due to the necessity that a soul become different according to the life it chooses. (618a–b)

The human being is envisioned in the midst of a polymorphous field of animation, and it is difficult to tell whether the differences among the many modes of humanity should be considered more or less conspicuous than those between the human and other-than-human animals. The "variety of human lives" underscores the instability, fragility, and relative indeterminacy of humankind: the "nature" of the human appears elusive, strained in its unity by profound discrepancies, thereby tending to recede into darkness. In the context of the aliveness of the cosmos, within the vibrantly animated organism of the all, what is illuminated is the fluid interpenetration of human and other forms of life, well beyond continuity and contiguity, making definitions and contours, not to mention all humanistic/anthropological privileges, tremble. The human and other animals share the deep syntax of aliveness and are embedded in the same conditions.[12]

The question of life is here exposed in its most elementary implications. Prior to constituting the subject matter of the zoologist or biologist or natural scientist, life is intimately known by living beings in its many shapes and registers. Not only is each life configured according to a certain mode of animality, but, inscribed in each life, in each mode of animality, is an archaic acquaintance with other forms of life, with lives configured otherwise: each one life knows other lives from within, as it were, in virtue of having lived in and as them. And of course "knowing" here means bearing a trace too remote, too layered and uncanny, to be simply spoken and owned. All shapes having passed through all shapes, each being bears the trace of a profound, if obscure, familiarity—a bond that no aversion, no revulsion can altogether obliterate. And we are led to wonder what it might mean for a human being to intuit the unfathomable, inhuman stratification he or she rests on; how the knowing of life, the living of life may be altered, may expand, evolve or intensify, in light of the impression of having lived in and as an animal, of having resided (however transiently) in the shape and body of different animals; what trials and what deepening may be at stake in such a passage and in such a dwelling.

For, indeed, the infinite circulation from life to death and back to another mortal life does not entail the radical renewal of the *psychē* each time. At each return, the *psychē* is *almost* undone by oblivion—but not quite. In other words, it is not indifferent and undifferentiated life that is reborn into ever-new lives and life forms—but *psychai* that retain some structure from previous vicissitudes. The context of the myth makes clear that, on the one hand, the *psychē* is nothing beyond the lives it has traversed: aside from them, it has no "ordering," because of "the necessity that a soul become different according to the life it chooses" (618b). On the other hand, the *psychē* carries out the task of choosing according to the way in which it has lived previously. We shall have to comment, albeit briefly, on the circularity evident here: choice can alter the trajectory of the soul's journey, and hence transform it; yet choice occurs according to what the soul has become, according to the kind of configuration that, lifetime after lifetime, has come to inhere in the soul *in some way*. But let us first notice that the spatio-temporal adventures of the *psychē* mold it, leaving marks on it that, if not in the order of conscious memories, can still be understood in terms of retention: mnestic traces carved in the *psychē* through its undergoings. This means that each one life, in any of its forms, harbors variegated mnemonic sedimentations due to earlier passages through other lives and kinds: each *psychē* is somehow differentiated, each one life is life itself inflected. It means as well that the genuinely ethical considerations outlined so far are by no means the exclusive prerogative of the human domain, but must be situated within life as a whole and viewed in connection with life's necessity and justice—with necessity and justice as the pulsating heart of life.

As for the circularity of choice, let us limit ourselves to the following observation. It is on the ground of the psychological shapes assumed through living that choices are made. How one lives or has lived determines how one will go on living—determines choices at every turn and every passage, whether to the next life or to the next moment. In death, and on the ground of previous life, the choice leading to the next life is formulated. This would seem to imply utter continuity and repetitiveness, choices made automatically, with no room for development, evolution, let alone surprises. At the limit, this would entail the impossibility of choice genuinely understood, in its disruptive power. However, as anticipated above, choice does name the potential for dramatic change. It can distinctively sustain spatio-temporal articulation both as jointure and as unprecedented, even traumatic, redirection. The myth locates in death the paradigmatic moment of choice and concern for the next initiative. At a certain remove from worldly involvements, choice takes shape and the return to this world is prepared. In part choosing occurs predictably: not out of nothing, choice to some extent results from given conditions and, thus, confirms certain automatisms and linear developments. And yet, choice can be in part interruptive, break patterns of mere reactivity, and promote action. Socrates goes on citing the story narrated by Er:

> And the messenger [*angelos*] from that place then also reported [*ēngelle*] that the spokesman said the following: "even for the one who comes forward last, if

he chooses intelligently and lives earnestly, a life to content him is laid up, not a bad one. Let the one who begins not be careless [*ameleitō*] about his choice. Let not the one who is last be discouraged." He said that when the spokesman had said this the one who had drawn the first lot came forward and immediately chose the greatest tyranny, and, due to thoughtlessness and gluttony, chose without having considered everything adequately; and it escaped his notice that eating his own children and other evils were fated to be a part of that life. When he considered it at leisure, he beat his breast and lamented the choice, not abiding by the spokesman's forewarning. For he didn't blame himself for the evils but chance, demons, and anything rather than himself. He was one of those who had come from the heaven, having lived in an orderly city in his former life, participating in virtue by habit, without philosophy. And, it may be said, not the least number of those who were caught in such circumstances came from heaven, because they were unpracticed in labors. But most of those who came from the earth, because they themselves had labored and had seen the labor of others, weren't in a rush to make their choices. On just this account, and due to the chance of the lot, there was an exchange of evils and goods for most of the souls. (619b–d)

Thus, for the most part the *psychai* oscillate between wise choices and deleterious ones. On the one hand, those who have lived well, but unconsciously and as if by chance, after death take the road across the sky and travel lightheartedly. But, coming from a frictionless crossing and lacking the practice of confronting difficulties, they will likely choose poorly when their turn comes and will be bound to inauspicious lives. Conversely, those who have lived unjustly and have traveled through the dust with much labor are now ready to choose cautiously, taking their time. It is this leisurely solicitude, this posture of care and attention (*meletē, cura*), that will support their choice and grant them a safe return to a balanced life. Here, however, lies the possibility of stabilizing this otherwise fleeting insight: the caution and care prompted in this circumstance by having suffered much can become an exercise that, through consistent practice, may allow for repeatedly propitious choices. It may allow, in other words, for a flight from captivity, from the inexorable succession of oscillations between extremes (felicitous choice, wretched choice). The name of such an exercise is philosophy, and it entails careful reflection (the capacity to look on), along with an ever more refined acquaintance with impulsive motility—a familiarity progressively making room, as it were, making the mechanics of impulsivity less binding, making it possible to step back from immediate absorption in compulsion, impatience, and rashness. The text is emphatic in this respect: the ability to choose "intelligently" and the habit of living "earnestly" are both required (619b).

Philosophy, if one were to indicate it most succinctly, may become manifest as that moment of syncopation, that countermovement with respect to the cadence of things, that allows not so much for abstraction but rather for the time and margins sufficient to contemplate the situation more comprehensively and so act out of a watchful rootedness in the surroundings. At stake, then, is an exercise of alertness, requiring a deepening adherence to life, the cultivation of consciousness, and thereby the capacity for choosing lucidly (618b–619b).

Only when choice genuinely becomes an ethical variable and no longer follows the logic of automatism and reaction, only then does it become possible, however marginally, to catch a glimpse of life's circulation in its irreducibility to mechanical metabolism. Yet, the ethical variable, leading to the variation named freedom and unpredictability, is a rare phenomenon. For the most part, the myth exposes the mechanicity of human life, life developing along courses altogether unsurprising because both thoughtless and perceptually untrained.

In this way, then, the myth casts light on the embrace of death and life, and on life resurfacing from the disappearance and invisibility of death. In the scene teeming with a multitude of animal shapes, life returning makes itself manifest: life as a whole, as the body of many. It is a story of reemergence to light, to the rippled and luminous surface, the thin veil undulating over the abyss. The angel is the one capable of this vision of life undying and unending:

> He said that this was a sight surely worth seeing: how each of the several souls chose a life. For it was pitiable, laughable, and wonderful to see. For the most part the choice was made according to the habituation of their former life. He said that he saw a soul that once belonged to Orpheus choosing a life of a swan out of hatred for womankind; due to his death at their hands, he wasn't willing to be born, generated in a woman. He saw Thamyras's soul choosing the life of a nightingale. And he also saw a swan changing to the choice of a human life; other musical animals did the same thing. The soul that got the twentieth lot chose the life of a lion; it was the soul of Ajax, son of Telamon, who shunned becoming a human being, remembering the judgment of the arms. And after him was the soul of Agamemnon; it too hated humankind as a result of its sufferings and therefore changed to the life of an eagle. Atalanta's soul had drawn one of the middle lots; she saw the great honors of an athletic man and couldn't pass them by but took them. After this soul he saw that of Epeius, son of Panopeus, going into the nature of an artisan woman. And far out among the last he saw the soul of the buffoon Thersites, clothing itself as an ape. And by chance Odysseus's soul had drawn the last lot of all and went to choose; from memory of its former labors it had recovered from love of honor; it went around for a long time looking for the life of a private man who refrains from busying himself [with public affairs]; and with effort it found one lying somewhere, neglected by the others. It said when it saw this life that it would have done the same even if it had drawn the first lot, and was delighted to choose it. And from the other beasts, similarly some went into human lives and into one another—the unjust changing [*metaballonta*] into savage ones, the just into tame ones, and there were all kinds of mixtures. (619e–620d)

The souls that most recently traversed the lives of and as singers (Orpheus, Thamyras) flow into new lives as birds, swift and winged like words. A rapacious bird, the eagle, is perceived with a sense of kinship by the soul recalling its past as a warrior from heroic ancestry—and the same is true for the lion. The reverse is also said to occur: other animals similarly *choose* human lives somewhat by affinity (again, choice apparently belongs in the dynamics of life as such, not solely in the human domain). The life of Atalanta the Artemidean huntress resolves to continue on in the guise of a male athlete of great repute, thus maintaining the focus on physical activity, while stepping out of a withdrawn life and into the splendor of notoriety. The soul that lived as Epeius, who built the Trojan horse, devises a way of cultivating its taste and skill in handicraft, but in an altogether different register, as a woman. In each single occurrence of choice, we note the unmistakable function of previous conditions, whether transformatively affirmed or rejected. But of course the most striking episode concerns Odysseus of many turns, surprisingly exemplifying the ability to take one's time, examine carefully, and perform the choice out of an enduring contact with even the most challenging circumstances: Odysseus the philosopher, endowed with vivid memory, unyielding to oblivion, capable of weeping and of recounting his own story. Odysseus suffered much and at last learned to navigate life's perilous waters, even in solitude, his anguish unseen.[13] In the image of this most controversial Homeric hero, it becomes clear to what degree, pronouncements against poetry notwithstanding, Plato has made the archaic poetic heritage his own and given it his voice.[14]

One last remark is in order, at least to make explicit that which has been only operatively implied so far, namely, the abiding mystery designated by the word *psychē*. I have throughout nonchalantly translated it as soul (*anima*), as if what that means were obvious. Yet the *psychē* that, in *Republic* as well as *Timaeus* and *Phaedrus*, in(de)finitely undergoes the cycles of death and rebirth, suffering change and everlasting, is not in the order of what will come to be called the "personal soul." Discrete life, in its finitude and singularity, is altogether mortal ("ephemeral"). What is immortal is the soul as life, as that which lives, whose assignment is living: it is life itself that is immortal, which goes on living and returns in ever-new guises, under ever-new names. Thus, neither is individual life granted any stable and lasting subsistence, nor is life immortal, life "itself" that invincibly abides, to be understood in terms of abstract simplicity. What enjoys infinite duration is inextinguishable precisely through constantly becoming other, flowing into ever-new cycles of regeneration. It is only in light of relentless mobility and mutability that abiding is envisioned. This means, above all, that the unity of life as a whole, undying, can by no means be understood in categorial terms. The one reveals itself *only* as self-differing and ever becoming, *only* as composite.[15] It should then be added, moreover, that embodiment (i.e., being materially embedded) belongs to the individual no more than immortality does: while matter is always this or that, encountered in one individual shape or another, still, it is never simply fixed in one such shape and thereby never simply the property of an individual. Matter indefinitely transcends any one individual, and the individual (if individual there be) should be understood in light of such a dispossession, relative to embodiment and aliveness alike.

Immortality, then, is nothing other than the impermanence of bodily guises and material arrangements, permanently decomposing and recomposing. Life returning is indefinitely layered, the precipitate of indeterminately many lives, passages through death, and returns to life—the indefinite accretion of mortal fragments. Life immortal cannot be viewed as amorphous, indifferent, inertial. It must somehow bear traces of individual lives and the ways they were lived; for the soul's vicissitudes and trajectories, from life to death and back to life, depend on such traces cryptically codified and recorded, as it were.[16] Without such lineaments, life would be nothing; it would not be. What we called the ethical variable, the ability to choose, to give oneself direction and not be simply impacted upon and reactive, rests precisely on this. How one lived will determine how life will subsequently go on, trespass its own confines, undergo metamorphosis, and come back otherwise, as an other.

Again, even in light of these considerations on traces mnemonically or immemorially retained and physically inscribed, we cannot speak of a personal, individual soul. For, in the first place, the soul always returns to a new life, always resurfaces from disappearance and involves a multitude—constant exchanges with the surroundings, participation in that which exceeds it, implication in the relentless circulation and communication, physical and otherwise, within the cosmos. Secondly, and most remarkably, the soul is a gallery of portraits, mostly dilapidated and unreadable: a community in time, a temporal proliferation stratified and crystallized within "one" and the "same," as it were. If there should be anything individual and individuated in a soul, it would have to do with something that cannot simply be undone but is more deeply carved in the soul: it would have to do with the architectural integrity and relative stability, and hence the resilience, yielded by the exercise of philosophy, which is a practice of freedom. But any mode of individuality and individuation would have to rest on the acknowledgment of utter divisibility: on the awareness of the unfathomable crowd unrecognizably resonating in any one life. After all, philosophy is crucially a matter of recollection, an effort to remember even the irretrievably dismembered, thereby saving it—in the fragile and defenseless form of a myth.

Thus the soul presents a collective character, both synchronically and in diachronic/genealogical terms. Among other things, this perspective opens new vistas on the phenomenon of empathy, illuminating it as a matter not merely of shared structures (neuro-, bio-, and physiological), but above all of shared vicissitudes—of having gone through certain lives and archaically, obscurely, in the hidden receptacles of one's aliveness, bearing the *pathos* of that, "knowing" what that is/was like. Empathy would emerge in the awareness of sharing an experiential field, manifold and choral.

Each one is many: not simply a collection but a collectivity; not simply a synergy of diverse aspects but a historical and prehistorical unfolding in which the nameless crowd of the dead is harbored, along with the seeds of the unborn. The commitment to this remembrance and to this saving, at once unlikely and necessary, has everything to do with the possibility of community.

Notes

The translation of the epigraph is mine.

1. *The Symposium and the Phaedrus: Plato's Erotic Dialogues*, trans. W. S. Cobb (Albany: State University of New York Press, 1993).

2. On the *vexata quaestio* of the conclusion in mythical form, see, for example, Ronald R. Johnson, "Does Plato's Myth of Er Contribute to the Argument of the *Republic*?" *Philosophy and Rhetoric* 32, no. 1 (1999): 1–13.

3. On *logos* as living, see also *Statesman* 277c, *Phaedrus* 275d–e, 276a–b, 276b–277b, 277e–278b.

4. Here and throughout, I have followed Allan Blooms's translation of *The Republic of Plato* (New York: Basic Books, 1968), although with frequent emendations.

5. *Pace* Heidegger, who, precisely by reference to the myth at the end of the *Republic* and to Aristotle's remark on the subject matter of *sophia* being "excessive, wondrous, difficult, and daimonic" (*Nicomachean Ethics* 6, 1141b4–8), asserts in the 1942–43 lecture course on Parmenides the irrelevance of the question of life for philosophy: "The Greeks, to whom we owe the essence and name of 'philosophy' and of the 'philosopher,' already knew quite well that thinkers are not 'close to life.' But only the Greeks concluded from this lack of closeness to life that the thinkers are then the most necessary—precisely in view of the essential misery of man. The Germans would not have had to be the people of thinkers if their thinkers had not known the same things" (*Parmenides*, trans. A. Schuwer and R. Rojcewicz [Bloomington: Indiana University Press, 1992], 100).

6. In *Orpheus and Greek Religion* (London: Methuen, 1935), W. K. C. Guthrie casts light on the Orphic background of Plato's myth and, in particular, recalls the inscription on a gold funerary plate from Thurii, in Southern Italy (end of the fourth century BCE), suggestively resonating with the itinerary of the *psychai* according to Er: "But so soon as the spirit hath left the light of the sun,/ Go to the right as far as one should go, being right wary in all things./ Hail, thou who hast suffered the suffering. This thou hadst never suffered before./ Thou art become god from man./ A kid thou art fallen into milk./ Hail to thee journeying the right hand road/ By holy meadows and groves of Persephone" (172–173). More broadly, Mircea Eliade notes that, in terms not only of his mythical visions but also of his consistent turns to eidetic or archetypal orders, "Plato could be regarded as the outstanding philosopher of 'primitive mentality,' that is, as the thinker who succeeded in giving philosophic currency and validity to the modes of life and behavior of archaic humanity" (*Cosmos and History: The Myth of Eternal Return*, trans. W. R. Trask [New York: Harper, 1959], 34).

7. See Hilda Richardson, "The Myth of Er (Plato, Republic, 616b)," *Classical Quarterly* 20, nos. 3–4 (1926): 113–133, who paradigmatically articulates a morphological analysis of the cosmos and delineates the terms of the debate surrounding it. See, furthermore, J. S. Morrison, "Parmenides and Er," *Journal of Hellenic Studies* 75 (1955): 59–68.

8. In *Logic of Imagination* (Bloomington: Indiana University Press, 2012), 230–243, John Sallis weaves the myth of Er into his discussion of "Natal Mortality." In turn, Sara Brill, in *Plato on the Limits of Human Life* (Bloomington: Indiana University Press, 2013), 155, at once retains and semantically reconfigures the language of geo- or topographical analysis, underscoring the centrality of the question of life in its ethical dimension: "The landscape of Er's tale marks out the shifting terrain of choice."

9. The image of the radiant column and of the light "binding the heaven" and "holding the entire revolution together" (616b–c) may be related to the fiery imagery of the Pythagoreans, who envisioned fire at the center as well as surrounding the cosmos (see E. Zeller, *Die Philosophie der Griechen in ihrer geschichtlichen Entwicklung*, 4th ed. [Leipzig: Reisland, 1876], 403–407). Fire, called "mother of the gods" and associated with Hestia by the Pythagoreans (Aëtius II.7.7, *Dox. Gr.*, ed. Diels [Berlin: Reimer, 1879], 336–367), comes thus to be linked to the figure of the goddess seated at the center of the scene and presiding over becoming and its revolutions. More broadly, the imagery of light may indicate the comprehensive animation (the soul) of the cosmos, and thus the generativity and life that infuse the cosmic expanse. (The lexical parallels between *Timaeus* 34b and *Republic* 616b suggest that the latter, with its emphasis on light, is describing the cosmic soul.) In this regard, see again Richardson, "The Myth of Er (Plato, *Republic*, 616b)."

10. On the mathematics of the myth of Er, see R. S. Brumbaugh, "Colors of the Hemispheres in Plato's Myth of Er (*Republic* 616e)," *Classical Philology* 46, no. 3 (1951): 173–176, and "Plato Republic 616e: The Final 'Law of Nines,'" *Classical Philology* 49, no. 1 (1954): 33–34.

11. Aëtius (II.7.1) notes in Parmenides the confluence of Dikē and Anankē, the "*daimon* who steers (*kubernetis*)" and the "holder of the keys" (*Dox. Gr.*, 335–336). In turn, Simplicius remarks on the similarity between Parmenides's goddess and Anankē in Plato's myth, particularly as they lie at the very heart of life's unfolding and govern the ventures of the *psychai* (in *On Aristotle's Physics* 39.17–21). See also Richardson, "The Myth of Er (Plato, *Republic*, 616b)."

12. In the *Statesman* such a communion or communication is factually affirmed: in the age of Cronos human beings and the rest of living beings, peacefully coexisting and tame (271d–e), could discourse with each other and share in this way their becoming (272b–c).

13. On Odysseus as prefiguring the philosopher, consider the following passage from Book 6: "Rather, just like a human being who has fallen in with wild beasts and is neither willing to join them in doing injustice nor sufficient as one man to resist all the savagery, one would perish before he has been of any use to city or friends and be of no profit to himself or others. Taking all this into the calculation, he keeps quiet and practices what is his own, as a man in the storm, when dust and rain are blown about by the wind, stands aside under a little wall. Seeing others filled full of lawlessness, he is content if somehow he himself can live his life here pure of injustice and unholy deeds, and take his leave from it graciously and cheerfully with fair hope" (496d–e).

14. The character of Odysseus will enjoy lasting prominence in later Platonic and Neoplatonic circles, and well beyond, precisely as a figure of deftness in navigating life and sheer determination to survive—features especially evident if contrasted with another mythical character, Narcissus, who was deceived by water and lost himself in it. This is paradigmatically evident in Plotinus and Porphyry (*De antro nympharum*). See Pierre Hadot, *Plotin, Porphyre: Études néoplatoniciennes* (Paris: Les Belles Lettres, 1999), 225–266; J. Pépin, "The Platonic and Christian Ulysses," in *Neoplatonism and Christian Thought*, ed. D. J. O'Meara (Albany: State University of New York Press, 1982), 3–18; and Julia Kristeva, *Histoires d'amour* (Paris: Denoël, 1983), particularly chapter 3.

15. In this connection, see *Symposium* 207d–208b and *Phaedrus* 245c ("every soul is immortal, for that which is ever moving or ever changing is immortal").

16. See also *Timaeus* 90e–92c.

14 Of Beasts and Heroes

The Promiscuity of Humans and Animals in the Myth of Er

Francisco J. Gonzalez

PLATO'S REPUBLIC, WHICH throughout nine books offers us the description of a utopian city meant to serve as a model in heaven, concludes with a very strange or *atopos* myth about a very *atopos* place: a place that is neither above nor below, neither here nor there, but a place of transition where souls choose their next lives to be reincarnated in a transitionless instant. In this "daimonic" place where normal dichotomies such as soul and body or this world and the beyond seem no longer to hold, we find human and animal lives tossed indiscriminately into the choice pool. What is more, we see animal lives chosen not by criminals nor even by mediocre human beings, but by great poets and heroes. Finally, among the souls choosing we find swans and other animals that are in no way prevented from choosing a human life for their next round of incarnation. The result is what the myth itself describes as an incredible and tragicomic spectacle. It is therefore no wonder that this myth, in this as well as in other ways, has disconcerted Plato's readers, or at least those who have chosen to pay attention. After an examination of the text and the questions or problems it presents, I will consider some of the readings that have been proposed, with particular attention to their philosophical assumptions, and then propose a somewhat different reading. One thing that will emerge clearly is that Plato is certainly not a Platonist when it comes to defining the relation between humans and animals.

The Problem: The Strange Status of Animals in the Myth of Er

There will be no attempt here to provide an interpretation of the myth as a whole and of its function in the *Republic:* this is something I have undertaken elsewhere.[1] Instead, the focus will be entirely on what can be described as the promiscuity of human and animal lives in the myth. The crucial texts and the problems they pose are the following:

1. The patterns of lives (τὰ τῶν βίων παραδείγματα) among which the souls are to choose include all kinds of animals as well as all sorts of human lives (Ζῴων τε γὰρ πάντων βίους καὶ δὲ καὶ τοὺς ἀνθρωπίνους ἅπαντας, 618a). There is no suggestion here of any superiority of human lives over animal lives. All the emphasis is on the *diversity* of lives (εἶναι δὲ παντοδαπά, 618a).
2. At 620a–c, different heroes are described as choosing the lives of animals: the soul of Orpheus chooses the life of a swan (κύκνου βίον αἱρουμένην), Thamyras the life of a nightingale, Ajax the life of a lion, Agamemnon the life of an eagle, and Thersites the life of an ape. It is significant that in this context other heroes are described as choosing human lives: Atalanta chooses the life of a great athlete and Odysseus chooses the life of an ordinary citizen. The *kind* of life seems more important than whether it is an animal or human life.[2]
3. If the soul of Orpheus chooses the life of a swan, Er also sees a swan "changing over into the choice of a human life [ἰδεῖν δὲ καὶ κύκνον μεταβάλλοντα εἰς ἀνθρωπίνου βίου αἵρεσιν]" (620a). That this is not a passing joke is made clear when the general principle is stated that "other animals change over in the same way to humans and to each other, the unjust ones to the savage, the just to the tame, with all possible mixtures in between [καὶ ἐκ τῶν ἄλλων δὴ θηρίων ὡσαύτως εἰς ἀνθρώπους ἰέναι καὶ εἰς ἄλληλα, τὰ μὲν ἄδικα εἰς τὰ ἄγρια, τὰ δὲ δίκαια εἰς τὰ ἥμερα μεταβάλλοντα, καὶ πάσας μίξεις μίγνυσθαι]" (620d). What we seem to have here is a complete indiscriminateness in the multiplicity of human and animal lives. Indeed, it would seem implied that there is no absolute difference between an animal and a human soul. The souls choosing their lives are presumably in themselves neither human nor animal: they choose either human or animal lives, moving back and forth between them.[3] It is therefore highly significant that the patterns of lives are said not to contain any particular determination of the soul as that will be conditioned by the kind of life chosen: ψυχῆς δὲ τάξιν οὐκ ἐνεῖναι διὰ τὸ ἀναγκαίως ἔχειν ἄλλον ἑλομένην βίον ἀλλοίαν γίγνεσθαι (618b). It seems that there are therefore no animal souls or human souls in the Myth of Er, only human and animal lives that condition the character of the soul and are in turn chosen according to the character of the soul. Furthermore, as already noted, when it comes to the character the soul acquires, the character of the life, rather than whether it is human or animal, is what appears decisive.
4. This whole scene of the choice of lives, rather than being described as morally edifying, is described as pitiful, comic, and strange (ἐλεεινήν τε γὰρ ἰδεῖν εἶναι καὶ γελοίαν καὶ θαυμασίαν, 620a). The reason given is that the choice,

rather than being based on knowledge and careful deliberation, is conditioned by the habit of previous lives (κατὰ συνήθειαν γὰρ τοῦ προτέρου βίου τὰ πολλὰ αἱρεῖσθαι, 620a). This is presumably why even animals can "choose." This is indeed the other striking thing about the myth: there appears to be no difference between how humans and animals choose their next lives. Both, like the swan described in the quotation above, "change over into" their choice of their next life through the character formed in the previous life.

There are of course other passages in Plato's dialogues that describe transmigration as occurring between humans and animals. The differences as well as the similarities between these passages and the Myth of Er will further clarify the problems the latter poses. To consider first the *Phaedo* 81e–82b, what we find there is simply a description of humans with different characters becoming different kinds of animals. What is striking there and offers the clearest parallel to the Myth of Er is the suggestion that people who have the popular and social virtues of moderation and justice will become social animals like bees or ants *and also the same kind of human beings*. Here, as in the Myth of Er, what matters is not whether one becomes animal or human, but only what *kind* of animal or human one becomes. In the myth of the *Phaedrus,* on the other hand, we appear to find the suggestion of an unbridgeable difference between human and animal souls and therefore a significant difference with the Myth of Er: "From there [the choice and allotment of second lives], a human soul can enter a wild animal, and a soul that was once human can move from an animal to a human being again. But a soul that never saw the truth cannot take a human shape" (249b).[4] Here only a certain kind of soul can enter a human body, so that an animal can become a human being only if its soul had occupied a human form earlier. But even here we have not so much a distinction between human and animal souls as rather a hierarchy of souls, with some capable of taking either human or animal form and some capable of taking only animal form. Something similar is found in a famous passage of the *Timaeus* on the generation of animals. There the different animals come to be through the descent of souls on account of their ignorance. But there is also the suggestion of a continual movement back and forth according to the degree of ignorance: νοῦ καὶ ἀνοίας ἀποβολῇ καὶ κτήσει μεταβαλλόμενα (92c).[5] At an earlier passage (42b–c) reincarnation as an animal appears to be described as punishment for a soul that has failed to master its desires and emotions and therefore fallen into wickedness. But the punishment here is not simply turning into an animal, but becoming "some wild animal that resembled the wicked character he had acquired."[6]

What is absent from all of these texts is any suggestion that animal life would in itself constitute a punishment for a soul having previously lived a human life;[7] absent too, then, is any assertion of the moral superiority of humans over animals (we are given no reason to think that a wild human tyrant is better than a sociable bee) as well as any claim of an absolute, unbridgeable difference between humans and animals. Yet there are two respects in which the Myth of Er goes even further. First, whereas in the *Phaedrus* and the *Timaeus* there is a ranking in terms of wisdom and ignorance, any such ranking is absent from the Myth of Er. Secondly, in the latter myth it is not only humans who can become animals but *heroes* or what we could call *super-humans*.[8]

Surprisingly, the strange status and role of animals in the Myth of Er has received very little attention in the literature. For a thorough engagement with the problems it raises we must go all the way back to the commentary of Proclus. Proclus has the virtue of finding these texts deeply troubling, though also the failing of seeking to eliminate what is troubling in them in ways that are not fully convincing. I will then turn to alternative readings that, together with that of Proclus, appear to represent the full range of possibilities, as the following outline can show:

1. There is an absolute distinction between human and animal, the soul of the one never becoming in truth the soul of the other. (Proclus)
2. As the principle of life, the soul is the same for humans and animals, but humans are distinguished from animals by the rational activity that supervenes on the soul. (Plotinus)
3. Both Proclus and Plotinus are wrong to read the myth literally: what is said about animals in the myth is said only metaphorically to make a moral point about human life. (Ficino)
4. What makes movement of a soul between animal and human forms possible is that animals possess a certain degree of responsibility or rationality. (Brisson)

We can thus interpret the myth either as keeping human and animal souls completely distinct or as attributing to humans and animals a common soul while keeping them distinct through the supervening activity of reason or as implying that humans and animals share even this rational activity. Or one can reject all of these readings in maintaining that the passages are to be read metaphorically and that they thus make no literal claim regarding the relation between humans and animals but only use animals to make a moral point about humans. Yet after considering all of these readings I will suggest another reading that, while sharing some points with these, still remains distinct. On this reading, which I will call the "tragicomic" reading, the point is to blur the line separating us from animals, not in order to make animals rational but in order to suggest the precariousness and limits of our own rationality. A lesson of both ancient comedy and ancient tragedy that Plato is echoing here is that not even heroes are so different from beasts.

Proclus:
Human and Animal Souls Only Joined While Absolutely Distinct

The central thesis of Proclus's interpretation in his commentary on the *Republic* is that when Plato describes a human soul as entering an animal body he does not mean that the soul actually becomes the soul of that body (natural structural differences, he explains, are incompatible with such a thesis) but rather that through a similar way of life it attaches itself to an animal understood as a body already possessing its own soul. In other words, Plato "makes our soul inhabit not the bodies of irrational beings, but beings that are already living animals [οὐ τοῖς σώμασιν ἐνοικίζει τοῖς τῶν ἀλόγων τὴν ἡμετέραν ψυχήν, ἀλλὰ τοῖς ἤδη ζῴοις οὖσιν]" (310.29–311.1).[9] There is thus for Proclus no possibility of a human soul becoming the soul of an animal body. Instead, if a human soul chooses the life of a swan, the result will be the joining, through a purely external relation, of the soul of a human to the soul of a swan. We are thus in this case to imagine a swan with its own internal swan soul being possessed from without by a human soul. The crucial passage in which Proclus expresses this idea is the following: "When the soul in us is joined to the soul in the animal through position, it animates the irrational animal from the outside, next to it in position [ἡ δὲ ἐν ἡμῖν πρὸς τὴν ἐν ἐκείνοις ἐν σχέσει γενομένη ψυχοῖ τὸ ἄλογον ἔξωθεν ἐφεστῶσα σχετικῶς]" (310.17–18). Proclus goes on to argue that the soul can join itself in this way even to gods and spirits without becoming a god or spirit. The soul is carried (φέρεσθαι) through such relations up to the Good or down to Tartarus, having no fixed rank, so that it seems to be fused with all things (συμφύεσθαι πᾶσι).

The attraction of such an interpretation is not hard to see: it keeps the human soul completely distinct from the animal soul, allowing between the two only an external relation of "position." But what is the textual support for such an interpretation? All that Proclus can really offer is that the text describes the human soul as coming to inhabit not the body of an animal but simply a "swan," a "monkey," and so on, by which must be meant *the whole animal* as a compound of body and soul. In contrast, Proclus argues, when Plato wishes to speak of a soul taking on a body, as in the case of the soul of Epeius taking on the body of a woman, he speaks of the soul entering "the *physis* of a skillful woman" (620c; cited by Proclus at 311.9). The problem, of course, is that within the Myth of Er there is no difference in the language used to describe the choice of a human life and that used to described the choice of an animal life: we are not told, for example, that while Atalanta will become a great athlete, Thersites will only be "joined" to the life of a monkey.

An important implication of Proclus's reading, though again one that receives no direct support from the text, is that only a *human* soul can pass from animals to humans and from humans back to animals. Here Proclus must turn for support to *Phaedrus* 249b and the claim there that no soul that has not seen being could enter a human form. Yet, for reasons already noted in the above discussion of this passage, it cannot really support Proclus's strong thesis. Having seen being does not prevent a human soul from truly becoming an animal through the kind of change in knowledge and ignorance described in the *Timaeus;* nor does it prevent an animal, through the same kind of change, from becoming again human. Furthermore, the point made in the *Phaedrus,* as already noted, is nowhere to be found in the Myth of Er itself. Proclus finds himself at odds with the text again when he turns to the transmigration of souls from animals to other animals. Proclus expectedly argues that even the souls that transmigrate between animals are *human* souls (322.25–325.10). His argument comes down to the fact that irrational animals could not make a choice of life. Yet, as we have seen, precisely such a choice is attributed in the text to a swan.

But then, why, on Proclus's view, believe that animals have their own souls? Why not conclude that all animals are inhabited by human souls? As we have seen, Proclus cannot allow a human soul to be truly "in" an animal body. He thus needs to maintain that animals have their own souls *in order to keep human beings and animals as distinct as possible.* In directly confronting the question of whether all animals receive their animation from a human soul or have their own proper soul, Proclus tries to resolve an apparent tension between the view he finds expressed in the *Timaeus* that animals are animated by human souls and the view he finds in the *Phaedrus* that there are souls that have not seen being and therefore cannot enter human form. As already suggested by the passage quoted above, his solution is to speak of two modes of animation: an animal is animated from within by its own soul and from without by a human soul. Among the reasons Proclus proceeds to give for why it is reasonable that animals should have their own souls, one is particularly revealing: if all animals were animated only by human souls, then the descent of the human soul into animals would not be *against* nature (παρὰ φύσιν), unless one were to claim that all animals as such exist against nature, which would be absurd (336.20–337.13). This argument assumes that the descent of human souls into animals is against nature, and Proclus insists that this is Plato's own view; yet the evidence he offers, that is, that this sort of animation is attributed by Plato to souls that have sinned (ἁρματουσῶν ψυχῶν, 337.5), is, as we have seen, a view of which there is no trace in the Myth of Er. The conclusion Proclus nevertheless reaches by means of this and other arguments is that animals have their proper souls according to nature and as commonly defining them before the advent of a human soul in some of them.

As should be fully clear by now, Proclus's interest lies in keeping humans as rational beings completely distinct from animals as irrational beings, and this requires an absolute and unbridgeable distinction between human and animal souls. Transmigration between humans and animals is admissible only if interpreted as human souls "visiting," as it were, animals that as such remain completely distinct from them. Yet it is precisely such an absolute distinction between human and animal souls that the Myth of Er not only gives no hint of but seems directly to undermine. As noted above, the myth does not even give us any grounds for speaking of *human* or *animal souls,* only of human and animal *lives,* where even this distinction is not the most important one (that being instead the moral character of the life, human or animal). Indeed, in all of the Platonic texts considered, there appear to be only souls that, while not in themselves human or animal, can end up in a human or animal life depending on their vision of being, alterations in their relative degree of knowledge or ignorance, and the disposition of their character in a prior life. But in this case the reading of Proclus proves the most incompatible with the texts.

Yet all this is not what gives Proclus the greatest difficulty in interpreting the Myth of Er. The passage that Proclus explicitly describes as full of absurdity on the face of it, though he adds that it must appear so only to those approaching it without sufficient thought (τοῖς ἀπερισκέπτως αὐτὰ μετιοῦσίν, 312.10–11), is the one that describes *heroes* as choosing the lives of animals. This passage cannot be taken at face value by Proclus because, while he grants that all human souls can descend into animals, he excludes the souls of heroes, claiming that they can descend only as low as humans (330.18–332.27). Furthermore, Proclus takes it to be obvious that the passage represents a shocking insult to heroes otherwise apparently admired by Plato; indeed, according to Proclus, Plato owes many of his own doctrines to that very Orpheus described as choosing to be a swan (340.23–28)! He also takes the passage to contradict Plato's critique of the poets for depicting the heroes in a less than heroic way, that is, as subject to extreme passions (313.1–4). For all of these reasons, it is Proclus's stated intent in the ensuing commentary to free Plato of this "blasphemy [δυσφήμια]" (313.9) toward the heroes.

Proclus's solution is to characterize the passage as a kind of riddle: through the names of the heroes Plato is hinting at (αἰνίσσεσθαι) particular forms of life (ζῴων εἴδη) that, while appearing like the heroes, are in fact dissimilar to them due to the addition of certain irrational passions (διὰ δέ τινας παθῶν προσθήκας, 313.13–14). If Er had spoken clearly instead of in enigmas, he would have said that he saw a soul *like* (οἵαν) that of Orpheus or *like* that of Thamyras (314.11–13). So it is not really Orpheus who chooses the life of a swan but rather a soul that might look like that of Orpheus in being musical, one that pursues the passion for music without reason or philosophy. The moral given is therefore the following: "Not even the musical life can save the soul without freedom from passion, but as in the case of the erotic life, it can lead upwards only with philosophy [οὐκ ἄρα οὐδὲ ὁ μουσικὸς βίος σῴζει τὴν ψυχὴν ἄνευ ἀπαθείας, ἀλλὰ καθάπερ ὁ ἐρωτικός, καὶ οὗτος ἀνάγει μετὰ φιλοσοφίας]" (315.11–13). Such musical souls descend into irrational animals because their passion is unphilosophical and even unmusical in the truest sense (πάθος δὲ αἴτιον ἄμουσον καὶ ἀφιλόσοφον τῆς εἰς ἄλογα ζῷα πορείας, 316.5–6). This is so because only philosophy can save one from the passions (and the animals, of course, do not philosophize). As for the names "Achilles" and "Agamemnon," they represent respectively the life of bravery, but joined with rivalry, and the life of rule, but joined with contempt for other humans (317.1–11). So in each case there is an irrational passion that drags the soul down to irrational animality. Proclus indeed explains later that one can have qualities such as musicianship and bravery and rule, either rationally or irrationally (ἔστι γὰρ ταῦτα καὶ ἀλόγως ἔχειν καὶ λογικῶς, ποιεῖ δὲ ἀλογίαν ἐμπαθὴς ζωή, καὶ ἀνθρωπίνην ἀπαθής, 319.22–24). Interestingly, Proclus treats the case of Thersites separately, though he gives the same type of explanation: the mixture of the laughable with villainy and weakness is what joins his soul to the monkey (319.1–24). Even Odysseus, though not choosing an animal life, is still said to represent not the actual hero but only a type of life (the prudent one, 320.5).

Proclus thus performs an extraordinary feat of alchemy with the text. What the text describes as the tragicomical spectacle of great heroes choosing animal lives is transformed into the morally edifying tale of how extreme and irrational passions can cause one to lose one's humanity and descend into the irrational life of an animal. Of course, nothing in the text suggests that the heroes mentioned are only symbols for vicious lives deserving punishment, and nothing can recommend such a reading beyond Proclus's moral indignation. Indeed, the main merit of Proclus's interpretation is in his demonstration of how resistant the text is to such an interpretation. As has already been noted, the Myth of Er not only seems to recognize no fundamental difference between human and animal souls but also offers no moral judgment on animal lives. The choice of an animal life is not depicted as punishment for anything, just as the choice of lives as such is given no function of punishing or rewarding past behavior. When Proclus proceeds to argue that the souls descended from heaven cannot enter an animal body, just as a soul cannot proceed up to heaven from an animal body (325.11–327.2), he is making a claim that has no basis in the text. If a soul descended from heaven can, after a few thousand years of bliss in reward for virtue, choose a life that involves eating one's own children and many other horrors (619c), why could it not choose the life of a swan (a much better fate, surely!). Proclus can make the myth morally edifying only by turning it into a riddle that means the opposite of what it says. Morality and human distinction can be saved only by interpreting heroes turning into animals as bad souls that are punished by being "attached" to animals. Proclus thereby shows, unintentionally and indirectly, how non-human-centered and amoral, not to say immoral, Plato's myth is.

Plotinus: The Homogeneity of the Soul and the Task of Being Human

What Plotinus has to say on the topic of transmigration is so obscure and so scattered among his texts that some have even denied he takes the view seriously.[10] Yet recent interpretations have found a distinct and consistent doctrine in Plotinus that appears inspired at least in part by the Myth of Er. Furthermore, it is a doctrine that appears diametrically opposed to that of Proclus in maintaining that the rational activity that defines human beings, rather than being a distinct type of soul, is an act that supervenes on the soul understood as the principle of life.

Where the question of the transmigration of human souls into animals receives the fullest discussion by Plotinus is *Ennead* VI. 7. The first important passage in this treatise is VI. 7. 4, 33–38; 5, 1–2:

> The human being is rational life. But how can there be life without the soul? For either the soul will provide the rational life and the human being will be an activity of the soul and not its being, or the soul will be the human being. But if the rational soul is the human being, how will it not be a human being when it enters another form of life? It is necessary for the human being to be another formal principle apart from the soul [Ζωὴ τοίνυν λογικὴ ὁ ἄνθρωπος. ἆρ᾽οὖν ζωὴ ἄνευ ψυχῆς; ἢ γὰρ ἡ ψυχὴ παρέξεται τὴν ζωὴν τὴν λογικὴν καὶ ἔσται ὁ ἄνθρωπος ἐνέργεια ψυχῆς καὶ οὐκ οὐσία, ἢ ἡ ψυχὴ ὁ ἄνθρωπος ἔσται. ἀλλ᾽ εἰ ἡ ψυχὴ ἡ λογικὴ ὁ ἄνθρωπος ἔσται, ὅταν εἰς ἄλλο ζῷον ἴῃ ἡ ψυχή, πῶς οὐκ ἄνθρωπος; Λόγον τοίνυν δεῖ τὸν ἄνθρωπον ἄλλον παρὰ τὴν ψυχὴν εἶναι].

The problem here is that if the soul that possesses reason were as such identical to a human being, it would remain a human being upon entering an animal. As we have seen, Proclus would accept such a consequence, but Plotinus implies that it would be absurd: the soul of a human being would need to cease to be human upon entering another form of life. This suggests that for Plotinus choosing the life of an animal would mean becoming that animal and not simply being attached to it from the outside.[11] The solution Plotinus offers is that the human being is not to be identified with the soul as such, but only with the rational activity of this soul. In this case the same soul could inhabit a human and then an animal, but in the latter case it would no longer exercise the rational activity that is the being of a human. In this case, the difference between humans and animals is not a difference in the being of the soul, but only one between the different activities that can be exercised by the soul. As Pierre Hadot has noted, this makes of the human being "a composite . . . not of a soul and a body, but of a soul and a formal reason that causes the human being to be a human being and that joins a soul to make of it a human soul: this *logos* is chosen by the soul which determines itself to be and act according to this type of being."[12] What enables this same soul to choose an animal life is that it contains within itself not only the *logos* of a human but also the *logoi* of all other animals. This is the point of another passage found later in the same treatise: "But if it take on the body of an animal, one might wonder how, given that it is the formal reason (*logos*) of a human being. Or it was all things and at different times exercises its activity according to a different formal reason" (VI. 7. 6, 21–23). The suggestion here is that the soul contains the *logoi* of all animals and therefore can activate one or the other at different times. This is stated more explicitly in another passage that follows shortly after: "When the soul that was suspended [from superior beings] as a human follows the soul that has chosen animal nature, it gives forth the formal reason of that animal that was already within it. For it possesses [this formal reason] and its activity is inferior" (VI. 7. 6, 33–36). There appears to be an implied distinction here between a lower sensitive soul and a higher intelligible soul, but the important point for our purposes is that the higher intelligible part contains within itself, and therefore can give forth, the formal reason not only of a human being but of any other animal. Neither ceasing to be the same soul nor remaining a human soul, it is active with a different *logos* when its lower sensitive part enters the body of an animal.[13] Because the soul possesses within itself all forms of animal life, it is not against its nature to take on the body of an animal.[14] Here the contrast with Proclus could not be sharper.

Plotinus goes on to elaborate on this idea by describing how the soul of all, because it is a *logos* containing all, sketches in advance all possible animal forms before souls reach them, like a set of illuminations projected upon matter (VI. 7. 7, 8–12). As Hadot has suggested, it is hard not to see here an echo of the choice of lives in the Myth of Er.[15] There is also another interesting parallel. If Plato's myth describes transmigration not only between humans and animals but also, to Proclus's shock, between heroes and animals, Plotinus's view takes this too into account and therefore does not need to resort to riddles or enigmas. The soul is described by Plotinus as possibly choosing not only the *logos* of a human or of an animal but also the *logos* of a *daimon*! (VI. 7. 6, 26–33) Because of all the kinds of *logoi* it contains within itself, and because its being is not defined or determined by any of them, the soul can choose lives ranging from semi-gods to the lowest animals.

The crucial and striking consequence of Plotinus's view, and the one that brings it most into line with what we have seen to be the explicit sense of the Myth of Er, has been stated most succinctly by Jean Derrida: "the soul of a human being is not solely or simply human."[16] As we have seen, a human being for Plotinus is neither the soul nor the being of the soul but an activity of the soul carried out according to one of its immanent *logoi*. Derrida stresses the instability this creates in the human identity: "the human is an act or project before it is a genus or species, and as *rational life* it is perhaps condemned to remain a problem, a paradox and even an oxymoron. It is not given to us as something accomplished and it is not as such that we should seek it."[17] The important point for our present purposes, however, is that the soul of a human being for Plotinus is not a different soul in nature or being from that of an animal: what distinguishes the one from the other is an activity added to the soul, which activity is in each case the exercise of only one of the many *logoi* the soul contains.[18] What characterizes the Plotinian soul, as many commentators have recognized, is its *homogeneity* across all forms of life.[19] It is to this extent a faithful reading of the Myth of Er, though ironically so, since it does not explicitly offer itself as an interpretation of the myth at all.[20] This is not, however, to say that it is completely faithful. There is still on Plotinus's view a sharp distinction between the *logos* and corresponding activity of a human being and the *logos* and corresponding activity of an animal, along with the judgment that the latter is radically inferior and can therefore count as a punishment; as we have seen, neither of these elements can be found in the Myth of Er. Even in a text like the *Timaeus* where the inferiority of animal life in relation to human life is clearly asserted, we do not see them distinguished according to two different kinds of activities, but rather according to different degrees of the same activity (from greater understanding to greater ignorance).

Ficino and the Metaphorical Reading

A reading of the Myth of Er, and of transmigration in general, that departs explicitly and fundamentally from those of both Proclus and Plotinus is the "metaphorical" reading defended by Marsilio Ficino in *Platonic Theology,* Book 17. In his discussion of the soul's status before entering and after leaving the body, Ficino considers the views of the academies of Plotinus and Proclus, summarizing succinctly the difference between them on the specific question of the incarnation of human souls in animals: "Finally, having laid aside its human shape, the soul submits to the body of the beast which it has made itself most resemble by its behavior, whether it inserts itself into the fetus of the beast and becomes the soul belonging to the beast's body, as Plotinus, Numenius, Harpocratius, and Boethius suppose; or whether it unites itself to the beast's soul and becomes the beast's companion, as Hermias, Syrianus and Proclus believe."[21] Here we see that the opposed doctrines we have found in Proclus and Plotinus were seen as defining two different schools of thought, each with its own adherents. At one point Ficino attributes the following motivation to Proclus and his school: they "were ashamed to hurl a celestial soul down into the bodies of beasts; and in order to punish monstrous vices with due punishment, they supposed that sacrilegious souls hover over beasts' souls yet do not rule over beasts' bodies, since if a soul has become brutish it will not be purged but totally infected" (XVII. 4. 4; p. 49).

Ficino himself, however, rejects the positions of both the Roman (Plotinus) and Lycian (Proclus) academies, as he calls them, and sides instead with the Greek academies, both the dogmatic and the skeptical. With the former he believes that Plato did affirm certain things about the soul, but with the latter he agrees that much is said "poetically" and therefore is not to be taken literally. "So treading in the footsteps of Xenocrates and Ammonius, we do not deny that Plato made some affirmations about the soul [*affirmavisse quaedam de anima*], but much that he says about the soul's circuit, being poetic [*tamquam poetica*], we take to mean differently than the words appear to signify [*aliter intelligimus quam verba videantur significare*]" (XVII. 4. 1; p. 45, translation modified). As for what Ficino refuses to take literally, we soon discover it to be species-to-species migration (*vera de specie in speciem transmigratio*), since, he argues, "not just any soul can enter any body [*non poterit anima quaelibet corpus quodlibet ingredi*]" (XVII. 4. 2). Indeed, according to Ficino, the Pythagorean views found in Plato's dialogues are not something he affirmed in his own person (XVII. 4. 5). His argument is that in the only place where he is speaking for himself, the *Laws* and the *Letters*, Plato does not affirm these things: "In the *Laws* Plato does not assert that men's souls cross over into beasts" (XVII. 4. 7; p. 55). We see here, of course, the problem with such a "metaphorical" reading; where do we find expressed Plato's real views and how do we determine this? That Plato is the Athenian Stranger or that the *Seventh Letter* was written by Plato and would be an appropriate context for discussing transmigration are all debatable assumptions, to say the least.

When it comes to the last book of the *Republic*, Ficino therefore offers the following allegorical interpretation: "In the last book of the *Republic* the soul of Thersites crosses over, not into the body of an ape, but into an ape. In such instances one understands Plato to mean a change of habit and life rather than of species or body [*habitus vitaeque potius quam specie vel corporis permutatio*]" (XVII. 4. 7; p. 55). One sees Ficino here make an interpretative move similar to that made by Proclus, since both insist that the transmigration is described as being into the animal as a whole and not into the body of the animal. Yet the conclusions reached are diametrically opposed: whereas Proclus concluded that the human soul is only joined from the outside to the composite of soul and body that is the animal, Ficino concludes that no real transmigration takes place, the animal as a whole standing simply for a change of habit or way of life. To say that Thersites changed into an ape is only to say that he began behaving like an ape. Yet one must wonder if Ficino is entitled to speak even of a *change* here: the text suggests, as we have seen, that if Thersites changes into an ape it is because he *already had* a character and way of life like that of an ape. On Ficino's reading, therefore, transmigration appears to become no more than a symbolic representation of the character one already has. Ficino therefore appeals to the analogies of the *Republic* (the image of a human body encasing a manifold of beasts, 588b–e) and the *Phaedrus* (Socrates's comparison of himself to Typhon [230a] and the image of the soul as a chariot pulled by two horses [246a–b]) to suggest precisely that the "beasts" are already within us: "But if the beasts are within us, then we cross over from man to beast and from beast to beast inside ourselves too, not outside" (XVII. 4.11; p. 61). There is at most, therefore, an inner transmigration constituted by a change in character. Ficino therefore concludes that either we take Plato not to have affirmed at all things like the transmigration of souls or we refrain from interpreting his words literally (*verum longe aliter quam verba designent, exponenda esse censibimus*) (XVII. 4. 14).

The appeal of Ficino's metaphorical interpretation is not hard to see: it renders possible the most unqualified anthropocentrism or, if one prefers, "humanism." Because the only "beasts" I have to worry about are within me, I do not have to worry about any threat from without that could render problematic my human nature. I can act like a beast without there being the slightest danger of my becoming a beast. Even the man who acts most like an ape is separated from actual apes through an abyssal and essential difference. The distinction here between man and beast is so absolute and so impermeable that the latter can be only a symbol or metaphor for the former. In this way Ficino has the same motive he attributes to Proclus, that is, that of not wanting to see celestial souls hurled down into the bodies of beasts, but he goes even further in this direction: while Proclus still allows the human soul to "hover over" beasts' souls, Ficino does not permit even this kind of external relation. Yes, Ficino allows "beasts" into the human soul, but these are not real "beasts," only symbols of human traits. The real beasts are kept very far away.

Some Modern Readings: From Allegory to Literalism

Modern readings of the Myth of Er tend to be closer to Ficino than to Proclus and Plotinus to the extent that they usually do not emphasize a literal interpretation of transmigration. However, it is often hard to see what exactly in this case they make of the talk of transmigration between humans and animals. Stephen Halliwell's reading of the Myth of Er favors treating it as "an allegory of the life of the soul in *this* world," but as he says little of the role of animals in the myth, it is unclear what becomes of them on this reading.[22] What he does say appears only to question the literal meaning and the moral point of the transmigration between humans and animals: "What, for example, are the future prospects of just souls that choose reincarnation as tame animals (620d)? Will the circumstances of their animal lives enhance or impede their possibilities of moral progress when the next cycle of existence comes around? If Er's own reactions to the mass spectacle of reincarnation are any guide, no overall inference can be drawn from the process; its mixed results encompass the pitiful, the ridiculous, and the amazing (620a), lending a tragicomic aura to the cosmic scene" (468–469). If we have an allegorical reading here, Halliwell appears to drop Ficino's moralizing and to leave the point of the story open. This characterization of the scene as "tragicomic" is something that I will explore below in the conclusion.

Pinotti appears to defend a metaphorical reading, as the very title of her article suggests: "Animals in Plato: Metaphor and Taxonomy." Pinotti does indeed speak of a "symbolic zoology" in Plato and explicitly characterizes this as an anthropocentric use of animals. Yet what sets her sharply at odds with Ficino is that she also finds in Plato, in contrast to this anthropocentric use, another use that "entails an alignment of the human with the animal, a deconstruction of the hierarchical relation given between the one and the other."[23] What this other use suggests, as Pinotti continues to explain, is that "between the human and the animal there exists no radical difference, but rather an ontological, and for this reason troubling, proximity."²⁴ Thus, for Pinotti, the symbolic use of animals, rather than ruling out any permeability of the boundary between human and animal, as it does for Ficino, exists in Plato side by side with a radical questioning of this boundary. After all, maybe the reason why I can be said to act like a beast is that I am not in fact so far from being a beast. A reading similar to that of Pinotti can be found in the book by Jean Frère, Le Bestiaire de Platon. While this "bestiary" documents a symbolic use of animals in Plato's dialogues, Frère does not reach the conclusion of a radical separation between human and animal in Plato. On the contrary, he concludes: "Thus the animal soul [*psychisme*] possesses a profound kinship with the human soul [*psychisme*]" (114). One can therefore say that modern interpreters, while sharing Ficino's starting point, arrive at the opposite position.

Another one of the few modern articles that address directly the status of animals in Plato, that by Luc Brisson, again suggests by its title a metaphorical reading: "The Animal Body as the Sign of the Value of a Soul in Plato."²⁵ Yet Brisson's thesis, it turns out, is not that animals are nothing more than symbols of the value of a human soul but rather that *all bodies,* animal and human, are signs of the value of the corresponding soul. The character of any soul, in other words, is reflected in the body it has. Brisson can thus write that "the entirety of human beings and animals that live in the air, on the earth and in the water constitute a vast system of signs."²⁶ But if humans are signs along with all other living things, they lose any kind of radical ontological distinction from and priority to animals. Animals cannot be mere metaphors for humans because humans are themselves mere metaphors. Furthermore, what both are metaphors or signs of is a certain quality of the soul. But note that if humans and animals are only signs of different qualities or values of the soul, the soul of the one does not differ in being or essence from the soul of the other. Even if the souls expressed in human bodies are *better* than the souls expressed in animal bodies, this very distinction of better and worse implies that we are talking about the same kind of soul in both cases. Indeed, Brisson's thesis of all forms of life as a system of signs leads in the end to the most literal reading possible of the Myth of Er, that is, a reading that completely undermines any essential difference between humans and animals. If animals in the myth can choose human lives, that is both because they literally have a rational part of the soul, and so are in some way intelligent beings, and because they have moral responsibility. All this entails, as Brisson specifies, that they cannot be killed without committing cannibalism.²⁷ To claim that the faculties of reason and choice are *better* developed in us than in animals and that our bodies are signs of this fact is still to assume that animals have these faculties. Ironically, therefore, Brisson's metaphorical reading leads exactly to what Ficino sought to avoid with his: taking literally the myth's description of animals choosing alongside humans lives both human and animal.

The Comedy of Human Animals

We have seen that three features of the account of animals in the Myth of Er required special hermeneutical violence from Proclus: the absence of any moral or even hierarchical distinction between human and animal lives; the choice of animal lives by *heroes;* the choice of human lives by animals. Yet the other interpretations we have considered ignore some or all of these features. Ironically, the worst in this regard is the moralizing metaphorical or allegorical reading. If we are dealing with allegory here, what is the moral point of having animals choose human lives or godlike heroes choose animal lives? And why, most seriously, does the myth so scrupulously avoid making the moral point supposedly behind the allegory? On the other hand, the most seriously literal reading, that is, that of Brisson, appears best able to take account of these features, though it appears to offer little toward the understanding of why heroes are shown choosing animal lives, given that he still wants to maintain a value distinction between human and animal souls. Most seriously, his interpretation comes at the cost of humanizing animals, that is, making them rational and morally responsible. This in the end only appears to be another form of anthropocentrism: instead of being turned into symbols for our own human traits, animals are now made to be in reality just like us.

Yet it is not the aim here to conclude with a decision regarding which interpretation is best. It is possible that the point of a myth as strange as the Myth of Er is to raise problems without giving us ready solutions. In this case, even Proclus's reading, however untenable it may in the end prove, is yet a proper response to the myth in confronting it as a problem. Indeed, the variety of different competing interpretations considered here may only show how well the myth has succeeded in presenting the relation between humans and animals as a problem. Perhaps the main failing of each interpretation is precisely that it in the end claims to find a solution where the myth offers none. Perhaps the myth blurs and complicates the distinction between human and animal precisely to short-circuit, as it were, any possible doctrine about this relation. A myth, after all, is not a doctrine but a story that provides meaning without answers. What I wish to suggest in closing is that the meaning of the scene in which heroes choose animal lives and swans choose human lives is to be found in precisely that aspect of the scene that the text explicitly draws attention to but that the interpretations considered here mostly ignore: its *tragicomic* character. It is a scene strange and amazing, but also pitiful and comic.

That the boundary between humans and animals should be blurred by having humans act like animals and animals act like humans, that, in other words, this boundary should be transcended in an emphasis on character, is hardly something peculiar to Plato's dialogues in ancient Greece: it is also a well-known feature of Old Comedy. The animals in the Myth of Er appear to be close cousins of Aristophanes's birds, frogs, and wasps. This is not the place for a detailed study of Aristophanes's use of animals, but a recent study by Kenneth S. Rothwell Jr. of animal choruses in Greek comedy reaches what is in the present context the important and revealing conclusion: "The animals of these [comic] choruses were presented as creatures that, like Dionysus, abolished the difference that separates men [sic] from animals, yet unlike Dionysus they do not shatter the social order in so doing; instead, they confirm it."[28] Two points are made here that find their parallels in Plato. First, comedy undermines any essential distinction between humans and animals as the Myth of Er in particular has been seen to do. Secondly, animals in comedy, rather than threatening the human world through their proximity (by threatening humans with a descent into bestiality, for example), peacefully share this world. Likewise, in the Myth of Er, human and animal lives lie side by side and humans and animals interchange lives without tension or conflict. This happy promiscuity is presumably one thing that makes the scene so comic.

Yet it is also a pitiful spectacle, and this suggests that we should find something tragic as well as comic in great heroes choosing the lives of animals. There is a suggestion here of the fragility of all those virtues that we take to make us distinctly human. If the separation between hero and beast is so fluid, how secure are all those qualities we admire in heroes? If abolishing the boundary between humans and animals can make animals *sociable* and thus part of our human world, it can also make us *unsociable* and thus render this world fragile. After all, the heroes who choose animal lives in the myth of Er are described as doing so *out of hatred of the human world*. Orpheus hates women for what they did to him (μίσει τοῦ γυναικείου γένος, 620a); Ajax rejects being a human being (φεύγουσαν ἄνθρωπον γενέσθαι, 620b) on account of the judgment made about his armor; Agamemnon hates the human race (ἔχθρᾳ τοῦ ἀνθρωπίνου γένους, 620b) on account of his own suffering. Here the choice to become an animal is the expression of a tragic failure in the human world. For this reason it is significant that the proximity of humans and animals is a feature of Greek tragedy as well as comedy. An article by Chiara Thumiger has shown how in ancient Greek tragedy animals are "presented in a proximity, rather than in opposition to man, instantiating human experiences and emotions; they signpost moments of crisis; in summary, they offer a paradigm and a counterpoint to the human story. The representation of the animate world that is the result has humans and beasts at the two extremes of the same continuum with much of human experience dangerously placed in the muddled area in between the two."[29] It is this dangerous placement in a muddled area between human and animal that we find expressed also in the Myth of Er. Thumiger indeed sees this representation of animals in poetic texts as "confirmed by the evidence offered by Platonic philosophy, where a dignified view of animals is found. Plato allows animals a degree of *logos* (as the doctrine of *metempsychosis*, the transmigration of the soul from one organism to the other, including human to animal, testifies). The opposition in Plato is between animals (human and non-human) and plants, or between contrasting elements in the soul, rather than between humans and other creatures."[30] Because both ancient Greek tragedy and comedy blurred or even undermined the separation between human and animal, Plato is able to use a tragicomic myth to suggest their proximity in a way that makes this proximity both encouraging and frightening.

Plato's own tragicomedy could therefore be intended to suggest that the boundary between human and animal is a fragile one, not only because animals are perhaps more rational than we normally assume, but because the rationality and even humanity of human beings is itself so fragile. At the conclusion of a dialogue that has created the model of both a city and a soul ruled entirely by reason, we need comedy to remind us of both our comic foolishness and our tragic limits. We mostly choose not according to reason, but according to habit, and the habits we have are not so different from those that characterize animals. In the cycle of generation, human becomes animal and animal becomes human indiscriminately. Is this not what is both celebrated and lamented by the god of both comedy and tragedy, Dionysus? This indiscriminateness is especially ironic at the end of a dialogue on justice, given that what was at least sometimes seen as distinguishing humans from animals was precisely the sense of justice. Consider, for example, the following passage from Hesiod: "Perses hear me out on justice, and take what I have to say to heart; cease thinking of violence. For the son of Cronos, Zeus, has ordained this law to men: that fishes and wild beasts and winged birds should devour one another, since there is no justice in them: but to mankind he gave justice which proves for the best" (*Works and Days* 274–280).[31] Socrates exhorts us to justice, but our kinship with animals might be meant to suggest that this justice is a difficult task, rather than an inalienable property of the human species. Indeed, the passage in Hesiod is itself ironic, since his exhortation to Perses to cease thinking of violence suggests that the justice that distinguishes us from animals is a fragile one that can be lost. In this respect Plotinus was right to emphasize the homogeneity of life and characterize being-human or rationality as a task rather than a species-defining property.[32] What he missed was the tragic point that this rationality is so fragile that even heroes can come to hate being human. As for the brilliant and utterly humorless Proclus, as well as the equally humorless and moralizing Ficino, we must imagine Plato responding to both with a good fit of laughter.

Notes

1. Francisco J. Gonzalez, "Combating Oblivion: The Myth of Er as Both Philosophy's Challenge and Inspiration," in *Plato and Myth: Studies on the Use and Status of Platonic Myths*,

ed. Catherine Collobert, Pierre Destrée, and Francisco J. Gonzalez (Leiden, Netherlands: Brill, 2012), 260–278.

2. One can also say that the *kind* of animal is more important. As Jean Frère claims, "La métempsychose selon Platon est métamorphose sélective. Certaines espèces animales n'entrent point dans le cycle des réincarnations" (*Le Bestiaire de Platon* [Paris: Éditions Kimé, 1998], 112).

3. As Patrizia Pinotti rightly observes, though without explicit reference to the Myth of Er, "Non di uomini e di animali si tratta, per Platone, ma di anime, di corpi e dei destini loro riservati lungo la scala dell'essere ed entro il ciclo delle metensomatosi" ("Gli animali in Platone: metafore e tassonomie," in S. Castignone and G. Lanata, *Filosofi e animali nel mundo antico* [Pisa: ETS, 1994], 104).

4. Plato, *Phaedrus*, trans. Alexander Nehamas and Paul Woodruff (Indianapolis: Hackett Publishing, 1995).

5. As Catherine Osborne observes, "There is, then, for Timaeus, no fundamental difference between men and women, or between men and animals. Women and animals are simply those of us who fail to live up to our full potential; we are nature's under-achievers, though the reason seems to be that we find ourselves in bodies that make it extremely hard to achieve better" (*Dumb Beasts and Dead Philosophers: Humanity and the Humane in Ancient Philosophy and Literature* [Oxford: Oxford University Press, 2007], 56). Francis Wolf therefore argues that "ni par le haut ni par le bas, le règne de l'animal n'est clairement délimité. Il n'y a pas d'animal dans le *Timée*" ("L'Animal et le Dieu: Deux Modèles pour l'Homme," in *L'Animal dans l'Antiquité*, ed. B. Cassin and J.-L. Labarrière [Paris: J. Vrin, 1997], 160). Wolf also notes that there is no Greek word for "animal," as the semantic range of *zōion* includes humans, demons, and gods as well what we would call "animals" (157–158). But Wolf finds this to be in tension with other texts in both Plato and Aristotle that "invent" the animal to define the human in opposition.

6. Plato, *Phaedo*, in *Plato: Complete Works*, ed. John M. Cooper, trans. Donald J. Zeyl (Indianapolis: Hackett Publishing, 1997).

7. In none of these texts is incarnation in animal form a *punishment*. Indeed, as Erland Ehnmark in particular has emphasized, in the Myth of Er rebirth in any form is not understood as a punishment and is not claimed to be avoidable by the best souls ("Transmigration in Plato," *Harvard Theological Review* 50, no. 1 [1957]: 15–16). One can make a bad choice and suffer the consequences, but this is not presented as punishment for some prior misdeed; even the man who rashly chooses the life of a tyrant who will eat his children *came from heaven*.

8. Strangely, Jérôme Laurent, while discussing all the other texts cited here, says nothing about the Myth of Er texts ("L'Animalité de L'Homme Selon Platon," *Archai* 11 [2013]: 79–90). This would have allowed him to pursue further the affinity between human and animal in Plato that he otherwise draws attention to. This is also the case with Pinotti ("Gli animali in Platone"), who makes only passing reference to the Myth of Er.

9. References will be to the page and line numbers in Proclus Diadochus, *In Platonis Rem Publicam Commentarii*, ed. W. Kroll, vol. 2 (Leipzig: Teubner, 1901; reprinted Amsterdam: Verlag Adolf M. Hakkert, 1965). All translations are my own, though I have occasionally consulted for help with difficult passages the French translation published as *Commentaire sur la République*, trans. with notes A. J. Festugière, vol. 3 (Paris: J. Vrin, 1970).

10. See Audrey N. M. Rich, "Reincarnation in Plotinus," *Mnemosyne* 10 (1957): 232–238. Rich takes up two questions: Did Plotinus believe in reincarnation? Rich argues, against other scholars, that he did. Did Plotinus believe that human souls can transmigrate into animal bodies? On the side of a negative answer, according to Rich, is that Porphyry and Iamblichus themselves rejected this doctrine and that Proclus in his commentary refers to Plotinus as someone who interpreted the doctrine in a purely moral sense (236). This last point seems simply wrong:

in the passage in question (310. 9) Proclus refers to Plotinus as supporting his own view that what draws human souls to animals is a similar *pathos*. Nowhere does Proclus suggest that Plotinus took the doctrine of transmigration any less literally than he himself did. What Proclus does do is ignore the significant difference we will find below between Plotinus's account of transmigration and his own. In any case, Rich, while acknowledging that some passages in the *Enneads* may be interpreted metaphorically, takes as decisive VI. 7. 6, discussed below, since there Plotinus attempts to explain *how* a human soul can transmigrate into an animal: "this happens when the lower self deliberately chooses an animal nature, whereupon the λόγος or seminal reason of the animal body is bestowed upon it by the higher soul" (237). The same, Rich claims, applies to IV. 7. 14, where Plotinus asserts that even souls descended into animal bodies are immortal. Furthermore, Rich takes Plotinus at VI. 4. 6 to be explicitly accepting the theory of transmigration as his own since he there refers to the teaching of the soul's descent into animal form as one he has inherited from the ancient philosophers who best inquired into the soul and one with which he must bring his own doctrine into agreement. Jérôme Laurent goes so far as to write: "Une chose est sûre: alors que pour Platon, la métempsychose apparaît comme une thèse marginale, voir comme nous l'avons dit, simplement parénétique, chez Plotin cette doctrine correspond au coeur même de sa psychologie" (*L'Homme et le monde selon Plotin* [Lyon, France: ENS Éditions, 1999], 126).

11. There is a passage elsewhere in Plotinus that might appear in tension with this idea. At Ennead I. 1. 11 Plotinus addresses the idea that there exist in savage animals human souls that have sinned: if so, he writes, "that which is separated in the soul does not belong to the animals, but while being present is not truly present to them, but their self-perception grasps only the image of the soul together with the body [οὐ τῶν θηρίων γίνεται τοῦτο, ὅσον χωριστόν, ἀλλὰ παρὸν οὐ πάρεστιν αὐτοῖς, ἀλλ' ἡ συναίσθησις τὸ τῆς ψυχῆς εἴδωλον μετὰ τοῦ σώματος ἔχει]" (10–12). This is an obscure and difficult passage, to say the least, but as Jean-François Pradeau has interpreted it (*Plotin, Traités 51–54* [Paris: Flammarion, 2010], 230), the part that remains separate is the intelligible part that does not descend. Animals are incapable of perceiving this part, perceiving only the sensible soul that is its image. As becomes clearer below, this distinction between a sensible part of the soul and an intelligible part that remains undescended does not contradict the central idea of the homogeneity of the soul throughout all forms of life. See note 13 below.

12. "un composé..., non d'une âme et d'un corps, mais d'une âme et d'une raison formelle qui fait que l'homme est l'homme et qui s'ajoute à l'âme pour en faire une âme humaine: ce *logos*, c'est l'âme qui le choisit, elle se détermine à être et à agir selon ce type d'être" (Pierre Hadot, *Plotin, Traité 38* [Paris: L'Éditions du Cerf, 1988], 219; my translation).

13. Giannis Stamatellos makes much of this distinction ("Plotinus on Transmigration: A Reconsideration," *Journal of Ancient Philosophy* 7, no. 1 [2013]: 49–64). He attributes to Plotinus a dual-aspect monism according to which the soul, while a unified whole, has a higher intelligible part and a lower sensible part (55). He then insists that transmigration involves for Plotinus only the lower perceptible part of the soul (58). This is how he reads the passage at I. 1. 11 cited in note 11 above: "It is only the lower part of the soul—an image of soul—that transmigrates" (61). He cites the example from I. 1. 12 where a part of Heracles is said to remain below (Hades) even as a part of him ascends to the intelligible world. "The higher part of the soul, the intelligible part on which the σπουδαῖος constantly attends and contemplates, remains undescended and uninvolved in transmigration" (61). But even if we grant that the higher intelligible part of the soul does not descend into the animal body (how could it, given that it is intelligible?) and therefore in this sense does not strictly speaking itself transmigrate, it is surely wrong to characterize it as "uninvolved in transmigration." It is this intelligible part of the soul that produces from within itself the *logos* of the animal whose body the lower part

of the soul will enter. The crucial qualification and correction to Stamatellos's argument was therefore already made by Laurent (*L'Homme et le monde selon Plotin*): "Mais c'est bien cette âme supérieure qui délègue sa partie inférieure tantôt dans tel corps, tantôt dans tel autre; c'est elle qui a différents 'reflets'. Cette possibilité d'incarnations multiples suppose que l'âme supérieure soit grosse de différentes raisons formelles qui vont présider à tour de rôle aux différentes incarnations" (131).

14. "Mais c'est justement que l'âme raisonnable possède en elle tous les *logoi* des animaux (6, 23 et 35) et c'est elle qui fournit à l'âme inférieure la raison (*logos*) de l'animal, parce qu'elle la possède en elle. Autrement dit, l'âme possède en elle tous les types possibles de forme de vie animale. Il n'est donc pas pour elle contre nature de prendre un corps de bête (7, 4)" (Hadot, *Plotin, Traité 38*, 227). In a note to the text, Hadot writes: "La métempsychose consiste dans le fait que l'âme raisonnable suit l'âme inférieure dans son incarnation bestiale" (103n88).

15. Hadot, *Plotin, Traité 38*, 229.

16. "l'âme d'un humain n'est pas seulement ou simplement humaine" (Jean Derrida, *La Naissance du corps (Plotin, Proclus, Damascius)* [Paris: Galilée, 2010], 71; my translation).

17. "l'humain est un acte ou un projet avant d'être un genre ou une espèce, et comme *vie rationelle*, il est peut-être condamné à rester un problème, un paradoxe et même un oxymore. Il ne nous est donc pas donné comme quelque chose de tout fait, et ce n'est pas comme cela que nous devons le chercher" (ibid., 73).

18. This difference in activity is what is expressed in another passage that alludes to transmigration: "When [the soul comes to be] in what is irrational, the power of sensation being dominant has led it there. When [it comes to be] in a human, all its movement either is in the rational part or comes from the intellect, as it possess its own proper intellect and an innate wish to think or to be moved as a whole [ὅταν δ'ἐν ἀλόγῳ (ψυχὴ γίνηται), ἡ τοῦ αἰσθάνεσθαι δύναμις κρατήσασα ἤγαγεν. ὅταν δὲ εἰς ἄνθρωπον, ἢ ὅλως ἐν λογικῷ ἡ κίνησις, ἢ ἀπὸ νοῦ ὡς νοῦν οἰκεῖον ἐχούσης καὶ παρ' αὐτῆς βούλησιν τοῦ νοεῖν ἢ ὅλως κινεῖσθαι]" (V. 2. 2, 7–10). See also III. 4. 2, 16–17 and IV. 3. 12, 32–39.

19. "Plotinus' treatment of transmigration diminishes the ontological differences between psychic classes and hierarchies. Whereas for Plotinus transmigration is based on the non-hierarchical unity and homogeneity of the soul, later Neoplatonists refuted transmigration through greater emphasis on a hierarchical ontology, in which the existence of the human soul possesses a higher rank than that of other animals. Since, for Plotinus, the soul is a homogenous and single intelligible source of life, all transmigrations into various life forms are possible, and so all ensouled bodies are rational and immortal" (Stamatellos, "Plotinus on Transmigration," 57–58). Francesco Fronterotta likewise observes: "L'homogénéité entre les âmes établit donc une certaine affinité rationnelle parmi toutes les réalités existantes, même si chaque âme comporte des différences spécifiques qui font la particularité de chaque être animé . . ." (*Plotin, Traités 38–41*, ed. Luc Brisson and Jean-François Pradeau [Paris: Flammarion, 2007], 124n55). Laurent expresses the same idea as follows: "Les âmes immortelles peuvent changer de niveau psychique: il y a une racine commune et en ce sens une nature commune pour l'ensemble des âmes" (*L'Homme et le monde selon Plotin*, 127).

20. On the homogeneity of all souls, see also *Ennead* IV. 3. 8–9

21. Marsilio Ficino, *Platonic Theology*, vol. 6: *Books XVII–XVIII*, Latin text ed. James Hankins with William Bowen, trans. Michael J. B. Allen (Cambridge, Mass.: I Tatti Renaissance Library, 2006), XVII.3.10, 41.

22. "The Life-and-Death Journey of the Soul: Interpreting the Myth of Er," in *The Cambridge Companion to Plato's* Republic, ed. G. R. F. Ferrari (New York: Cambridge University Press, 2007), 469. Goldschmidt held essentially the same view of the myth: "Le futur du mythe traduit notre condition présente; la vertu, cet 'unique nécessaire', ne s'acquiert ni ne se perd

dans un 'instant critique', mais au cours d'une longue série d'efforts ou d'abandons; le jeu décisif ne se joue pas dans l'au-delà, mais à chaque instant du présent" (*La Religion de Platon* [Paris: Presses Universitaires de France, 1949], 85). Goldschmidt insists that all of the supposedly unchangeable elements of our lives can be said to be "chosen": "Tous les éléments inchangeables de notre vie, ceux dont nous pouvons user d'une manière plutôt que d'une autre, mais qu'il nous est impossible de supprimer, sont 'choisis'" (89). But not surprisingly, the role of animals simply disappears on this reading.

23. "comporta un allineamento dell'umano all'animale, la disarticolazione del rapporto gerarchico dato tra l'uno e l'altro" ("Gli animali in Platone," 104; my translation).

24. "tra humano e animale non si dà differenza radicale, piuttosto un'ontologica, e per questo inquietante, prossimità" (ibid., 104; my translation).

25. Luc Brisson, "Le Corps Animal Comme Signe de la Valeur d'Une Âme chez Platon," in *L'Animal dans l'Antiquité*, ed. B. Cassin and J.-L. Labarrière (Paris: J. Vrin, 1997), 227–245.

26. "l'ensemble des êtres humains et des animaux qui vivent dans l'air, sur terre et dans l'eau constituent un vaste système de signes" (239; my translation).

27. Brisson, "Le Corps Animal Comme Signe de la Valeur d'Une Âme chez Platon," 242–243). See also Richard Sorabji: "Plato's extension to animals of a rational part of the soul is suggested by his repeated supposition that animals are reincarnated humans. Reversing Darwin, he made humans precede animals" (*Animal Minds and Human Morals* [Ithaca, N.Y.: Cornell University Press, 1993], 10).

28. Kenneth S. Rothwell Jr., *Nature, Culture, and the Origins of Greek Comedy: A Study of Animal Choruses* (Cambridge: Cambridge University Press, 2006), 185. See also H. S. Lonsdale, "Attitudes towards Animals in Ancient Greece," *Greece and Rome* 26 (1979): 146–159, 154.

29. Chiara Thumiger, "ἀνάγκης ζεύγματ'ἐμπεπτώκαμεν: Greek Tragedy between Human and Animal," *Leeds International Classical Studies* 7, no. 3 (2008): 9–10.

30. Ibid., 4.

31. Cited by Lonsdale, "Attitudes towards Animals in Ancient Greece," 156.

32. Laurent notes something similar when he writes: "Selon Platon, l'homme n'est pas une fois pour toutes et par essence un animal distinct des autres, mais c'est un animal qui choisit d'être différent des autres animaux et y arrive par la vertu et la pratique de la philosophie" ("L'Animalité de L'Homme Selon Platon," 80).

Contributors

CLAUDIA BARACCHI is professor of moral philosophy at the Università di Milano-Bicocca. Among her many publications are *Aristotle's Ethics as First Philosophy* (2011), *Of Myth, Life, and War in Plato's* Republic (IUP, 2002), and *L'architettura dell'umano. Aristotele e l'etica come filosofia prima* (2014).

JEREMY BELL is a postdoctoral research fellow at the Fox Center for Humanistic Inquiry at Emory University. He specializes in ancient philosophy, with a focus on the relationship between practices of care and systems of governance. He is preparing a book manuscript entitled *Plato's Politics of Care*, which examines the central role of care in Plato's philosophical, ethical, and political thought.

SARA BRILL is associate professor of philosophy and director of the Classical Studies Program at Fairfield University in Fairfield, Connecticut. She is the author of *Plato on the Limits of Human Life* (IUP, 2013) as well as articles on tragedy and the Hippocratic corpus.

S. MONTGOMERY EWEGEN received his PhD in philosophy from Boston College in 2011. He is assistant professor of philosophy and classics at Trinity College and is the author of *Plato's* Cratylus: *The Comedy of Language* (IUP, 2013).

FRANCISCO J. GONZALEZ is professor of philosophy at the University of Ottawa. His publications include *Dialectic and Dialogue: Plato's Practice of Philosophical Inquiry* (1998) and *Plato and Heidegger: A Question of Dialogue* (2009).

DREW A. HYLAND is Charles A. Dana Professor of Philosophy Emeritus at Trinity College, where he has been on the faculty since 1967. He is the author of some ten books, most recently *Plato and the Question of Beauty* (IUP, 2008).

DAVID FARRELL KRELL is emeritus professor of philosophy at DePaul University and Brauer Distinguished Visiting Professor of German Studies at Brown University. He writes fiction and philosophy, often confusing the two. He is the author of *Derrida and Our Animal Others: Derrida's Final Seminar, the Beast and the Sovereign* (IUP, 2013).

CHRISTOPHER P. LONG is associate dean for Graduate and Undergraduate Education and professor of philosophy and classics in the College of the Liberal

Arts at the Pennsylvania State University. He is the author of an enhanced digital book, *Socratic and Platonic Political Philosophy: Practicing a Politics of Reading* (2014), and two other monographs, *Aristotle on the Nature of Truth* (2011) and *The Ethics of Ontology: Rethinking an Aristotelian Legacy* (2004). He is the host of the Digital Dialogue podcast (thedigitaldialogue.com), blogs at www.cplong.org, and can be reached on Twitter @cplong.

MARINA MCCOY is associate professor of philosophy at Boston College. She is the author of *Plato on the Rhetoric of Philosophers and Sophists* (2008) and *Wounded Heroes: Vulnerability as a Virtue in Greek Tragedy and Philosophy* (2013). Her work focuses on the relationship between rhetoric and philosophy in ancient Greek thought and on the relationship between philosophy and literature.

HOLLY MOORE is assistant professor of philosophy at Luther College. Her research focuses on the interaction between the philosophy and the methodology of Plato's dialogues. She is currently working on a book project entitled *Plato's Mimetic Methodology*, which examines the way that the methods employed throughout the dialogues reflect and respond to Plato's intellectual inheritances.

MICHAEL NAAS is professor of philosophy at DePaul University. He works in the areas of ancient Greek philosophy and contemporary French philosophy. His most recent book is *The End of the World and Other Teachable Moments: Jacques Derrida's Final Seminar* (2014).

HEIDI NORTHWOOD is dean of liberal arts and professor of philosophy at Wilfrid Laurier University in Brantford, Ontario, Canada. Her publications include articles on Aristotle's embryology and Sophocles's *Ajax*. She is currently working on Plato's treatment of the arts (liberal and mechanical) in *Republic, Philebus,* and *Gorgias*.

H. PETER STEEVES is professor of philosophy and director of the Humanities Center at DePaul University, where he specializes in phenomenology, ethics, and philosophy of science. He is the author of several books, including: *Founding Community: A Phenomenological-Ethical Inquiry* (1998), *Animal Others: On Ethics, Ontology, and Animal Life* (1999), and *The Things Themselves: Phenomenology and the Return to the Everyday* (2006).

THOMAS THORP is professor of philosophy at Saint Xavier University in Chicago. He has published essays on Homer, Solon, and Plato, and is the author (with Brian Seitz) of *The Iroquois and the Athenians: A Political Ontology* (2013). Other bestial works include a recently published philosophical study of Yellowstone's wolves ("Eating Wolves"). He is the founding director of Greater Yellowstone College.

Plato's Animals Index

Aesop's Fables: Socrates recalls the myth (or fable) of the lion and the fox (*Alcibiades I* 122e–123a; see Aesop fable 147); Socrates says that during his time in prison he has been setting Aesop's myths to music (*Phaedo* 61b).

Animals (ζῷα) and painting (ἡ ζωγραφία): the beauty of animals or painting (*Philebus* 51c); speech organized as a living being (*Phaedrus* 264c, 265d–266b, 276a–b, 277e–278b); speech, writing, and painting (*Phaedrus* 275d–e); speech, writing, and husbandry (*Phaedrus* 276b–277a); portraying living beings by speech or by painting (*Statesman* 277c–d).

Animals as property: Spartans called wealthy because of their slaves (or helots), horses, flocks, and herds (*Alcibiades I* 122d); ox or sheep as property to be sold or sacrificed (*Euthydemus* 301e–302a); owning bees (*Laws* 843d–e); how to treat animals or lifeless objects that kill or "murder" (*Laws* 873e); owners are responsible for what their slaves or animals—mules, horses, or dogs—do to the property of others (*Laws* 936d–e); dogs, horses, quails, and cocks as examples of coveted possessions (*Lysis* 211d).

Animals and virtue: boars as courageous (*Euthydemus* 294d); animals as courageous—lion, leopard, boar, stag, bull, monkey (*Laches* 196e–197c); natural virtue of children and animals (*Laws* 710a); animals and children have a courage that comes naturally and without reason (*Laws* 963e); question raised by Solon's poem of whether humans can be friends with dogs or horses (*Lysis* 212e); in the myth told by Protagoras (*Protagoras* 320d–323a) every animal (save humans) is said to have been given a certain virtue or power (a *dynamis*)—swiftness or thick skin, etc.—as well as its own food and power of generation to help it survive; humans are compensated by fire (321d) and, later, "respect and right" (322c); on the specific virtue or *aretē* of a dog or horse (*Republic* 335b); on the horse and dog as high-spirited, courageous animals (*Republic* 375a); the spirited part of soul can be seen in both animals and children (*Republic* 441a–b); animal part of humans bound with laws (*Statesman* 309c–310a); all animals, according to Erixymachus, experience love (*Symposium* 186a, 188a); all animals, according to Diotima, love and procreate with a view to immortality (*Symposium* 207a–b).

Ant (ὁ μύρμηξ): those who practice civil virtues are reincarnated into some "social [πολιτικόν] and gentle [ἥμερον]" species, such as bees, ants, or wasps, or back into the human species (*Phaedo* 82b); the earth is large and humans living around the Mediterranean are like ants or frogs around a pond (*Phaedo* 109a–b).

Ape/Monkey (ὁ πίθηκος): Socrates mockingly proposes a hierarchy of beauty that runs from pots to mares, monkeys, and maidens to gods (*Hippias Major* 288e–289b); animals as courageous—lion, leopard, boar, stag, bull, monkey (*Laches* 196e–197c); in the transition from timocracy to plutocracy men become more like apes than lions (*Republic* 590b); in the myth of Er, Thersites, the ugliest of men, chooses the life of an ape (*Republic* 620c).

Bee (ἡ μέλιττα): there are mountains with food only for bees (*Critias* 111c); poets are like bees culling honey (*Ion* 534b); like a swarm (ὁ ἐσμός) of bees that migrates (*Laws* 708b); legislating for beekeepers (*Laws* 842d); attracting bees by rattling pans (*Laws* 843d–e); on the essence or being of bees (*Meno* 72a–c); those who practice civil virtues reincarnated as bees, ants, or wasps (*Phaedo* 82b); Socrates compared to a stinging bee (*Phaedo* 91c); quote from Homer (*Republic* 363b); philosopher as leader or king bees or leaders of the hive (τὸ σμῆνος) (*Republic* 520c); ὁ κηφήν: on the drones—some stinging (malefactors) and some stingless (beggars)—that help turn the oligarchy into a democracy (*Republic* 552c–d, 554b–c, 554d, 555e) and a democracy into a tyranny (563e–564b, 572e–573b); ὁ μελιττουργός: the prudent beekeeper knows how to cut out diseased cells (*Republic* 564c); colonies are like bees that create new hives elsewhere (*Statesman* 293d); there is no naturally born statesman who would be like the ruler of a swarm of bees (τὸ σμῆνος) (*Statesman* 301d–e).

Bird (ὁ/ἡ ὄρνις): on the correct names of birds (*Cratylus* 392a–b); interlocutors compared to children trying to catch birds (*Euthydemus* 291b); the family is like a flock of birds, patriarchal government resembles rulership in a covey of birds (*Laws* 680d–e); in Athens game birds are trained by being carried around by their owners (*Laws* 789b); mother birds protect their young (*Laws* 813e–814c); birds as sacrificial animals (*Laws* 956a); on the superiority of prophetic madness to augury or the reading of bird signs (οἰωνιστική) (*Phaedrus* 244c–d)—from ὁ οἰωνός, bird of prey; philosopher is a like a bird gazing upward, neglecting the things below (*Phaedrus* 249d); the Ibis in the myth of writing (*Phaedrus* 274c); augurs trust in birds (*Philebus* 67b); one must not imitate the "cries of dogs, sheep, and birds" (*Republic* 397a); selective breeding is beneficial to humans as it is to dogs, cocks, horses, and birds (*Republic* 459a–b); Plato compares himself to a bird in a cage (*Seventh Letter* 348a); Socrates is compared, by means of a quote from Aristophanes's *Clouds* 362, to a kind of water fowl (ὁ βρένθος) (*Symposium* 221b); types of knowledge are like species of birds (*Theaetetus* 197b–d).

Boar (ὁ κάπρος): interlocutors (ironically) likened to valiant boars (*Euthydemus* 294d); "then your father is a boar and a dog" (*Euthydemus* 298d); animals as courageous—lion, leopard, boar, stag, bull, monkey (*Laches* 196e–197c).

Bull (ὁ ταῦρος): sacrifice of bulls (*Critias* 119d–120a); animals as courageous—lion, leopard, boar, stag, bull, monkey (*Laches* 196e–197c); Socrates's wide open, "bull-like" eyes (*Phaedo* 117b); on not imitating the sounds of bulls (*Republic* 396b).

Cosmos as animal (as ζῷον): the cosmos or universe as a "living being" (*Statesman* 269d) or "living creature" (*Timaeus* 30b).

Cow/Ox (ὁ/ἡ βοῦς): oxen as sacrificial animals (*Alcibiades II* 149c); on cows and their natural offspring (*Cratylus* 393b–c); eristic argument involving an ox (*Euthydemus* 301a); ox or sheep as property to be sold or sacrificed (*Euthydemus* 301e–302a); on Heracles driving off the oxen of Geryones (*Gorgias* 484b); the bad statesman is compared to a herdsman who inherits tame animals, such as oxen, horses, and donkeys, and makes them wild (*Gorgias* 516a); on a fisherman's device made from an ox's horn (*Ion* 538d); on whether the cowherd or the rhapsode knows best how to pacify cows (*Ion* 540c); cows do not rule over cows but are ruled by humans (*Laws* 713d); beast of burden (τὰ ὑποζύγια) used for work (*Laws* 761a); on the sacrifice of oxen (*Laws* 782c); on the unity of things such as an ox (*Philebus* 15a); oxen found in pairs (*Philebus* 56d–e); pleasure comes in fifth, even if cattle and horses would rank it first (*Philebus* 67b); things profitable to humans are not always profitable to cattle, horses, and dogs (*Protagoras* 334a); Thrasymachus mocks Socrates for believing that neatherds consider only the good of their cattle (*Republic* 343b); cattle and oxen needed for plowing and building (*Republic* 370e); guardians who have served are given free reign of the pasture (perhaps like oxen) to philosophize (*Republic* 498a); on not confusing an ox with a horse (*Theaetetus* 190c).

Crane (ὁ γέρανος): cited as another example of an animal (besides humans) that, if it could think, would oppose itself to all other animals (*Statesman* 263d).

Dog-faced baboon (ὁ κυνοκέφαλος): Protagoras argues that humans, not the swine or the dog-faced baboon, are the measure of all things (*Theaetetus* 161c, 166c).

Dog (ὁ/ἡ κύων): conclusion of an eristic argument: "then your father is a boar and a dog" (*Euthydemus* 298d–e); expression "by the dog" (*Gorgias* 461a, 466c, 482b, *Hippias Major* 287e, *Phaedo* 98e, *Phaedrus* 228b, *Republic* 399e); better to ride a horse poorly or perform actions with a dog poorly voluntarily than involuntarily (*Hippias Minor* 375a); those who pursue a subject in dialogue are compared to hounds on the trail (*Laws* 654e); were evil men able to bribe the gods, it would like wolves giving bits of their prey to watchdogs in order to devour the flock (*Laws* 906d–e); owners are responsible for what their slaves or animals—mules, horses, or dogs—do to the property of others (*Laws* 936d–e); philosophers like dogs howling at the moon (*Laws* 967d); roosters, quails, horses, and dogs as example of possessions (*Lysis* 211e); question raised by Solon's poem of whether humans can be friends with dogs or horses (*Lysis* 212e); Socrates in argument is like a Laconian hound (*Parmenides* 128c; see *Laws* 654e); a dog is an example of a creature of varying sizes between the extremes of the big and the small (*Phaedo* 89e–90a); things profitable to humans are not always profitable to cattle, horses, and dogs (*Protagoras* 334a); on the specific virtue or *aretē* of a dog or horse (*Republic* 335b); on the horse and dog as high-spirited, courageous animals (*Republic* 375a); in well-raised guard dogs opposite qualities—such as tameness and spiritedness—can exist together (*Republic* 375e); the dog can distinguish friend from enemy (*Republic* 376a); Achilles in the *Iliad* insults Agamemnon by saying he has the "eyes of a dog" (cited at *Republic* 390a); one must not imitate the "cries of dogs, sheep, and birds" (*Republic* 397a); guardians are like sleepless hounds (*Republic* 404a); the guardians must be raised like dogs that will protect the flock, lest they become wolves that will attack it (*Republic* 416a); a well-prepared army is like a pack of hard and wiry hounds (*Republic* 422d); spirit is called back by reason much like a dog is called back by a shepherd (*Republic* 440d); selective breeding is as beneficial to humans as it is to dogs, cocks, horses, and birds (459a–b); guardians keep guard and hunt together like hounds (*Republic* 466c–d); those who strip the dead in battle are like dogs barking at stones that have hit them (*Republic* 469e); young men who taste dialectic are like ill-trained puppies who take pleasure in biting others indiscriminately (*Republic* 539b); in a democracy even dogs, horses, and donkeys do what they want (*Republic* 563c); old expression regarding "dogs barking at their masters" as a sign of the quarrel between poetry and philosophy (*Republic* 607b); a wolf (the wildest of all creatures) resembles a dog (the tamest), that is, the sophist resembles the philosopher (*Sophist* 231a); dogs are not to be considered gregarious or herd animals (*Statesman* 266a); colors perhaps appear differently to dogs than to men (*Theaetetus* 154a); ὁ/ἡ σκύλαξ: guardians must be like "well-bred hounds" (*Republic* 375a); male and female dogs will guard together (*Republic* 451d); children are given a taste for war like young dogs are given a taste for blood (*Republic* 537a).

Dolphin (ὁ δελφίς): in Atlantis (*Critias* 116e); as rescuers (*Republic* 453d–e).

Domesticated vs. wild animals: the bad statesman is compared to a herdsman who inherits tame animals, such as oxen, horses, and asses, and makes them wild (*Gorgias* 516a); after the flood only a few goats and oxen remained for herdsmen (*Laws* 677a–e); men had plenty of flocks and herds for meat and milk, and they also hunted (*Laws* 679a); herdsman and farmers protect their animals and crops from wild beasts (*Laws* 680e–681a); sheep do not rule over sheep, or goats over goats, or cows over cows, but are ruled by humans (*Laws* 713d); vegetarian cultures (*Laws* 782c); regulating the sale of livestock (*Laws* 849b–d); question raised by Solon's poem of whether humans can be friends with dogs or horses (*Lysis* 212e); the generation of animals, both wild and tame (*Menexenus* 237d); ability of animals to nourish their offspring (*Menexenus* 237d–238a); relation between shepherd and sheep is not one of mutual benefit, says Thrasymachus (*Republic* 343a–344c); shepherds in the ideal city (*Republic* 370d–e; see 399d for shepherds using piccolos); hunters in the city (*Republic* 373b); swineherds (*Republic* 373c); meat-eating (*Republic* 373c, 404c–d); selective breeding is beneficial to humans as it is to dogs, horses, and birds (*Republic* 459a–b); a wolf (the wildest of all creatures) resembles a dog (the tamest), that is, the sophist resembles a philosopher (*Sophist* 231a); animals that are tame and can even speak with humans in the Age of Cronos become fierce and antagonistic to humans in the Age of Zeus (*Statesman* 272b–c, 274b–c).

Donkey/Ass (ὁ ὄνος): it is absurd to believe that there can be offspring of horses and donkeys—namely, mules—and yet no horses or donkeys (*Apology* 27e); the bad statesman is compared to a herdsman who inherits tame animals, such as donkeys, horses, and oxen, and makes them wild (*Gorgias* 516a); by being careless in argument one may "get a toss off the donkey" (*Laws* 701d); gluttons can be reincarnated as donkeys or asses (*Phaedo* 81e); a rhetorician can convince a crowd that a donkey is a horse (*Phaedrus* 260c); in a democracy even dogs, horses, and donkeys do what they want (*Republic* 563c); horses and donkeys can cross-breed (*Statesman* 265d); Alcibiades mocks Socrates for speaking always of "pack-asses" (*Symposium* 221e) and the like; those who fail in argument are like those in the children's game who must "sit down and play donkey" (*Theaetetus* 146a).

Eagle (ὁ ἀετός): quote from Homer's *Iliad* (*Ion* 539b); Agamemnon in the afterlife chooses the life of an eagle (*Republic* 620b).

Fish (ὁ ἰχθύς): fishermen are the best judges of words about fishing (*Ion* 538d); humans are like fish in the sea, our world is to the upper world what the sea is to our world (*Phaedo* 109c–111a); quote from the *Iliad* (*Republic* 363c); Socrates comments that in the *Iliad* the Greeks feasted on not fish but roasted meat (*Republic* 404b); fishing by trident as opposed to with hooks (*Sophist* 220e–221a); on the generation of the "tribe of fishes" (*Timaeus* 92b).

Fox (ἡ ἀλώπηξ): Aesop fable about a lion and a clever fox (*Alcibiades I* 123a); Archilochus as fox, "shifty and bent on gain" (*Republic* 365c).

Frog (ὁ βάτραχος): humans like ants or frogs around a pond (*Phaedo* 109a–b); perhaps Protagoras was in intellect no better than a tadpole (*Theaetetus* 161c–d).

Gadfly (ὁ μύωψ): Socrates as gadfly (*Apology* 30e); ὁ οἶστρος: the tyrant is driven by the gadfly of desire (*Republic* 577e).

Goat (ὁ/ἡ αἴξ): on the tragic goat and Pan as goatlike in his lower parts (*Cratylus* 408c–d); goats do not rule over goats but are ruled by humans (*Laws* 713d); goat-stag as an example of a mixed animal often represented by painting (*Republic* 488a).

Hawk (ὁ ἱέραξ): tyrants, robbers, and other kinds of unjust men pass in their next lives into the bodies of predators such as hawks, wolves, and kites (*Phaedo* 82a).

Hierarchy of creatures: from the inanimate pot to the animal (mare, monkey) to the human and the gods (*Hippias Major* 287e–289d); sexual pleasures found in all animals (*Laws* 636b–d); humans rule over oxen and goats, not oxen over oxen or goats over goats (*Laws* 713d); ivory comes from a lifeless body (*Laws* 956a); humans and animals have pleasure and pain (*Philebus* 32a); the life of pleasure comes in fifth, even if cattle and horses would rank it first (*Philebus* 67b); animals on the divided line (*Republic* 510a); animal puppets and references in the myth of the cave (*Republic* 514b, 532b–c); colors appear differently to men than to dogs (*Theaetetus* 154a); both animals and human have perceptions, but only the latter have reflection (*Theaetetus* 186c).

Horse/Mare (ὁ/ἡ ἵππος): horsemanship (ἡ ἱππική) as an example of an art (*Alcibiades I* 124e, *Euthyphro* 13a–b, *Hippias Major* 284a); Socrates argues that believing in the affairs of horses implies believing in horses, just as believing in the affairs of daimons implies believing in daimons (*Apology* 27b); Socrates compares himself to the victor of a horserace (*Apology* 36d); on horses, lions, and their natural offspring (*Cratylus* 393b–c); reference to horses in *Iliad* (*Cratylus* 407d); a statue of winged horses in honor of Poseidon (*Critias* 116d); horse races in Atlantis (*Critias* 117c); horses used in war (*Critias* 119a–b); Polus is said to be worthy of his name, "colt [πῶλος]" (*Gorgias* 463d); the bad statesman is compared to a herdsman who inherits tame animals, such as donkeys, horses, and oxen, and makes them wild (*Gorgias* 516a); Socrates mockingly proposes a hierarchy of beauty that runs from pots to mares and monkeys, and from maidens to gods (*Hippias Major* 288c–289d); horse—along with cock and quail—as an example of a beautiful animal (*Hippias Major* 295c–d); better to ride a horse poorly voluntarily than involuntarily (*Hippias Minor* 375a); charioteering (*Ion* 537a–e, *Lysis* 208a); Clinias says that Thessaly is flat and conducive to riding on horseback, while Crete is rugged and so more suited to running (*Laws* 625d); an army is like a herd of colts at grass (*Laws* 666e); discourse must sometimes be reined in like a horse (*Laws* 701c; see 693d); a team of horses as an image of obedience (*Laws* 708d); implied analogy between the state and a horse (*Laws* 753e); both boys and girls must learn to ride horses (*Laws* 794c); teachers for horse racing (*Laws* 804c); why there are few horses and little chariot racing in Crete (*Laws* 834b–d); owners are responsible for what their slaves or animals—mules, horses, or dogs—do to the property of others (*Laws* 936d–e); roosters, quails, horses, and dogs as example of possessions (*Lysis* 211e); question raised by Solon's poem of whether humans can be friends with dogs or horses (*Lysis* 212e); horse races honoring the dead (*Menexenus* 249b, see also *Laws* 947b–e); Meno and Thessalians known for their horsemanship (*Meno* 70a–b); on the horsemanship of Themistocles's son (*Meno* 93c–d); Pericles trained his sons in horsemanship (*Meno* 94b); Antiphon devotes his time to horse-training (*Parmenides* 126c–127a); Parmenides compares himself to the old race horse in Ibykus's poem, compelled to run around the course of dialectic (or love) one more time (*Parmenides* 137a); one can be reminded of a person by seeing the image of a horse associated with that person (*Phaedo* 73e); horse as an example of a composite thing (*Phaedo* 78e); a rhetorician can convince a crowd that a donkey is a horse (*Phaedrus* 260c); the soul is compared to charioteer and two horses—one good, one bad (*Phaedrus* 246a–250c, 253c–257b); pleasure comes in fifth, even if cattle and horses would rank it first (*Philebus* 67b); things profitable to humans are not always profitable to cattle, horses, and dogs (*Protagoras* 334a); on the torch race being run on horseback (*Republic* 328a); a horse trainer is the person best suited to buy a horse (*Republic* 333c); on the specific virtue or *aretē* of a dog or horse (*Republic* 335b; see 352e); on the hollow, bronze horse in the myth of Gyges (*Republic* 359d–3); the horse and dog as high-spirited, courageous animals (*Republic* 375a); on not imitating the sounds of bulls or horses (*Republic* 396b); both men and women guardians should learn to ride horses (*Republic* 452c); selective breeding is beneficial to humans as it is to dogs, cocks, horses, and birds (*Republic* 459a–b); children should be brought to view battles and put on horses in order to flee dangers (*Republic* 467d, 537a); in a democracy even dogs, horses, and donkey do what they want (*Republic* 563c); the horseman knows best the quality of reins and bridles (*Republic* 601c); "horse" as mere nouns that of themselves do not make discourse (*Sophist* 262b–c); Alcibiades recounts being on horseback during the battle of Delium, while Socrates fought on foot (*Symposium* 221a); compare to the body as a Trojan horse through which we perceive (*Theaetetus* 184d); on the possibility of confusing an ox with a horse (*Theaetetus* 190c; see 195d).

Human (as) animal: *anthrōpos* as the only animal able to "look up" (*Cratylus* 399c); humans as the only animal able to perceive order—and so the only one able to sing and dance (*Laws* 653e, 664e); other animals have only frenzied movement and cries (*Laws* 672c); without education humans are the "wildest [ἀγριώτατον] of all earth's creatures," but when trained right they become "tame [ἥμερον]" animals (*Laws* 766a); slaves often treated like animals with goads and whips (*Laws* 776d–777a); human life much more than the life of beasts (*Laws* 806e–807d); children go to teachers like sheep to the shepherd or the slave to master (*Laws* 808d); the child is an intractable animal that must be bridled (*Laws* 808e); humans sate themselves like beasts (θηρίῳ) (*Laws* 831b–e); the ability to make laws and live by them is what distinguishes humans from the most savage of beasts (*Laws* 874e); humans can be like "ravening beasts [θηριώδεις]" (*Laws* 906b–c); anarchy must be removed from the lives of both men and beasts (*Laws* 942c); "fierce loves [ἀγρίων ἐρώτων]" (*Phaedo* 81a–b); myth of the soul as charioteer and horses (*Phaedrus* 246a–256d); man who "gives himself up to pleasure and like a beast [a four-footed animal: τετράποδος] proceeds to lust and begetting," not at all "revering [σέβεται]" what he is looking at (*Phaedrus* 250e); desire is "a raging and savage [ἄγριον] beast of a master" (*Republic* 329c); desire "drives [a part of the soul] like a beast [θηρίον] to drink" (*Republic* 439b); spirit is called back by reason much like a dog called back by a shepherd (*Republic* 440d); the spirited part of soul is seen in both children and animals (*Republic* 441a–b); gymnastics without music makes one "savage [ἄγριός]"(*Republic* 410d); the misologist ends acts "like a beast by violence [βίᾳ] and savagery" (*Republic* 411d–e); tyrant's unruly desires make him like a beast (*Republic* 571c); men with eyes bent down feast like cattle [βόσκονται] (*Republic* 585e); image of the soul (like Cerberus, the Scylla, and Chimera) as several forms (human, lion, many-headed beast) grown together in one (*Republic* 588b–e); person with lusts "like a beast [θηρίον]" (*Seventh Letter* 335b).

Hunting (ἡ θήρα): generals as man-hunters (*Euthydemus* 290b); dialogue as hunt (*Laches* 194a–b, *Lysis* 218c, *Republic* 432 b–c, *Sophist* 264a); definition and kinds of hunting (*Laws* 822d–824c); lover as hunter of his beloved (*Lysis* 206a–b); Socrates as bloodhound in argument (*Parmenides* 128c; see *Laws* 654e); Socrates as hunter of Alcibiades (*Protagoras* 309a); on the following of tracks (*Republic* 365d); hunters in the city (*Republic* 373b); gymnastics and hunting for the body (*Republic* 535d, *Laws* 763b); sophist as a hunter of youth (*Sophist* 221c–223b).

Imitating animals: on whether the imitation of an animal's cry (for example, a cock or a sheep) would constitute a name for that animal (*Cratylus* 423b–c); humans should imitate animals in eschewing homosexuality (*Laws* 636b–c, 836b–e); one must be familiar with animal bodies—and especially the human body—to represent them correctly (*Laws* 668d–e); caution with regard to combining the cries of beasts and men (*Laws* 669d); patriarchal government is like a covey of birds (*Laws* 680d); ruler is like a shepherd who must separate the ill-bred from the rest flock (*Laws* 735b–d); humans should imitate mother birds who protect their young (*Laws* 813e–814c); humans must follow nature in sanctioning only procreative sex (*Laws* 838c–840e); one should not imitate bulls or horses (*Republic* 396a–b), or the "cries of dogs, sheep, and birds" (*Republic* 397a); humans should follow female guard dogs and let women share in the tasks of the male (*Republic* 451d); all animals fight better in front of their offspring, and humans should imitate them (*Republic* 467b).

Kite (ὁ ἰκτῖνος): tyrants, robbers, and other kinds of unjust men pass in their next life into the bodies of predators such as kites, hawks, wolves, and kites (*Phaedo* 82a).

Leopard (ἡ πάρδαλις): animals as courageous—lion, leopard, boar, stag, bull, monkey (*Laches* 196e–197c).

Lion (ὁ λέων): Aesop fable about a lion and a clever fox (*Alcibiades I* 123a); fable of a fawn (Socrates) before a lion (Charmides) (*Charmides* 155d); horses, lions, and their natural offspring (*Cratylus* 393b–c); Callicles and the natural rule of young, strong as lions, over the weak (*Gorgias* 483e–484a); animals as courageous—lion, leopard, boar, stag, bull, monkey (*Laches* 196e–197c); when ships are positioned for easy escape, soldiers become like lions fleeing deer (*Laws* 707a); proverb about "bearding a lion" (*Republic* 341c); image of the soul as composite human, lion, and many-headed beast (*Republic* 588e–589a); the guardian, like the lion or snake, can become irascible (*Republic* 590a–b); Ajax chose the life of a lion in the afterlife (*Republic* 620b); the word "lion" alone does not constitute discourse (*Sophist* 262b–c); sophists can look like lions (*Statesman* 291a).

Locust (ὁ τέττιξ): on their music (*Phaedrus* 230c); as muses (*Phaedrus* 237a, 258e–259d, 262d); on their mating habits (*Symposium* 191b–c).

Mixed or fabulous animals: Pan as half-goat (*Cratylus* 408c–d); sophist like a many-headed hydra (*Euthydemus* 297c); Centaurs, Chimaera, Gorgons, Pegasus (*Phaedrus* 229c–230a); half goat, half deer (ὁ τραγέλαφος)—goat-stag (*Republic* 488a); image of the soul (like Cerebus, the Scylla, and Chimaera) as several forms (human, lion, many-headed beast) grown together in one (*Republic* 588b–589a); sophists can look like lions, centaurs, satyrs, and other cunning beasts (*Statesman* 291a–b); Socrates "resembles the satyr Marsyas" (*Symposium* 215b–c, 216c–d, 221d–e, 222d).

Mule (ὁ ἡμίονος): it is absurd to believe that there are offspring of horses and donkeys—

namely, mules—and yet no horses or donkeys (*Apology* 27e); τὸ ὑποζύγιον: mule or beast of burden as a murderer (*Laws* 873d–e); owners are responsible for what their slaves or animals—mules, horses, or dogs—do to the property of others (*Laws* 936d–e).

Nightingale (ἡ ἀηδών): the nightingale (or swallow [ἡ χελιδών] or hoopoe [ὁ ἔποψ]) does not sing in lamentation (*Phaedo* 85a); in the myth of Er, Thamyras chose to be a nightingale for his next life (*Republic* 620a).

Oyster (τὸ ὄστρεον): we are imprisoned like an oyster in its shell (*Phaedrus* 250c); life without the memory of pleasure or the calculation of future pleasures would be the life not of a human but of a mollusk (πλεύμονος) or some other shellfish like the oyster (ὀστρεῖνων) (*Philebus* 21c–d); the body as a covering for the soul is compared to the shells that cover the sea-god Glaucus (*Republic* 611c–612a); on the creation of fish, shellfish, and other creatures of the sea (*Timaeus* 92b).

Pig/Swine/Sow (ὁ/ἡ ὗς): on the proverb "any pig would know" (*Laches* 196d); on the Crommyonian sow (*Laches* 196e); an error more appropriate for "guzzling swine" than men (*Laws* 819d); Glaucon calls the city of minimal necessity a "city of pigs" (*Republic* 372d); on the similarities between humans and (it is implied) pigs (*Statesman* 266b–c); Protagoras argues that humans, not swine or the dog-faced baboon, are the measure of all things (*Theaetetus* 161c, 166c).

Plover (ὁ χαραδριός): an example of the life of pleasure (*Gorgias* 494b).

Quail (ὁ ὄρτυξ): the quail—along with the cock and horse—as an example of a beautiful animal (*Hippias Major* 295c–d); roosters, quails, horses, and dogs as example of possessions (*Lysis* 211e); the question of whether humans can be friends with quails, dogs, or horses (*Lysis* 212d–e).

Reincarnation as animals: gluttons can be reincarnated as donkeys or asses (*Phaedo* 81e); those who are unjust, or tyrants, or robbers pass into the bodies of wolves, hawks, and kites—predators (*Phaedo* 82a); those who practice civil virtues are reincarnated as bees, ants, or wasps (*Phaedo* 82b); in the myth of Er, there are many possible future lives, both human and animal, for a human soul to choose from (*Republic* 618a); Orpheus chooses the life of a swan, and a swan chooses the life of a human (*Republic* 620a); Thamyras chooses to be a nightingale, Ajax a lion, Agamemnon an eagle, and Thersites an ape (*Republic* 620a–c); "some beasts entered into men and into one another, the unjust into wild creatures, the just transformed to tame, and there was every kind of mixture and combination" (*Republic* 620d); men reborn as women or animals (*Timaeus* 42b–c).

Rooster (ὁ ἀλεκτρυών): the rooster—along with the horses and quail—as an example of a beautiful animal (*Hippias Major* 295c–d); Socrates's famous last words, "Crito, we owe a cock to Asclepius. Pay it and do not neglect it" (*Phaedo* 118a); roosters, quails, horses, and dogs as example of possessions (*Lysis* 211e); "cocks" crowing (*Symposium* 223c); debaters are compared to gloating gamecocks (*Theaetetus* 164c).

Sacrifice (of animals): oxen or bulls as sacrificial animals (*Alcibiades II* 149c, *Critias* 119d–120a); ox or sheep as property to be sold or sacrificed (*Euthydemus* 301e–302a); on the ritual of sacrifice associated with voting (*Laws* 753d); on animal sacrifice (including human sacrifice), on the sacrifice of oxen, and on bloodless sacrifice (*Laws* 782c); birds as sacrificial animals (*Laws* 956a); on Socrates's wide open, "bull-like" eyes (*Phaedo* 117b); diairesis/division as the carving up or sacrifice of animals (*Statesman* 259d, 287c; *Phaedrus* 265d–266b).

Scorpion (ὁ σκορπίος): the sorcerer's art of charming scorpions, spiders, and snakes (*Euthydemus* 289e–290a).

Sea-urchin/Sea creature (*adj.* θαλάττιος, -α, -ον): if one is a mother, then one is a mother of all animals—including sea-urchins (*Euthydemus* 298d; see *Meno* 80a, *Philebus* 21c; *Republic* 611c).

Sheep (ὁ/ἡ ὄϊς): ox or sheep as property to be sold or sacrificed (*Euthydemus* 301e–302a); sheep do not rule over sheep but are ruled over by humans (*Laws* 713d); Thrasymachus mocks Socrates for believing that shepherds consider only the good of their sheep (*Republic* 343b); the guardians must be raised like dogs that will protect the flock, lest they become wolves that will attack it (*Republic* 416a); one must not imitate the "cries of dogs, sheep, and birds" (*Republic* 397a); were they not so raised they would be like wolves (*Republic* 416a); bloated and ill-prepared citizens are like fattened sheep that invite attack (*Republic* 422d).

Snake (ὁ ἔχις): the sorcerer's art of charming snakes, spiders, and scorpions (*Euthydemus* 289d–290a); the guardian, like the snake or lion, can become irascible (*Republic* 590a–b); Alcibiades compares the effect of Socrates's discourse to being bitten by a snake (*Symposium* 217e) or adder (ἔχιδνα) (*Symposium* 218a); ὁ ὄφις: rivers coil about the earth like serpents (*Phaedo* 112d); Socrates as snake-charmer (of Thrasymachus) (*Republic* 358b).

Socrates as animal: as an older stork to be cared for by its young (*Alcibiades I* 135e); as gadfly (*Apology* 30e); fable of a fawn (Socrates) before a lion (Charmides) (*Charmides* 155d); as torpedo fish (*Meno* 80a–d); as bloodhound in argument (*Parmenides* 128c); as prophetic swan (*Phaedo* 84e, 85a–b); as a stinging bee (*Phaedo* 91c); Socrates's wide open, "bull-like" eyes (*Phaedo* 117c); as a hungry animal led out of Athens (*Phaedrus* 230d–e); as snake-charmer (of Thrasymachus) (*Republic* 358b); Socrates "resembles the satyr Marsyas" (*Symposium* 215b–c, 216c–d, 221d–e, 222d); as Siren (*Symposium* 216a, 218b); Alcibiades compares Socrates to a snake (*Symposium* 217e–218a); Socrates is compared, by means of a quote from Aristophanes's *Clouds* 362, to a kind of water fowl (ὁ βρένθος) (*Symposium* 221b).

Spider (τὸ φαλάγγιαν): the sorcerer's art of charming spiders, snakes, and scorpions (*Euthydemus* 289e–290a).

Stag/Deer (ὁ/ἡ ἔλαφος): animals as courageous—lion, leopard, boar, stag, bull, monkey (*Laches* 196e–197c); when ships are positioned for easy escape, soldiers become like lions fleeing deer (*Laws* 707a); Achilles insults Agamemnon in the *Iliad* by saying he has the "heart of a fleet deer" (cited at *Republic* 390a); "stag" as an example of a noun that does not form a discourse (*Sophist* 262b–c); fawn (ὁ νεβρός): fable of a fawn (Socrates) before a lion (Charmides) (*Charmides* 155d).

Stork (ὁ πελαργός): Socrates as an older stork to be cared for by its young (*Alcibiades I* 135e).

Swan (ὁ κύκνος): Socrates as prophetic swan (*Phaedo* 84e); swan as Apollo's bird (*Phaedo* 85a–b); in the myth of Er, Orpheus chooses the life of a swan, while swans and other musical animals choose the life of a human (*Republic* 620a).

Torpedo fish (ἡ νάρκη): Socrates as torpedo fish (*Meno* 80a–d).

Wasp (ὁ σφήξ): those who practice civil virtues are reincarnated as bees, ants, or wasps (*Phaedo* 82b).

Wolf (ὁ λύκος): gods being open to bribes would be like wolves (i.e., bad men) giving bits of their prey to watchdogs (i.e., the gods) (*Laws* 906d–e); tyrants, robbers, and other kinds of unjust people pass in their next lives into the bodies of predators such as hawks, wolves, and kites (*Phaedo* 82a); the lover is like a wolf that devours lambs (*Phaedrus* 241d); rhetorician—Lysias—as wolf (*Phaedrus* 272c); the guardians must be raised like dogs that will protect the flock, lest they become wolves that will attack it (*Republic* 416a); were they not so raised they would be like wolves (*Republic* 415e–416a); tyranny comes in the form of a wolf (*Republic* 566a); a wolf (the wildest of all creatures) resembles a dog (the tamest), that is, the sophist resembles a philosopher (*Sophist* 231a).

Name and Subject Index

Aeschylus, 30, 47, 58n3, 92n9, 109n2
Aesop, 4, 13–26, 79, 105, 109, 111n23; life of, 14–16
Agamemnon, 92n9, 135, 220, 226, 232, 240
Agathon, 199–200, 202
Ajax, 220, 226, 240
Alcibiades, 49, 95n38, 132, 193
Allen, R. E., 53, 59n7, 93n19, 93n22, 94n29
anamnesis, 64, 66, 71. See also recollection
animals, wild and tame, 16, 28, 33, 50, 103, 108, 116, 118, 120–121, 124, 127, 129n9, 129n13, 129n15, 132, 134–135, 138, 141, 143n21, 145n35, 161, 164, 170, 186–188, 192n26, 220, 224nn12–13, 226–227, 237, 241
ants, 17, 18, 21, 227
Annas, Julia, 144n27, 160n30
ape, Thersites as, 220, 226, 236, 237. See also monkeys
Apollo, 13–15, 18, 44–45, 81–84, 87–91, 92n3, 92n5, 93nn14–15, 196
aporia, 5, 63–68, 70, 72, 74, 127, 195, 196
Aristophanes, 7–8, 14, 24n13, 61, 80, 87, 93n14, 190, 193–204, 205n2, 205n5, 240
Aristotle, 24n13, 24n15, 47, 58n1, 58n4, 61, 73, 75n6, 76n15, 80, 92n6, 92n8, 100, 110n10, 129n14, 131, 142n4, 175n27, 190, 191n16, 195, 204, 205, 223n5, 242n5
Aspasia, 31–32
Autolykos (father of Odysseus), 132–133, 136

Baracchi, Claudia, 93n20
Barney, Rachel, 157, 159n3, 160nn37–38
bats, 25n61
bees, 2, 17, 18, 20, 21, 27, 57, 227
beetles, 20
Belfiore, Elizabeth, 125, 130n24
Berry, Christopher, 159n2
Berthiaume, Guy, 191n12
birds, 9, 21, 25n61, 27–29, 56, 81–84, 92n6, 93nn13–15, 170, 175n25, 220, 240, 241
Blackham, H. J., 16, 24n13
Bloom, Allan, 130n21, 144n27, 159n1, 223n4
boars, 132, 161
Brague, Remi, 172n1
Brann, Eva T. H., 143n23, 145n35, 145n39
Brill, Sara, 224n8

Brisson, Luc, 228, 238, 239, 244n19, 245n25, 245n27
bulls, 2, 24n38, 47, 100, 109
Burkert, Walter, 151, 159n4, 159nn6–7, 159n9, 159n12, 159n14, 159n17, 183, 191nn14–15, 192n23
butterflies, 20
Buxton, Richard, 133, 143nn12–14, 143n16, 159n19

camels, 17, 21
cats, 29
Cephalus, 132, 135, 210–211
Cerberus, 142n5, 145n35
Chantraine, Pierre, 172n1
chickens, 2, 17, 20, 21, 96, 110n19
chōra, 163, 165–166, 169, 175n24
cicadas, 2, 27, 98–99, 110n4, 180, 194, 205n2
Clayton, Edward, 14–16, 21, 23n7, 24nn13–15, 24n17
Cole, Susan Guettel, 153, 159n19, 160n22, 160n24
comedy, 96, 101, 104, 110n19, 151, 195, 198, 228, 240–241
Compton, Todd, 14–15, 21, 23nn3–4, 111n23
Cornford, F. M., 92n3
cosmos, 3, 4, 7, 8, 10n2, 21, 30, 32–33, 74, 110n19, 162–166, 169–170, 172, 173n13, 175n32, 216–217, 222, 224n9
cows, 21, 47, 161
crabs, 20, 110n9
cranes, 21
crickets, 17, 27
crocodiles, 17
Cronos, 30, 32, 33, 38, 158, 241; Age of Cronos, 28, 32–34, 129n15, 224n12
Cynics, 106, 110n6

deer, 20
Delphic Oracle, 82, 85–86, 102, 104
Demeter, 6, 33, 150, 152–153, 157
democracy, 24n13, 59n10, 102–103, 107, 122–123, 126, 130n17, 135
Democritus, 132
Derrida, Jacques, 57, 59n11, 67–69, 73, 75n3, 75n9, 75nn11–12, 76nn17–19, 95n33, 190n3, 204, 205n7

257

Derrida, Jean, 234, 244n16
Descartes, René, 68
desire, 6–8, 15, 27, 48–51, 65, 70–74, 97, 105, 117–118, 121–125, 130nn18–19, 130n22, 134, 137, 139, 142, 152, 155, 158, 175n31, 195, 198–204, 211, 227; desire as beast, 123–124
Detienne, Marcel, 153–154, 160n21, 160n25, 160nn28–29, 191n13
Devereux, Daniel, 155, 160n32
diairesis (division), 7, 34, 179, 181–189, 191n8
Diogenes Laertes, 96, 110n7, 110nn10–11, 111n21
Diogenes of Sinope, 5, 96, 101–106, 109, 110nn7–8, 110nn10–11, 110n16, 111n21, 111n24
Diotima, 150, 195, 199–201, 203, 212
dogs, 2, 5, 6, 21, 27, 29, 31, 39, 101, 104–106, 110n6, 110n19, 111n22, 131–141, 142n5, 144n25, 144n27, 144n30, 145n32, 145n35, 188, 192n26; guardians as dogs, 1, 133, 135–140, 144n29
donkeys, 2, 17, 19, 20, 161
Dorter, Kenneth, 182, 191nn10–11

eagles, 9, 31, 20, 220, 226
earthworms, 20
education, 6, 35, 37, 119–120, 128n1, 137–140, 144n30, 150, 168, 172, 174n15
Ehnmark, Erland, 242n7
eidos (form, idea), 32, 34, 55, 64–65, 69–71, 101, 104, 106, 156, 172, 181, 189–190, 200
Eliade, Mircea, 223n6
epimeleia (care), 1, 5, 6, 9, 32, 44–45, 49, 51, 57, 85, 99, 116–128, 129n7, 129nn9–10, 129n12, 135, 150, 155
eros, 6, 8, 37, 48–49, 71–72, 130n22, 156–158, 171, 175n31, 181, 184, 193–205, 209

Ficino, Marsilio, 8, 228, 235–238, 241, 244n21
fish, 5, 17, 20, 21, 28, 60–73, 75n3, 75n8, 241; aporia-fish, 4, 62, 68, 69, 71, 72
Flacelière, Robert, 92n11, 93n15
foxes, 2, 14, 17, 20, 21, 23, 132
Frère, Jean, 9n1, 238, 242n2
Freud, Sigmund, 71
frogs, 17–21, 24n38, 240
Fronterotta, Francesco, 242n19

gadfly, 1, 3–5, 43–58, 59nn8–10, 91, 97–109, 115–119, 125, 128n4, 172
geese, 18
Gibbs, Laura, 23n2, 24nn19–24, 24nn27–37, 25nn39–41, 25nn44–70, 26nn71–76
Glaucon, 6, 126, 135–142, 143n23, 144n29, 145n36, 145nn38–39, 149–152, 155–156, 160n21, 160n38

goats, 21, 184
gods, 3, 6, 9, 13, 17, 18, 26n76, 27–34, 44–45, 51, 57, 81–90, 92n5, 92n7, 93n13, 93n15, 98, 104, 117, 118, 123, 132, 149–152, 163–167, 174n13, 183–185, 193–197, 202–203, 210–211, 216, 224n9, 224n11, 229, 241, 242n5; Demiurge, 34, 163, 165, 166, 169, 170, 170n13, 175n24; Titans, 30, 32, 33
Goldschmidt, Victor, 244n22
Good beyond Being, 36, 56–57, 70–71, 73, 106, 134, 140–142, 145nn38–40, 229
Gordon, Jill, 130n25, 174n17
Gorgias, 60, 62, 72
Gottfried, Bruce, 110n4
Gregory, Justina, 117, 128n3
Grube, G. M. A., 53, 59n7
Guthrie, W. K. C., 61, 75n3, 223n6

Hadot, Pierre, 224n14, 233–234, 243n12, 244nn14–15
Halliwell, Stephen, 237
hares, 16, 20, 24n20
hawks, 2, 16, 17, 24n18, 92n13
Heath, John, 100, 109n2, 110n5
Heidegger, Martin, 68, 89, 223n5
Henderson, Jeffrey, 151, 159n15
hens. See chickens
Hephaestus, 33, 202
Heraclitus, 49
Herodotus, 14, 153
Hesiod, 16, 160n38, 163, 170, 174n20, 175n26, 175n29, 175n32, 241
Hölderlin, Friedrich, 32–33
Homer, 23n3, 100, 111n23, 132, 135, 143n10, 143n18, 143n22, 144n30, 183, 221
horses, 1–3, 5, 6, 17, 21, 44–47, 49–52, 58, 71, 96–98, 100, 101, 108, 116–121, 125, 127, 128n1, 128n4, 129n9, 129nn12–13, 130n23, 130n25, 134, 136, 180, 236
Howland, Jacob, 94n30, 144n29
human beings, 6, 8, 21, 28–30, 36, 53, 58, 80, 83, 89, 90, 98, 109n2, 118, 120, 121, 136, 150, 152, 162, 166–172, 174n17, 174nn21–22, 180, 194, 195, 197, 198, 202–204; human body, 23, 33, 161, 227, 236; humans as or like animals, 1, 7, 18, 21, 31, 48, 52, 71, 80, 100, 116, 118, 128, 139, 141, 165, 166, 169; reincarnated as or from animals, 2, 216–218, 220, 221, 225–241, 242n8, 242n10, 243n11; as opposed to animals, 2, 3, 9, 57–58, 99, 105, 181–182, 187–188, 198–199, 201
hyenas, 25n61
Hyland, Drew A., 145nn39–40

irony, 110, 197, 203, 235, 241; animal irony, 105; Socratic irony, 51, 53, 55–56, 87, 93–94, 101, 104
Isaac, Erich, 186, 192n24

Jowett, Benjamin, 39n1, 53, 59n7, 61

Kahn, Charles, 21, 173n4
Kant, Immanuel, 68, 92n10, 203
kites, 2, 17, 21
Kurke, Leslie, 21–22, 23n3, 26n77

Lacan, Jacques, 68
Lamb, W. R. M., 61, 74n1, 130n26, 190n1
Laurent, Jérôme, 242n8, 243n10, 244n13, 244n19, 245n32
Lawlor, Leonard, 75n10
Levinas, Emmanuel, 68
lions, 1, 2, 14, 16, 17, 21, 23n2, 24n38, 45, 124, 143n20, 161, 216, 220, 221, 226
locusts, 2. *See also* cicadas
logos (argument, speech), 5, 13, 59n9, 67, 69–72, 74, 79–81, 84–91, 92nn6–7, 93n19, 95n37, 97–100, 105, 108, 109, 110n4, 123–125, 138, 145n33, 161, 164, 169, 180–182, 188, 190n3, 195, 204, 209, 211, 215, 223n3, 233–235, 244; animal as *alogon*, 67, 92n7, 229, 231
Long, Christopher P., 92n6, 143nn22–23, 144n24, 145n36
Lopez, Barry, 131, 142n1
Lycaon, 133, 141
Lysias, 99, 126, 180–181, 191n21, 201, 209

Matthews, Gareth, 75n3
mageiros (butcher or sacrificer), 7, 20, 154, 181, 183–185; butchery, 179, 183–184, 186
McKeen, Catherine, 154, 155, 159n13, 160n31, 160n33
metaphor, 2, 44, 51, 52, 55–58, 100, 102, 103, 107, 119, 123–124, 235–239
mice, 16, 19, 20, 25n61, 102, 110n10
Miller, Mitchell, 145n39, 174n23, 182, 191n10
Minotaur, 108–109
monkeys, 2, 17, 20, 229, 232, 237. *See also* ape, Thersites as
Muses, 15, 37, 82, 99
music, 4, 13–14, 16, 19–21, 23, 25n43, 79, 80, 82–83, 89–91, 92n3, 92n5, 92n8, 95, 109, 138, 144n31, 149, 216, 220, 231
myth, 1, 3, 4, 9, 13, 15, 16, 28, 29, 33, 37, 99, 133, 145n35, 158, 161, 172n2, 174n21, 180, 181, 194–195, 200, 204, 209–211, 213, 223n2, 223nn5–6, 241; of Er, 8, 209–224, 226–245

Naas, Michael, 75n9
Nehamas, Alexander, 190n4, 242n4
Nietzsche, Friedrich, 2, 32, 171
nightingales, 9, 16, 24n18, 220, 226

Odysseus, 132–133, 143n11, 220, 221, 224nn13–14, 226, 232
Olympiodorus, 91
Orpheus, 220, 226, 231, 240
Osborne, Catherine, 242n5
Osborne, Robin, 160n21, 160n28
ostriches, 25n61
oxen, 21, 127, 184
oysters, 2, 21, 27–29, 180

Pandora, 170, 174n20, 175n26
Pappas, Alexandra, 75n7, 143n19
Parker, Robert, 192n25
Parmenides, 1, 28, 35, 224
Pausanias, 133, 143nn16–17
Pericles, 102
Persephone, 223n6
Peterson, Sandra, 144n27
philosopher kings, 137, 139, 144nn27–28
plants, 9, 10n2, 21, 36, 151–152, 157, 164, 174n14, 241
phronēsis (wisdom), 29–30, 120, 123–126, 129n14, 189
physis (nature), 32, 37, 125, 171, 229, 230
pigs, 2, 6, 17, 149, 150–154, 158; city of sows, 6, 149–158
Pindar, 72, 133, 143n13
Pinotti, Patrizia, 237–238, 242n3
poetry, 4, 79, 83, 92n5, 96, 100, 107, 156, 221, 235, 240; poets, 13–14, 60, 72, 82–84, 86, 88, 145n34, 154, 163, 193, 205n2, 225, 231
Polemarchus, 132–138, 142, 144nn26–27
polis, 1, 54, 97–98, 100, 102, 116–118, 121–123, 126–127, 128n4, 129n10, 129n15, 152–153, 155, 157, 161, 210; *polis* as horse, 1, 97, 115–118, 121, 127
Pradeau, Jean-François, 243n11, 244n19
prophecy, 14, 83, 86, 90, 105–106, 202; animals as prophetic, 5, 6, 14, 29, 45, 56, 81–86
plants, 9, 10n2, 21, 29, 32, 36, 151–152, 157, 164, 174n10, 241
Plato, dialogues cited: *Alcibiades I*, 1, 14, 23n2, 128n5; *Apology*, 1, 5, 16, 43–48, 50–55, 57–58, 59n7, 79–80, 84–91, 92n2, 93n17, 93nn19–20, 93n22, 94n30, 95n34, 97–98, 101, 103, 106, 115, 118–120, 123, 125, 127, 128nn1–2, 128n4, 129n7, 129n10, 155, 160n34; *Cratylus*, 92n5, 92n7,

93n18; *Crito*, 2, 16, 81, 90, 92n4; *Euthyphro*, 129n12; *Gorgias*, 10n2, 16, 130, 144n24; *Ion*, 83; *Laws*, 6, 9, 10n2, 47–49, 119, 123, 129n7, 129nn9–10, 161, 192n24, 236; *Menexenus*, 4, 29, 31; *Meno*, 1, 60–76, 83, 128n5; *Phaedo*, 1–5, 8, 13–15, 17–21, 23, 25n42, 56, 79–81, 83, 86, 88–91, 92nn2–3, 94n22, 94n28, 95n39, 108, 128nn1–2, 172n2, 227; *Phaedrus*, 2, 6, 7, 10n2, 49–51, 57–58, 82, 84, 95n33, 98, 125–126, 128n1, 130n22, 161, 172n2, 179–180, 182–184, 188, 190nn3–4, 191n21, 195, 201, 204, 209, 221, 223n3, 224n15, 227–228, 230, 236; *Philebus*, 25n43, 26n76, 128n1; *Protagoras*, 10n2, 24n26, 26n76, 92n7; *Republic*, 1–2, 6–8, 10n2, 16, 37, 48, 73, 86, 97, 99, 106, 111n26, 119, 121, 122, 124–127, 128n1, 130n17, 130nn22–23, 131–145, 149–161, 164, 171–172, 173n9, 209–224, 226–245; *Seventh Letter*, 236; *Sophist*, 7, 10n2, 19, 25n43, 34, 161, 182, 185, 188–189; *Statesman*, 4, 6–7, 10n2, 27–39, 127, 129n11, 129n15, 130n17, 179, 181–183, 185, 189, 223n3, 224n12; *Symposium*, 1, 7–8, 26n79, 37, 49, 86–87, 150, 193–205, 209, 212, 224n15; *Theaetetus*, 17, 24n27, 49, 56, 84, 120, 150; *Timaeus*, 4, 10n2, 27–29, 32, 34, 39, 50, 161–175, 191n6, 221, 224n9, 224n16, 227–228, 230, 235
Plotinus, 8, 224n14, 228, 232–235, 237, 241, 242n10, 243n11, 243n13
plovers, 9, 21
Plutarch, 75n8
Porphyry, 224n14, 242n10
Proclus, 228–237, 241, 242n9, 243n10, 244n16
Prometheus, 24, 33
Pseudo-Aeschylus, 30
psychē (soul), 1–3, 5, 6, 8, 10n2, 15, 17, 18, 25n43, 34, 36–37, 44, 48–51, 56, 58, 64, 66, 71–74, 81, 84, 97, 99, 109, 116, 123–127, 129n7, 129n11, 130nn23–24, 134, 138–140, 143n21, 144n29, 145n37, 155–156, 161, 163–170, 173n10, 173n12, 174n14, 174n18, 174n23, 175nn27–28, 180–181, 200–202, 204, 210–222, 223n6, 224n9, 224n11, 225–240, 242n7, 242n10, 243n11, 243nn13, 244n14, 244nn18–20, 244n22; animal souls, 18, 36, 74, 161, 165, 167, 175n28, 181, 204, 212, 217, 220, 221, 225–241; depicted as horses and charioteer, 2, 6, 50–51, 125, 180, 204
Pythagoras, 92n3

ravens, 20
recollection, 64, 66–67, 71, 72–73, 75n9, 130n25, 191n22, 222

Reeve, C. D. C., 94n23, 94n25, 94n27, 95n35, 144n27
reincarnation, 3, 8, 17, 18, 167, 181, 225, 227, 230, 232–237, 241, 242n7, 242n10, 243n13, 244n19, 245n27
Rich, Audrey N. M., 242n10
Richardson, Hilda, 223n7, 224n9, 224n11
roosters. *See* chickens
Rosen, Stanley, 144n27
Rothwell, Kenneth S., 16, 24n13, 240, 245n28

sacrifice, 3, 7, 108, 133, 150–154, 158, 160n28, 179–192, 195–196, 210
Sallis, John, 75n3, 93n19, 93n21, 94n24, 143n23, 173n8, 224n8
Sandford, Stella, 174nn21–22, 175n24
Santayana, George, 131, 132, 142n6
satyrs, 14, 25n61
Saxonhouse, Arlene W., 143n21, 144n32, 145n34, 157, 160n35
Schleiermacher, Friedrich, 34–36, 39n2
sheep, 21, 135, 138, 144n32; shepherds or herdsmen, 16, 28, 34, 135, 138–140, 143n22, 144n32, 152
Skemp, J. B., 36, 173n4, 174n14, 191n8
snakes, 1, 2, 20–21, 31, 45, 143n21, 150, 154
Socrates: and Aesop, 4, 13–23, 23n7, 24n14, 24n17, 25n42, 79, 105, 109; as bee, 18, 20, 57; and Diogenes of Sinope, 96, 101–106, 109, 110nn7–8, 110nn10–11, 110n16, 111n21, 111n24; as fawn, 1; as gadfly, 1, 3–5, 43–59, 96–109, 115–119, 125, 128, 128n4, 172; as midwife, 56, 150, 155; as snake, 1; as stork, 1, 9; as swan, 1, 3, 5, 18, 20, 44–45, 79–95; as torpedo fish, 1, 4–5, 44, 47, 60–76, 103
sophists, 1, 17, 33–34, 184–185, 187–188, 192n26
Sorabji, Richard, 245n7
sows. *See* pigs
Stamatellos, Giannis, 243n13, 244n19
Steel, Carlos, 172n3
stingrays, 1–4, 27, 44, 57, 61–62, 66, 73, 74n2, 75n3, 76n12, 103
Stone, I. F., 59n10, 103, 110n12
stags, 20
swans, 1–5, 18, 20, 44–45, 56, 80–86, 89–91, 92n8, 93nn14–15, 94n22, 161, 220, 225–227, 229–232, 239

technē, 153, 171, 185
Thamyras, 220, 226, 231

Thesmophoria, 6, 150–154, 157–158, 159n5, 159n8, 159n10, 160n25, 160n29, 160n36
Thucydides, 102
Thumiger, Chiara, 240, 245n29
torpedo fish, 1–4, 27, 44, 57, 61–62, 66, 73, 74n2, 75n3, 76n12, 103
tortoises, 20–21
thumos (spirit), 64, 70–72, 74, 130n23, 156
tragedy, 96, 205n5, 228, 240–241, 245n29
translation, 4, 36, 43–44, 47–48, 52–55, 58, 59n7, 59n9, 66, 73, 75n3, 93n14, 93n19, 115, 130n21, 145n33, 151, 173n5, 221
transmigration. *See* reincarnation
Tredennick, Hugh, 59n7
truth, 5, 9, 16, 57, 70, 73–74, 98–99, 104–106, 141, 156, 227, 228; and prophecy, 79–80, 83–91, 92n6, 93n18, 93n22, 94n27, 95n35
tyranny, 1, 17, 48–50, 97, 102–103, 121–124, 130nn17–18, 130n20, 141, 158, 217, 219, 228, 242n7; the tyrant as wolf, 6, 132, 134–136, 143n21

Vernant, Jean-Pierre, 160n25, 175n29, 183, 191n13
Versnel, H. S., 157, 159n5, 159n8, 159n10, 160n29, 160n36
virtue, 15, 45–46, 51, 55, 57–58, 60–66, 70–72, 74, 98–99, 102, 106, 109n2, 117–118, 120, 129n14, 134–136, 138, 216–217, 219, 232, 240; animals and virtue, 3, 16–17, 120, 134–135, 138, 227

war, 13, 30, 127, 141, 149–150, 152–156, 162, 172, 212–213; *polemos*, 175n32
wasps, 2, 17, 20, 21, 240

West, Thomas G., 53, 59n7
wild animals. *See* animals, wild and tame
Wolf, Cary, 9n1
Wolf, Francis, 242n5
wolves, 1–2, 6, 17, 20, 31, 99–100, 103, 108, 131–141, 142n2, 142n5, 142n8, 143nn12–14, 143n16, 143n19, 143n21, 144n25, 161, 188, 192n26; Thrasymachus as wolf, 1, 99–100, 108, 132, 134–138, 141, 143n21
women, 31–32, 67, 150–159, 160nn24–25, 160nn28–29, 174n20, 200, 217, 240; in relation to animals, 27, 29, 162, 167–168, 170, 175n25, 220, 242n5; in relation to men, 2, 34, 37, 39, 50, 54, 93n20, 133, 139, 168–171, 174n21, 174n23, 242n5; in politics, 38, 160n2; reincarnation as, 221, 229
Wood, Robert E., 145n35
Woodruff, Paul, 190n4, 242n4

Xenophanes, 173n7, 209
Xenophon, 94nn29–30, 94n32, 129n9, 142n8

Zeitlin, Froma, 170, 175n26, 175n29
Zeus, 18–20, 24n33, 26n76, 30–31, 33, 35, 38, 47, 133, 196, 241
Zhuang-zi, 184–185, 191nn18–19
zōion (animal, living being), 3, 7, 10n2, 172n1, 181, 242n5; cosmos as a *zōion*, 3–4, 7, 10n2, 30, 32, 162, 164–166, 169–170, 173n13, 217, 224n9; human as *zōion echon logon*, 70; *logos* as a *zōion*, 181
Zuckert, Catherine, 91n1, 175nn30–31

www.ingramcontent.com/pod-product-compliance
Lightning Source LLC
Chambersburg PA
CBHW031805220426
43662CB00007B/533